PAPER TO PETAL

PAPER TO PETAL

75 Whimsical Paper Flowers to Craft by Hand

REBECCA THUSS and **PATRICK FARRELL**

Foreword by **MARTHA STEWART**

NEW YORK

FAUX BOIS TREE PEONIES *Previous spread:* These flowers were made with double-sided white crepe paper that was painted using a fan brush. Petal #208 was used for both petal layers, 6 in the first layer and 9 in the second layer. Centers were made from *Buds* (p. 131) surrounded by microbead *Glittered* (p. 137) fringe and Petals #42 cut from painted single-ply crepe. Leaves #52 were cut from metallic silver and copper single-ply crepe and brown florist crepe papers and then *Wrinkle Pleated* (p. 134).

MERRY-GO-ROUND *Opposite:* This 10" (25.5cm) bloom was made with apricot/light apricot double-sided crepe paper that was painted using different styles of striping paintbrushes. Fourteen Petals #220 make up the first layer of petals, and 17 Petals #218 make up the second layer. The center was made from a spun-cotton mushroom cap, covered in mixed aqua glitter and surrounded by individual florets made from Petal #264 in yellow double-sided crepe. Leaves #50 were cut using a deckle edger from gray decorative paper.

Published in the United States by Potter Craft, an imprint of the Crown Publishing Group, a division of Random House, Inc., New York.
www.crownpublishing.com
www.pottercraft.com

POTTER CRAFT and colophon are registered trademarks of Random House, Inc.

Library of Congress Cataloging-in-Publication Data
Thuss, Rebecca.
Paper to petal: 75 whimsical paper flowers to craft by hand / by Rebecca Thuss and Patrick Farrell.
pages cm
Includes index.
1. Paper flowers. I. Farrell, Patrick, II. Title.
TT870.T545 2013
745.54—dc24 2012048675

ISBN 978-0-385-34505-7
eISBN 978-0-385-34506-4

Printed in China

Additional text by Kathryn Thuss
Text design and photographs by THUSS + FARRELL
Jacket design and photographs by THUSS + FARRELL

10 9 8 7 6 5 4

First Edition

for poet

FOREWORD

I have been crafting for years and years, and I am always looking for old and new books that will enable me, with specific how-to instructions, to make something beautiful, prettily and perfectly. *Paper to Petal* is just such a book, a manual so carefully conceived, so beautifully illustrated and photographed, so innovative and creative, that it is impossible not to want to try each and every one of the 75 flower projects Rebecca Thuss and her husband, Patrick Farrell, have developed and photographed. This book is a labor of love as is so clearly evidenced by the whimsical combinations of colors and materials, by the referencing of old-fashioned manuals and workbooks, and by the modern interpretations and reimaginings of old-world techniques.

Paper flower making is several hundred years old—my Polish ancestors fashioned peonies and roses from paper to embellish costumes and homes, and handed down those skills to their children and grandchildren. Young, early American women were taught to fashion flowers from paper, wax, and other materials as were young ladies in England and on the Continent. Paper flowers were crafted in Japan and China to embellish headdresses and beautify shrines and altars. Special papers were developed that permitted stretching and pulling and shaping, and wires and tapes were created to aid in the making of these blooms and foliage.

The authors have taken all they have learned and reimagined this craft in new and surprising ways—new types of papers have been introduced, paints and other materials employed, to change and enliven old techniques, and traditional flower forms have been thrown to the winds and new designs incorporated that are inspired by nature, by color, by materials, and by imagination.

I studied each and every page, happy to see a reinterpretation of nature, knowing that if she could, Mother Nature herself would want to evolve the poppy, all the foliage, and the hellebore and the lily and all other flowers to mimic what the authors have created.

Martha Stewart

CUT-FROM-THE-GARDEN BOUQUET This lush bouquet is made with the coral poppies from project #75, Butterfly Nest, and assorted foliage from project #17, Multifarious Foliage. A handful of emerald green twisted paper ribbon leaves smeared with glitter glue were tucked in.

History

Paper crafts and paper flowers have been a longtime tradition in many countries, including Mexico, Korea, Japan, and China. The variety of paper-art techniques developed over the centuries—origami and kirigami in Japan and hanji/mulberry paper flower crafts in Korea—is simply amazing. Often paper flowers were used as decorations in ceremonial events and celebrations, and as a social group-oriented folkcraft. Paper-flower crafting was also popular in the Victorian era and in the United States during the 1920s and 1930s, and then again during the mid-twentieth century. Flowers were created and used during times of the year when fresh flowers weren't obtainable. When crepe paper became even more readily available, the range of instruction booklets expanded. These now vintage booklets are wonderful sources of inspiration.

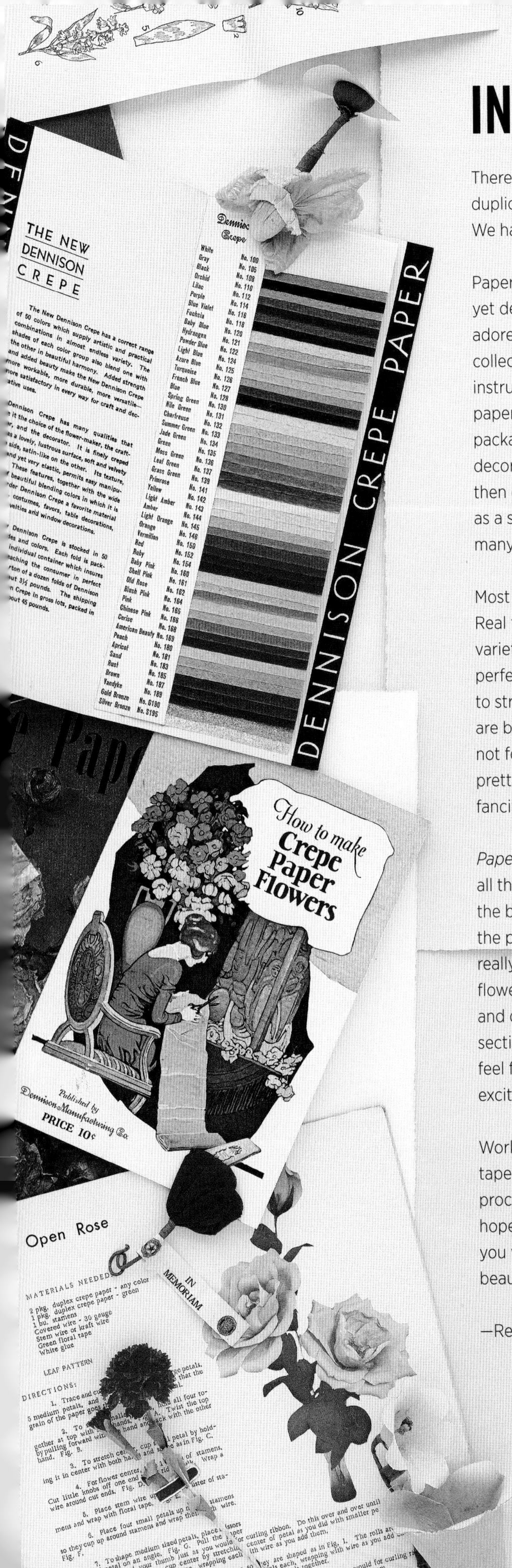

INTRODUCTION

There is an intangible element in the handmade; an aspect of individuality that can't be duplicated. It's why my husband, Patrick, and I have crafted things by hand our entire lives. We have always been drawn to the beauty, charm, and personality of handmade items.

Paper flowers embody the best of these traits. Like real flowers, they are substantial yet delicate; impermanent yet artful. I have always loved vintage paper ephemera and adore the patina of aged paper. While in art school I began amassing what is now a large collection of vintage crepe paper, paper flowers, party nut cups, and old paper-flower instruction booklets. Over time I've become ever more inspired by the art of making paper flowers and the history of this craft. I find myself continually making them to adorn packages and give them as gifts, for photography sets and projects, party and holiday decorations, and to simply enjoy at home. I learned basic skills from my vintage books and then developed my own techniques through years of experimentation. During my ten years as a style director at *Martha Stewart Weddings* magazine I had the opportunity to craft many paper-flower projects that were featured in editorial stories.

Most vintage paper-flower instruction books are rooted in creating forms found in nature. Real flowers provide an endless source of inspiration. The shapes, colors, textures, and variety are incredible and exciting to use as a starting point for paper crafts. Nature has perfected imperfection, and the same principle can be applied to paper flowers. No need to strive for perfection; each hand that makes a flower will introduce lovely differences that are beautiful. I love using nature as a reference, but I also enjoy creating whimsical flowers not found in the natural world. When designing flowers, Patrick and I can get inspired by pretty much anything, allow our imaginations to run wild, and create something unique, fanciful, and most important, fun to make.

Paper to Petal is organized in five main sections. The first section, "The Flowers," features all the designs we created for this book. Each flower has a corresponding how-to later in the book that explains the construction process. The second section, "Materials," delineates the papers, tools, and paper-flower-specific supplies we like to use. That said, all you really need is paper, scissors, wire, and floral tape to make a simple version of any of these flowers. "Skills" outlines the parts of a flower, shows our layered method for flower making, and defines techniques that we have developed in addition to the classics. The final main section, "Templates," contains the petal and leaf shapes used in this book. We hope you will feel free to mix and match shapes and pair them with different materials to create new and exciting paper flowers, such as the ones we show on pages 2–13.

Working on this book has been an all-consuming love affair with paper, paint, and floral tape. We felt inspired while producing it, and we hope you feel inspired by the results. The process of creating and making flowers is easy, enjoyable, and truly rewarding. It is our hope that as you look at these projects and the techniques we've used to create them that you will come up with your own designs, color palettes, techniques, and individual ideals of beauty, whimsy, and style.

—Rebecca

Easily Made Flowers for Decorations

PAPER FLOWERS

Orange Blossom

Sweet Pea

April Showers

INSPIRED BY: A child's yellow raincoat. **COLOR:** A bright yellow flower matches the shade of the coat, paired with happy blue paper raindrop leaves. **SHAPE:** The pressed paper button glued to a paper-covered center is directly inspired by the buttons on the raincoat. Leaves are expressed as falling raindrops. **TEXTURE:** The entire flower, petals, leaves, and stem have been painted with multiple coats of acrylic gloss medium to create a wet and shiny finish. A few dotted cellophane leaves add an additional layer of translucency. **MOOD:** Youthful and bright. **MADE WITH:** Petal #144 in yellow double-sided crepe. Leaves #91 and #92 in shades of blue florist crepe and dotted cellophane.

Pixie Bell

INSPIRED BY: Our daughter. **COLOR:** Pale shades of crepe inspired by her strawberry blond hair; blue glitter centers inspired by her blue eyes; leaves inspired by her gray-and-white-striped leggings. **SHAPE:** The triple petals of each bloom curl up like the swirls and twirls of her hair. **TEXTURE:** The ball centers are covered in blue glitter. They are surrounded by delicate gray "eyelashes" (pips). **MOOD:** Charming and sweet with a bold hint. **MADE WITH:** Petal #134 in apricot/light apricot double-sided crepe. Leaf #62 in silver painted white double-sided crepe. Glitter covered spun-cotton ball on a stem wire, gray pips.

Pattern Plays

INSPIRED BY: Favorite handbags. **COLOR:** A direct color interpretation for both flowers. Red and white and a multicolor splatter palette. **SHAPE:** Thicker papers create a sense of structure. The leaves on the red flower are shaped like the side ties of the handbag. **TEXTURE:** Fabric patterns were replicated onto paper. The glossy wood bead detail on the red bag inspired a wood bead center. **MOOD:** Sophisticated and lighthearted. **MADE WITH:** *Red flower:* Petals #129 and #130 and Leaves #142 and #143 in red/brick red double-sided crepe. Acrylic paint was dotted on using a striping brush. *Splatter flower:* Petals #129 and #130 and Leaf #131 in apricot/light apricot double-sided crepe were painted with six different acrylic paint colors using a spray bottle.

GET INSPIRED

When designing paper flowers, we always begin with a nugget or spark of inspiration. This can be as simple as a color or as complex as an emotion. Nature is, of course, a great starting point for floral crafting, but you can find inspiration anywhere. Combining the basic elements of flowers—petals, leaves, stamen—with an inspiring item or idea, such as a candy cane or a beautiful sunset, and making something new from paper and a few materials can be incredibly satisfying. Find something that speaks to you, perhaps an object, place, or experience, and turn it into a component of your flower. Once you have an idea for a paper flower project, choose the materials that will allow you to best express it.

This process is a useful way to narrow your focus before designing and crafting. Along with the ideas, skills, and projects we have created in this book, consider the following questions to help guide you to create unique flower designs of your own, inspired by something you love.

Color

Identify something that appeals to you and ask yourself the easiest question: What color is it? Is it one color or multiple colors? Assess bright colors versus pastels, light versus deep colors, solid versus graduated tones. You can choose to be literal and mimic colors as closely as possible, or interpret them loosely. Paper and paint come in every shade. Find an exact color match in the paper type you want to work with, or use paint and colorings to achieve your desired shades and tones.

Shape

Examine the shape and form of your inspirational object. Is it rounded and curved, or pointy and spiky? Perhaps it is jagged or ruffled? These impressions can influence your petal, leaf, and overall flower shape. If your object is round and fluffy, you might craft a multilayered, rounded-petal bloom from tissue paper. If your object is a tall and thin vintage glass vase, perhaps make a long-stemmed bloom with translucent, narrow petals.

Texture

Texture and pattern add levels of detail and finish to a project. Do you have a favorite patterned plaid scarf? Render your flower in plaid wrapping paper. Is your inspiration a fuzzy teddy bear? Glue soft crepe confetti to the petals and center. Adding additional materials, like pips and pressed-paper ornaments, raffia, paper ribbon, and glitter, can provide even more levels of texture and interest.

Mood

The last question helps frame an overall direction. What is the mood and vibe of your object? How do you feel when you look at it? Is there a history to it? Is it from a certain time period? Is it happy or spooky? Does it remind you of a favorite book or movie? Does it seem modern or old-fashioned? The answers can help steer your design and material choices. Perhaps your flower can have a wild personality such as a kooky curled stem with an assortment of petal colors, or a romantic, vintage sensibility, with aged and drapey tissue-paper petals and faded leaves.

Look at your favorite items or concepts to inspire the creation of paper flower crafts that feel personal and special to you.

The FLOWERS/

1 / FRECKLE PASTEL

The pastel hues and big petals of this 9" (23cm) flower have a soft and feminine feel. The pale colors are grounded with burnished, copper-colored crepe leaves. **INSPIRED BY:** Pastel cupcake sprinkles. **MADE WITH:** Single-ply, double-sided, and florist crepe; vintage pips. **GREAT FOR:** Centerpieces, weddings, spring or summer decorations, and home decor. **HOW-TO:** p. 140.

2 / PARTY FLOWER

Oversized flowers make spectacular party decor. Hang one or more from a color cord on a wall or door, or even suspend it from the ceiling. This example is 16" (40.5cm) wide. **INSPIRED BY:** Our lively daughter. **MADE WITH:** Tissue; metallic polyester film; cardboard; card stock. **GREAT FOR:** Parties, birthdays, and weddings. **HOW-TO:** p. 141.

3 / CHEERLEADERS

Pom-poms are one of the simplest paper flowers to make. Fringing scissors make this project quick work. We paired the pastel shades with bright leaves. **INSPIRED BY:** Cheerleading pom-poms! **MADE WITH:** Tissue; single-ply, double-sided, and florist crepe. **GREAT FOR:** Gift trimming, party favors, and large arrangements. **HOW-TO:** p. 142.

4 / CRUMPLED POPPIES

We used a mixture of tissue and crepe to re-create the charmingly crinkled and rumpled, "just out of bed" look that poppies have in the early stages of bloom. *Opposite:* These flowers look lively in a bright and saturated palette. **INSPIRED BY:** Opening poppies. **MADE WITH:** Tissue; single-ply, double-sided, and florist crepe. **GREAT FOR:** Gift trimming, favors, weddings, and other special events. **HOW-TO:** p. 143.

5 / TWISTED-RIBBON TULIPS

Bring a tulip bed to your table. Two different paper-ribbon styles are combined to create blooms with leaf colors not found in nature. The stems are anchored in floral foam set inside terra-cotta pots covered with golden rocks. **INSPIRED BY:** Arching tulips. **MADE WITH:** Lightweight and twisted paper ribbons. **GREAT FOR:** Spring holidays, parties, home decor, and centerpieces. **HOW-TO:** p. 144.

6 / BOOKWORM BOOKMARKS

Bookworms have munched their way through these blooms. The knotted centers are reminiscent of vintage ribbon bookmarks. We let the book covers inspire each palette. **INSPIRED BY:** Bookmarks and bookworms! **MADE WITH:** Single-ply and double-sided crepe; cotton ribbon; washi tape. **GREAT FOR:** Gifts and home decor. **HOW-TO:** p. 145.

7 / BABY BLOOMS

These flowers seem to be growing up right before your eyes. The palette for these blooms came directly from the confections in our favor bags. **INSPIRED BY:** A spring baby shower. **MADE WITH:** Tissue; single-ply, double-sided, and florist crepe; twisted paper ribbon. **GREAT FOR:** Favors, parties, centerpieces, and showers. **HOW-TO:** p. 146.

8 HYBRID HELLEBORE

This giant 15" (38cm) flower uses an eclectic mix of materials, including speckled Bleeding Art Tissue and a wild tangle of raffia around the center. Two-sided wired leaves are made from patterned papers and finished with fabric tape. **INSPIRED BY:** Unusual hellebore varieties. **MADE WITH:** Double-sided crepe; glassine; Bleeding Art Tissue; raffia; marbleized and decorative papers. **GREAT FOR:** Home decor, centerpieces, and events. **HOW-TO:** p. 147.

9 / FÊTE FLOWER & BIRTHDAY LEI

A fringed pastel rainbow flower sprouts a striped candle center, perfect for a birthday celebration. A handmade lei adorns the birthday girl. **INSPIRED BY:** Striped birthday candles and tropical flower leis. **MADE WITH:** Florist and double-sided crepe; tissue; twisted paper ribbon; a paper straw. **GREAT FOR:** Parties and events, gifts, favors. **HOW-TO:** p. 148.

10 / FLYING KITES

String-covered centers, kite-shaped petals, and fabric kite-tail "leaves" make lively flowers that are perfect for a child's party. Creasing double-sided crepe and embellishing it with felt-tipped markers give the petals kite-like detail. **INSPIRED BY:** Flying kites and Mary Poppins! **MADE WITH:** Double-sided crepe; cotton string; fabric. **GREAT FOR:** Children's parties, birthdays, kid's room decor, and centerpieces. **HOW-TO:** p. 149.

11/ CHIYOGAMI CHERRY BLOSSOMS

Fanciful cherry blossoms bloom from stems rather than branches in this playful centerpiece. The soft *Wrinkle Pleated* petals play off of the graphic floral patterned leaves. We'd love to see these perched on a windowsill as well. **INSPIRED BY:** Chiyogami/yuzen Japanese patterns. **MADE WITH:** Double-sided and single-ply crepe; vintage pips; patterned paper. **GREAT FOR:** Centerpieces, parties, and home decor. **HOW-TO:** p. 150.

Gail

A
C

12 / SMILEY'S MOBILE

Each flower hanging from the paper-trimmed hoop is crafted on a removable wire, so the cheerful flowers can be arranged in a vase when it's time to pack the crib away. **INSPIRED BY:** Happy faces. **MADE WITH:** Florist crepe; painted wood beads; wood hoop. **GREAT FOR:** A baby's or child's room, and shower gifts. **HOW-TO:** p. 151.

13 RAINBOW RUFFLE

These dramatic, two-feet-tall, soft, ruffled, multilayered blooms are simple to make and lovely to display. They would also look beautiful in a darker autumnal palette. **INSPIRED BY:** A vintage layered paper costume dress. **MADE WITH:** Single-ply and florist crepe. **GREAT FOR:** Large arrangements, centerpieces, and weddings. **HOW-TO:** p. 152.

14 / POLKA PETAL PARTY HAT

With a few kid-friendly ingredients this party hat is fun to craft and adds handmade cheer to a birthday party. Kids can make the spotted paper in any color combination, using dot-shaped stamping markers. **INSPIRED BY:** Classic birthday parties. **MADE WITH:** Double-sided crepe; pom-poms; pipe cleaners. **GREAT FOR:** Children's parties, birthdays, kids' craft project. **HOW-TO:** p. 153.

15 / SUNNY BEES

A triangular vase displays welcoming flowers made in shades of yellow with a layered look and wild personality. The mottled crepe leaf was created with a child's craft sponge brush. *Opposite:* A green-and-black variation has a very different feel. **INSPIRED BY:** Bumblebees. **MADE WITH:** Tissue; single-ply, double-sided, and florist crepe; vintage pips. **GREAT FOR:** Home decor, centerpieces, and summer decorating. **HOW-TO:** p. 154.

16 / WHITE PINE & JAPANESE PAPER PEONY

This elegant peony in three stages of bloom features patterned Japanese paper petals. Delicate pine sprays on found branches offer contrast. **INSPIRED BY:** Ikebana (the art of Japanese flower arranging). **MADE WITH:** Florist crepe; Japanese paper; paper twine; vintage pips from Japan. **GREAT FOR:** Home decor, gifts, centerpieces, and special events. **HOW-TO:** p. 155.

17 / MULTIFARIOUS FOLIAGE

In a world full of colorful flowers, this whimsical potted garden pays homage to all things green. We crafted our botanical specimens from varied shades of solid and hand-painted green papers. **INSPIRED BY:** Potted gardens. **MADE WITH:** Tissue; single-ply, double-sided, and florist crepe; decorative papers. **GREAT FOR:** Centerpieces, weddings and events, home decor, and gifts. **HOW-TO:** p. 156.

18 / SORBET BOUQUET

This soft and striking 15″ (38cm) bouquet gets its charm from the mix of textures and materials we've used to craft the flowers and foliage. **INSPIRED BY:** Sorbet shades. **MADE WITH:** vintage, single-ply, florist, double-sided crepe; tissue; decorative paper; vintage pips. **GREAT FOR:** Wedding bouquets and spring entertaining. **HOW-TO:** p. 158.

19 / THE SUNSET

Moved by the dazzling dawn and dusk colors that wash across the skies, we crafted tissue puff cloud blooms that are tinted by a setting-sun flower. **INSPIRED BY:** The setting sun. **MADE WITH:** Bleeding Art Tissue; tulle; florist crepe; water-soluble crayons. **GREAT FOR:** Home decor, centerpieces, parties, and baby gifts. **HOW-TO:** p. 160.

20 GEO WRISTLETS

Gemstone-shaped petals made from hand-speckled crepe surround stone bead centers, and sit in poufs of tissue and gold marbled paper fringe. **INSPIRED BY:** Geology, stone, and marble. **MADE WITH:** Double-sided crepe; printed tissue; marbled paper; stone beads. **GREAT FOR:** Bridesmaid corsages, parties and events, gifts, and favors. **HOW-TO:** p. 161.

21 / MULTIBLOOMS

A variety of shapes and crafting techniques come together in these fun and graphic multibloom stems. **INSPIRED BY:** Flowers with many blooms. **MADE WITH:** Single-ply, double-sided, and florist crepe; crepe streamers; twisted paper ribbon; glitter. **GREAT FOR:** Gifts, centerpieces, and home decor. **HOW-TO:** p. 162.

22 INKED IMPRINTS

This circle of blooms in a warm palette brings to mind a Moroccan sunset. Petals and leaves get their dynamic ornamental imagery from patterned rubber stamps. We used a single petal shape in three different sizes and different stamping configurations. **INSPIRED BY:** Moroccan motifs. **MADE WITH:** Single-ply and double-sided crepe; rubber stamps. **GREAT FOR:** Gift trimming and centerpieces. **HOW-TO:** p. 163.

23 / KINGFISHER & FLAMINGO

Two vibrant birds prompted these two different palettes and leaf design treatments. Both 9" (23cm) blooms are a similar design with multiple fringed feather-like layers. **INSPIRED BY:** Blue kingfisher and pink flamingo birds. **MADE WITH:** Tissue; single-ply and florist crepe; sparkle wrapping paper; tulle; raffia; pips; twisted paper ribbon. **GREAT FOR:** Home decor and parties. **HOW-TO:** p. 164.

24 / CRAYON COSMOS

Plaid patterns were drawn with water-soluble crayons across white and pink crepe paper and gently brushed with water to create a bleeding madras effect. Built with a continuous petal, these flowers are very simple to craft. **INSPIRED BY:** Madras plaid. **MADE WITH:** Double-sided crepe. **GREAT FOR:** Bouquets, weddings and parties, gifts, and Mother's Day. **HOW-TO:** p. 165.

25 / PETITE POTTER'S URN

Crepe paper nut cups are transformed into a sweet garden urn that is home to a bowing snowdrop bloom. The mint and olive green petals are made from the same paper as the leaves, giving this project a fresh feel. **INSPIRED BY:** Iron garden urns and snowdrops. **MADE WITH:** Double-sided and florist crepe; vintage pips; crepe paper nut cups. **GREAT FOR:** Wedding or party favors and gifts. **HOW-TO:** p. 166.

26 / FEATHERED FASCINATOR

The delicate yet slightly wild hand-cut paper feathers in this charming flower flutter lightly with just a bit of movement, and the soft peachy tones add to the feminine feel. **INSPIRED BY:** Vintage hats. **MADE WITH:** Single-ply and double-sided crepe; tissue; vintage pips; decorative paper. **GREAT FOR:** Accessories, wedding bouquets, and gifts. **HOW-TO:** p. 167.

27 FIZZ

These silvery-sheened flowers are made in a sophisticated palette with an organic and polished feel. Paint-dotted centers and lively wood-grain fringe lend the flower a fizzy quality. *Opposite:* Six additional color palettes are ready for gifting in cake boxes filled with shredded paper. **INSPIRED BY:** Fizzy drinks. **MADE WITH:** Single-ply and florist crepe; decorative papers. **GREAT FOR:** Centerpieces, gift trimming, and home decor. **HOW-TO:** p. 168.

28

GRAND MUM

This stand-alone specimen living in a fishbowl feels elegant and refined. Gold Dresden paper ornaments add a textured level of detail and a vintage look and feel. **INSPIRED BY:** A chrysanthemum kimono. **MADE WITH:** Double-sided and florist crepe; Dresden pressed-paper ornaments. **GREAT FOR:** Home decor, gifts, and centerpieces. **HOW-TO:** p. 169.

29 / COFFEE & CHOCOLATE

This lovely coffee-filter flower has ring-stained petals and spoon-shaped leaves. Bean buds are playfully growing on the stems. **INSPIRED BY:** Coffee beans and chocolate wrappers. **MADE WITH:** Coffee filters; embossed paper; single-ply crepe; gold twisted ribbon. **GREAT FOR:** Father's Day, birthdays, and gifts. **HOW-TO:** p. 170.

30 / PAINTERLY POPPIES

Invite kids to paint abstract designs onto sheets of double-sided crepe, then turn their artwork into imaginative flowers perfect for a grandparent or friend. Or paint them yourself! **INSPIRED BY:** A child's drawing. **MADE WITH:** Double-sided crepe; tinsel glitter. **GREAT FOR:** Gift trimming and home decor. **HOW-TO:** p. 171.

WALLIS

31 / CONFETTI CAKE

Sculptural yet soft, these flowers with their paper-confetti sprinkled centers and curled petals look chic and celebratory against the clean lines of the wedding cake.
INSPIRED BY: Tossed confetti!
MADE WITH: Double-sided and florist crepe; decorative paper.
GREAT FOR: Cake decor, parties, and weddings. **HOW-TO:** p. 172.

32 WILD MEADOW WREATH

Fun and easy to craft, this 15″ (38cm) wreath makes use of simple fringing techniques that bring to mind tall grasses waving in a warm summer breeze. Delicate pink flowers and speckled leaves are tucked in for softness and color. **INSPIRED BY:** A wildflower meadow. **MADE WITH:** Tissue; single-ply, double-sided, and florist crepe. **GREAT FOR:** Holidays, springtime, weddings, and other events. **HOW-TO:** p. 173.

33 / CAMELLIA METALLICA & GOLDEN WHEAT

Reflective metals inspire a soft interpretation in tissue and crepe. Long stems of golden paper wheat offset burnished shades of copper, silver, and gold in the flowers.

INSPIRED BY: Precious metals.

MADE WITH: Single-ply and florist crepe; tissue; and metallic paper.

GREAT FOR: Centerpieces, holiday decorations, home decor, and weddings. **HOW-TO:** p. 174.

34 VINTAGE SPRIGS

We made these flowers from a variety of vintage pips and collected vintage aged crepe. The palette of the time-worn paper is elegant, saturated, and subdued. A quick coil turns the stem into a napkin ring. **INSPIRED BY:** Vintage craft supplies. **MADE WITH:** Vintage crepe; vintage pips. **GREAT FOR:** Table settings and gifts. **HOW-TO:** p. 176.

35 / RINGING BELL GARLANDS

These two distinct garlands work together, but would look equally great alone. The coral bells garland features a simple, cuff-style bloom. The smaller flying bluebells garland is strung with small double flowers with wired speckled leaves. **INSPIRED BY:** Wedding bells. **MADE WITH:** Tissue; single-ply and florist crepe; twisted paper ribbon; marbelized paper. **GREAT FOR:** Weddings, holidays, and parties. **HOW-TO:** p. 177.

36 / FIVE-PETAL SWEETIES

The possibilities are endless with this simple flower. Play around with your favorite materials and create a mixture of beautiful blossoms. This small bloom also makes a great center for a more complicated flower. **INSPIRED BY:** Nature's variety. **MADE WITH:** Assorted crepe; pips. **GREAT FOR:** Anything and everything. **HOW-TO:** p. 178.

37 / COFFEE-FILTER FIREWORKS

Each flower is made from four paint-dyed coffee filters fringed into "fireworks" and embellished with metallic fringe. Tiny "sparklers" are crafted from patriotic crepe paper streamers. **INSPIRED BY:** Fireworks! **MADE WITH:** Coffee filters; streamers; silver metallic twisted ribbon; star garland. **GREAT FOR:** Birthdays, patriotic holidays, and parties. **HOW-TO:** p. 179.

38 / WILD STRAWBERRIES

Quirky colors and oversized blooms give personality to these strawberry vines. Place a few berry baskets along a runner and let the plants trail their way down the center of a picnic table. **INSPIRED BY:** Wild strawberry plants. **MADE WITH:** Single-ply, double-sided, and florist crepe. **GREAT FOR:** Centerpieces, favors, and weddings. **HOW-TO:** p. 180.

39 / SWEETS BLOOM

Inspired by a candy wrapper, simple line-work patterns were hand-drawn on crepe petals with a felt-tipped marker. Flowers growing straight up and out of cellophane bags are kept stable by the weight of hard candies. **INSPIRED BY:** Parisian rose hard candies. **MADE WITH:** Tissue; new and vintage single-ply crepe; wood bead. **GREAT FOR:** Party favors, weddings, and events. **HOW-TO:** p. 181.

40 PINSTRIPE & PIN DOT

We used felt-tipped markers to draw polka dots and lines in contrasting and complementary colors, resulting in these crisp and graphic flowers. **INSPIRED BY:** Stripe and dot patterns. **MADE WITH:** Double-sided crepe. **GREAT FOR:** Boutonnieres, bouquets, gift trimming, and centerpieces. **HOW-TO:** p. 182.

41

PARTY STICKS

Built on 40" (101.5cm) painted dowel stems, these fringy decorations are lively and dramatic. Consider an all-white palette for a wedding. **INSPIRED BY:** Vintage paper party garlands. **MADE WITH:** Tissue; single-ply and florist crepe; wood dowels. **GREAT FOR:** Home decor, centerpieces, holidays, and weddings. **HOW-TO:** p. 183.

42 / WHITE & BLACK WITH NEON POPS

Oversized mimosa-like pom-poms on lanky black stems and white neon-dipped lotus flowers make a frolicsome presentation. Use as a group or in individual arrangements. **INSPIRED BY:** A 1980s color palette. **MADE WITH:** Single-ply and double-sided crepe. **GREAT FOR:** Centerpieces, weddings, and home decor. **HOW-TO:** p. 184.

43 / GREEN THUMB GARDEN ROSE

A green rose with shell-pink foliage creates a unique reversal of nature. Petal tip textures emerge when the double-sided crepe is lightly brushed with diluted white paint, causing the colors to bleed. **INSPIRED BY:** Old-fashioned garden roses. **MADE WITH:** Double-sided crepe; tissue; pips. **GREAT FOR:** Gifts and home decor. **HOW-TO:** p. 185.

44 / SPOOKY RAVENS & KITTY CATS

These creepy "birds" with hand-painted striped petals and claw stems have landed on a tumble of bare branches. A cat eye garland with kitty ear petals keeps watch. **INSPIRED BY:** Halloween! **MADE WITH:** Single-ply and florist crepe. **GREAT FOR:** Halloween parties and decor. **HOW-TO:** p. 186.

45

LIGHTCATCHERS

These delicate flowers seem to float effortlessly atop glass stirring rods. Made from glassine, the translucent petals catch the light and, when overlapped, create beautiful new color combinations. **INSPIRED BY:** Stained glass. **MADE WITH:** Glassine paper; glass rods. **GREAT FOR:** Home decor and centerpieces. **HOW-TO:** p. 187.

46 / MEDALLION LADDER

Dramatic yet relatively simple to assemble, these suspended flowers make the perfect backdrop for a child's party, exchanging wedding vows, or a fun photo booth. This party decoration looks great in any color palette. **INSPIRED BY:** Korean paper flowers. **MADE WITH:** Single-ply and florist crepe; wood dowels. **GREAT FOR:** Parties and weddings. **HOW-TO:** p. 188.

47 PAINTER'S MUSE

Inspired by a floral painting from the 1970s, we rendered our version of these colorful flowers in luminous shades of tissue instead of paint. **INSPIRED BY:** A flea-market painting. **MADE WITH:** Tissue; florist crepe. **GREAT FOR:** Home decor, centerpieces, and wedding bouquets. **HOW-TO:** p. 189.

48 FADING FALL WREATH

From pumpkin orange to gold, honey to coffee, and finally plum to brown, this wreath embodies nature's transition from autumn to winter. **INSPIRED BY:** Changing seasons. **MADE WITH:** Florist and single-ply crepe; tissue; paper-covered pears. **GREAT FOR:** Autumn decor and holiday events. **HOW-TO:** p. 190.

49 / OMBRÉ PLUM BLOSSOMS

A tonal range of petite flowers in purple, plum, orchid, and lavender spill down an elegant branch. These blossoms are simply grouped by color and attached with hot glue to a found branch. **INSPIRED BY:** Ombré textile patterns. **MADE WITH:** Single-ply and florist crepe. **GREAT FOR:** Weddings, parties, and home decor. **HOW-TO:** p. 192.

50 / PEPPERED PEONY

Light single-ply crepe paper and feathers from a vintage hat sway in the slightest breeze giving these big 8" (20.5cm) blooms a light and fluttery feel. **INSPIRED BY:** A floral hat. **MADE WITH:** Vintage feathers; single-ply and florist crepe; tissue; Japanese paper. **GREAT FOR:** Centerpieces, home decor, and gifts. **HOW-TO:** p. 193.

51 / DUTCH BOTANICAL

This arrangement is a lush and varied collection of blossoms, buds, and leaves in a subdued yet vibrant palette. Texture and materials combine to give this arrangement an old-world quality. **INSPIRED BY:** Dutch master paintings. **MADE WITH:** Tissue; single-ply and double-sided crepe; pips. **GREAT FOR:** Centerpieces and home decor. **HOW-TO:** p. 194.

52/ **SUMMER SPECKLE**

Happy flowers with hand-striped leaves look lovely nestled together, especially when displayed in multiple arrangements. **INSPIRED BY:** A summer garden and striped beach towels. **MADE WITH:** Single-ply, double-sided, and florist crepe. **GREAT FOR:** Centerpieces, wedding bouquets, and home decor. **HOW-TO:** p. 196.

53 / WATER-DIPPED WATER LILIES

These blossoms are floating in hand-dyed paper confetti "water." The variegated petal effect is created with a simple dip in a shallow bowl of water, causing the double-sided crepe colors to bleed together. **INSPIRED BY:** Monet, water lilies. **MADE WITH:** Double-sided crepe; Venetian dew glitter; vintage pips. **GREAT FOR:** Centerpieces, weddings, and events. **HOW-TO:** p. 197.

54 LICORICE ALLSORTS

This abundant grouping is modern yet slightly old-fashioned when styled like a vintage arrangement. Black and white painted petals and leaves are punctuated with a bit of color. **INSPIRED BY:** Licorice allsorts candies. **MADE WITH:** Single-ply, double-sided, and florist crepe; twisted paper ribbon; pips. **GREAT FOR:** Home decor, centerpieces, and wedding bouquets. **HOW-TO:** p. 198.

The Party Book

55 / SEA SPRAY

Gift toppers are made from a mix of different aquatic-colored and textured materials, including polka-dot "bubbles," shell-inspired opalescent fringe, and cheesecloth "netting." These flowers come together quickly and look great in any color scheme. **INSPIRED BY:** The ocean. **MADE WITH:** Single-ply crepe, iridescent twisted ribbon; cheesecloth. **GREAT FOR:** Gift trimming and favors. **HOW-TO:** p. 200.

56 / PEPPERMINT SNO-CONES

A simple project made with painted continuous-petal flowers becomes a peppermint wonderland when each blossom is pinned to a cone with a decorative straight pin. **INSPIRED BY:** Striped peppermint candies and candy canes. **MADE WITH:** Single-ply and double-sided crepe; decorative pins; glitter. **GREAT FOR:** Holidays, centerpieces, and home decor. **HOW-TO:** p. 201.

57 TROMPETTES

Metallic crepe and a trumpet-like shape lend a vintage vibe to these classic-looking and chic holiday ornaments. Perched on a tree, whether feathered or fresh, or grouped together on a table, these glinty flowers feel celebratory and special. **INSPIRED BY:** Vintage holiday decorations. **MADE WITH:** Metallic florist crepe. **GREAT FOR:** Holiday decorating. **HOW TO:** p. 202.

58 / BLOOMING RUBY

Monochromatic shades of red, burgundy, and deep plum are grounded with paper-covered wire "roots." The petals, leaves, and bulb gleam and glint from a wash of glitter glue. **INSPIRED BY:** Forced bulbs. **MADE WITH:** Florist and single-ply crepe; glitter. **GREAT FOR:** Holiday and seasonal decorating, and gifts. **HOW-TO:** p. 203.

59 / STARBURST WREATH

A sparkling ring of pointy-star crepe petals, tinsel centers, and punched stars makes a shimmery New Year's decoration. Customize a paper banner for any holiday or event. **INSPIRED BY:** Holiday sparkle. **MADE WITH:** Printed single-ply crepe or tissue; card stock; tinsel. **GREAT FOR:** Winter holidays, weddings, and events. **HOW TO:** p. 204.

60 / MIXERS

Perfect for mixing in with more complicated flowers, these simple blossoms make it easy to fill out a larger arrangement or bouquet. They're charming in any color palette, and can stand alone as a sweet posy great for gifting. **INSPIRED BY:** Old-school florist filler flowers. **MADE WITH:** Single-ply, double-sided, and florist crepe. **GREAT FOR:** Arrangements, gifts, gift trimming, and favors. **HOW-TO:** p. 205.

61 / STARGAZER LILIES

These oversized lilies are the yin and yang of a celestial night. One lives in moonlight, the other in shadow. Printed tissue was adhered to crepe and stars were rubber-stamped in a pattern to create a star shower on curling petals. **INSPIRED BY:** Stargazer lilies and starry nights. **MADE WITH:** Single-ply, double-sided, and florist crepe; tissue; tulle. **GREAT FOR:** Home decor, centerpieces, and gifts. **HOW-TO:** p. 206.

62 DELFT & FLOW BLUE

Taking inspiration from the nature-infused patterns in blue-and-white china, we rubber-stamped white petals with floral-themed stamps in various shades of blue. **INSPIRED BY:** Blue-and-white china. **MADE WITH:** Double-sided crepe; tissue; rubber stamps. **GREAT FOR:** Gift trimming, home decor, centerpieces, and events. **HOW-TO:** p. 207.

63 / NOM DE BLOOM

This large monogrammed bloom would look beautiful nestled inside a shadow box. A tribute to all forms of glitter, this flower's iridescent nature is expressed with fine glitter, glitter paint, and glitter glue. **INSPIRED BY:** Vintage glittered leaves. **MADE WITH:** Single-ply crepe; glitter; pressed-paper leaves. **GREAT FOR:** Home decor, holiday decorations, and gifts. **HOW-TO:** p. 208.

64 / CANDY CENTER

Playful and sweet, these blooms pull double duty; first as a fun centerpiece, and then as a delicious takeaway. Origami leaves add a hint of pattern. **INSPIRED BY:** Our passion for Japanese candies. **MADE WITH:** Double-sided crepe; origami papers; cellophane bags. **GREAT FOR:** Favors, centerpieces, and a child's party. **HOW-TO:** p. 209.

65 / MARI-POPPY

The individual palettes for these abstract poppies were directly inspired by the unique colorways of a well-known poppy-print fabric. Tied with personalized tags, they make a fanciful seating-card arrangement for a special event. **INSPIRED BY:** Marimekko Unikko fabric. **MADE WITH:** Single-ply, double-sided, and florist crepe; paper ribbon. **GREAT FOR:** Seating and place cards, and gift trimming. **HOW-TO:** p. 210.

66 / LEFTOVERS BLOOM

Collected wrapping paper scraps are transformed into a patterned blossom. Take this idea further by making a wacky version with recycled holiday wrapping papers, a vintage magazine, or the funny pages. **INSPIRED BY:** Paper scraps in the studio. **MADE WITH:** Single-ply and florist crepe; tulle; wrapping paper. **GREAT FOR:** Home decor, centerpieces, birthday parties, and other events. **HOW-TO:** p. 211.

67 / CONFISERIES COLORÉES

Pastry shop eye candy influenced these layered flowers. Vintage and new doily petals pair up with tissue. Gold paper garlands cut with a craft punch trim the stems and allude to the decorations on our favorite macaron boxes. **INSPIRED BY:** Ladurée, Parisian pastry shops. **MADE WITH:** Tissue; florist crepe; decorative paper; doilies. **GREAT FOR:** Centerpieces, parties, and home decor. **HOW-TO:** p. 212.

68 / CORAL-COLORED REEF

Watery-hued aqua tulle and curled, thin leaves create a sense of movement that mimics the undulating waves of the sea. Embossed matte paper petals with a decorative edge add texture. **INSPIRED BY:** Coral reefs. **MADE WITH:** Single-ply and florist crepe; embossed paper; tissue; tulle. **GREAT FOR:** Centerpieces and home decor. **HOW-TO:** p. 213.

69 / TRIBAL TARGET

Aztec-inspired hand-painted flying arrow leaves spin around this oversized 11" (28cm) flower. Multiple rings of rustic and natural hues are punctuated with black and white. **INSPIRED BY:** Aztec and tribal patterns. **MADE WITH:** Single-ply and double-sided crepe; tissue; decorative paper. **GREAT FOR:** Home decor. **HOW-TO:** p. 214.

70 / I HEART YOU

With Valentine's Day gift giving in mind, we crafted (with love) a variety of heart-shaped petal flowers and leaves. **INSPIRED BY:** Hearts. **MADE WITH:** Double-sided crepe; decorative paper; vintage pips; Dresden paper ornaments. **GREAT FOR:** Valentine's Day, gifts, and gift trimming. **HOW-TO:** p. 215.

71 / DOUBLE SCOOP

Both children and adults will delight in these ice cream creations. Let your own tastes dictate the direction of the flavors. **INSPIRED BY:** Ice cream cones! **MADE WITH:** Single-ply crepe; Styrofoam; ribbed kraft paper. **GREAT FOR:** A child's party, birthdays, and centerpieces. **HOW-TO:** p. 216.

72 / CANDY STRIPES

Multiple small arrangements in aqua vases create a parade of color. White, curvy foliage complements the linear hand-painted striped petals. **INSPIRED BY:** Candy wrappers and swirled, striped lollipops. **MADE WITH:** Single-ply and double-sided crepe; decorative paper; yarn. **GREAT FOR:** Centerpieces, events, and gift trimming. **HOW-TO:** p. 217.

73 / SPARKS

A giant globe vase with embossed detail plays off the loose and graphic elements in these flowers. The fringe centers suggest a flickering flame and are crafted from ultrasuede fabric. **INSPIRED BY:** Fire sparks. **MADE WITH:** Single-ply and double-sided crepe; ultrasuede. **GREAT FOR:** Centerpieces and home decor. **HOW-TO:** p. 218.

74 / DELICATE DIP-DYE

Simple shapes are transformed with a quick and delicate paint dip. We used five different petal styles with a variety of dip treatments to create a range of softly graphic flowers. **INSPIRED BY:** Dip-dye textiles. **MADE WITH:** Single-ply and double-sided crepe. **GREAT FOR:** Centerpieces, home decor, and holidays. **HOW-TO:** p. 219.

75 / BUTTERFLY NEST

A cross section of a meadow displayed in a rustic log planter beckons paper butterflies to its curly stemmed pods and blooms. **INSPIRED BY:** A field of poppies and bachelor buttons. **MADE WITH:** Single-ply, double-sided, and florist crepe; tissue; pressed-paper butterflies. **GREAT FOR:** Weddings and events, centerpieces, and home decor. **HOW-TO:** p. 220.

2 3 4 5 6 7 8 9 10 11 12

MATERIALS/

CREPE PAPERS

Due to its inherent sculptural qualities, crepe paper is one of the most common materials used for making paper flowers. To produce crepe paper, tissue paper is coated in sizing and processed on a machine that makes gathers in the paper. This creates a material that is semirigid in the direction of the grain and expands to varying degrees across the grain. Easing the gathers apart enables the paper to be configured into various forms that maintain their shape. Crepe paper lengths are commonly known as *folds*.

Single-Ply (1)

Characterized by a translucent quality that lends itself to creating lifelike flowers, single-ply is the most delicate of the crepe paper weights available. Because of its lighter weight, single-ply can be less forgiving than thicker-weight crepe. It won't bounce back easily once worked with. Single-ply can be found in a wide range of colors, making it useful for all types of projects. Two primary brands of single-ply crepe paper are widely available. One is made in the United States and, because it is not colorfast, works well with water for color-bleeding techniques. The other is colorfast and fade resistant.

Streamers (2)

Crepe paper streamers are inexpensive, and because the grain runs with the short side of the roll, they are great for making smaller blooms. They make quick work of fringed centers and small continuous petal–style flowers. Basic colors are available, as well as printed options that can make interesting-patterned flowers.

Vintage (3)

Found on Etsy and eBay, and in the occasional antique shop, vintage crepe paper often has a beautifully faded and worn appearance that can result in unique creations. Interesting varieties of crepe paper were produced in the twentieth century that are not made today. Color palettes often feel more refined, prints are more festive, and generally the papers are of a high quality.

Printed (4)

Perfect for making whimsical flowers, printed crepe paper comes in a somewhat limited variety of patterns and colors. Generally single-ply, it can be laminated to other weights of crepe paper with paste glue to produce thicker sheets. Some of the best examples of printed crepe paper are vintage rather than new.

3

Double-Sided, 2-Ply (5)

Double-sided crepe, produced in Germany, is made by fusing together two layers of lighter-weight crepe. It is finely grained, with a generous amount of stretch and a two-toned appearance. Double-sided crepe absorbs paint well. It comes in a wide variety of warm-toned colors, with fewer options available on the cooler side of the spectrum.

Florist, Italian (6)

Florist crepe is the most sculptural of all the crepe papers because it has the greatest amount of stretch. When pieces are stretched completely, the result is a softer paper with lots of body that holds a shape well. Produced primarily in Italy and Asia, florist crepe is available in several weights most often noted as 100, 160, and 180 grams and a wide range of colors.

Metallic (7)

Though a bit harder to find, florist and single-ply crepe are available in a few metallic options. Gradated styles and foil finishes are fun to work with, especially for holiday projects.

About Crepe Paper Grain

Noting the paper's grain direction is especially important when working with crepe. The grain of crepe paper always runs in the direction of the gathers. When crafting with crepe paper, the grain should generally run lengthwise with a template unless a specific effect is desired. Petals or leaves cut with the grain will have support from the paper fibers, and the gathers will stretch out in the proper direction. If desired, cutting against the grain will give a floppy appearance to a petal or leaf shape.

4

5

ADDITIONAL PAPERS

Tissue (1)

Tissue paper is very inexpensive and comes in a wide range of colors and patterns. Delicate and light, it lends itself well to creating double-petal and cuff-style flowers. Tissue has no give—a petal's or leaf's shape is determined by how it is attached to a stem. Many layers can be cut at once—or, to aid in cutting intricate shapes, a sheet can be supported with a piece of heavier paper. Bleeding Art Tissue is made using pigments that are water-soluble. A variety of effects can be achieved by brushing, dipping, or spraying water onto the paper.

Decorative (2)

The world of decorative papers is seemingly inexhaustible and allows for exploration and unique discoveries for any project. Metallic, patterned, and graphic print papers can add interesting details to your flowers. Japanese and Indian papers often have texture that can add depth to your project.

Origami (3)

Origami papers are lightweight and come in a range of precut sizes that are easy to work with. A wide variety of colors and patterns make this paper a fun one to use in projects, especially when adding small details.

Paper Ribbon (4)

Made for crafting and gift trimming, paper ribbon often has a crinkly texture and comes in a variety of tones. It is very lightweight yet stiff and makes wonderfully delicate petals or leaves. Twisted paper ribbon can be untwisted and flattened into a highly textured crinkly sheet.

Glassine & Vellum (5)

Flowers made from translucent glassine and vellum papers have a wonderful luminous quality. Glassine has a slightly softer hand and is more translucent than vellum. Vellum is heavier and more matte than glassine and is great for making crisp leaves. Both papers stay sharply creased when folded, but overfolding vellum can cause the paper to crack.

Wrapping (6)

Generally inexpensive and easy to find, most crafters already have several options on hand. Wrapping paper is great for creating abstract and whimsical flowers and making double-sided leaves.

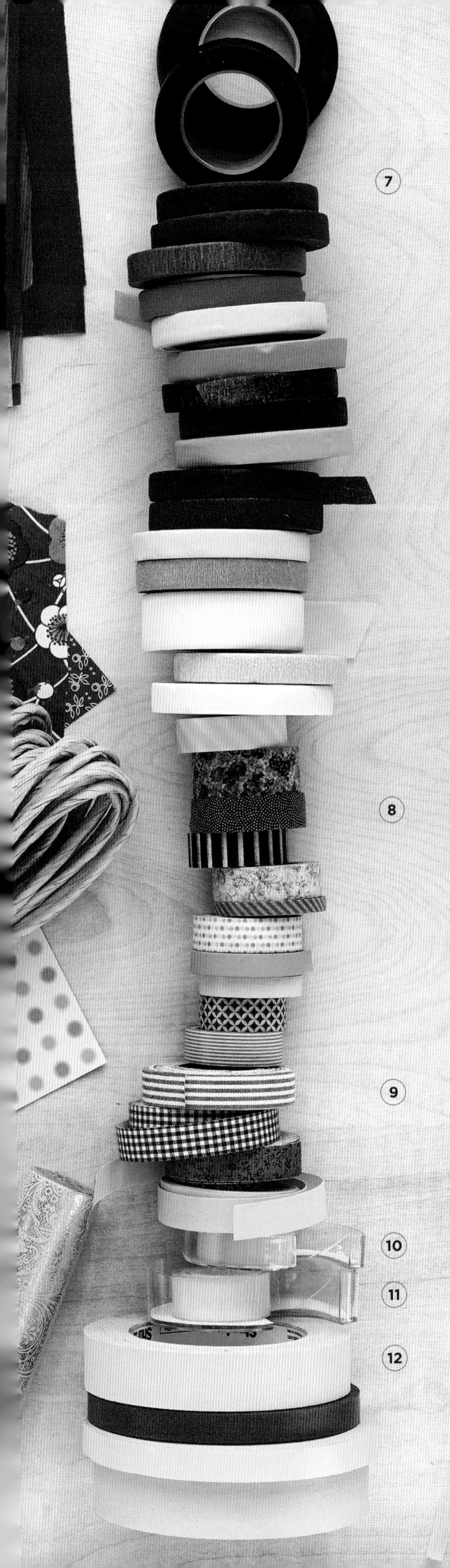

TAPES

Floral (7)

Floral tape (also known as stem wrap) is a slightly sticky, self-sealing tape with an embedded adhesive that is released when the tape is stretched. It is the primary material used for attaching petals and leaves and wrapping stems. Floral tape brands are few in number and have varying levels of adhesive quality. It is commonly found in ½" (13mm) widths in many colors, including metallic; 1" (2.5cm) widths are also available, but in a more limited selection of colors. Since floral tape can dry out over time, it should be stored in an airtight bag to preserve the moisture content.

Washi (8)

Washi tape, made for crafting and gift trimming, is less adhesive than other tapes and is easily removable. It comes in many colors and detailed patterns, providing beautiful options for finishing stems.

Fabric (9)

A strip of cloth or ribbon with an adhesive backing, fabric tape is perfect for finishing stems and adding a bit of pattern. It has a softer look and feel than floral tape.

Clear (10)

Invisible tape, cellophane, or gloss-finish gift wrap tape is ideal when a transparent tape is needed to complement other clear or translucent components in a project.

Double-Sided (11)

Double-sided tapes are made with adhesive on both sides. They are useful for starting flowers and adhering certain types of centers. Acid-free varieties are available.

Masking (12)

Masking tape is produced with varying levels of adhesive quality and in many colors from bright neon to pastel. It works well for securing pieces when building larger flowers.

ADHESIVES

White Craft Glue (13)

White craft glue is suitable for most crafting materials, including paper, fabric, and glitter. Thick white craft glue is used for making flower centers and works well for adding stability where needed. White "tacky" glue is best for adhering heavier items or when you need glue that sets quickly. Look for acid-free varieties.

Paste & Stick Glue (14)

Paste glues work well for adhering two layers of paper together. Their low moisture content won't cause thin papers to buckle as easily as other adhesives might. Glue sticks dry quickly, making them best for small areas and thin papers. Stick and paste glues both dry clear and remain flexible when dry.

Hot Glue (15)

Hot glue is a good choice when maximum stability is needed because it sets fast and is rigid when dry. Also, it will join porous and nonporous materials. In general, with hot glues the higher the glue's temperature the stronger the bond. Hot glue works well for securing or affixing flowers, rather than building them.

TOOLS

All-Purpose Scissors (1)

Having two pairs of quality scissors, one regular size (8"–9"/20.5cm–23cm) for general work and one smaller-size (4"–6"/10cm–15cm sharp-point) for intricate work, is recommended. A detail scissors with a two-fingered bottom handle and flexible grips can be easier to use when cutting curves. Designate scissors for paper and shears for fabric and ribbon to keep blades sharp.

Decorative Scissors (2)

Fringing scissors are designed with several conjoined blades that cut at the same time to make shredding, fringing, and paper confetti a simple task. Many styles of decorative-edge scissors can be found for adding creative finishing touches to projects. They vary in quality and generally have a short reach. A "deckle" edge scissors can create an organic-looking edge. A "cloud" or oversized scallop scissors softens the straight edges of cuff-style flowers. Pinking shears have a zigzag edge and a longer reach than decorative-edge scissors.

Rotary Cutter (3)

Useful for cutting through many layers of crepe or tissue at once, rotary cutters are time-savers when making multiples of a flower. They are sturdy enough to cut through an entire packet of crepe folds in one pass. Interchangeable rotary blades come in decorative edges as well.

Wire Cutters & Pliers (4)

A good pair of wire cutters for trimming wire stems and wired leaves is essential. Needle-nose pliers are optional, but are perfect for turning down any sharp wire edges or tips. In either case, look for a pair that are spring-loaded with rubber-coated handles.

Craft & Hole Punches (5)

Craft punches are available in a wide variety of shapes and sizes. Deep-edge punches are ideal for making delicate strands that can be added to stems and arrangements. While limited in their reach, traditional hole punches work well for adding precise holes to the edges of paper. In addition to a range of sizes including mini- and microcircles, they come in a variety of shapes such as stars and hearts. A Japanese screw punch, which takes interchangeable multiple-sized hole bits, will make holes through multiple layers of paper anywhere on a sheet.

Brushes & Painting Tools (6)

Having a selection of brushes from thick to fine to specialty allows more freedom for creativity when adding color to papers. Soft, nylon-bristle brushes are ideal for most purposes. Flat brushes work well for applying glue to larger areas, for adhering papers together, glittering, or creating wide stripes. Fan and feather brushes are great for making rougher, looser, and more organic stripes. An adjustable striping brush makes quick work of painting multiple stripes. If your budget allows, choose brushes that are well made. With proper care they will last for years. Decorative texture tools designed for children's art projects are fun to use and make excellent patterns for petals and leaves. Spray bottles with both adjustable and nonadjustable tips, filled with diluted acrylic paints or water, provide endless possibilities for painted speckle, spray, and stream effects.

Rubber Stamps (7)

Rubber stamps can add pattern, color, and detail to paper flowers. Thousands of designs are available from craft stores locally and online. Some stamps have clear acrylic mounts printed with a grid to aid in alignment and are designed to work with repositionable stamp designs. Stamp pad inks are available in an endless range of colors, sizes, and ink types. Many can be re-inked as they dry out.

Curling Tools (8)

Scissors, pencils, kitchen skewers, knitting needles, and toothpicks make great curling tools for all types of paper, especially crepe. Full beverage cans, tubes of glue, or thick markers work well for forming wire into curves.

Rulers & Cutting Mats (9)

Cork-backed rulers have a slip-resistant back that adds safety to precise cutting. Clear plastic quilting rulers simplify techniques with a see-through grid and measurements. Self-healing cutting mats protect the work surface from cuts and scratches and at the same time prevent cutting tools from dulling prematurely.

PAINTS & COLORINGS

Paints, Mediums & Watercolors (1)

Acrylic and watercolor paints offer flexibility when adding color. They dry fast and can be diluted with water. Acrylic mediums, both matte and gloss, can be used as thin paper adhesives or to add a specific sheen to a flower component. Matte medium is especially useful where an overall matte finish is desired when wrapping shapes in paper. Gloss medium can give otherwise matte-finished papers or parts a glossy coating.

Water-Soluble Crayons & Pencils (2)

Endless drawn and painted effects are possible with water-soluble crayons and pencils. They can be applied to paper dry or brushed with water and blended like watercolor paint.

Markers (3)

Markers are ideal for fine line work and come in every imaginable color, ink type, and width.

Glitter (4)

Glitter is available in several forms. Loose glitter comes in beautiful colors and different materials like glass, tinsel, shaped, flake, and even microbeads. Glitter glue, packaged in tubes, is metallic particles suspended in an emulsion that dries clear and remains flexible. Glitter paint is similar, with the exception that the particles are suspended in color pigments and can be used like paint.

STEMS & CENTERS

Covered Floral Wire (5)

There are two main types of covered stick floral wire, cloth-wrapped and paper-covered. They are most commonly available in 18" lengths. Cloth-wrapped wire is covered in thread and available in a range of gauges, or thicknesses. Tapes adhere well to the softer surface of cloth-wrapped wire, and the cloth can be colored with permanent markers. The higher the gauge number, the thinner and more pliable the wire. Paper-covered floral wire is a very textured, natural kraft-paper color, and commonly found in 18-gauge. Thin gauge wires are best for securing parts and thicker wires make better stems. Other materials for stems include tree branches and twigs, skewers, paper straws, pipe cleaners, wood dowels, and even glass rods like those used for mixing.

Cotton (6)

Flower centers can be created with cotton balls—full-sized, doubled-up, or separated into smaller pieces. Spun cotton, or Watte, most often made in Germany, come in various sizes and preformed shapes including balls, half-rounds, and bud shapes, They work well for intricately shaped centers and are fabricated with a hole in the base for inserting a wire stem.

Pips (7)

Pips (also known as peps) mimic stamen in real flowers and come in a variety of colors and styles both vintage and new. Typically made from a small amount of material made from glue and wood pulp or sawdust adhered to the end of a stiffened thread, they add lifelike qualities to paper flowers.

OTHER MATERIALS

Doilies & Coffee Filters (8)

Doilies make beautiful lacy petals. In addition to white there are color, patterned, metallic, and vintage options available. White and kraft-colored coffee filters absorb paint beautifully, and when painted have a distinctive look. Both are generally inexpensive and easy to find.

Notions & Millinery (9)

Beautiful and unique paper flower centers can be made from buttons, pom-poms, or any of the huge varieties of beads available. Vintage or new millinery fruit, flowers, and leaves can also be added to any project.

Cellophane & Polyester Film (10)

Adding cellophane or polyester film, commonly known as Mylar, can add texture, reflectivity, and shine to centers, petals, or leaves.

Fabric & Netting (11)

Using fabrics and/or netting is a way to add soft texture to paper flowers. Fabrics and netting can be used to make and cover centers, cut into petals and leaves, or layered with paper.

Ribbon, Raffia & Trimmings (12)

Ribbon and raffia are great materials for paper flower centers. Ribbon is available in an inexhaustible variety of widths, finishes, and colors. Natural and synthetic raffia fibers have an organic look and are available in a range of colors. Unique trimmings can be wrapped around stems for interesting effects.

Pressed-Paper Ornaments (13)

German-produced Dresden pressed-paper ornaments are made from die-cut paper-backed foil in different shapes, sizes, and themes. Dresden ornaments have a bas-relief sculptural quality to them, which can give instant detail to a project and add contrast when used with other papers. Embossed, die-cut scrap pictures include shapes and images such as flowers, animals, leaves, and butterflies and can be used as accents.

SKILLS/

ANATOMY OF A PAPER FLOWER

Making paper flowers is a fun and imaginative process often inspired by nature. Elements of real flowers can be used for reference depending on what type of flower you want to create. Most, if not all of the parts, can be considered optional.

CENTERS Often made from paper-covered cotton, fringe, pips, or any combination thereof, the center is the first component that gets attached to the stem.

STAMEN Vintage and new pips, as well as paper fringe, fill in for stamen, adding a lifelike quality to paper flowers.

PETALS Crafted from any type of paper, single, continuous, or cuff petals are applied in one or many layers and are usually the most prominent feature of a flower.

CALYX An optional element that adds finish to a paper flower. The calyx is at the junction where the petals attach to the stem.

STEM Generally made from cloth-wrapped or paper-covered floral wire, the stem must be strong enough to support the weight of the finished flower.

BUDS Buds can be crafted from paper-covered cotton or a small bundle of complementary materials. Buds can contribute to a more natural appearance in a flower arrangement.

LEAVES Crafted from all types of paper in varying shapes and sizes, and attached along the stem, leaves can add personality and texture.

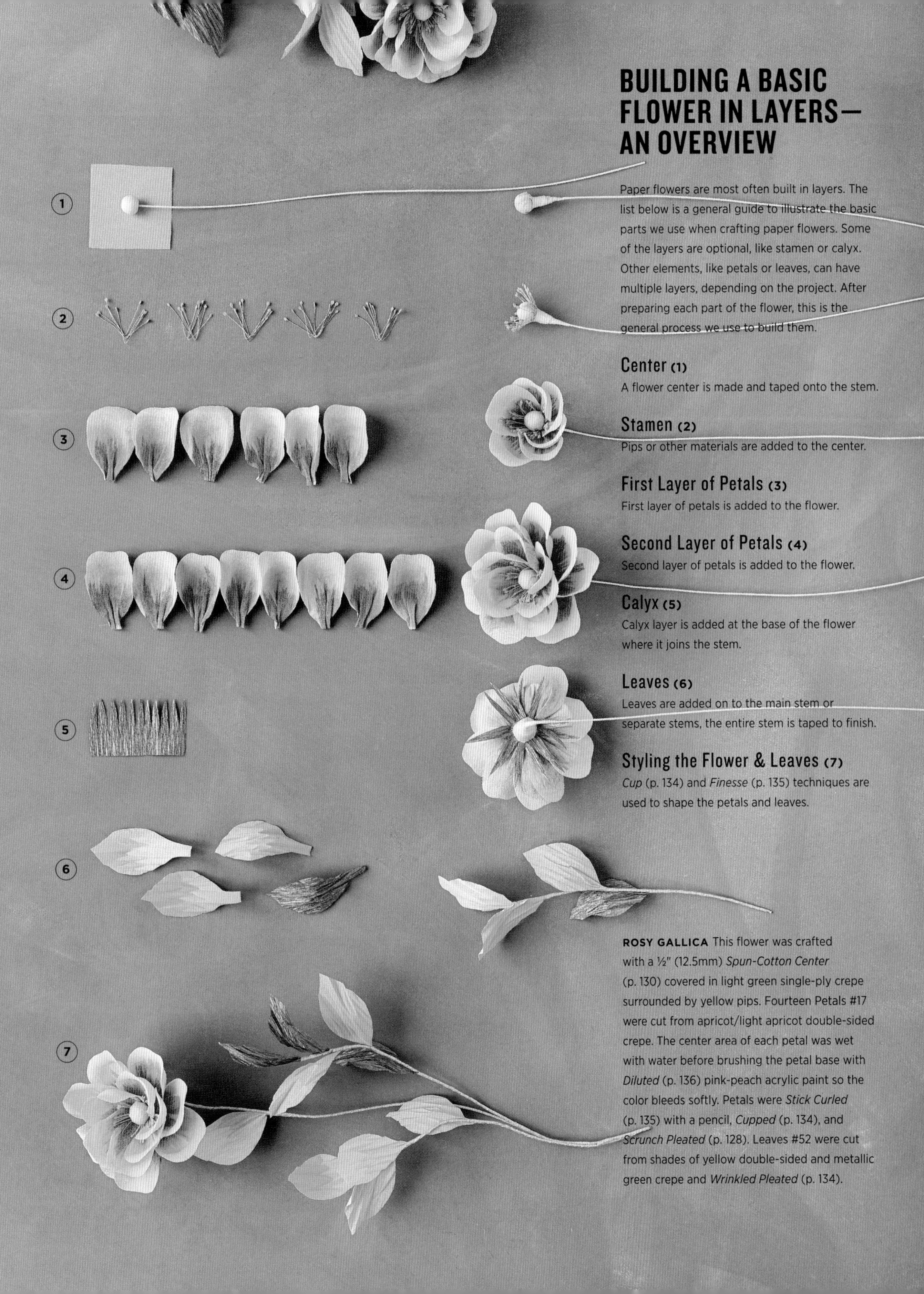

BUILDING A BASIC FLOWER IN LAYERS—AN OVERVIEW

Paper flowers are most often built in layers. The list below is a general guide to illustrate the basic parts we use when crafting paper flowers. Some of the layers are optional, like stamen or calyx. Other elements, like petals or leaves, can have multiple layers, depending on the project. After preparing each part of the flower, this is the general process we use to build them.

Center (1)
A flower center is made and taped onto the stem.

Stamen (2)
Pips or other materials are added to the center.

First Layer of Petals (3)
First layer of petals is added to the flower.

Second Layer of Petals (4)
Second layer of petals is added to the flower.

Calyx (5)
Calyx layer is added at the base of the flower where it joins the stem.

Leaves (6)
Leaves are added on to the main stem or separate stems, the entire stem is taped to finish.

Styling the Flower & Leaves (7)
Cup (p. 134) and *Finesse* (p. 135) techniques are used to shape the petals and leaves.

ROSY GALLICA This flower was crafted with a ½" (12.5mm) *Spun-Cotton Center* (p. 130) covered in light green single-ply crepe surrounded by yellow pips. Fourteen Petals #17 were cut from apricot/light apricot double-sided crepe. The center area of each petal was wet with water before brushing the petal base with *Diluted* (p. 136) pink-peach acrylic paint so the color bleeds softly. Petals were *Stick Curled* (p. 135) with a pencil, *Cupped* (p. 134), and *Scrunch Pleated* (p. 128). Leaves #52 were cut from shades of yellow double-sided and metallic green crepe and *Wrinkled Pleated* (p. 134).

PETAL STYLES & WORKING WITH TEMPLATES

Petal Styles

Single, continuous, and cuff are the three main styles we use to make petals for paper flowers. Single petals are individually cut petals that are layered when crafting a paper flower. Continuous petals are longer and cut from accordion-folded paper so they remain attached to one another at the base. Cuff petals are similar to continuous-petal styles, but there is little to no definition in the petal shape, and generally they do not require a template.

Single-Petal Templates

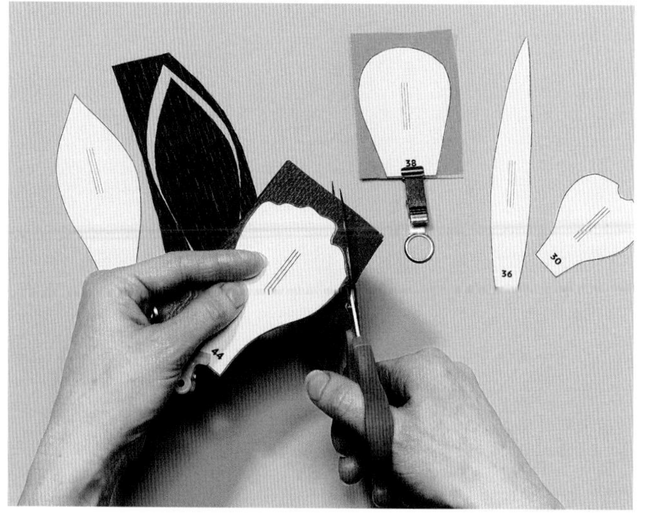

A single petal can be cut from one or several sheets of paper at a time. When cutting multiple sheets start with sheets cut slightly larger than the template, or alternatively, accordion-fold a longer strip of paper into several layers placing the template on top. Stabilize the template to the paper with a clip. Some symmetrical shapes are cut from half-shape templates by aligning the dashed fold line with the folded edge of the paper.

Continuous-Petal Templates

Continuous petals are cut from a strip of paper that has been accordion-folded to the width of the template. Align the base of the template with the bottom of the folded paper, clip the template to the paper, and cut around the template, leaving the base of the paper folds uncut. Our continuous-petal templates are demarcated with dashed lines where the folds should remain intact. The end result will be a series of petals that are connected at the base in one long piece—like a string of paper dolls.

Making Your Own Templates

Once you are comfortable working with templates, you can easily create your own petal and leaf templates using stiff paper and cutting tools. To create symmetrical shapes, cut out half of a shape using the paper's straight edge as a centerline for your design. When using a symmetrical template, align the centerline of the template with the folded edge of a sheet of paper that has been folded in half. The width of your template's base will dictate how the petal or leaf gets attached to the stem and the amount of bulk around the bottom of the flower.

CUTTING TECHNIQUES

Cutting Tips for All Papers

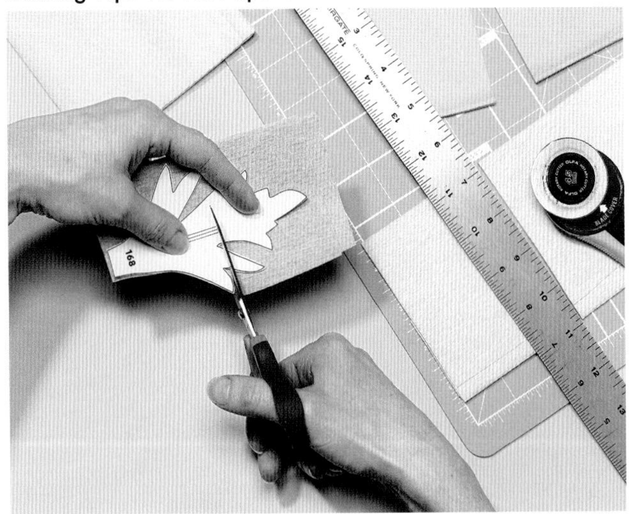

Snags occasionally occur when cutting paper, especially crepe. For more control, try moving the paper when cutting instead of the scissors. With long strokes, working close to the fulcrum of the scissors, keep your scissors hand stationary as you turn the sheet with your opposite hand. Using this method, 3–5 layers of thicker papers like double-sided and florist crepe and 6–10 layers of single-ply crepe or tissue can be cut at a time. To expedite straight cutting when working on a project, full folds of single-ply or double-sided crepe can be cut with scissors or a rotary cutter.

Using Decorative-Edge Scissors

Decorative paper edgers tend not to be as sharp as high-quality all-purpose scissors, occasionally catching and tearing the paper during cutting. Make sure to start the cut as close to the fulcrum of the scissors as possible. Cutting through a few sheets of single-ply crepe or tissue at once will often result in a cleaner cut than working with single sheets. If you desire a continuous and precise edge, make sure to realign the pattern before each cut.

Using Fringing Scissors

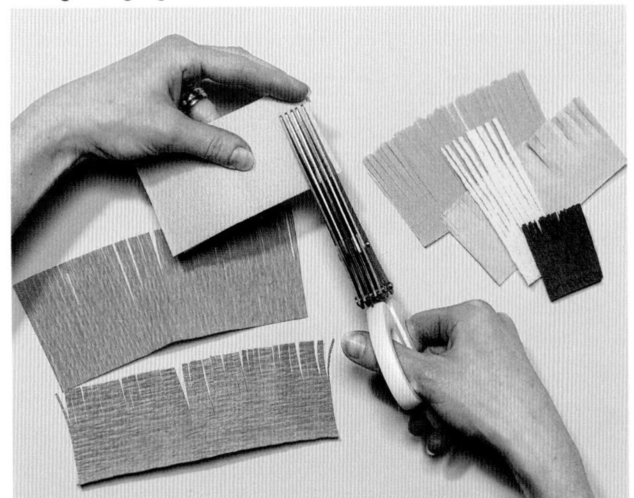

When working with fringing scissors, we have found that gently pulling the paper taut with the opposite hand as you cut gives the most precise results. When making centers and fringed accents, leaving an uncut base will allow you to easily gather the fringe together. In general, you can cut through 5 layers of single-ply crepe, 3 layers of double-sided crepe, 2 layers of florist crepe, and 6–8 layers of tissue at one time. Cutting with the grain will give the fringe more body, while cutting against the grain will result in a softer and more floppy fringe.

Hand Cutting Fringe

Hand fringing takes more effort, but gives more control over the thickness of the fringe. To cut fine fringe, hold the top of the paper between your index and middle fingers. Rest the bottom blade of the scissors against your ring finger while supporting the bottom of the paper between your thumb and ring finger. Begin cutting along the paper in the desired thickness, moving toward your supporting hand. Gently feed the uncut paper into the scissors with your thumb, maintaining the contact between the blade and your ring finger.

PREPPING PETALS & LEAVES

Scrunch Pleat (Single Petal or Leaf)

Begin *Scrunch Pleat* for single petals by holding one side of the base of a petal or leaf between your thumb and index finger, and the opposite side of the base between your other thumb and index finger. Scrunch the sides toward each other, creating multiple gathers. Press a bit to crease. This technique adds dimension and creates a thinner base and a slightly rounded petal. You can prescrunch your petals to condition the paper, and then *Scrunch Pleat* again as you attach each one to a stem.

Scrunch Pleat (Continuous & Cuff Petals)

Begin *Scrunch Pleat* for continuous and cuff petals by holding the base of one end of a strip of paper securely between the thumbs and index fingers of both hands. Start gathering the base of the paper using your index finger to feed the length of the paper past your thumb toward the opposite hand, supporting the pleats as you progress. Like *Scrunch Pleat* for single petals, this technique adds dimension. Prescrunching your continuous and cuff petals to condition the paper makes them a bit easier to work with when attaching to your flower stem using the *Gather and Wrap* (p. 132) method.

Single Pleat & Box Pleat

To make a *Single Pleat*, hold one side of the base of a petal or leaf between your thumb and index finger, and the opposite side of the base between your other thumb and index finger. Gently overlap the base onto itself at a slight diagonal, by approximately ¼" (6mm) or more. Press to crease. To make a *Single Pleat* with double petals, overlap and offset the petals, and pleat together. To make a *Box Pleat*, hold the piece in the same way as a *Single Pleat* but push the sides together to create a channel in the center of the base. Both methods add dimension and result in a thinner base.

Twist

To *Twist*, begin by *Scrunch Pleating* a petal or leaf base. Then hold it just above the base between the thumb and index finger of your nondominant hand and use the thumb and index finger of your dominant hand to twist the base of the petal away from you. Twist a few times. The twist creates a smaller contact point that will allow a petal or leaf to be a bit freer once it's attached to a flower's stem. This technique is great for securing double petals together before attaching them to a stem. To *Twist* double petals, overlap and offset petals before *Scrunch Pleating*, then twist.

STEMS & TAPING TECHNIQUES

Choosing Your Stem

The most important factor when choosing your stem is the weight of your finished flower. Make sure that the wire will support the finished piece. In general, we use 18-gauge or 20-gauge paper-covered or cloth-wrapped floral wire. Paper-covered wire has a thicker appearance and will generally hold more weight at the same gauge than cloth-wrapped wire. Cloth-wrapped wire gives your stems a thinner look. Stems are a matter of preference; try both to see which works best for you.

Floral Taping Tips

With some practice, floral tape is simple to use. Firmly but gently stretching the tape as you wrap is crucial to release the adhesive that makes it stick to itself. With one hand, hold and slowly twist the stem while applying pressure to the tape. The opposite hand stretches the tape as you work. Overlap the tape as you wrap, adding pressure with your fingers to prevent unraveling. Make a few fingernail scores at the end of each length of tape to help it adhere. When building a flower, keep a small pile of precut 3"–4" (7.5cm–10cm) strips of tape at the ready.

Using Floral Tape

Holding a stem with one hand, place a petal, leaf, or shape at the back of the stem, holding both between your thumb and index finger. Place the tape on the front of the stem and begin wrapping it around the stem, continuing to hold the petal in place and catching the base in the tape while spinning the stem. Wrap the tape around the base of the flower a few times. Continue wrapping down onto the wire at a slight diagonal, making sure to continually and gently pull the tape as you progress. Tape beyond the center, petal, or leaf and down onto the stem to secure.

Finishing Stems

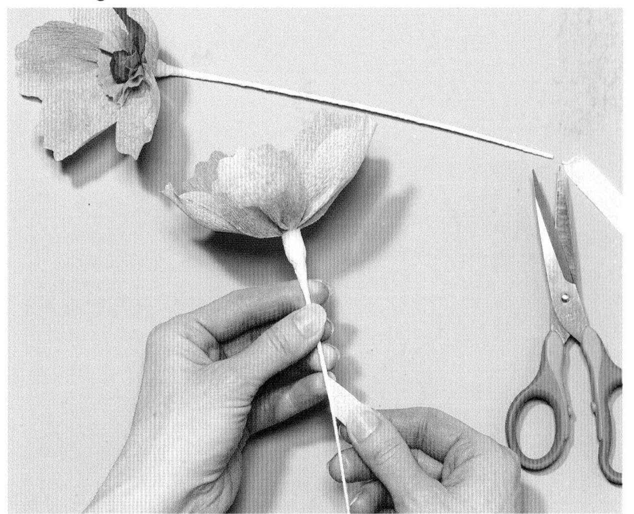

Cut a 12" (30.5cm) or longer piece of tape. Holding the stem in one hand, use your thumb to hold the end of the tape against the stem or flower base. Begin to twist the stem while firmly but gently stretching the tape with your opposite hand. Continue down the wire at a slight diagonal, continuing to stretch the tape as you progress. To finish the end, tape ⅛"–¼" (3mm–6mm) past the end of the wire, giving the extra tape a few twists. Then snip the tape just past the wire to cover sharp edges and prevent unraveling. Score the tape with a fingernail at the end of the wire.

MAKING BASIC CENTERS & BUDS

Cotton Ball Center

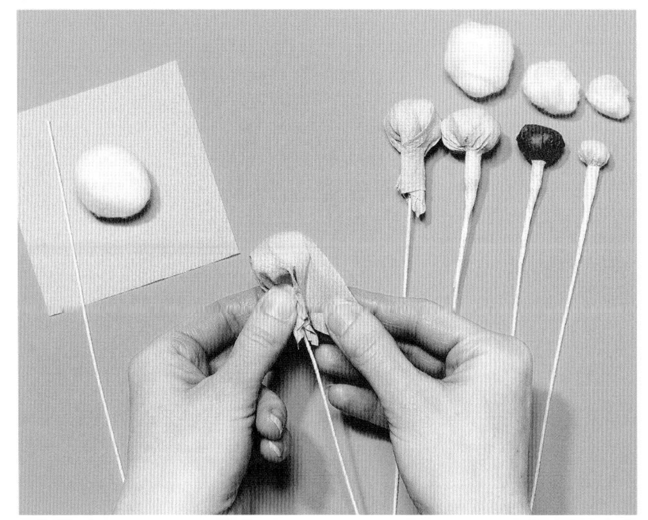

Centers can be made from one or several balls or torn pieces of cotton. Determine your center's size and cut a paper square, leaving a 1" (2.5cm) border around the cotton. With a stem in one hand, hold a cotton ball to the stem's end and center your paper on top of the cotton ball. Wrap the paper in half over and down the ball and pinch the two edges of the paper to the stem. Next, fold one remaining side down followed by folding in the two adjoining corners, like wrapping a package. Repeat on the opposite side, pinching any extra paper tightly to the stem. Secure with tape.

Spun-Cotton Center

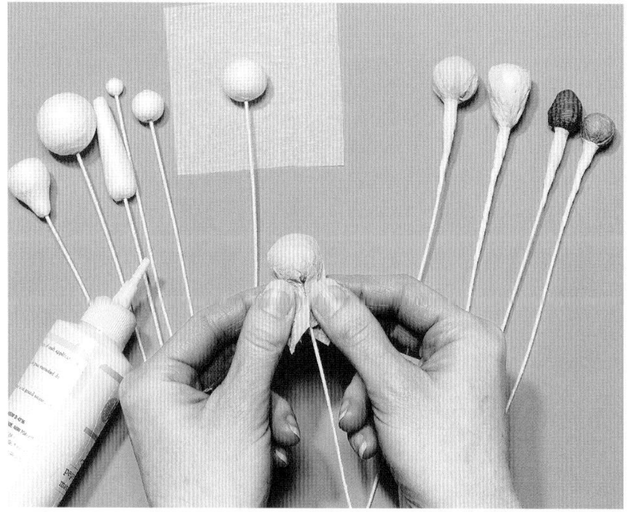

With a small amount of glue on the end of your stem, insert the stem into the hole in a spun-cotton center and let it dry. Cut a piece of paper larger than your center and fold it over the center using the same method as making a *Cotton Ball Center*. You can also center a piece of paper on top of your cotton and pull it down on all sides, smoothing the paper over the shape. Finish by twisting and pinching the paper at the base and taping it in place to secure. Lightweight crepe and tissue work well for centers, as they don't create added bulk.

Fringe Center

To make a basic *Fringe Center*, begin with a strip of paper, fringed with the grain, ¾ of the way down. *Gather and Wrap* (p. 132) the base of the strip around a stem and secure it with tape. The length of the strip will determine the size of your center. For a tailored appearance, tightly roll the base of the fringe around your stem. Secure longer pieces to the stem with glue before taping. Shorter fringe looks compact and graphic, while longer fringe looks wild and free-form. For different results, mix papers or use a decorative edger on the strip before cutting it into fringe.

Pip Center

A bundle of pips can be a center by itself, or pips can be added as accents. Most pips have double ends and can be folded in half to make use of all the tips. Make a basic *Pip Center* by bending a 24- or 26-gauge wire in half over 10–15 folded pips. Pull the wire down and twist it, then tape the joint to secure it, then attach the wired bundle to a stem with tape. Pips can also be used full-length by snipping off one set of ends and taping them to a wire. When using pips as an accent, hold and tape a few at a time to a completed center, spacing the pips as desired.

Rolled Center

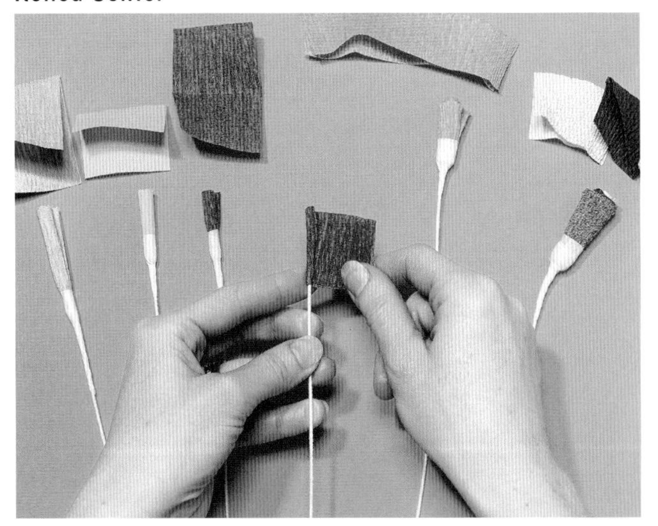

A basic *Rolled Center* starts with a 2" × 1½" (5cm × 4cm) piece of crepe, grain running with the height. Fold it in half, against the grain, and roll it onto a stem wire with the folded edge up, creating a visible coil. Tape the base to the stem to finish. Start with a longer piece of paper or add strips in succession to alter the size or style of a rolled center.

Alternative Centers

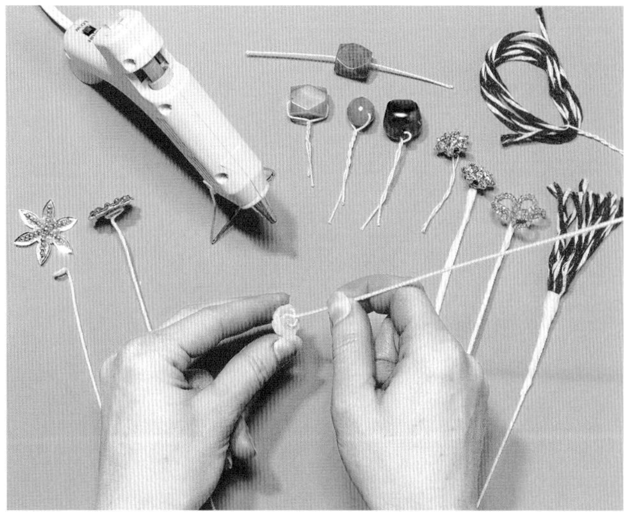

To create centers made of small objects like stones or buttons, first craft a small coil at the top of a wire and bend it perpendicular to the stem. Attach your object to the wire coil with hot glue. If you are using a bead or button with a center hole, thread a 24- or 26-gauge wire through the hole and twist it to secure before attaching it to the main stem wire with floral tape. White cloth-wrapped floral wire can be colored with markers or acrylic paints to match your object, if desired. A fabric or ribbon center can be attached to the stem with craft glue or wire and secured with floral tape.

Buds

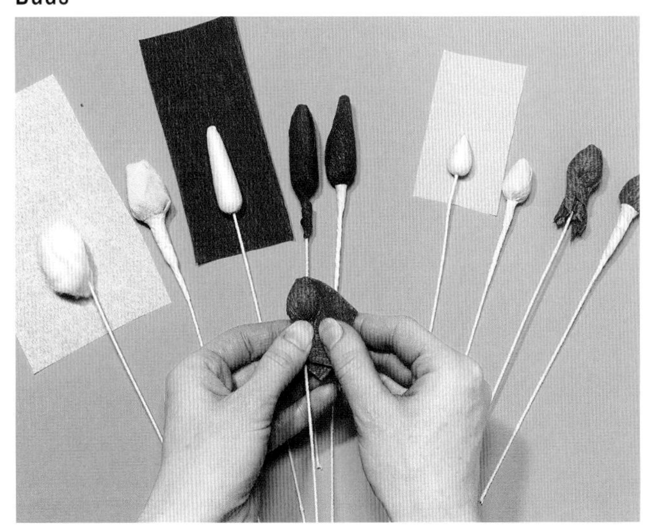

Simple buds can be made from elongated cotton balls or spun-cotton bud shapes. Follow the directions for making a *Cotton Ball Center* (p. 130) with the following exceptions. Cut the paper into a longer rectangle to work with bud shapes. After wrapping the paper over your bud, pinch the paper edges together at the top of one side and fold the piece diagonally and down around the stem, pinching the paper at the stem joint. Turn the piece around and repeat the motion on the remaining side. Pinch any extra paper tightly to the stem, twist, and wrap with tape.

Connected Buds

Simple *Cotton Ball Centers* (p. 130), as well as spun-cotton shapes and buds, can be crafted on short wires and then connected to a primary stem. We usually start with the first bud or ball on the end of the primary stem, adding randomly or evenly spaced buds or balls down the wire with the *Joining Stems* (p. 132) technique.

ATTACHING PETALS & LEAVES, JOINING STEMS

Attaching Single Petals

Place ⅜"-½" (9.5mm-13mm) of the base of a petal against a center or stem. While squeezing the pleat at the petal's base to the center or stem, tape around the base a few times, gently pulling the floral tape as you work, continuing down beyond the petal onto the stem. Overlap each petal slightly when you are attaching them as a layer. When attaching multiple petals at once, make sure the tape comes into contact with each petal as well as the base of the flower and the stem. Leave ¼"-½" (6mm-13mm) of space on the stem between the petal layers for a more lifelike and natural flower.

Gather & Wrap

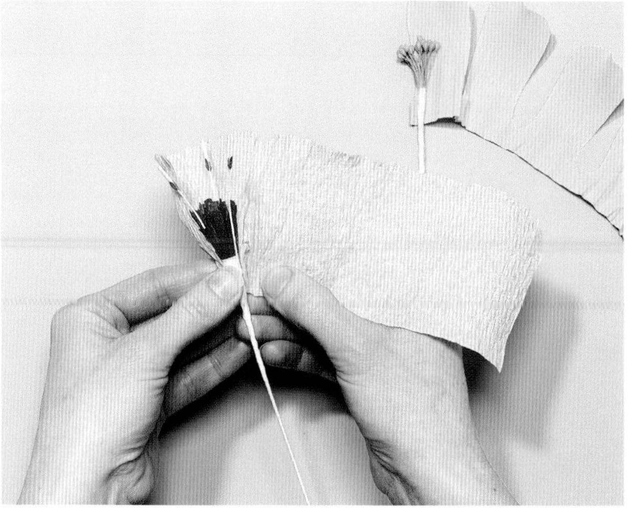

Use *Gather and Wrap* to attach continuous, cuff, and large single petals. Start by placing a flower center at the base of one end of a paper strip, supporting both between thumb and index finger. With your other hand, begin gathering the strip of paper against the stem while rotating the flower slowly as you pinch and wrap the paper around the stem until you reach the end of the strip. Hold it firmly together and tightly tape it (to prevent slipping) at the base of the flower center and down the stem. Continuous petals can be cut into multiple lengths to make attaching them easier.

Attaching Leaves

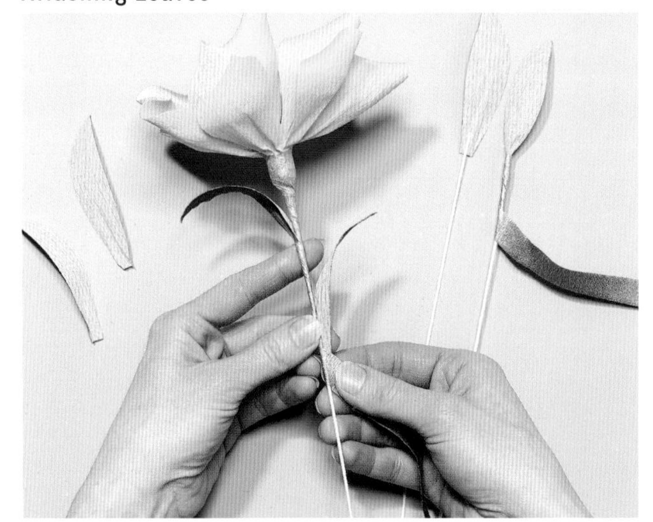

While holding the base of a *Single* or *Scrunch Pleated* (p. 128) leaf against your stem at a desired attachment point, use tape to bind the leaf to the stem, making sure to tape beyond the end of the leaf's base. An efficient way to add leaves is to attach them while final taping your stem. Start taping at the base of the flower, continuing down the stem and taping in leaves as you progress. To join a single leaf to the tip of a stem, *Single* or *Scrunch Pleat* the base of your leaf and nestle the wire in the gathers ¼"-½" (6mm-13mm). Then tape the base of the leaf tightly onto the stem.

Joining Stems

Finish all stems with floral tape before joining them together. Start with the smallest stem, working down to the larger ones. Hold two wires together at a desired contact point and use tape to bind them, tightly taping past the end of the smaller wire. Cover ½"-1" (13mm-2.5cm) of the smaller wire with tape, so that it cannot easily be pulled off the larger stem. Use enough tape to keep the wires together, but not so much as to create a bulky point on the stem. Larger groupings will require more tape and a larger contact point, 1"-4" (2.5cm-10cm) to support the weight of the parts.

WIRING PETALS & LEAVES, FINISHING STEMS

Wire One-Sided Leaves or Petals

Adding a wire to support leaves or petals will allow for more articulation and control when styling your finished flower. Begin with a cutout shape facedown on a work surface. Draw a thin line of craft glue down the center of your shape starting ¼"–1" (6mm–2.5cm) below the tip, depending on the shape's size. Set a straight wire on the glue line and let it dry. Wires can be wrapped with floral tape before gluing for a more finished look. You can include the leaf or petal base while taping a finished wired leaf or petal stem.

Wire Two-Sided Leaves or Petals

There are two methods for hiding a wire; both start with *Wire One-Sided Leaves or Petals*. Method one: Cover the back of your shape with paste or stick glue and place a wire down the center, leaving space at the tip. With a second, slightly larger sheet of paper, sandwich the papers together and smooth. When dry, trim the larger piece to fit your original shape. Method two: Cut a small paper strip and adhere with paste or stick glue to cover the wire and surrounding area. For both methods, finish the stem with floral tape, catching the leaf or petal base in the tape if desired.

Covering Stems/Decorative Stem Wrapping

Start with a finished stem before covering with crepe or decorative tape. Cut one or more ½" × 12" (13mm × 30.5cm) strips of paper as needed. *Grain runs with height; all dimensions are given as H × W.* Fully stretch florist crepe beforehand. Glue one end of a strip to the base of a flower. Begin winding the paper at a diagonal around the stem, overlapping slightly and adding a dab of glue every few inches. Wind the paper around the leaves, covering the floral tape. Add strips as needed, securing the ends with glue. Other wrappings include fabric and washi tapes that can be used over floral tape or wire.

Styling Stems

Leaving stems stiff and straight will give your flowers or leaves an angular and graphic appearance. Curving the wires will create a more lifelike and organic impression. Use your fingers to gently curve the wires in any direction or bend them around a jar, can, or dowel to create clean uniform curves.

PETAL- & LEAF-STYLING SKILLS

Cupping (Crepe Papers Only)

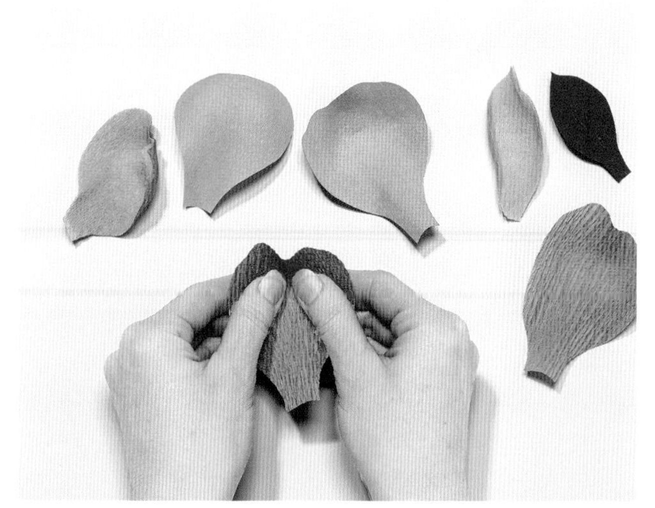

To *Cup*, lightly grasp the center of a petal or leaf at its widest point between the thumbs and index fingers of both hands. Gently slide your thumbs and index fingers away from one another, gently pulling from the center out, coaxing the folds of the paper apart. Leave a border to maintain the petal's structure. The number of strokes depends on the weight of the crepe and how cupped you want the shape to be. *Cupping* is one of the most important skills when working with crepe, so practice is recommended before using this technique on an assembled flower.

Fluting (Crepe Papers Only)

With the edge of a petal or leaf held between the thumbs and index fingers of both hands, gently move your hands in opposite directions, stretching the gathers apart. The result will be a gently ruffled edge. The more pronounced the paper's gathers, the more exaggerated the ruffling will be. *Fluting* florist crepe yields large ruffles, while single-ply and double-sided crepe papers yield subtle ruffles. Another common method we use is to single *Flute* the center of the top edge of a petal with one finger to create an indentation. You can *Flute* multiple stacks of paper parts at a time.

Table Pleat

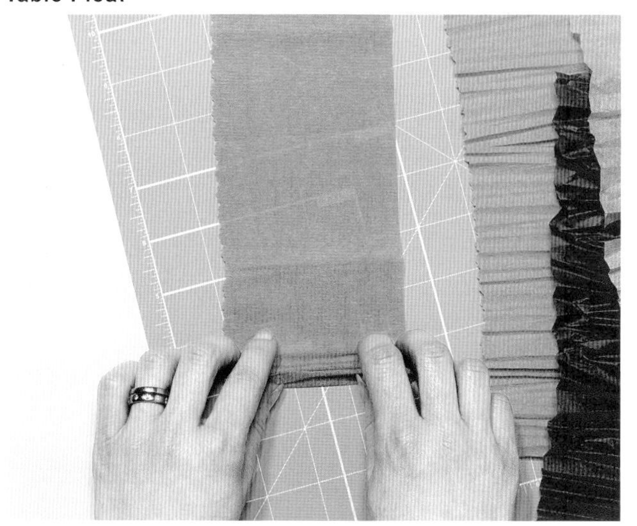

Table Pleat begins by placing a precut strip of paper on a slippery table or on top of a quilting ruler. Place your thumbs at one end of the paper, running lengthwise away from you. With your fingers, begin to drag the paper toward your thumbs, scrunching it together as you gather the entire length of the strip together. You can tightly press the pleating to create defined creases, or you can leave it loose and ruffled. This technique is ideal for continuous cuff-style flowers and large petals.

Wrinkle Pleat

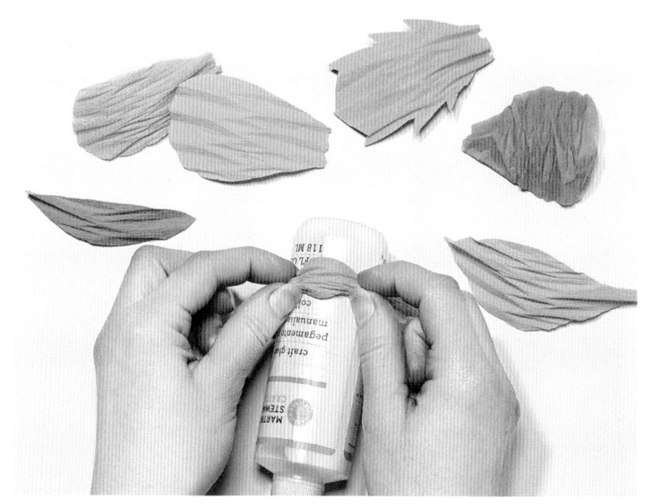

To *Wrinkle Pleat* lay a single petal or leaf on top of a rounded surface, like a can or bottle of glue. Make sure the paper's grain is running in the same direction as the curve of your surface. Use the *Table Pleat* technique on the entire petal, smoothing the paper around the curves of the bottle or can. To finish, firmly pinch and press the pleating to create defined wrinkles and a gentle curve, and gently pull open the petal or leaf.

Scissor Curl

The *Scissor Curl* is the same technique you may have used to curl ribbon when wrapping a gift. Begin by holding the base of a petal or leaf in one hand and the top blade of a scissors between your thumb and index finger in the opposite hand. While supporting the paper gently on top with your thumb, drag the blade of the scissors along underside of the length of the piece in the direction of the paper's grain. Work gently not to tear the paper, and use multiple strokes for a thicker piece of paper or to increase the curl.

Stick Curl

A toothpick, skewer, pencil, or thin and rounded object will work well for a *Stick Curl*. Simply roll the paper, with or against the grain, tightly around the object, taking care that the tip of the leaf or petal stays flat. The more you roll, the deeper the curl will be. The smaller or larger your object is, the tighter or looser your curl will be. You can curl the top edge of a petal or leaf, or one or more side edges to create diagonal curls.

Styling Fringe

The body and weight of a paper will affect how fringe behaves. Thicker papers will stand up straighter and thinner papers will flop over more. *Scissor Curling* adds shape and bend to fringe. Curling fringed paper that has been accordion-folded will yield sections of curls that move in opposite directions once the sheet is unfolded. Curling cut lengths of fringed paper creates fringe that moves in one direction. When working with delicate papers, curling is best done with your fingers. Gently scrunching a length of fringe will give it a playful look.

Finessing & Stretching

To *Finesse*, gently stretch, *Cup* (p. 134), or *Flute* (p. 134) to create sculptural effects in the petals and leaves of the finished flower. Techniques can be combined on different areas of a flower to add character. Stretching florist crepe before working with it will remove some, most, or all of the gathers, depending on how much it is stretched. Stretching reduces bulk and creates a softer look and feel. When working with a cut strip of crepe, you can stretch it out and cut the petals or leaves, or alternatively, cut the pieces and then stretch them.

ADDING COLOR

Adding Color/Tips

Adding color is a way to personalize your flowers and make them artful. Allow painted or dipped papers to dry fully before working with them. Laundry or cooling racks work well to aid drying. Pieces can also be dried on paper towels, garbage bags, and drop cloths. Paper towels wick moisture and a bit of color, possibly affecting saturation, an effect that is sometimes desired. Most papers will buckle when painted, especially crepe. When dry, crepe can be stretched and petals can be gently *Scissor Curled* (p. 135) a small amount to reduce buckling, if desired.

Diluting Paint

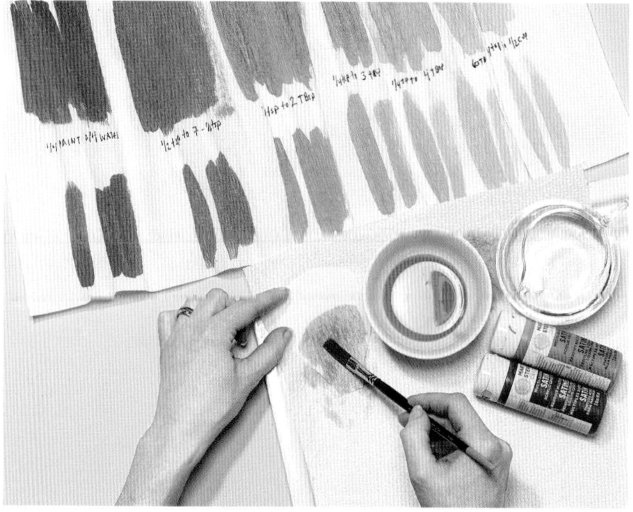

In most projects we use diluted acrylic paints, sprayed or painted on, that soak into the paper. There are a few basic formulas for diluting paints, but any shade of paint can work for a project. A basic formula is ¼ tsp (1.25mL) of paint to 3–6 tbsp (45mL–90mL) of water, or about a 1:50 ratio. To create a pale wash, ¼ tsp (1.25mL) of paint to ⅓–½ cup (80mL–120mL) or more of water works well. For a more heavily pigmented wash, ¼ tsp (1.25mL) to 1–2 tbsp (15mL–30mL) of water will yield a strong color that still soaks into the paper. When diluting darker colors, less paint can be used.

Painting

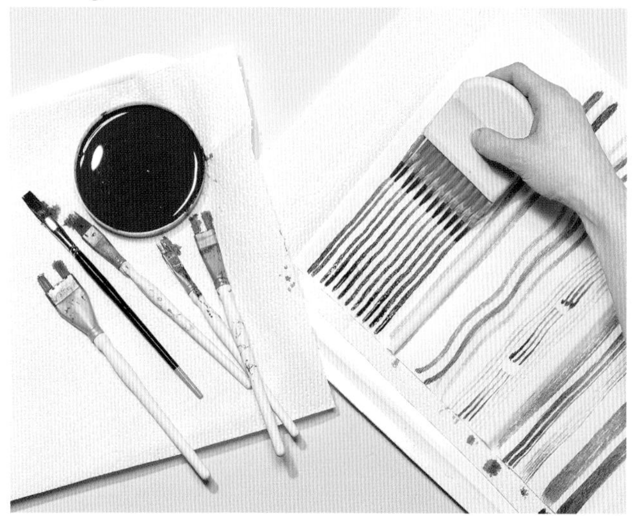

Hand-painting works beautifully on all types of crepe, tissue, and decorative papers. We usually dilute paints before working with them. Paint an entire piece of crepe and then cut the petals and leaves, or cut the shapes and then paint them individually. Both methods work equally well. Decorative brushes, like striping, feather, and fan shapes, yield wonderful organic or graphic patterns on crepe paper. Delicate brushes can be used to add small details of paint to finished flowers, adding character.

Spraying

Coloring paper with diluted paints in spray bottles is fast, fun, and simple. Mix paints and water thoroughly in smaller containers before filling the bottles. Depending on the type of spray bottle, working close to the paper will often create a finer mist, while spraying from farther away will make larger droplets. Vary the angle at which you spray to combine droplet sizes and layer colors in passes for texture. Spraying works well with all crepe weights as well as tissue and other papers. Noncolorfast crepe and other papers can also be sprayed with plain water to create a mottled texture.

Dip-Dyeing

Dip-dyeing can be done with larger strips of paper or cut pieces in acrylic or watercolor paint that has been diluted to the desired opacity. It is a good idea to test the color, allowing a test strip to dry fully, as some colors will dry lighter than expected. Dipped crepe papers soak up paint quickly, and the color will continue to spread after the paper is removed from the paint. Remove the paper before the color reaches the desired finish point, give it a gentle shake to remove excess paint, and lay it on paper towels or cooling racks to dry.

Water-Soluble Crayons & Pencils, Markers

Water-soluble crayons and pencils work especially well on crepe papers. Simply draw and then brush with water in the direction of the grain. Pigments are altered by the amount of water, brush type, and blending technique. Felt-tipped markers make adding color to papers very easy. They bleed slightly into crepe paper, creating a nice soaked-in effect. Crayons, pencils, and markers can drag or pull on crepe when drawing against the grain. For stability, support the paper with the fingers of your opposite hand.

Rubber Stamps

Stamping works well on single-ply and double-sided crepe as well as tissue and other decorative papers. When stamping on crepe, keep in mind that the pattern may change when the paper is cupped or stretched. Repeating a stamped design creates a custom pattern that can be as simple or as intricate as desired. Stamping on florist crepe is generally not recommended because the grain gathers are too deep to maintain the design. Some ink pads have a longer drying time; it's important to let the ink dry fully to prevent smearing.

Glittering

Flower centers, petals, leaves, and stems can all be glittered. There are a few types of glitter products that can be used when making flowers. Apply loose glitter by covering your surface with craft glue, sprinkling glitter over the glue, and shaking off the excess before setting aside to dry. Glitter glue, which comes in a tube, is great for drawing precise lines or smearing on paper with a finger to create thin, organic glittery washes. Glitter paint can be used just like regular paint, undiluted, for adding decorative borders or washes of color.

2 3 4 5 6 7 8 9 10 11 12
168

HOW-TOS/

Skill Levels

ABOUT SKILL LEVELS To help you get started, we have rated the projects in this book by skill level. All of the projects in this book are attainable and enjoyable, but these general guidelines can help you decide what to make if you are new to crafting paper flowers. That said, a level 2 or 3 project can be simplified by omitting steps, petal layers, or processes like adding color.

1 Level 1 projects incorporate our basic flower-building skills such as using floral tape, making basic centers, petal and leaf pleating, *Gathering and Wrapping*, *Cupping*, and attaching petals. In addition, you should be comfortable using tools like fringing scissors and decorative paper edgers.

2 Level 2 projects build on level 1 projects by combining skills and incorporating more steps and petal layers. Leaf and stem treatments may be slightly more involved or require additional steps like *Joining* or *Covering Stems*. Some multiflower projects are made from level 1 flowers but are rated level 2 for the number of flowers required.

3 Level 3 projects are larger in size and require multiple steps. They require more skills and petal layers as well as color techniques. A good understanding of flower-building and styling skills is ideal. Practice and precision is recommended to build larger, multilayered flowers, and spacing petals evenly will allow you to achieve the effects shown.

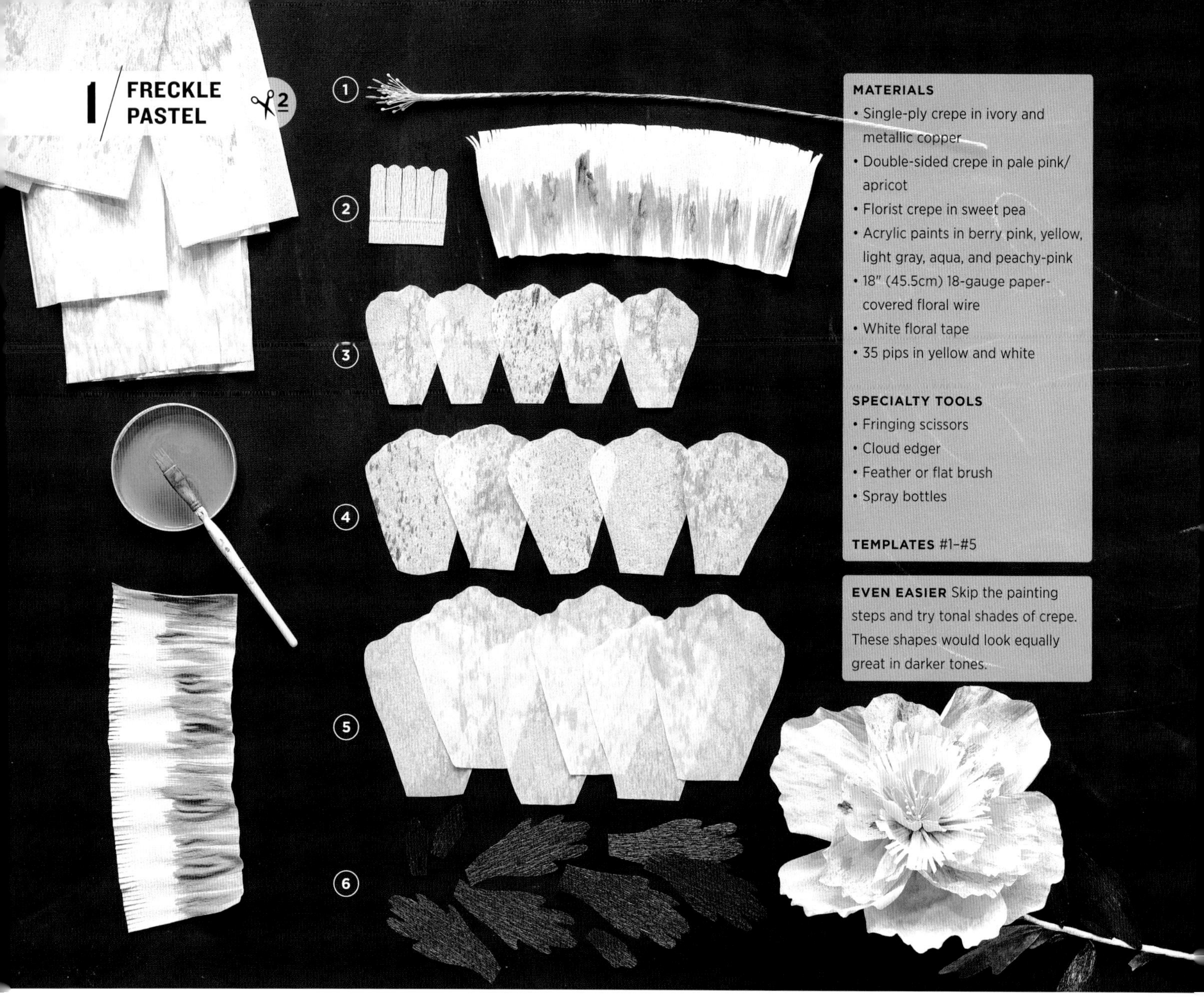

ADD COLOR *Grain runs with height; all dimensions are given as H × W. Dilute* (p. 136) the berry pink, yellow, light gray, and aqua acrylic paints and fill 4 spray bottles with them. Cut 4 pieces of ivory single-ply crepe, 4 folds wide. Lightly spray each with 1 color. Vary spraying distance to vary size of speckles. Cut a 4" × 10½" (10cm × 26.5cm) strip from pale pink/apricot double-sided crepe. *Dilute* the peachy-pink acrylic paint. Using a feather brush, gently paint halfway up the height of the paper. This will become your cuff petal. Set pieces aside to dry.

CUT Cut a 2½" (6.5cm) square from sweet pea florist crepe. Cut 1 side across the grain with a cloud edger, then cut with the grain ¾ of the way down at each notch made by the edger, to create continuous petals. Cut the painted cuff petal ½" (13mm) on the unpainted side edge with fringing scissors. Petal #1: Cut 5 from pink-speckled crepe. Petal #2: Cut 3 from pink-speckled and 2 from yellow-speckled crepe. Petal #3: Cut 4 from aqua-speckled and 2 from gray-speckled crepe. Leaf #4: Cut 6 from metallic copper crepe. Leaf #5: Cut 3 or more from metallic copper crepe.

BUILD Secure each layer with floral tape. **1.** Make a *Pip Center* (p. 130) with full-length pips. **2.** *Gather and Wrap* (p. 132) a 5-petal piece around the center, then gently *Cup* (p. 134). *Scrunch Pleat* (p. 128) cuff petal, and *Gather and Wrap* it around the center. *Cup* base of cuff petal and fan out the fringed rim. **3.** *Scrunch Pleat* Petals #1, then secure them to the center, spreading them evenly around the flower. Gently *Cup* and *Flute* (p. 134). **4 and 5.** Repeat step 3 with Petals #2 and #3, following color order as shown. Finish stem. **6.** *Scrunch Pleat* each leaf, attach 1 leaf 3" (7.5cm) from base of flower. Continue adding leaves randomly as you finish the stem. Slightly *Cup* the leaves.

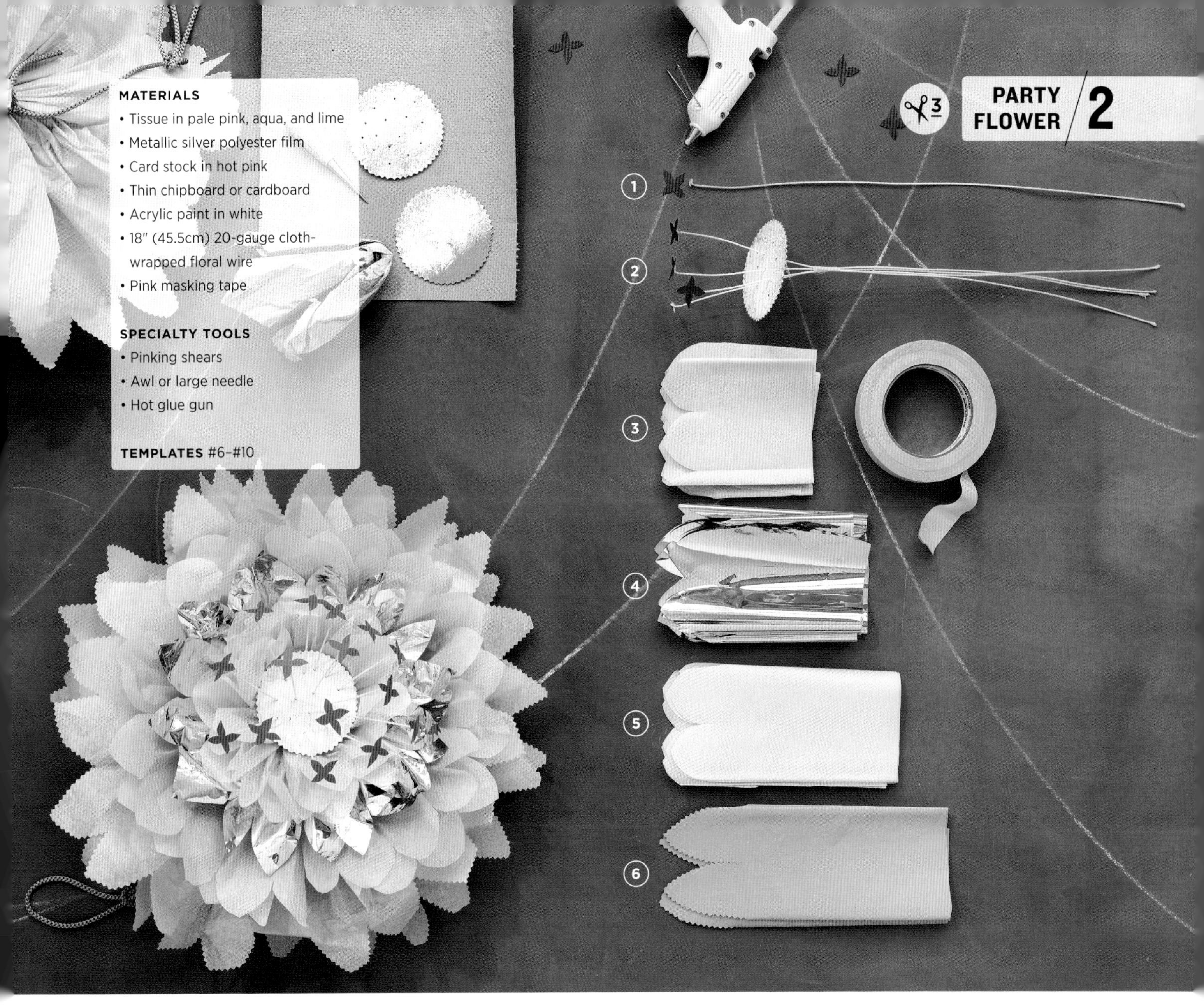

CUT *Grain runs with height; all dimensions are given as H × W.* Trace a 2¾"–3" (7cm–7.5cm) circle on chipboard using a glass and cut it out with pinking shears. Floret #6: Cut 15 from pink card stock. Petal #7: Cut four 5½" × 24" (14cm × 61cm) strips from lime tissue, accordion-fold to fit template, and cut a continuous petal. Petal #8: Cut three 7" × 24" (18cm × 61cm) strips from silver film, accordion-fold to fit template, and cut a continuous petal. Petal #9: Cut four 9" × 24" (23cm × 61cm) strips from aqua tissue, accordion-fold to fit template, and cut a continuous petal. Petal #10: Cut four 11" × 24" (28cm × 61cm) strips from pink tissue, accordion-fold to fit template, and cut a continuous petal with pinking shears.

ADD COLOR Using a crumpled paper towel, blot and rub white acrylic paint on the chipboard disc. Set aside to dry.

BUILD Secure all layers with masking tape. **1.** Create a coil at the end of a full-length wire and bend the coil perpendicular to the wire. Hot-glue a pink floret to the coil. Repeat with remaining florets and wires, making 15 total. **2.** Using an awl, make 15 randomly spaced holes in the white disc. Thread 5 wires in the holes closest to the center leaving 3½"–4" (9cm–10cm) sticking out from the top as shown. Gather wires together 1½" (4cm) from the base of the center and secure. Continue to thread remaining 10 wires evenly around the center, 5 wires at a time, gathering each group at the same point as the first set and securing. The tape is the attachment point for the petals. **3.** *Gather and Wrap* (p. 132) 1 Petal #7 ¼ of the way around the center and secure. Repeat with remaining 3 petals, ¼ each, to complete the layer. **4.** *Gather and Wrap* 1 Petal #8 ⅓ of the way around the center and secure. Repeat with remaining 2 petals, ⅓ each, to complete the layer. **5.** Repeat step 3 with Petals #9. **6.** Repeat step 3 with Petals #10. Leave stem long or trim. Finish stem.

PROJECT NOTE We trimmed our stem to 1½" (4cm) and wrapped masking tape to cover the exposed paper and wire. Tie a loop of satin cord around the base for hanging.

3 / CHEERLEADERS

MATERIALS

- Single-ply crepe in pale pink, pale peach, and pale yellow
- Double-sided crepe in light yellow/yellow
- Florist crepe in bright pink and bright peach
- Tissue in bubblegum pink, pale pink, peach, pale peach, pale yellow, and yellow
- 18" (45.5cm) 18-gauge paper-covered floral wire
- Floral tape in pink

SPECIALTY TOOLS

- Fringing scissors
- Scallop edger

TEMPLATES #11, #12

TRY THIS This flower can be made on longer stems. Try all white papers with pastel leaves or darker holiday colors with metallic leaves.

CUT *Grain runs with height; all dimensions are given as H × W.* Cut all fringe with fringing scissors. Cut a 3½" × 13" (9cm × 33cm) strip from pale pink single-ply crepe. Fold into quarters widthwise and fringe with the grain ⅔ of the way down. Cut two 3½" × 30" (9cm × 76cm) strips each from bubblegum and pale pink tissue. Fold into quarters widthwise and fringe with the grain ⅔ of the way down. Unfold all strips. Leaves #11 and #12: Using a scallop edger, cut 1 each from yellow double-sided crepe. Cut a 9" (23cm) stem wire.

BUILD Secure all layers with pink floral tape. **1.** *Gather and Wrap* (p. 132) pale pink crepe around stem. **2.** Repeat step 1 with bubblegum pink tissue strips. To make wrapping easier hold stem upside down to let fringe fall downward; this keeps the fringe out of the way. **3.** Repeat step 1 with pale pink tissue strips. Finish stem with tape. **4.** *Single Pleat* (p. 128) Leaves #11 and #12. Begin a second layer of tape, attach Leaf #11 3" (7.5cm) down from flower. Continue taping, attach Leaf #12 1" (2.5cm) lower. Finish stem.

PROJECT NOTE We made the peach pom-pom with pale peach single-ply crepe and two tones of peach tissue and leaves of bright pink florist crepe. The yellow pom-pom was made with yellow single-ply crepe and two tones of yellow tissue and leaves of bright peach florist crepe.

CUT *Grain runs with height; all dimensions are given as H × W.* Cut a 2½" × 12" (6.5cm × 30.5cm) strip from black single-ply crepe; fringe with fringing scissors, with the grain, ¾ of the way down. Petal #13: Cut a 2¾" × 5½" (7cm × 14cm) strip from cream/lemon yellow double-sided crepe, accordion-fold to fit template, and cut a continuous petal. Cut two 4" × 18" (10cm × 45.5cm) strips, 1 from peach single-ply crepe, 1 from peach tissue; trim 1 side of strips lengthwise with a cloud edger. Leaf #14: Cut 1 from lavender tissue. Cut a 9" (23cm) stem wire.

BUILD Secure all layers with floral tape. **1.** Make a *Fringe Center* (p. 130) with fringed black crepe. **2.** *Gather and Wrap* (p. 132) the continuous petal around the center, with cream side of crepe facing in. Gently *Cup* (p. 134) petals. **3.** *Table Pleat* (p. 134) peach crepe strip. *Gather and Wrap* halfway around the center. **4.** *Table Pleat* peach tissue strip; overlap crepe by 2" (5cm). *Gather and Wrap* the remainder of the way around, overlapping opposite end by 2" (5cm). **5.** *Scrunch Pleat* (p. 128) Leaf #14. Attach 2" (5cm) from flower base, as you finish stem. To finish flower, make a few large *Flutes* (p. 134) in the crepe petals, creating a slight wave motion. Crumple and twist petals in a counterclockwise motion to give the flower a sense of movement.

PROJECT NOTE We made these flowers in additional versions. One with pink tissue and single-ply crepe, light pink and darker pink florist crepe centers, and turquoise single-ply crepe leaves. The second is black metallic tissue and black single-ply crepe, white fringe single-ply crepe center, omitting layer two, with a yellow tissue leaf. Our arrangement (shown on p. 21) features blooms in saturated shades of crepe and tissue crafted on longer stems.

5 / TWISTED-RIBBON TULIPS

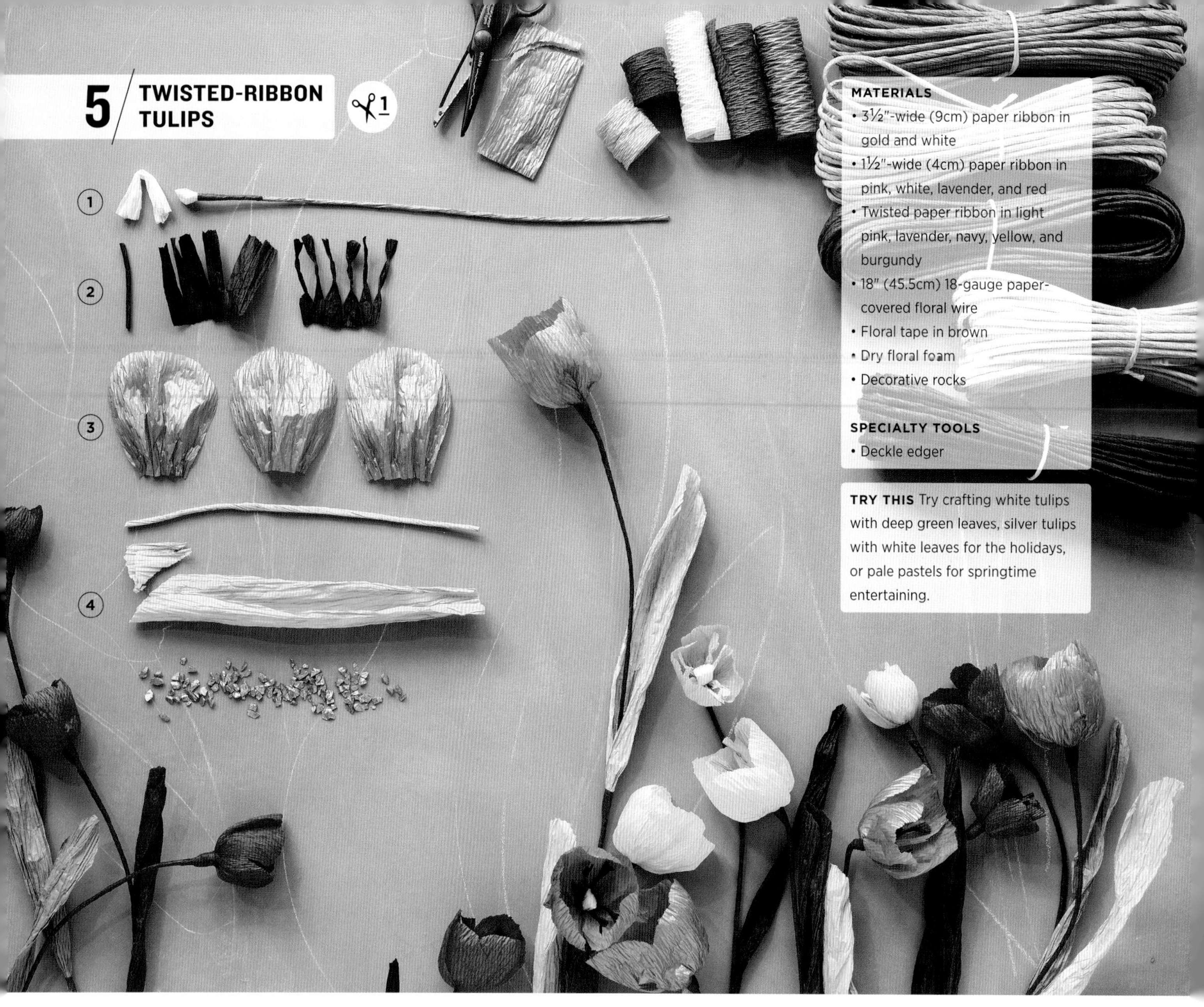

MATERIALS

- 3½"-wide (9cm) paper ribbon in gold and white
- 1½"-wide (4cm) paper ribbon in pink, white, lavender, and red
- Twisted paper ribbon in light pink, lavender, navy, yellow, and burgundy
- 18" (45.5cm) 18-gauge paper-covered floral wire
- Floral tape in brown
- Dry floral foam
- Decorative rocks

SPECIALTY TOOLS

- Deckle edger

TRY THIS Try crafting white tulips with deep green leaves, silver tulips with white leaves for the holidays, or pale pastels for springtime entertaining.

CUT Cut a 3" (7.5cm) length of 3½" (9cm) white paper ribbon. Cut a 2¾" (7cm) length of navy twisted paper ribbon; untwist it completely. Make 5 cuts, ¾ of the way down to make 6 connected strips. To make the petals: Cut three 4" (10cm) lengths of 3½" (9cm) gold paper ribbon; fold each in half lengthwise. Starting 1½" (4cm) from the top of each piece on the unfolded side, round off top corner with a deckle edger. Repeat with remaining pieces to create 3 petals. To make leaves: Cut a 12" (30.5cm) length of pink twisted ribbon; untwist completely and fold in half lengthwise. Starting 1½" (4cm) from the top of each piece on the unfolded side, round off top corner with a deckle edger.

BUILD Secure all layers with floral tape. **1.** Roll white paper ribbon lengthwise, scrunching loosely; bend in half. Center the wire between the fold, twist paper around the wire, creating a small loop, and secure. **2.** With navy ribbon, twist 1 strip from the base up toward the top, leaving the last ½" (13mm) untwisted, to create an abstract stamen; repeat with remaining 5 sections. *Gather and Wrap* (p. 132) around center. **3.** *Scrunch Pleat* (p. 128) base of each gold petal, attach evenly around center. Gently round petals by hand. **4.** Finish stem. *Scrunch Pleat* leaves. Attach 1 leaf 3" (7.5cm) from end of stem, secure, finish remainder of stem with tape. *Style Stems* (p. 133).

PROJECT NOTE Multiple tulips were made from a selection of paper and twisted paper ribbons. We made a smaller bloom using the following measurements: Petals: 3" (7.5cm) length of 1½" (4cm) paper ribbon. Stamen: 2¼" (5.5cm) in length. Leaf: 10" (25.5cm) in length. To resemble our arrangement, trim wires to different lengths and vary the curve in your stems. Anchor stems in containers filled with dry floral foam and cover with gold decorative rocks.

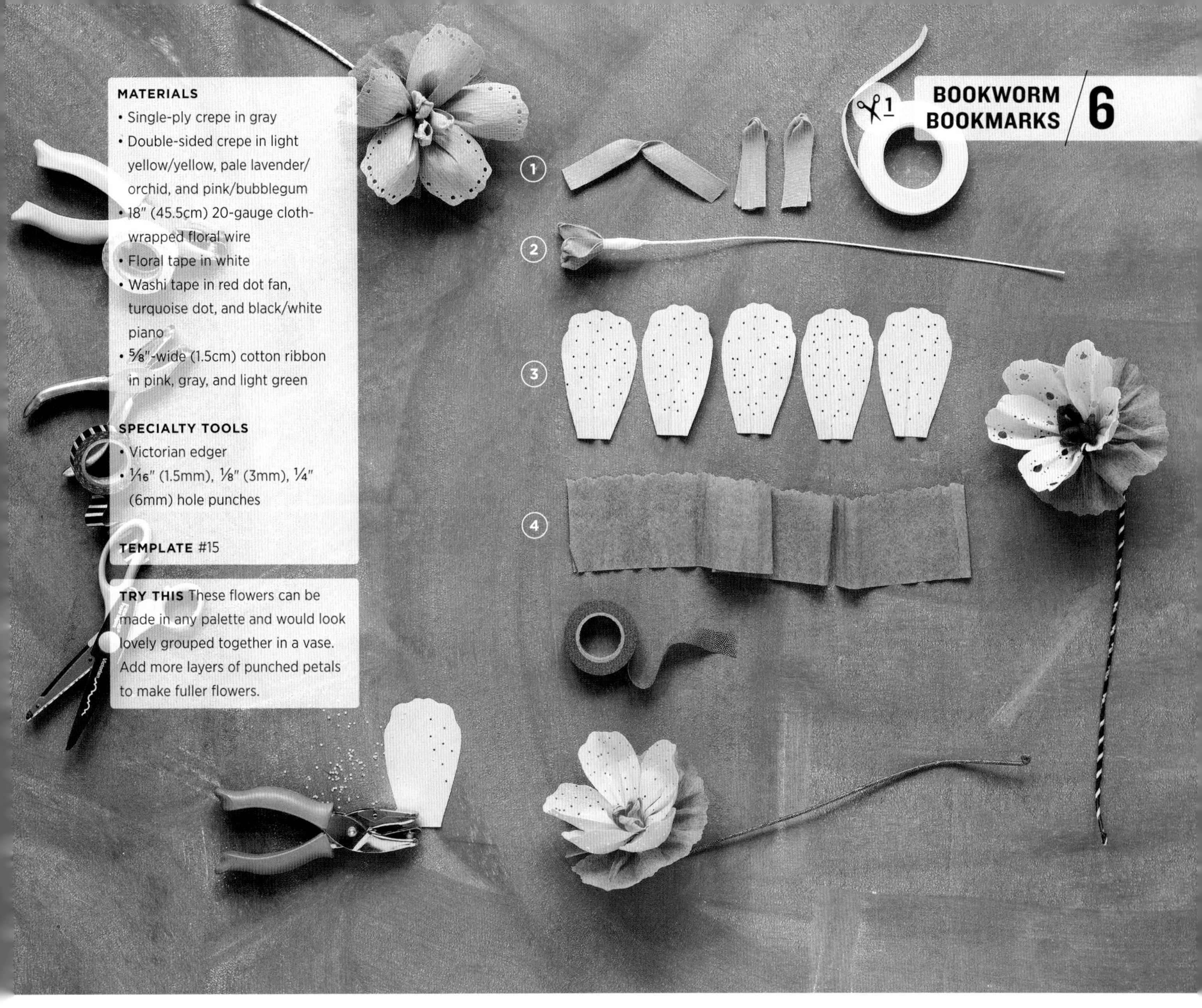

BOOKWORM BOOKMARKS / 6

MATERIALS

- Single-ply crepe in gray
- Double-sided crepe in light yellow/yellow, pale lavender/orchid, and pink/bubblegum
- 18" (45.5cm) 20-gauge cloth-wrapped floral wire
- Floral tape in white
- Washi tape in red dot fan, turquoise dot, and black/white piano
- ⅝"-wide (1.5cm) cotton ribbon in pink, gray, and light green

SPECIALTY TOOLS

- Victorian edger
- 1/16" (1.5mm), ⅛" (3mm), ¼" (6mm) hole punches

TEMPLATE #15

TRY THIS These flowers can be made in any palette and would look lovely grouped together in a vase. Add more layers of punched petals to make fuller flowers.

CUT *Grain runs with height; all dimensions are given as H × W.* Cut three 5" (12.5cm) lengths of pink cotton ribbon. Petal #15: Cut 5 from light yellow/yellow double-sided crepe. Using a ⅛" (3mm) hole punch, create random holes or patterns in petals. Cut a 3" × 18" (7.5cm × 45.5cm) strip of gray single-ply crepe. Trim one long edge with a Victorian edger. Cut a 13" (33cm) length of stem wire.

BUILD Secure all layers with floral tape. **1.** Twist 1 ribbon length in the middle twice and fold it in half as shown. Repeat with 2 remaining lengths, to make 3 total. **2.** Group the folded ribbons together and secure them to the stem wire to make a center. **3.** Gently *Cup* (p. 134) and *Scrunch Pleat* (p. 128) the petals, then attach them evenly around the center. **4.** *Scrunch Pleat* and *Gather and Wrap* (p. 132) the gray strip of single-ply crepe around the center and gently *Flute* (p. 134). Finish stem with floral tape and cover stem with washi tape. Curl stem end tightly as shown.

PROJECT NOTE Flowers were made in additional crepe colors: pale lavender/orchid and pink/bubblegum. Petals were punched with larger hole punches for variety in hole size and pattern. Stems were covered with turquoise dot and black/white washi tape. The pink and yellow flower petals were cupped in, and the lavender petals were cupped out.

7 / BABY BLOOMS

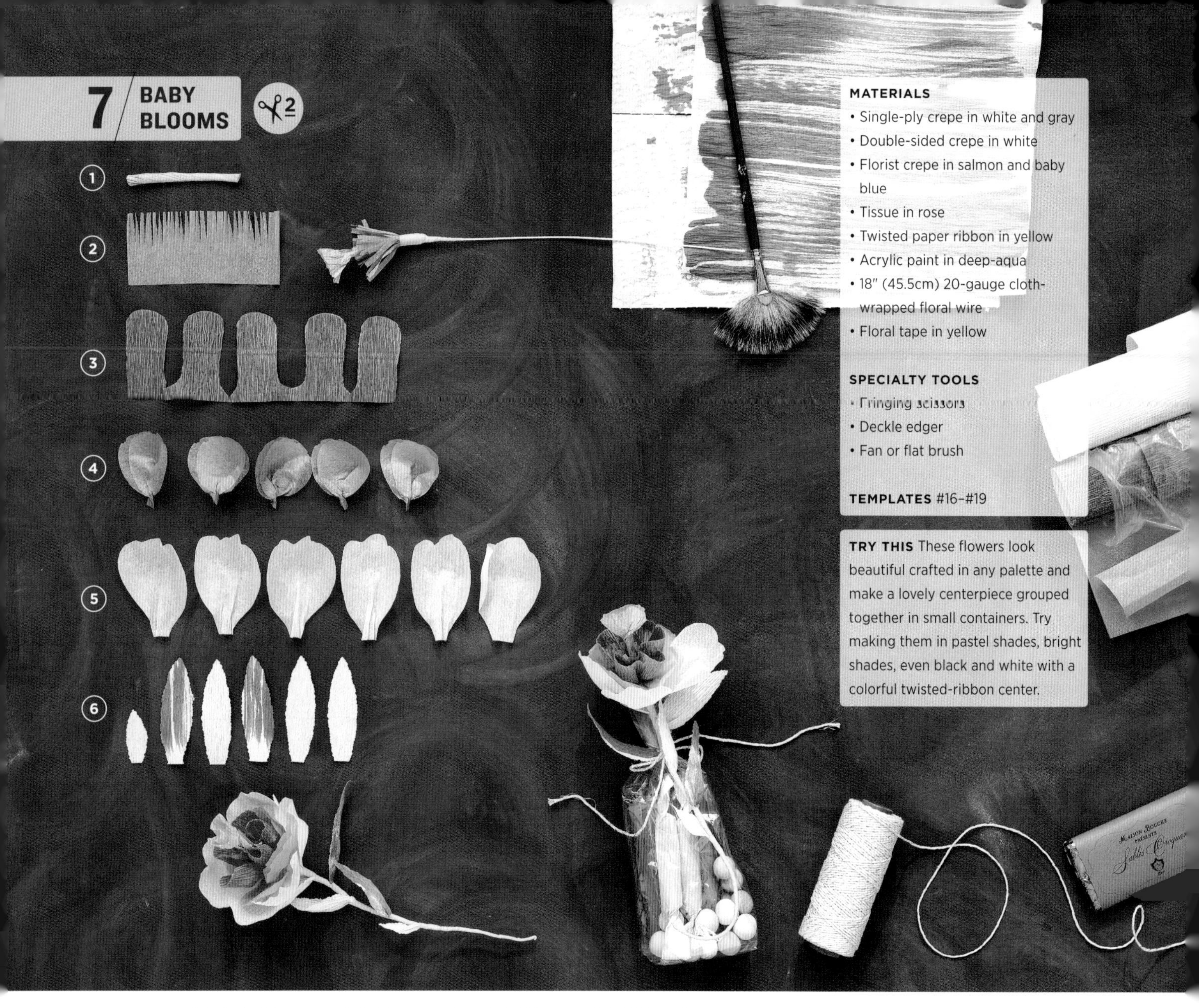

MATERIALS

- Single-ply crepe in white and gray
- Double-sided crepe in white
- Florist crepe in salmon and baby blue
- Tissue in rose
- Twisted paper ribbon in yellow
- Acrylic paint in deep-aqua
- 18" (45.5cm) 20-gauge cloth-wrapped floral wire
- Floral tape in yellow

SPECIALTY TOOLS

- Fringing scissors
- Deckle edger
- Fan or flat brush

TEMPLATES #16–#19

TRY THIS These flowers look beautiful crafted in any palette and make a lovely centerpiece grouped together in small containers. Try making them in pastel shades, bright shades, even black and white with a colorful twisted-ribbon center.

ADD COLOR *Dilute* (p. 136) the aqua acrylic paint. Cut 2 folds from white double-sided crepe. Using a fan brush, loosely paint aqua stripes, with the grain, on white double-sided crepe as shown.

CUT *Grain runs with height. All dimensions are listed as H × W.* Cut a 3" (7.5cm) length of yellow twisted paper ribbon. Cut a 2" × 4½" (5cm × 11.5cm) strip from gray single-ply crepe. Using fringing scissors, fringe ¾ of the way down with the grain. Petal #16: Cut a 3" × 9" (7.5cm × 23cm) strip from salmon florist crepe, accordion-fold to fit template, and cut a continuous petal. Petal #17: Cut 10 from rose tissue. Petal #18: Cut 6 from white single-ply crepe. Leaf #19: Using a deckle edger, cut 2 from aqua painted crepe, 3 from blue florist crepe—hand cut a half-sized petal from blue florist crepe as shown. Cut a 10" (25.5cm) stem wire.

BUILD Secure all layers with floral tape. **1.** Untwist and fan out the top ½" (13mm) of the yellow paper ribbon and secure ½" (13mm) of the opposite end to the wire to make a center. **2.** *Gather and Wrap* (p. 132) the gray single-ply crepe fringe at the base of the paper ribbon where the stem wire is attached. **3.** *Scrunch Pleat* (p. 128) and *Gather and Wrap* Petal #16 evenly around center and secure. *Cup* (p. 134) gently. **4.** With Petal #17, layer 2 petals and offset each slightly, and *Twist* (p. 128). Repeat step 4 with remaining Petals #17 to make 5 pairs total. Attach evenly around center and secure. **5.** With Petals #18 *Cup* gently and *Scrunch Pleat*, attach evenly around center. **6.** While finishing stem attach Leaves #19 randomly.

PROJECT NOTE We filled our bags with caramels, mints, and a chocolate bar. Using a piece of twine tie the bag closed and tie the flower on. Curve the bottom of the flower stem.

HYBRID HELLEBORE 8

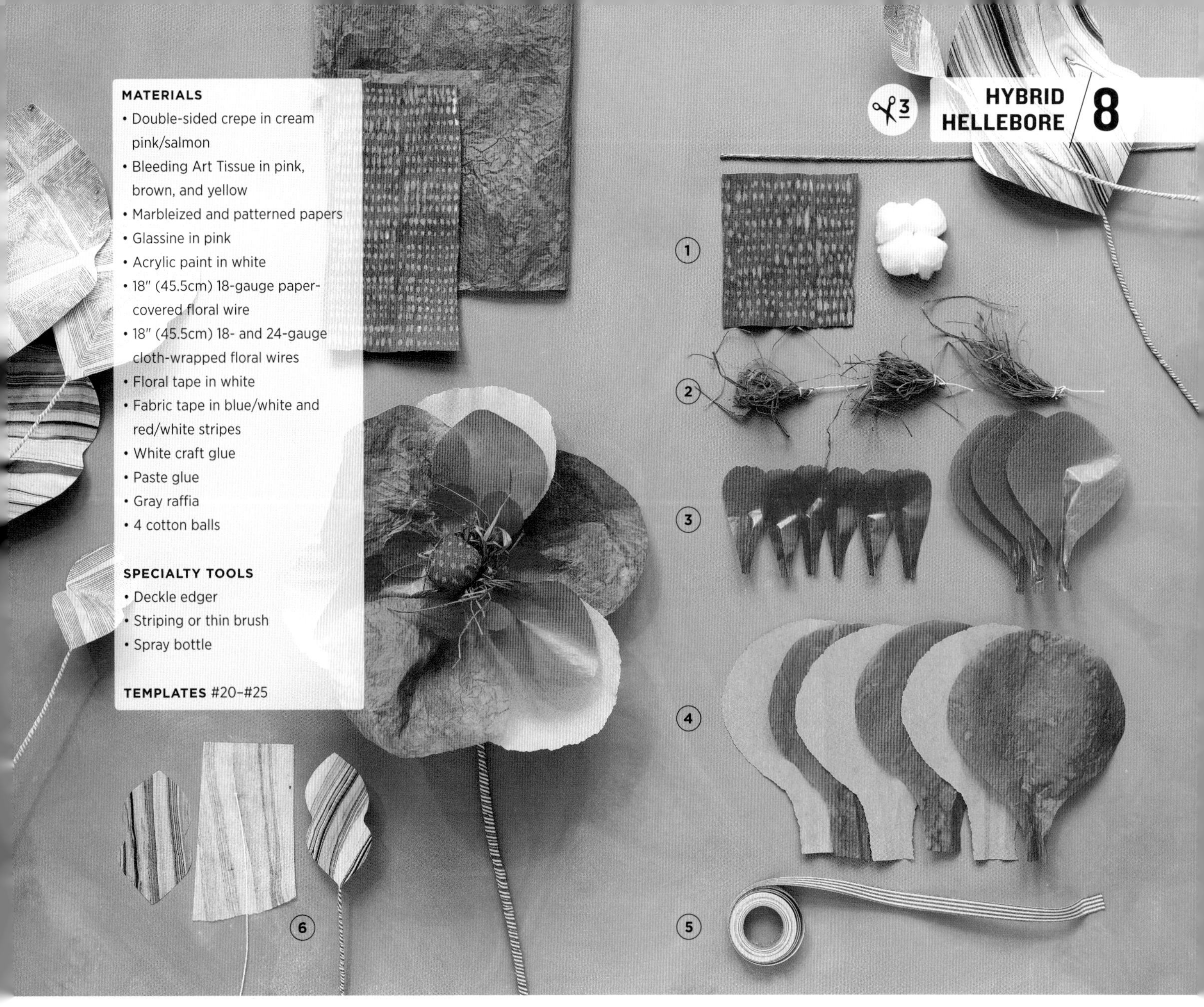

MATERIALS

- Double-sided crepe in cream pink/salmon
- Bleeding Art Tissue in pink, brown, and yellow
- Marbleized and patterned papers
- Glassine in pink
- Acrylic paint in white
- 18" (45.5cm) 18-gauge paper-covered floral wire
- 18" (45.5cm) 18- and 24-gauge cloth-wrapped floral wires
- Floral tape in white
- Fabric tape in blue/white and red/white stripes
- White craft glue
- Paste glue
- Gray raffia
- 4 cotton balls

SPECIALTY TOOLS

- Deckle edger
- Striping or thin brush
- Spray bottle

TEMPLATES #20–#25

ADD COLOR Unfold 2 pieces of pink Bleeding Art Tissue over a drop cloth. Tear up 1 yellow and 1 brown piece of tissue into 2"–4" (5cm–10cm) pieces and scatter them on top of 2 pink sheets. Generously spray with water and let dry. Once dry, peel off yellow and brown pieces, leaving 2 sheets of mottled pink tissue. Cut 2 folds of double-sided crepe. *Dilute* (p. 136) the white paint. Use a striping brush to paint a dotted pattern over the length of crepe. Set pieces aside to dry.

CUT *Grain runs with height.* Cut a 5½" (14cm) square from dotted double-sided crepe. Cut three 5" (12.5cm) hunks of raffia. Cut three 4" (10cm) lengths of 24-gauge cloth-wrapped wires. Petal #20: Cut 6 from pink glassine. Snip off top with a deckle edger. Petal #21: Cut 3 from pink glassine. Petal #22: Using a deckle edger, cut 3 from Bleeding Art Tissue and 3 from cream pink/salmon double-sided crepe. Leaves #23, #24, and #25: Cut 1 each from marbleized and decorative paper and 1 each of a slightly larger shape to make a double-sided leaf.

BUILD Secure all layers with floral tape. **1.** Make a *Cotton Ball Center* (p. 130) with the dotted crepe square and 4 cotton balls. **2.** With 1 hunk of raffia and a 4" (10cm) length of wire, fold the raffia in half over the wire, bending the wire in half and twisting it to secure. Bend 1 arm of the wire up, wrapping it around the base of the raffia to keep from unraveling. Repeat with remaining raffia hunks. Secure all 3 raffia stamen wires evenly around center. **3.** *Single Pleat* (p. 128) Petals #20, secure evenly around center. Repeat with Petals #21. **4.** *Box Pleat* (p. 128) the base of 6 Petals #22, secure evenly around center, alternating crepe with Bleeding Art Tissue. Finish stem. **5.** Wrap stem with fabric tape, secure end with craft glue. **6.** *Wire Two-Sided Leaves* (p. 133) to full-length 18-gauge cloth-wrapped wire to make 6 leaves total. Set aside to dry. Wrap stem with fabric tape to finish, secure end with craft glue. *Style Stems* (p. 133) and curve leaves gently over a glue bottle.

PROJECT NOTE To make the flower or leaf stems longer if desired, attach a second wire 1½" (4cm) from the base of the first wire and secure it with glue and tape before you fully finish the stems.

9 / FÊTE FLOWER & BIRTHDAY LEI

✂2

MATERIALS

- Double-sided crepe in white, golden yellow/melon
- Florist crepe in mauve, daffodil, dark pink, light pink, rose, blue nuance
- Tissue in pale pink, bubblegum, strawberry, sunny, lemon, aqua sparkle
- Twisted paper ribbon in light pink
- Acrylic paint in pink
- 18" (45.5cm) 18-gauge paper-covered floral wire
- Floral tape in white and silver
- White craft glue
- Striped paper straw
- Thick yarn
- Metallic eyelash yarn in rose, aquamarine, and purple
- Bakers twine in pink
- Metallic pom-poms

SPECIALTY TOOLS

- Fringing scissors
- Yarn needle

TEMPLATES #26–#28

TRY THIS The Fête Flower would make a fun children's centerpiece for a birthday party. Make multiples in any color palette and display each bloom in an individual container.

CUT *Grain runs with height; all dimensions are listed as H × W.* Cut straw to 6.5" (16.5cm). Petals #26 and #27: Cut 1 #26 and 2 #27 from yellow/melon double-sided crepe. Cut a 4" × 30" (10cm × 76cm) strip from all colors of tissue, 2 from aqua sparkle tissue. Fold each 4 times. Using fringing scissors, fringe ¾ of the way down. Cut three 8" (20.5cm) lengths of twisted paper ribbon. Untwist and fold in half lengthwise. Using scissors, round off 1 end beginning 2" (5cm) down from corner opposite folded edge to make a leaf. Repeat to make 3 leaves. Petal #28: Cut two 3" × 7" (7.5cm × 18cm) strips each from all florist crepe colors, accordion fold to fit template and cut. Cut a 3" × 11" (7.5cm × 30cm) strip from white double-sided crepe. Cut seventeen 5" (12.5cm) lengths of pink bakers twine. Cut four 2" (5cm) lengths each of all colors of eyelash yarn. Cut two 24" (61cm) lengths of thick yarn.

ADD COLOR *Dilute* (p. 136) the pink paint. *Dip-Dye* (p. 137) 1" (2.5cm) of 1 long edge of white double-sided crepe and let it dry.

BUILD Secure all layers with white floral tape unless noted. **1.** *Scrunch Pleat* (p. 128) 3 flames together and glue inside rim of straw. Glue 18-gauge wire 1" (2.5cm) inside opposite end of straw and let dry. Secure joint. **2.** *Scrunch Pleat* folded light pink tissue strip, *Gather and Wrap* (p. 132) around center and secure. Repeat with folded bubblegum tissue. **3.** Repeat step 2 with strawberry and sunny tissue. **4.** Repeat step 2 with lemon and 2 pieces of aqua sparkle tissue. **5.** *Scrunch Pleat* twisted paper ribbon leaves. Add leaves 1" (2.5cm) apart, 5" (12.5cm) from base, while finishing stem with silver tape. **6.** Glue eyelash yarn strips to lower left corner of Petals #28, let dry. *Scissor Curl* (p. 135) petals out. **7.** *Gather and Wrap*, curl out and eyelash yarn in. Secure with bakers twine. Repeat with all florist crepe colors and trim excess twine. **8.** Thread twine through a pom-pom and knot end. Repeat with 2 more pompoms. Gather 3 pom-poms and tie together as shown. **9.** *Gather and Wrap Dip-Dyed* crepe around the pom-poms, maintaining the knot above the papers' end, and secure them with twine. **10.** Tie yarn together as shown, leaving 3" (7.5cm) tails. Thread the center of 6 florets on each length of yarn grouping pairs together. Using bakers twine tails, tie *Dip-Dyed* floret to the yarn knot and trim tails. Tie top of lei to desired length.

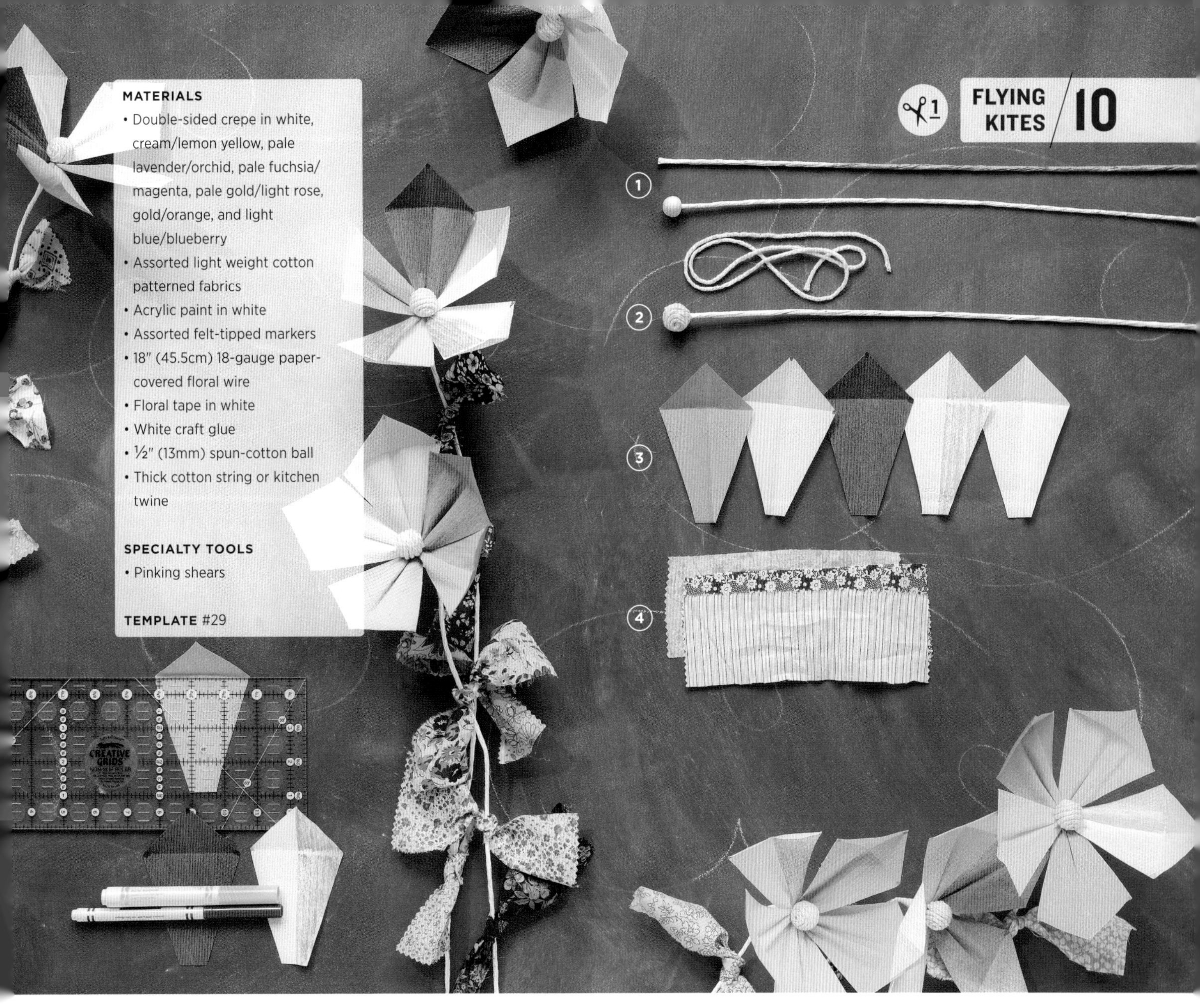

FLYING KITES / 10

MATERIALS

- Double-sided crepe in white, cream/lemon yellow, pale lavender/orchid, pale fuchsia/magenta, pale gold/light rose, gold/orange, and light blue/blueberry
- Assorted light weight cotton patterned fabrics
- Acrylic paint in white
- Assorted felt-tipped markers
- 18" (45.5cm) 18-gauge paper-covered floral wire
- Floral tape in white
- White craft glue
- ½" (13mm) spun-cotton ball
- Thick cotton string or kitchen twine

SPECIALTY TOOLS

- Pinking shears

TEMPLATE #29

CUT *Grain runs with height. All dimensions are listed as H × W.* Choose 5 different colors of double-sided crepe. Petal #29: Cut 1 from each color. Cut a 3" × 7" (7.5cm × 18cm) strip from 3 lightweight cotton fabrics. Trim short edges with pinking shears.

ADD COLOR Paint the paper-covered wire with white acrylic paint. Set aside to dry.

BUILD Secure all layers with floral tape. **1.** Glue the spun-cotton center onto the stem wire and let it dry. **2.** Coat the spun-cotton ball with a thick layer of glue. Wind a 24" (61cm) length of string parallel to the stem by placing an end of the string at the center of one side of the ball and begin to tightly coil the string around the ball. Spiral the string past the stem around the entire ball, and cut the end on the opposite side. Push both ends into glue to secure. Let dry. **3.** Fold each Petal #29 in half with the grain, and crease firmly with your finger to make the first kite crease. Lay a ruler over top of each petal widthwise, lining the ruler up with the points on either side of the kite shape. Fold top of petals over the edge of the ruler against the grain to create the second kite crease. Using felt-tipped markers, randomly color different sections of kite petals in the direction of the grain. Mimic the construction of old-fashioned kites by adding a dot of color to the 3 top corners of each kite petal, leaving some uncolored. *Box Pleat* (p. 128) each kite petal and secure it evenly around the center with floral tape. **4.** Tie on each fabric strip randomly along stem.

PROJECT NOTE To make taller kites: Attach 2 painted wires together with a dab of glue, overlapping them 1¼" (3cm), and securing with floral tape. Cover the tape seam with a kite tail. Our kite stems were set in large spools of kitchen twine made stable with heavy fishing weights affixed with strong tape inside the bases.

11 CHIYOGAMI CHERRY BLOSSOMS

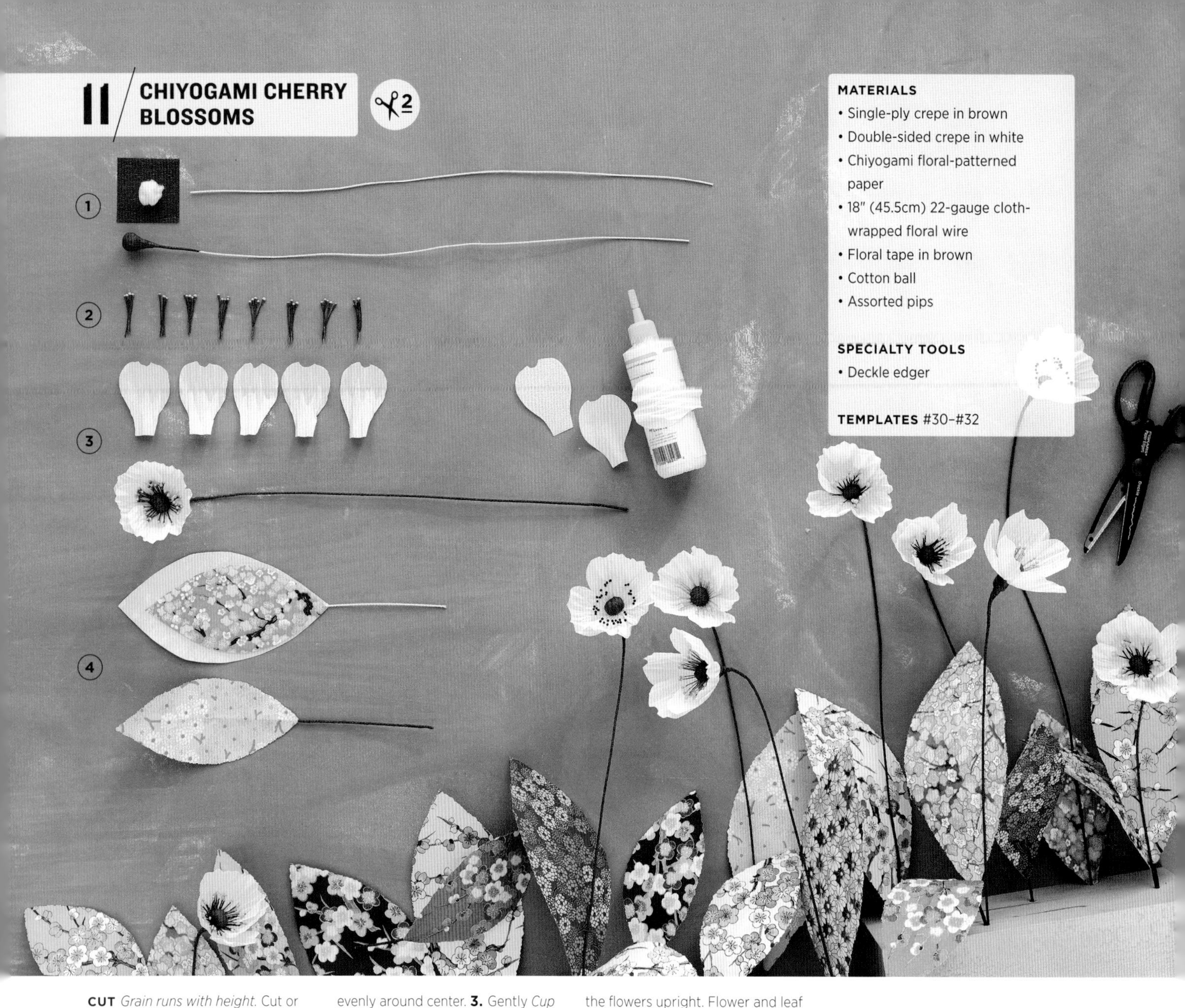

MATERIALS

- Single-ply crepe in brown
- Double-sided crepe in white
- Chiyogami floral-patterned paper
- 18" (45.5cm) 22-gauge cloth-wrapped floral wire
- Floral tape in brown
- Cotton ball
- Assorted pips

SPECIALTY TOOLS

- Deckle edger

TEMPLATES #30–#32

CUT *Grain runs with height.* Cut or tear 1 cotton ball into 3–4 pieces. Cut a 2" (5cm) square from brown single-ply crepe. Petal #30: Cut 5 from white double-sided crepe. Cut 20 pips in half. Leaves #31 and #32: Cut 1 each from chiyogami paper. Cut 1 each with a loose border ½" (13mm) larger than the template. Cut a 16" (40.5cm) and two 9" (23cm) stem wires.

BUILD Secure all layers with floral tape. **1.** Make a *Cotton Ball Center* (p. 130) with a brown singly-ply crepe square, 16" (40.5cm) wire, and a small piece of cotton. **2.** Attach pips in small groups and secure them evenly around center. **3.** Gently *Cup* (p. 134) and then *Wrinkle Pleat* (p. 134) all white double-sided crepe Petals #30. *Scrunch Pleat* (p. 128) base and attach evenly around center and secure. Finish stem. **4.** *Wire Two-Sided Leaves* (p. 133) #31 and #32, using 9" (23cm) wires and the slightly larger pieces of paper to match as shown. When dry, trim excess to leaf shape using a deckle edger and curve over a bottle. Cover exposed stems with tape.

PROJECT NOTE We drilled 1¼" (3cm) deep holes using a $^3/_{16}$" drill into 4" × 10" (10cm × 25.5cm) basswood carving blocks to keep the flowers upright. Flower and leaf stems were trimmed to different heights for variety. Additionally, we used 11 different chiyogami floral and cherry blossom patterned papers and 8 different colors of vintage pips.

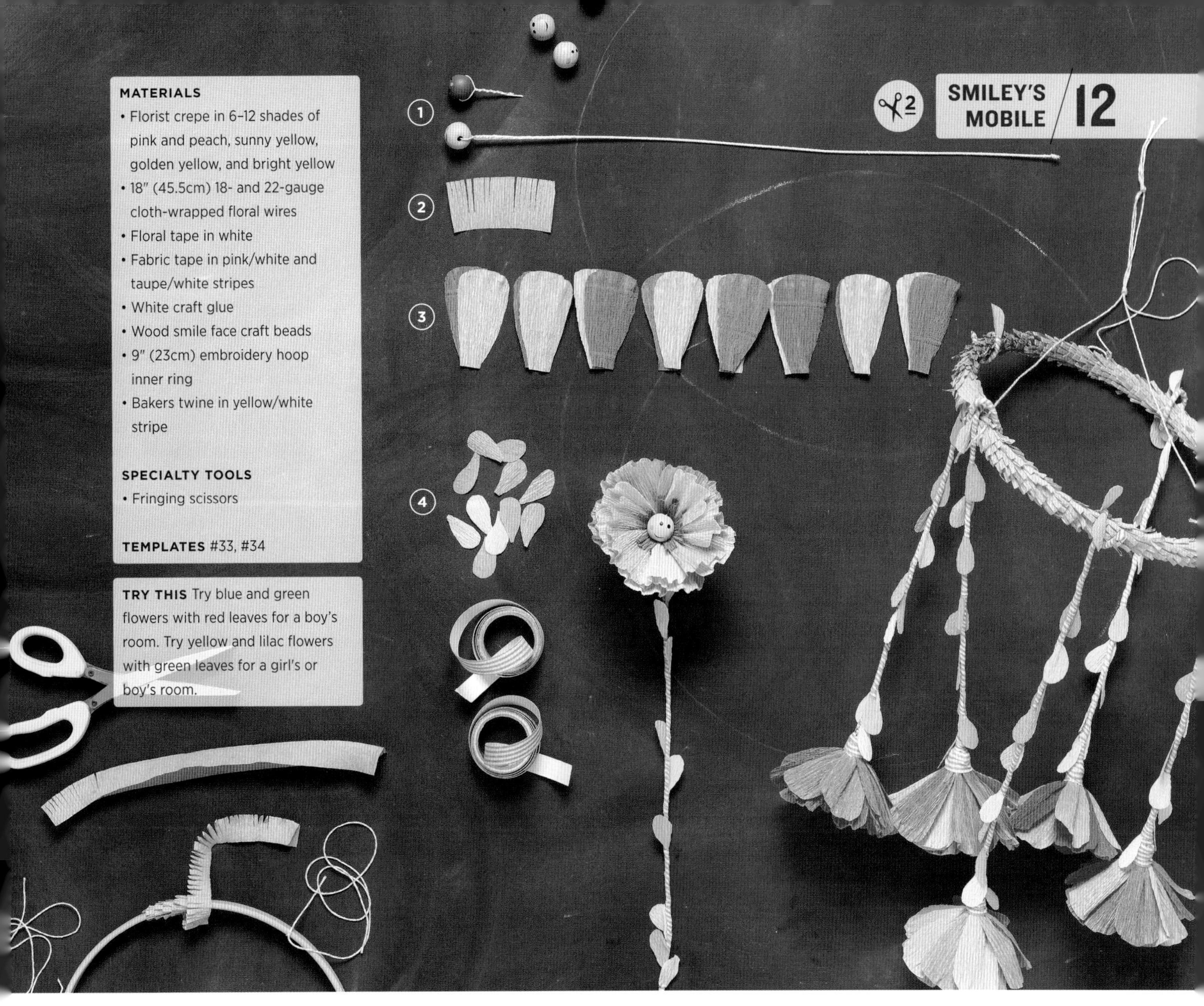

SMILEY'S MOBILE / 12

MATERIALS

- Florist crepe in 6–12 shades of pink and peach, sunny yellow, golden yellow, and bright yellow
- 18" (45.5cm) 18- and 22-gauge cloth-wrapped floral wires
- Floral tape in white
- Fabric tape in pink/white and taupe/white stripes
- White craft glue
- Wood smile face craft beads
- 9" (23cm) embroidery hoop inner ring
- Bakers twine in yellow/white stripe

SPECIALTY TOOLS

- Fringing scissors

TEMPLATES #33, #34

TRY THIS Try blue and green flowers with red leaves for a boy's room. Try yellow and lilac flowers with green leaves for a girl's or boy's room.

CUT *Grain runs with height; all dimensions are given as H × W.* Cut all fringe with fringing scissors. For each flower: Cut a 4" (10cm) length of 22-gauge wire. Pick 3 shades of pink and peach crepe. Choose a color and cut a 1½" × 3" (4cm × 7.5cm) strip; fringe with the grain ¾ of the way down. Petal #33: Cut 8 each from the 2 remaining colors (16 petals total). Leaf #34: Cut 10 total from 2 or 3 different yellow crepes. Cut six 1½" × 11" (4cm × 28cm) strips from 3 pink crepes, 2 from each color. Fold in half lengthwise, fringe with the grain on the folded side ¾ of the way down. Cut 1 of each color in half widthwise.

BUILD Flower: Secure all layers with floral tape. **1.** With face pointing up, thread 4" (10cm) wire through bead, pull down, and twist ends together tightly. Secure to full-length 18-gauge stem wire. **2.** *Gather and Wrap* (p. 132) a 1½" × 3" (4cm × 7.5cm) fringe strip around bead to make a center. **3.** *Flute* (p. 134) top edges of Petals #33. Pair opposite pink petals together offsetting slightly as shown. *Scrunch Pleat* (p. 128) 8 pairs. Attach pairs evenly around center. Finish stem. **4.** Working with 10" (25.5cm) lengths of fabric tape, wrap base of flower and continue down stem, randomly attaching *Scrunch Pleated* Leaves #34, adding more tape as needed. Repeat 5 more times with remaining color combinations to make 6 flowers total. Curl ends of wire and dab with glue to secure fabric tape. **Hoop:** Cut 3 lengths of 25" (63.5cm) bakers twine. Tie ends to hoop, spacing evenly around the circle. With 1 long piece of folded fringe, affix the end to the hoop with glue. Wrap fringe around hoop, overlapping slightly as shown. Secure end with glue. Repeat process with a shorter piece in a different color. Alternate colors and lengths; cover twine, until hoop is fully wrapped. Gather pieces of twine and adjust in your hands until the hoop hangs level. Tie a knot 10" (25.5cm) above hoop. Tie another knot 3" (7.5cm) above first knot, to create a hanging loop. Trim ends. Attach flowers at alternating heights evenly around circle by wrapping wires around hoop.

PROJECT NOTE Our prepainted wood beads were purchased, but you could paint your own smiley face on any type of bead.

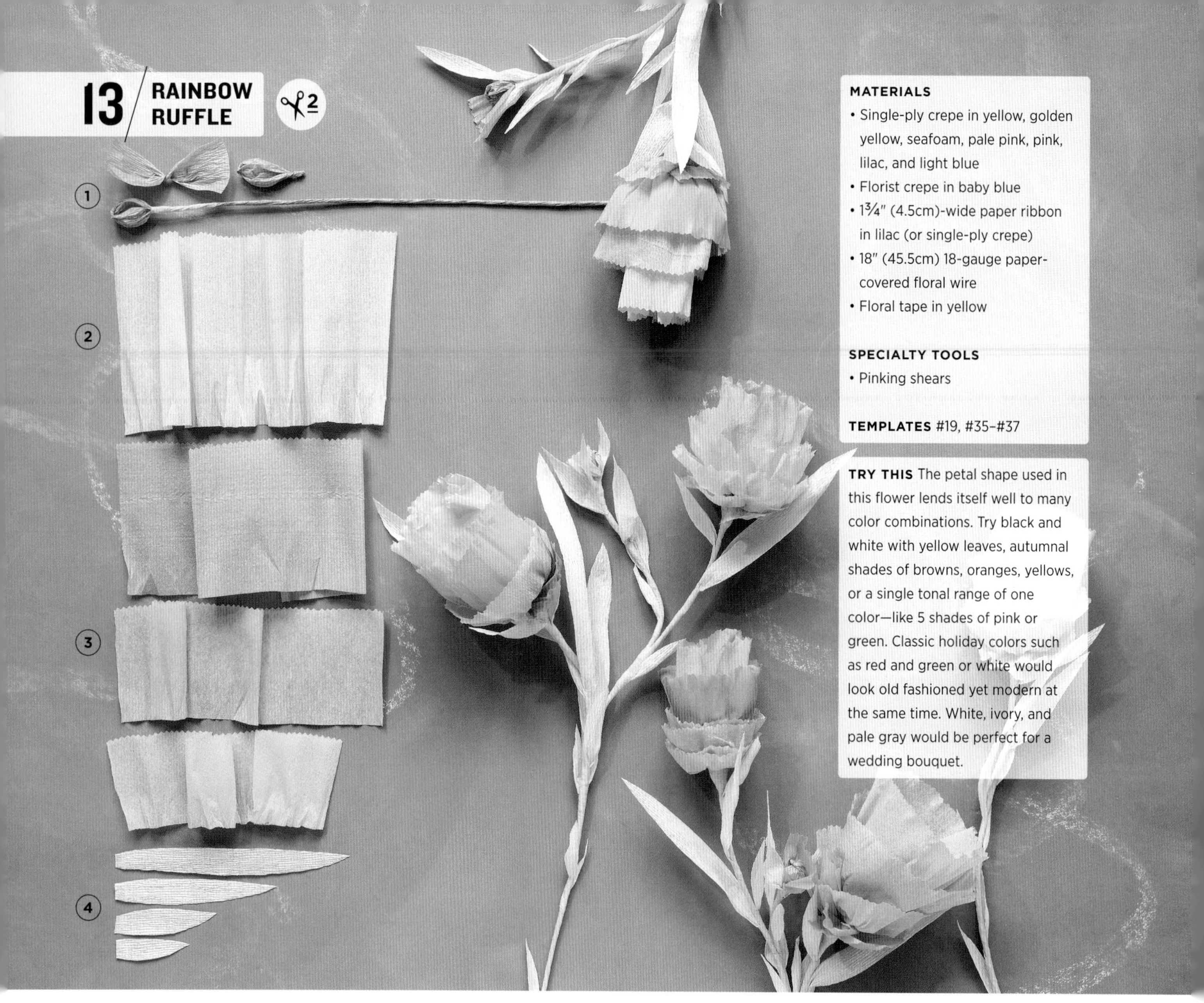

13 / RAINBOW RUFFLE

2

MATERIALS

- Single-ply crepe in yellow, golden yellow, seafoam, pale pink, pink, lilac, and light blue
- Florist crepe in baby blue
- 1¾" (4.5cm)-wide paper ribbon in lilac (or single-ply crepe)
- 18" (45.5cm) 18-gauge paper-covered floral wire
- Floral tape in yellow

SPECIALTY TOOLS

- Pinking shears

TEMPLATES #19, #35–#37

TRY THIS The petal shape used in this flower lends itself well to many color combinations. Try black and white with yellow leaves, autumnal shades of browns, oranges, yellows, or a single tonal range of one color—like 5 shades of pink or green. Classic holiday colors such as red and green or white would look old fashioned yet modern at the same time. White, ivory, and pale gray would be perfect for a wedding bouquet.

CUT *Grain runs with height; all dimensions are given as H × W.* Cut a 4" (10cm) length of lilac paper ribbon. Cut a 6" × 14" (15cm × 35.5cm) strip from yellow single-ply crepe. Cut a 5" × 14" (13cm × 35.5cm) strip from lavender single-ply crepe. Cut a 3½" × 14" (9cm × 35.5cm) strip from pink single-ply crepe. Cut a 2½" × 14" (6.5cm × 35.5cm) strip from seafoam single-ply crepe. Trim all strips on one long side with pinking shears. Cut 3 each of Leaves #19, #35, #36, and #37 from the baby blue florist crepe.

BUILD Secure all layers with floral tape. **1.** Twist paper ribbon 2 or 3 times in the middle, like a bow tie as shown. Fold down creating a loop with the twist at the top. *Scrunch Pleat* (p. 128) the base and secure it to a wire to make a center. **2.** *Gather and Wrap* (p. 132) yellow crepe evenly around the base, overlapping ends 2"–3" (5cm–7.5cm). *Finesse* (p. 135) on the inside of the base of the cuff to form a bell shape. **3.** Repeat step 2 for each strip, taking care to not align the seams. Overlap ends slightly less with each layer. **4.** *Scrunch Pleat* all leaves and attach randomly as you finish the stem.

PROJECT NOTE In our arrangement we mixed up the color combinations by adding in light blue, golden yellow, and a brighter pink single-ply crepe. We attached multiple flowers to one another by *Joining Stems* (p. 132). We also made small buds using the same center and a 2" × 2½" (5cm × 6.5cm) strip of pinked edge single-ply crepe; *Gather and Wrap* it halfway around the center. To make a smaller flower, use these measurements for the following steps: **2.** 5" × 12" (12.5cm × 30.5cm). **3.** 4" × 12" (10cm × 30.5cm), 3" × 12" (7.5cm × 30.5cm), 2½" × 12" (6.5cm × 30.5cm).

ADD COLOR Cut 2 folds from light salmon/light rose double-sided crepe. Stamp random dots with dot marker stampers as shown. Set aside to dry.

CUT *Grain runs with height; all dimensions are given as H × W.* Petal #38: Cut 4 from dotted pink/salmon double-sided crepe.

BUILD 1. Wrap a pipe cleaner in half tightly over a pom-pom and twist a few times at the base to secure to make a center. **2.** *Cup* (p. 134) gently and *Scrunch Pleat* (p. 128) Petals #38 and attach them evenly around center, securing 1 or 2 at a time with masking tape.

PROJECT NOTE Cut 8½" (21.5cm) semicircles from paper and join the straight edges with double-sided tape or glue to make the party hat cone. Trim the brim with a wave edger. Punch holes and thread with the stem of a flower, bend the stem 90 degrees and secure with masking tape inside the hat. Punch holes on either side at the base of the hat and thread with cord to create ties. Additional colors of flowers were made with white double-sided crepe and a yellow dot stamper and yellow/melon double-sided crepe and a pink dot stamper.

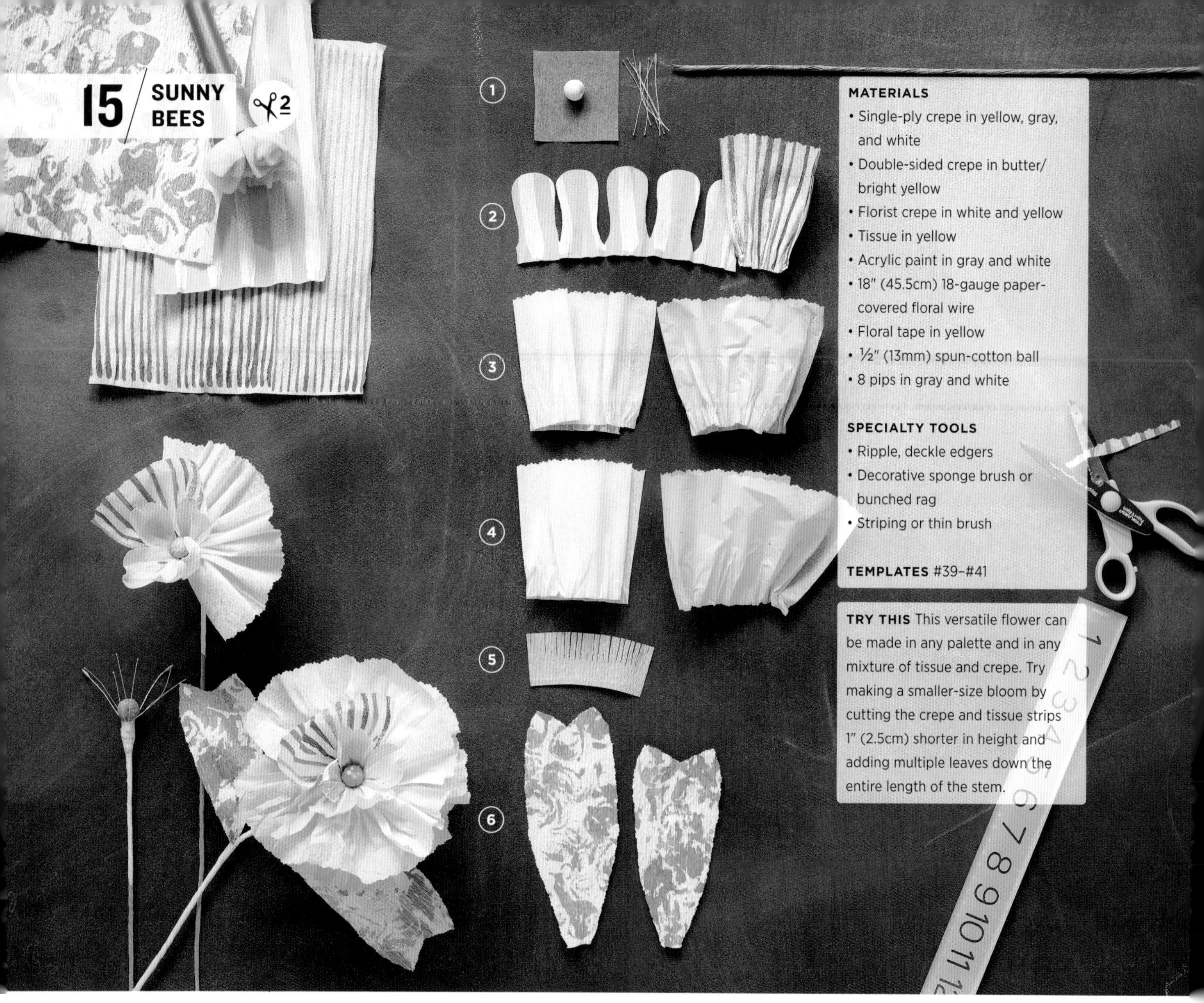

15 / SUNNY BEES

MATERIALS

- Single-ply crepe in yellow, gray, and white
- Double-sided crepe in butter/ bright yellow
- Florist crepe in white and yellow
- Tissue in yellow
- Acrylic paint in gray and white
- 18" (45.5cm) 18-gauge paper-covered floral wire
- Floral tape in yellow
- ½" (13mm) spun-cotton ball
- 8 pips in gray and white

SPECIALTY TOOLS

- Ripple, deckle edgers
- Decorative sponge brush or bunched rag
- Striping or thin brush

TEMPLATES #39–#41

TRY THIS This versatile flower can be made in any palette and in any mixture of tissue and crepe. Try making a smaller-size bloom by cutting the crepe and tissue strips 1" (2.5cm) shorter in height and adding multiple leaves down the entire length of the stem.

ADD COLOR *Dilute* (p. 136) the white and gray acrylic paints. Cut 1 piece, 2 folds wide, from butter/ bright-yellow double-sided crepe. Paint ¾"-wide (2cm) white stripes with the grain ½"–¾" (13mm–2cm) apart. Cut 1 piece 2 folds wide from white single-ply crepe. Paint thin gray stripes with the grain using a striping brush. Cut a 10" (25.5cm) piece from white florist crepe. Using a sponge brush, blot gray acrylic paint to create a pattern. Set pieces aside to dry.

CUT *Grain runs with height; all dimensions are given as H × W.* Cut a 2½" (6cm) square from gray single-ply crepe. Petal #39: Cut a 3" × 8" (7.5cm × 20.5cm) strip from striped yellow double-sided crepe, accordion-fold to fit template, and cut a continuous petal. Cut a 4" (10cm) square from gray striped crepe, trim 1 end across the grain using a ripple edger. Cut 2 pieces each 3½" × 12" (9cm × 30.5cm) from yellow single-ply crepe and yellow tissue; trim 1 long side using a ripple edger. Cut a 1½" × 3½" (4cm × 9cm) strip from the yellow florist crepe. Using fringing scissors, fringe with the grain ¾ of the way down to make a calyx. Leaves #40 and #41: Using deckle edger cut 1 each from sponge painted crepe.

BUILD Secure all layers with floral tape. **1.** Make a *Spun-Cotton Center* (p. 130) with gray single-ply crepe, add pips evenly around center. Paint 2 small white dots on the center, let dry. **2.** *Gather and Wrap* (p. 132) Petal #39 and *Cup* (p. 134). *Flute* (p. 134) the top of each petal. *Gather and Wrap* the 4" (10cm) gray striped crepe square ¼ of the way around the center. **3.** *Scrunch Pleat* (p. 128) all yellow crepe and tissue strips. *Gather and Wrap* 1 piece of yellow crepe halfway around the center, repeat with 1 piece of yellow tissue around the remaining half, overlapping both ends slightly. **4.** Repeat step 3 with remaining crepe and tissue strips. *Flute* and *Finesse* (p. 135) both layers. **5.** *Gather and Wrap* fringed calyx around base. **6.** *Scrunch Pleat* leaves. Attach Leaf #40 4" (10cm) from flower base and Leaf #41 2" (5cm) below Leaf #40 while finishing stem. Gently *Cup* both leaves.

PROJECT NOTE (see p. 35) Our green version has an extra green florist crepe petal with a painted white stripe. The centers are made with black striped white double-sided crepe, and the petals are crafted with mint and chartreuse tissue.

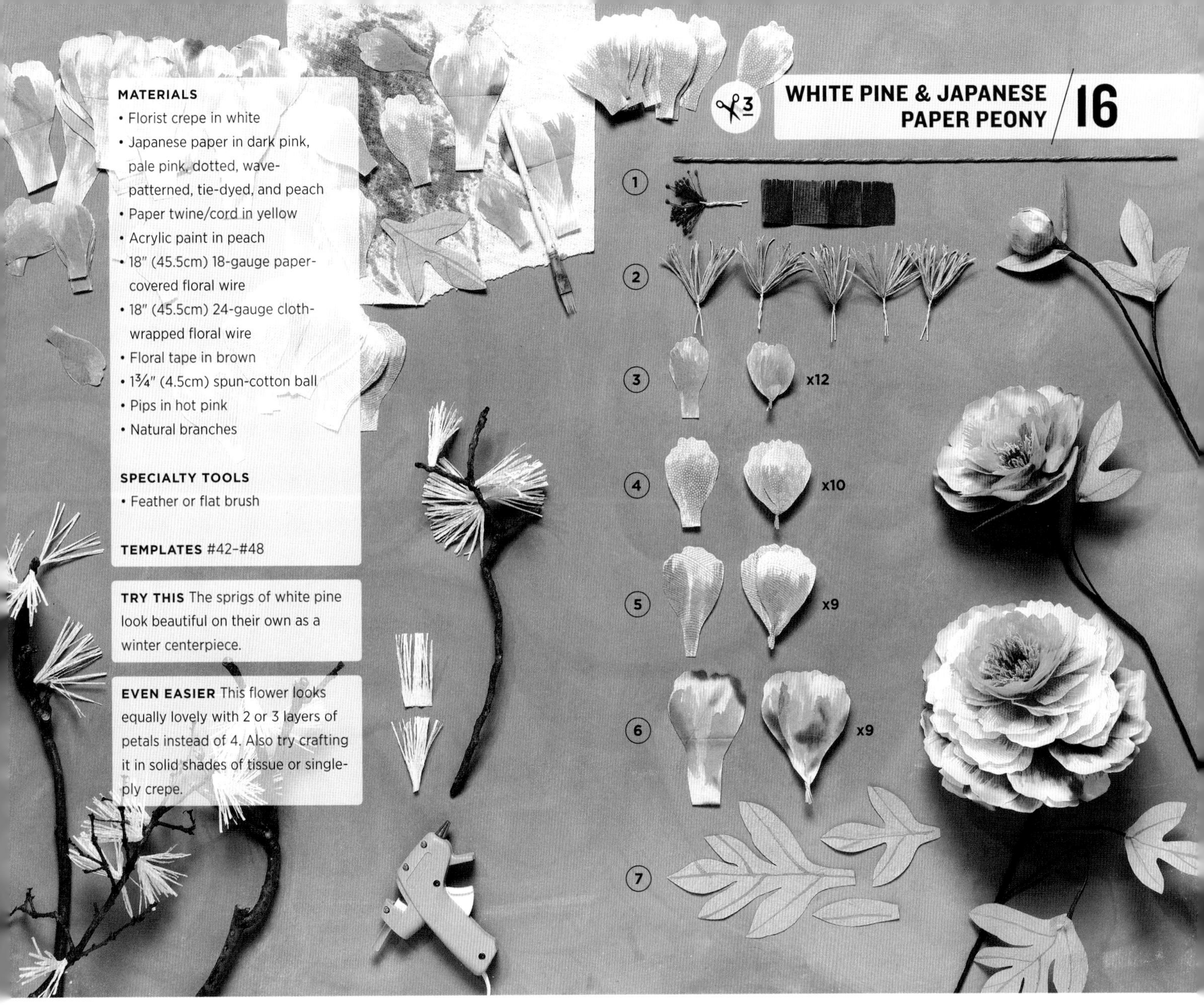

WHITE PINE & JAPANESE PAPER PEONY / 16

MATERIALS

- Florist crepe in white
- Japanese paper in dark pink, pale pink, dotted, wave-patterned, tie-dyed, and peach
- Paper twine/cord in yellow
- Acrylic paint in peach
- 18" (45.5cm) 18-gauge paper-covered floral wire
- 18" (45.5cm) 24-gauge cloth-wrapped floral wire
- Floral tape in brown
- 1¾" (4.5cm) spun-cotton ball
- Pips in hot pink
- Natural branches

SPECIALTY TOOLS

- Feather or flat brush

TEMPLATES #42–#48

TRY THIS The sprigs of white pine look beautiful on their own as a winter centerpiece.

EVEN EASIER This flower looks equally lovely with 2 or 3 layers of petals instead of 4. Also try crafting it in solid shades of tissue or single-ply crepe.

CUT *Grain runs with height; all dimensions are given as H × W.* Cut a 1½" × 5" (4cm × 12.5cm) strip from dark pink speckled paper, fold in half twice widthwise, finely *Hand Cut Fringe* (p. 127) with the grain ¾ of the way down. Cut seventy-five 4" (10cm) lengths of yellow cord. Cut six 4" (10cm) lengths of 24-gauge wires. Petal #42: Cut 24 from pale pink paper. Petal #43: Cut 20 from dotted paper. Petal #44: Cut 18 from wave paper. Petal #45: Cut 18 from tie-dyed paper. Cut 1 each of Leaves #46, #47, and #48 from peach paper. Cut fifteen 2½" × 1" (6.5cm × 2.5cm) strips from prestretched sheets of white florist crepe. Finely *Hand Cut Fringe* ¾ of the way down with the grain. Cut two 9" (23cm) lengths of 24-gauge wire.

ADD COLOR *Dilute* (p. 136) the peach acrylic paint. Flip half of each petal type over. Using a feather brush, paint the bottom ¾ of all the petals, leaving the tip unpainted as shown. Paint the veining on the leaves. Let the petals and leaves dry on paper towels.

BUILD Secure all layers with floral tape. **1.** Make a *Pip Center* (p. 130) with 25 pink pips. *Gather and Wrap* (p. 132) pink paper fringe around center. **2.** Make 5 *Pip Centers* with 15 lengths each of yellow cord, secure evenly around center. **3.** Create 12 pairs of Petal #42 by layering 2 slightly offset petals together, painted sides up, mirroring petal shapes as shown, and *Twist* (p. 128). Secure pairs evenly around center. Leave a ½" (13mm) space on stem between layers. **4.** Repeat step 3 with Petal #43, make 10 pairs. **5.** Repeat step 3 with Petal #44, make 9 pairs. **6 and 7.** Repeat step 3 with Petal #45, make 9 pairs. *Scrunch Pleat* (p. 128) all leaves. Finish stem, attaching Leaf #48 1" (2.5cm) below flower base. Attach Leaves #46 and #47 to separate wire tips, finishing each stem. Randomly *Join Stems* (p. 132) of leaves to the main stem.

PROJECT NOTE Make pine spray by *Scrunch Pleating* a piece of fringed white crepe and attach to the branch with a dot of hot glue. Hot glue multiples where desired onto branches. To make smaller peony, complete steps 1 and 2 with 3 yellow cord centers. Complete steps 3 and 7 with half the number of petals. To make the bud, make a *Spun-Cotton Center* (p. 130) using any of the rice papers and surround with 2 Petals #42. Attach 2 Leaves #48 to stem.

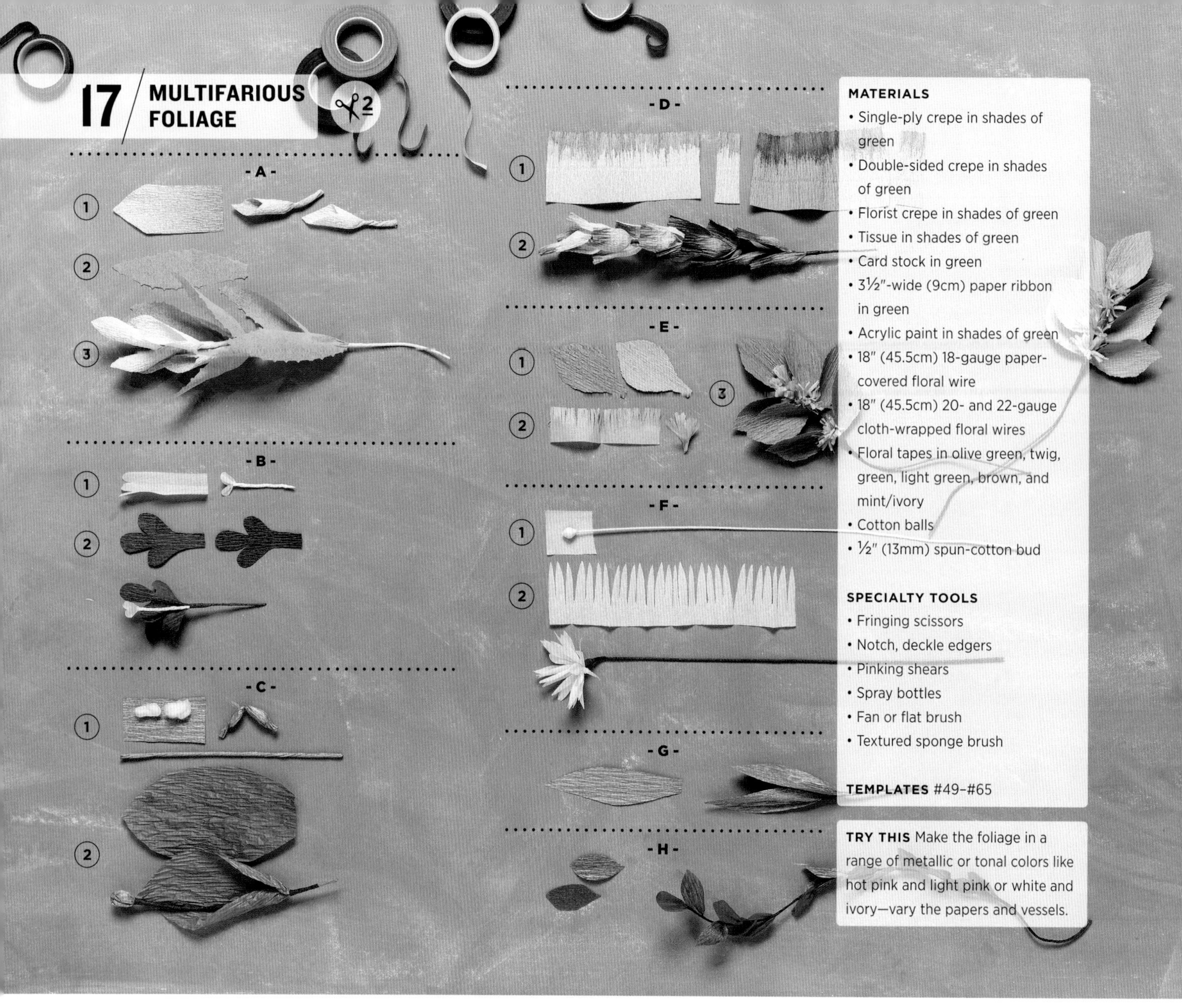

NOTE *Dilute* (p. 136) and paint; let parts dry. *Grain runs with height; all dimensions are given as H × W.* Secure all layers and finish stems with floral tape. Use floral tape colors as desired. Cut wires to desired lengths. Cut fringe with fringing scissors.

A 1. Leaf #49: Cut from green gradated florist crepe. Place a finger halfway down from the pointed end, wrap sides around finger, pinch, and twist excess tightly to make base as shown. **2.** Leaf #50: Cut from apple green single-ply crepe with notch edger. **3.** *Scrunch Pleat* (p. 128) leaves. Secure 4 or 5 Leaves #49 at top section of stem followed by 5 or 6 Leaves #50.

B 1. Cut a 2½" × 1¼" (6.5cm × 3cm) piece from white single-ply crepe. Fold in thirds with the grain, cut scallop across 1 short end; unfold. Cut ½" (13mm) down at notches with the grain. Roll tightly; fold down scallops. Attach to a wire. **2.** Leaf #51: Spray olive and moss florist crepe with olive paint. Cut 1 each. *Scrunch Pleat* and secure to stem.

C 1. Make a coffee bean bud (step 5, p. 170) with a 3½" × 2" (9cm × 5cm) green metallic crepe piece; secure to a 6" (15cm) length of wire. **2.** Cut a 7" (18cm) length of olive paper ribbon, fold in half lengthwise, round off corners opposite fold to make a leaf. Finish stem, secure leaf 1½" (4cm) from base of stem.

D 1. Cut a 3½" × 12" (9cm × 30.5cm) strip from light green florist crepe, paint lime green stripe as shown. Repeat with olive crepe and kelly green paint. Trim painted edge with pinking shears. Cut into 1" (2.5cm) sections. **2.** *Scrunch Pleat* unpainted side; space blooms 1" (2.5cm) apart, attach while finishing stem.

E 1. Leaf #52: Cut 7 from mint/olive double-sided crepe with a deckle edger. **2.** Cut four 1½" × 6" (4cm × 15cm) strips from chartreuse tissue, fringe with the grain ¾ of the way down. *Scrunch Pleat* leaves and strips. **3.** Attach 1 leaf to a wire tip, then attach fringe at base of leaf. Attach 2 leaves opposite each other, then attach fringe at base. Repeat with remaining pairs.

F 1. Make a *Spun-Cotton Center* (p. 130) with a 2" (5cm) white single-ply crepe square and ½" (13mm) bud. **2.** Petal #53: Cut a 3" × 11" (7.5cm × 28cm) strip from white single-ply crepe, accordion-fold to fit template, and cut. *Gather and Wrap* (p. 132) around center.

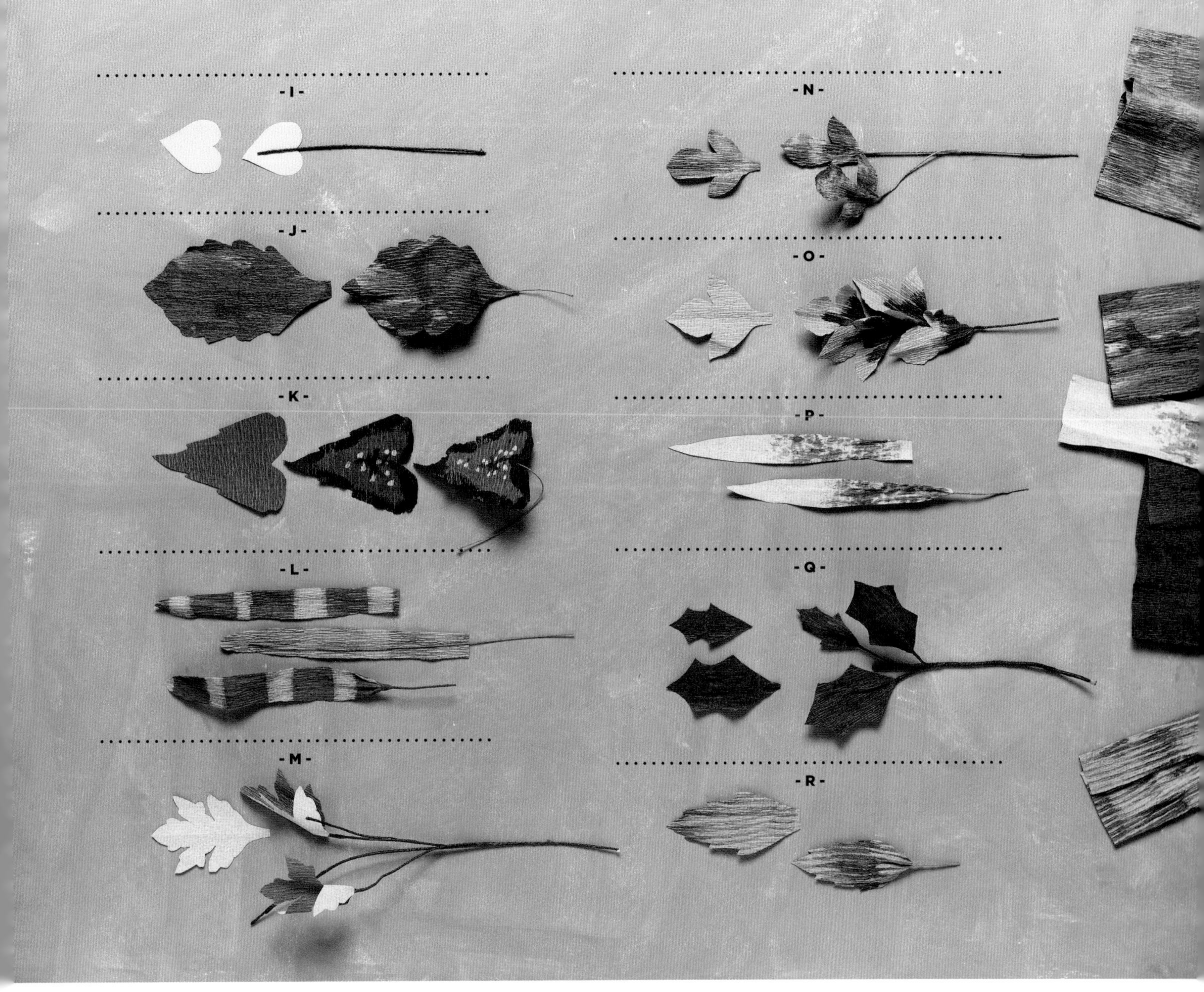

G Leaf #50: Cut 2 from metallic yellow crepe. *Scrunch Pleat*, secure to wire while finishing stem.

H Leaf #54: Cut multiples from green metallic and kelly green single-ply crepe. Secure randomly to a thin wire while finishing stem.

I Leaf #55: Cut from pale green card stock. *Wire One-Sided Leaf* (p. 133) with taped stem. *Style Stems* (p. 133), *Join Stems* (p. 132).

J Leaf #56: Loosely paint white stripes on forest green florist crepe as shown, cut leaves. *Wire One-Sided Leaves*.

K Leaf #57: Cut from olive florist crepe. Paint plum border and white dots as shown. *Wire One-Sided Leaves*, *Flute* (p. 134) edges.

L Leaf #58: Paint 1½"-wide (4cm) kelly green stripes across the grain on pale green florist crepe, cut 2 leaves. *Wire Two-Sided Leaves* (p. 133). Double the template length to make longer leaves.

M Leaf #59: Cut 2 from mint/olive double-sided crepe. *Scrunch Pleat* and secure to the wire tip, *Cup* (p. 134). *Join Stems*, add covered wires to mimic branches.

N Leaf #60: Spray light green florist crepe with dark green paint, cut 2 leaves. *Scrunch Pleat*, secure to wire tips, *Join Stems*.

O Leaf #61: Cut 4 from medium green florist crepe. Paint the leaf base with plum acrylic paint as shown. *Scrunch Pleat* and secure 1 leaf to the wire tip before securing the others down the stem.

P Leaf #62: Sponge-paint half of mint/olive double-sided crepe with green paint as shown, cut leaves. *Scrunch Pleat*, secure to wire tip.

Q Leaves #63 and #64: Spray moss florist crepe with green paint, cut 3 leaves. *Scrunch Pleat*, secure to tip of short wire. *Join Stems* to a thicker covered wire.

R Leaf #65: Paint dark green stripes on light green florist crepe, cut leaves. *Scrunch Pleat*, secure to tip of wire.

PROJECT NOTE All stems were secured in pots filled with dry floral foam covered with natural and basil Spanish moss.

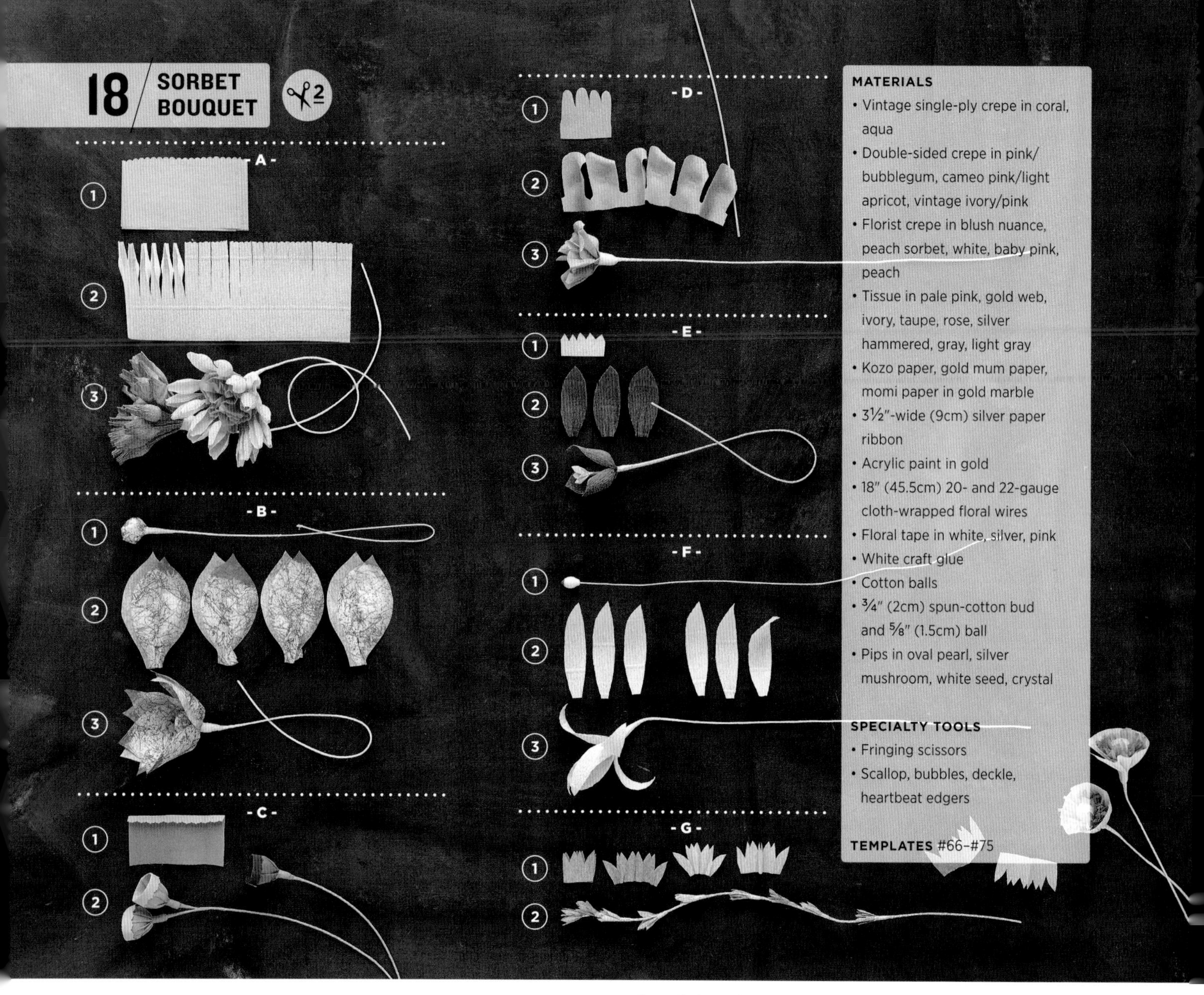

NOTE *Grain runs with height; all dimensions are given as H × W.* Cut fringe using fringing scissors, with the grain, ¾ of the way down. Secure all layers and finish stems with floral tape unless noted.

A 1. Cut a 3½" × 30" (9cm × 76cm) strip from pale pink tissue. Trim 1 long side using a scallop edger. *Scrunch Pleat* (p. 128) and *Gather and Wrap* (p. 132), secure to a wire tip. **2.** Cut a 4" × 10" (10cm × 25.5cm) strip from blush nuance florist crepe. Trim 1 long side using scallop edger. *Hand Cut Fringe* (p. 127) ½" (13mm) wide. *Cup* (p. 134) the top ⅓ of petal fringe leaving tip uncupped. **3.** *Scrunch Pleat* and *Gather and Wrap* strip, secure around center.

B 1. Make a *Cotton Ball Center* (p. 130) with a 3" (7.5cm) gold web tissue square. **2.** Petal #66: Cut 8 from gold web tissue. Brush tips with gold metallic acrylic, let dry. Pair petals with pattern facing out, offset slightly, and *Scrunch Pleat* together, to make 4 pairs. **3.** Secure evenly around center.

C 1. Cut a 2½" × 4" (6.5cm × 10cm) strip from vintage ivory/pink double-sided crepe. Trim 1 long edge using heartbeat edger, fold over ¼" (6mm), and crease. **2.** Glue ¼" (6mm) of a stem wire to the inside bottom left edge of strip, let dry. *Gather and Wrap* evenly around wire, overlap edge slightly, secure with pink tape. *Finesse* (p. 135) base to create bell shape as shown. Tuck outer folded flap under inner flap. Repeat steps 1 and 2 using a 3" (7.5cm) wire. *Join Stems* (p. 132) as shown.

D 1. Petal #67: Cut 1 from pink/bubblegum double-sided crepe. *Gather and Wrap* to wire tip and secure. **2.** Petal #68: Cut a 2½" × 10½" (6.5cm × 27cm) strip from pink/bubblegum double-sided crepe, accordion fold to fit template, cut. Using a skewer, *Stick Curl* (p. 135) corners out diagonally and *Cup*. **3.** *Scrunch Pleat* and *Gather and Wrap* securing evenly around center.

E 1. Petal #69: Cut 1 from cameo pink/light apricot double-sided crepe. *Gather and Wrap* to wire tip, fan out, secure with silver tape, 1½" (4cm) down. **2.** Petal #70: Cut 3 from peach sorbet florist crepe. Gently *Cup* and *Scrunch Pleat*. **3.** Secure evenly 1½" (4cm) down from top with silver tape.

F 1. Glue a ¾" (2cm) bud to wire tip. Paint the tip with gold acrylic. **2.** Petal #71: Cut 6 from white florist crepe. *Scissor Curl* (p. 135) and *Scrunch Pleat*

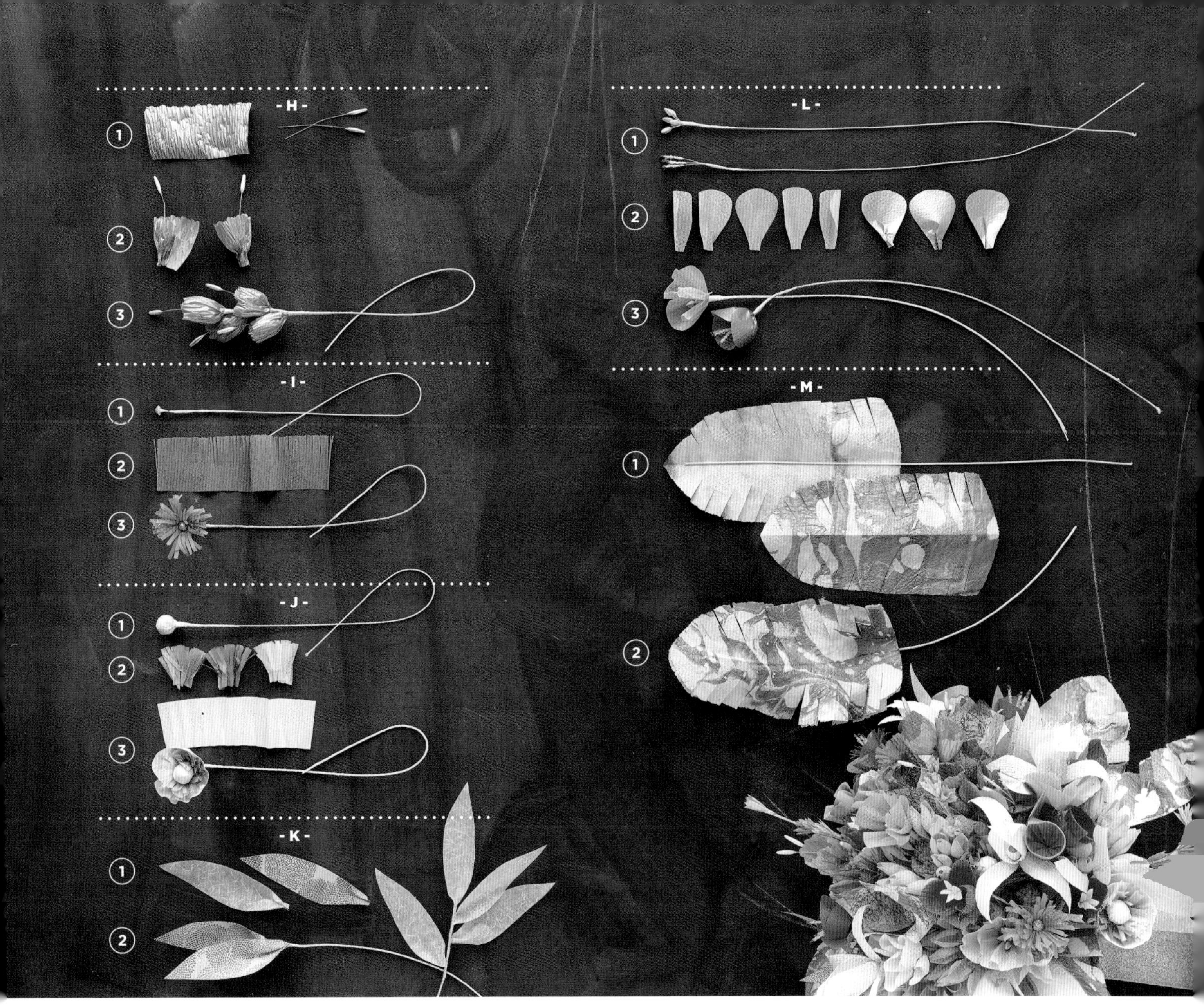

all petals. **3.** Secure 3 petals, curl in, evenly around the center. Secure the remaining 3 petals, curl out at opposite points.

G 1. Petal #72: Cut eight 1½" × 3" (4cm × 7.5cm) strips from stretched florist crepe, 4 from baby pink, 4 from peach. Fold each in half widthwise and cut. **2.** *Scrunch Pleat* petals and secure 1 petal to a 22-gauge wire tip with silver tape. Randomly attach remaining petals while finishing stem.

H 1. Cut four 2" × 3½" (5cm × 9cm) lengths of silver paper ribbon. Trim 1 long edge each using bubbles edger. **2.** *Gather and Wrap* around an oval pearl pip overlapping by ½" (13mm) to make a floret. **3.** Secure 1 to a stem wire tip with silver tape. Secure 3 florets ¾" (2cm) apart while finishing the stem.

I 1. Make a *Pip Center* (p. 130) with 1 silver mushroom pip. **2.** Cut a 2" × 8" (5cm × 20.5cm) strip from vintage coral single-ply crepe. Trim 1 long edge using deckle edger and fringe. **3.** *Gather and Wrap* around the center, secure with silver tape. *Scissor Curl* the fringe out.

J 1. Make a *Spun-Cotton Center* (p. 130) with a 3" (7.5cm) ivory tissue square and one ⅝" (1.5cm) ball. **2.** Cut three 1½" × 7" (4cm × 18cm) strips from taupe and ivory tissue. Fold each in quarters and fringe. Keep folded, *Scrunch Pleat* then secure evenly around the center. **3.** Cut a 2" × 7" (5cm × 18cm) strip from white double-sided crepe. *Scrunch Pleat* then *Gather and Wrap* evenly around the center, overlapping slightly, and secure. *Cup* gently.

K 1. Leaf #73: Cut 2–5 each from kozo and gold mum papers; *Scrunch Pleat*. **2.** Secure 1 leaf to a wire tip with silver tape. Attach remaining leaves randomly while finishing the stem with silver tape.

L 1. Make 2 *Pip Centers*, 1 with 3 folded white seed pips, 1 with 3 crystal pips. **2.** Petal #74: Cut 5 from aqua single-ply crepe, 3 from silver hammered tissue; *Scrunch Pleat*. **3.** Secure aqua petals evenly around white pip center with silver tape. Repeat with silver tissue petals and crystal pip center.

M 1. Leaf #75: Cut 2 from gold marbled momi paper using deckle edger. *Wire Two-Sided Leaf* (p. 133), glueing center area only. **2.** Finish stem with silver tape, *Style Stems* (p. 133) as shown.

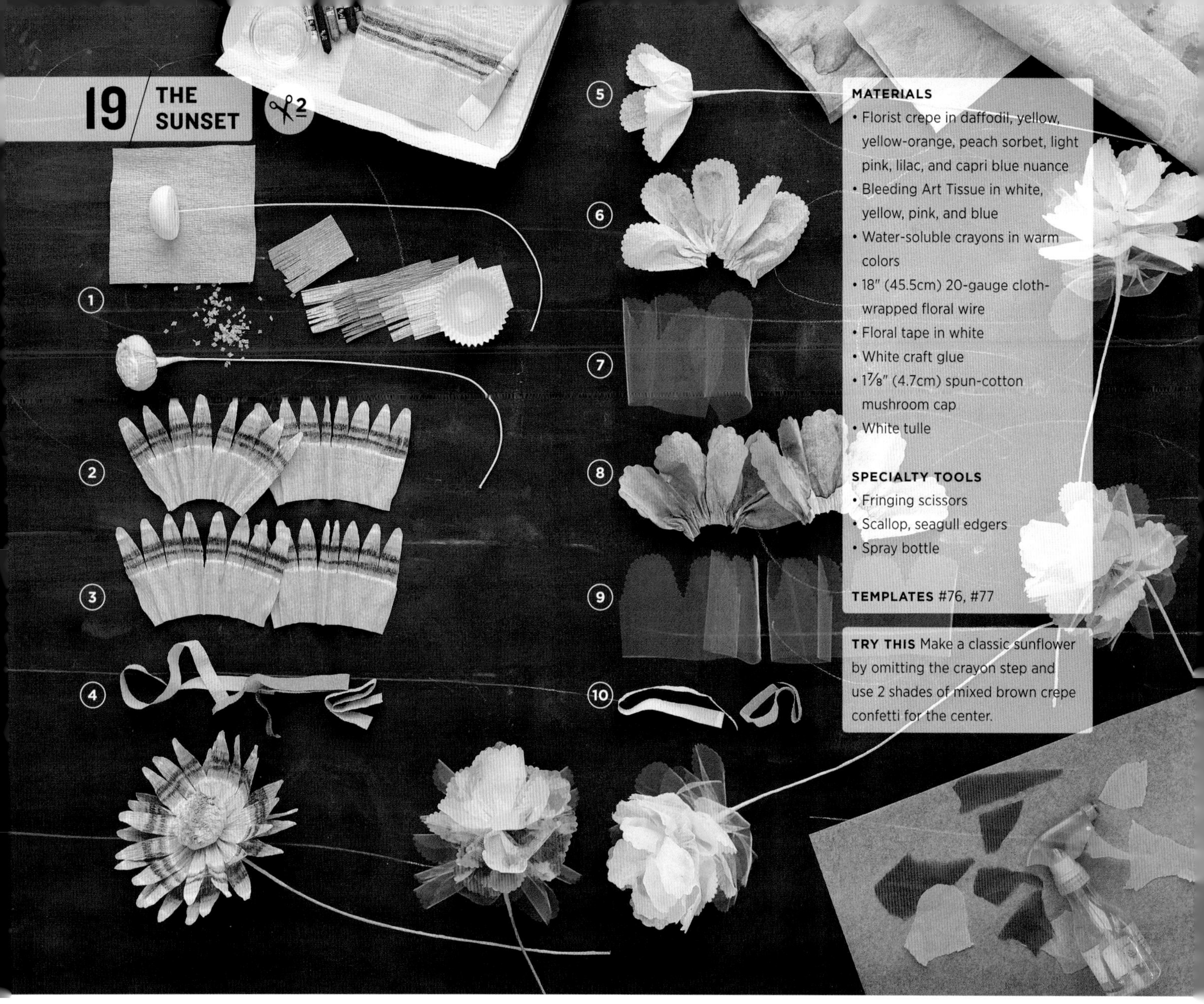

ADD COLOR Over a drop cloth, scatter torn pieces of blue Bleeding Art Tissue on a white piece of tissue. Spray with water and let dry. Peel off tissue pieces. Cut four 4½" × 7½" (11.5cm × 19cm) strips from stretched daffodil crepe. With 6 shades of water-soluble crayons draw stripes against the grain as shown. Brush each strip with water and dry on paper towels.

CUT *Grain runs with height; all dimensions are given as H × W.* Cut a 6" (15cm) square from daffodil crepe. Petal #76: Restretch daffodil crepe strips, fold in half to fit template, align stripes in petal area and cut. Cut 4" × 2" (10cm × 5cm) pieces from yellow, daffodil, yellow-orange, peach sorbet, light pink, and lilac crepe. Using fringing scissors fringe with the grain ¾ of the way down and cut across the grain to make confetti. Petal #77: Cut four 4" × 12" (10cm × 30.5cm) strips from blue and white tissue. Accordion-fold strips in pairs to fit template. Cut 1 pair using scallop edger, 1 pair using seagull edger. Cut three 4" × 12" (10cm × 30.5cm) strips from white tulle, accordion-fold to fit template and cut using scallop edger. Cut two ½" × 8" (13mm × 20.5cm) strips each from daffodil, peach sorbet, lilac, and capri blue nuance crepe, stretch strips.

BUILD Secure all layers with floral tape. **1.** Make a *Spun-Cotton Center* (p. 130) with mushroom cap and daffodil crepe square. Brush top with glue. Sprinkle confetti in rows as shown: yellow, daffodil, yellow-orange, peach sorbet, light pink, and lilac. Let dry. **2.** *Scrunch Pleat* (p. 128) and evenly *Gather and Wrap* (p. 132) 1 daffodil crepe strip halfway around center, secure. Repeat with second strip around remaining half. **3.** Repeat step 2 with 2 daffodil crepe strips, offset starting points. Finish stem. **4.** *Cover Stem* (p. 133) with thin crepe strips: daffodil, peach sorbet, lilac. **5.** *Scrunch Pleat* and evenly *Gather and Wrap* 1 tissue strip on wire tip and secure. **6.** Repeat step 5 below first layer. **7.** Leave ½" (13mm) of space on stem and repeat step 5 with tulle strip. **8.** Repeat step 7 using 1 tissue strip halfway around stem, secure. Repeat with second strip around remaining half. **9.** Repeat step 7 with 2 more tulle strips. Finish stem. **10.** *Cover Stem* with blue nuance and lilac crepe strips.

PROJECT NOTE Additional colors of clouds were crafted by making different tonal ranges of Bleeding Art Tissue in yellow and pink.

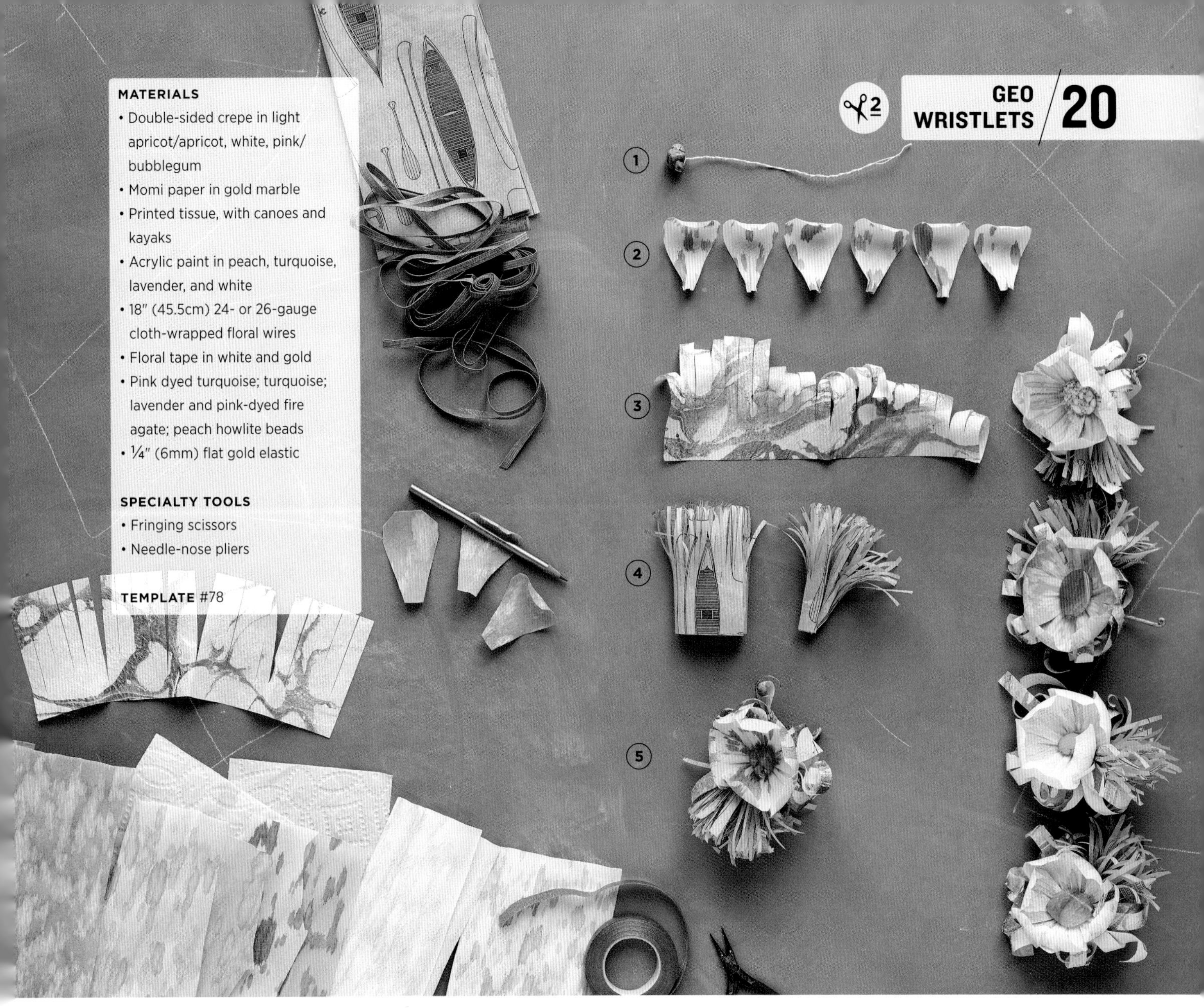

ADD COLOR *Dilute* (p. 136) the peach acrylic paint. Cut 1 piece 3 folds wide from light apricot/apricot double-sided crepe. Drop and dribble paint onto crepe to create large droplets and splatters. Set aside to dry.

CUT *Grain runs with height; all dimensions are given as H × W.* Petal #78: Cut 6 from painted double-sided crepe. Cut a 4" × 10" (10cm × 25.5cm) strip from gold marbled momi paper and *Hand Cut Fringe* (p. 127) ½" (13mm) wide ¾ of the way down. Cut a 3½" × 15" (9cm × 38cm) strip from canoes and kayaks tissue and fold in thirds. Using fringing scissors, fringe ¾ of the way down. Cut a 15" (38cm) length of gold elastic.

BUILD Secure all layers with white floral tape unless noted. **1.** Thread wire through bead, twist at base as shown to make a center. **2.** Very gently *Scissor Curl* (p. 135) each petal to smooth out buckling from paint. *Stick Curl* (p. 135) with a pencil, top edge of petal in, then *Cup* (p. 134) gently. *Scrunch Pleat* (p. 128) each petal. Attach 2 petals at opposite sides of bead and secure. Attach additional petals 2 at a time on either side. **3.** *Scissor Curl* gold marbled momi paper with pattern facing out. *Scrunch Pleat* and *Gather and Wrap* (p. 132) around base and secure. **4.** Fold fringe piece in half as shown, *Scrunch Pleat* to make a petal, and secure to base. **5.** Trim stem to 3½" (9cm). Finish stem with white tape, then cover in gold tape. Curl stem end on itself with pliers. Tie gold elastic to stem, make a knot, and tie again to make a bracelet.

PROJECT NOTE Additional color combinations: Turquoise bead with turquoise paint on white double-sided crepe. Lavender dyed fire agate bead with lavender paint on white double-sided crepe. Pink dyed fire agate bead with white paint on pink/bubblegum double-sided crepe. Peach howlite bead with light peach paint on light apricot/apricot double-sided crepe. To ensure wristlets stay together while wearing, squeeze glue in between layers and at the base and let fully dry before wearing.

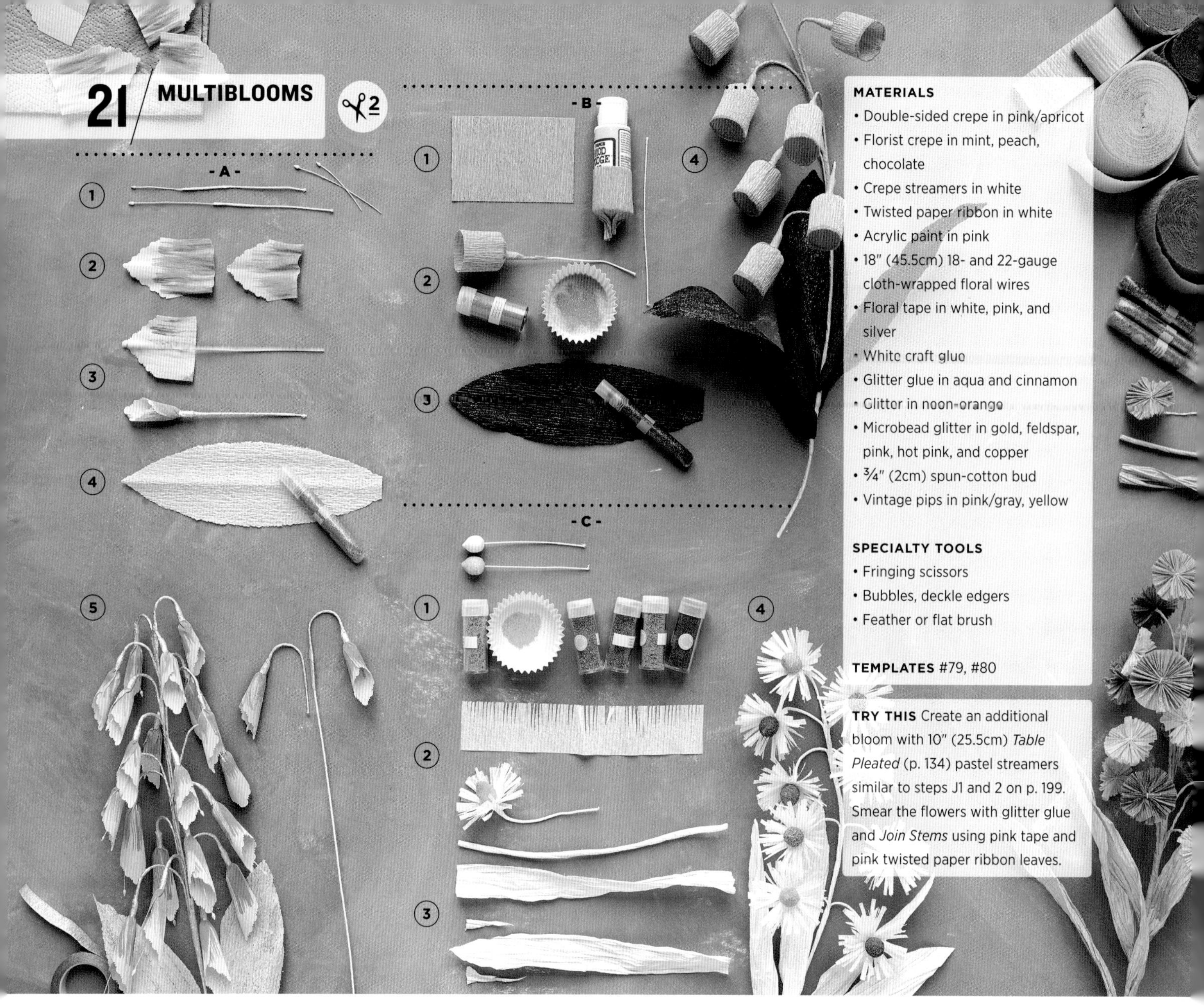

21 / MULTIBLOOMS

✂ 2

MATERIALS

- Double-sided crepe in pink/apricot
- Florist crepe in mint, peach, chocolate
- Crepe streamers in white
- Twisted paper ribbon in white
- Acrylic paint in pink
- 18" (45.5cm) 18- and 22-gauge cloth-wrapped floral wires
- Floral tape in white, pink, and silver
- White craft glue
- Glitter glue in aqua and cinnamon
- Glitter in neon-orange
- Microbead glitter in gold, feldspar, pink, hot pink, and copper
- ¾" (2cm) spun-cotton bud
- Vintage pips in pink/gray, yellow

SPECIALTY TOOLS

- Fringing scissors
- Bubbles, deckle edgers
- Feather or flat brush

TEMPLATES #79, #80

TRY THIS Create an additional bloom with 10" (25.5cm) *Table Pleated* (p. 134) pastel streamers similar to steps J1 and 2 on p. 199. Smear the flowers with glitter glue and *Join Stems* using pink tape and pink twisted paper ribbon leaves.

NOTE *Grain runs with height; all dimensions are given as H × W.* Secure all layers and finish stems with floral tape: A. silver, B. pink, C. white, *Scrunch Pleat* (p. 128) all leaves and secure.

A 1. Attach 1 pink/gray pip to a 3½" (9cm) length of 22-gauge wire. Repeat to make 12. Attach 1 yellow pip to a 4½" (11.5cm) length of 22-gauge wire. Repeat to make 8. **2.** Petal #79 (long and short): Cut 8 long, and 12 short from the pink/apricot double-sided crepe. Trim the point using the bubbles edger. *Dilute* (p. 136) the pink acrylic paint. Using a feather brush, paint the bottom of each petal. **3.** Position the wire as shown, place index finger ½" (13mm) from the straight end, wrap each side over your finger, and then twist the excess around the wire and secure. Repeat with all petals, pink/gray pip with the short petal, and yellow pip with the long petal. **4.** Leaf #80: Cut 3 from the mint florist crepe using a deckle edger; smear with aqua glitter glue. **5.** *Style Stems* (p. 133). Secure 1 short flower to an 18-gauge wire tip. *Join Stems* (p. 132) of all the petals to the main stem, starting with the short flowers. Tape additional 18-gauge wire pieces to the base portion of the stem to thicken and add support. Secure 3 mint florist crepe leaves.

B 1. Cut seven 2¾" × 4½" (7cm × 11.5cm) strips from peach florist crepe. Cut seven 6" (15cm) 22-gauge wires. Form a cylinder with the grain, using half of strip, around base of 1¼" (3cm) bottle, form crepe over base, twisting end. Remove, insert wire, secure. Glue sides together. Repeat, make 7. **2.** Dip edge in glue and apply neon-orange glitter. Repeat, all flowers. **3.** Repeat step A4 with chocolate florist crepe and cinnamon glitter glue. **4.** *Style Stems, Join Stem* of 1 flower to 18-gauge wire tip, secure. *Join Stems* of remaining flowers to main stem. Secure 3 chocolate florist crepe leaves.

C 1. Cut nine 4½" (11.5cm) 22-gauge wires. Glue 1 spun-cotton bud to each wire tip. Coat bud with glue, apply microbead glitter. Repeat using all colors, make 9. **2.** Cut a 9" (23cm) length of white streamer and fringe it, with the grain, ¾ of the way down. *Gather and Wrap* (p. 132) it around the bud and secure. Repeat, make 9. **3.** Cut two 10" (25.5cm) lengths of white twisted paper ribbon and untwist. Cut in half lengthwise. Round off the open corners of 1 end to make a leaf. **4.** *Join Stem* of 1 flower to an 18-gauge wire tip. *Join Stems* of the remaining flowers to the main stem. Secure 4 leaves.

INKED IMPRINTS / 22

MATERIALS
- Single-ply crepe in white, yellow, goldenrod, buttercup, pink, and blue
- Double-sided crepe in white and orange/dark orange
- 18" (45.5cm) 20-gauge cloth-wrapped floral wire
- Floral or washi tape in pink, blue, yellow, and white
- Cotton balls
- Assorted rubber stamps and stamp pads

TEMPLATES #81–#83

TRY THIS For the holiday season try crafting with white stamps on red crepe. For a summer garden wedding centerpiece try making these flowers in shades of green, white, and brown. Rust, gold, and lavender would be lovely for an autumn gathering.

CUT *Grain runs with height; all dimensions are given as H × W.* Cut a 3½" (9cm) square from white single-ply crepe. Cut a 1½" × 4" (4cm × 10cm) strip from goldenrod single-ply crepe. Petal #81: Cut 5 from white double-sided crepe. Cut 1 piece of white double-sided crepe large enough to accommodate 2 or 3 stamped leaves. Cut a 6" (15cm) length of stem wire.

ADD COLOR Ink rubber stamps generously. Stamp in the center of crepe square. Stamp in the center of each Petal #81, re-inking each time. Stamp 2 or 3 leaf shapes on white double-sided crepe. Let papers dry.

BUILD Secure all layers with floral tape. **1.** Make a *Cotton Ball Center* (p. 130) with white crepe square, centering the stamped area over the top of cotton ball. **2.** *Gather and Wrap* (p. 132) goldenrod cuff petal around center. **3.** *Single Pleat* (p. 128) Petals #81 and secure evenly around base, gently *Cup* (p. 134). **4.** Cut out around leaf stamps leaving a base, and *Single Pleat* each leaf. Finish stem with tape, attaching leaves randomly to stem.

PROJECT NOTE To complete this project we used 2 additional sizes of petals, Petals #82 and #83. We varied the number of petals in the flowers by making 4- and 6-petal versions in addition to the 5-petal flower. We used different stamps and mixed up their placement on the petals and centers. In addition, to create wider as well as tighter flowers, we varied the attachment point of the petal onto the stem. All petals have been gently cupped, and a few flowers feature a single *Flute* (p. 134). We kept the palette tonal with orange, pink, white, and red inks and shades of orange single-ply and double-sided crepe.

23 KINGFISHER & FLAMINGO

MATERIALS

- Single-ply crepe in fuchsia, magenta, turquoise, and teal
- Florist crepe in light pink, magenta, fuchsia, and coral
- Tissue in rose, dark pink, aqua, and teal
- Wrapping paper in pink and aqua sparkle
- 3½"-wide (9cm) paper ribbon in hot pink and turquoise
- Twisted paper ribbon in hot pink and turquoise
- 18" (45.5cm) 18-gauge paper-covered floral wire
- 1" (2.5cm) floral tape in white
- 2" (5cm) spun-cotton carrot
- 12 pips in pink
- Aqua raffia
- Pink sparkly tulle

SPECIALTY TOOLS

- Fringing scissors

TEMPLATE #84

CUT *Grain runs with height; all dimensions are given as H × W.* Cut fringe with the grain using fringing scissors. Cut a 6" × 3" (15cm × 7.5cm) strip from fuchsia single-ply crepe. Petal #84: Cut 3 from coral pink florist crepe. Cut three 7" (18cm) lengths of pink paper ribbon. Cut three 4" (10cm) squares each from magenta and fuchsia florist crepe, sparkly tulle, rose and dark pink tissue. Fringe all pieces ¾" (2cm) on one side. Cut four 5" × 4" (12.5cm × 10cm) pieces each from light pink and coral florist crepe, fuchsia single-ply crepe, and wrapping paper. Fringe all pieces ¾" (2cm) on one side. Cut ten 5" (12.5cm), 8" (20.5cm), and 12" (30.5cm) lengths each of pink twisted paper ribbon. Untwist, and cut each length into 4 equal strips lengthwise. Round off both sides of 1 end with scissors. Cut five ¾" × 12" (2cm × 30.5cm) strips from magenta single-ply crepe. Cut an 8" (20.5cm) length of stem wire.

BUILD Secure all layers with floral tape. **1.** Glue a spun-cotton carrot to the tip of a full-length wire, let dry. Lay on bottom half of fuchsia crepe with ½" (13mm) overhang past base of carrot as shown. Roll paper around center, twist around wire. Tightly twist paper at top of carrot, fold down toward stem, smoothing out paper, and secure to finish center. Snip 1 end off pips; evenly secure around center. **2.** *Scrunch Pleat* (p. 128) Petals #84, secure evenly around center. **3.** Create soft paper ribbon loop by folding in half widthwise, *Scrunch Pleat* ends together, secure evenly around center. **4.** *Scrunch Pleat* tulle and magenta florist crepe petals together in pairs. *Scrunch Pleat* tissue petals. Attach petals overlapping while spreading evenly alternating tissue and crepe/tulle. **5.** *Scrunch Pleat* pink florist crepe and pink tissue petals. Alternate petals, and attach evenly around center. **6.** Leave a ¾" (2cm) space on stem between layers, repeat step 5 with light pink and coral florist crepe. **7.** Repeat step 5 with fuchsia crepe and wrapping paper. **8.** With an 8" (20.5cm) length wire, overlap with stem end by 1½" (4cm). Dab glue between wires, secure with tape. Finish stem with tape, randomly attaching various length *Scrunch Pleated* leaves. *Cover Stem* (p. 133), winding around leaves, with magenta crepe strips.

PROJECT NOTE We created the same flower in shades of turquoise, aqua, and teal and changed the leaf styles. Use aqua raffia in place of pips.

CRAYON COSMOS 24

✂2

MATERIALS

- Double-sided crepe in white, cream/lemon yellow, watermelon/watermelon ice, and fuchsia/magenta
- Water-soluble crayons
- 18" (45.5cm) 18-gauge cloth-wrapped floral wire
- Floral tape in yellow
- ½" (13mm) spun-cotton ball

SPECIALTY TOOLS

- Deckle edger
- Pinking shears

TEMPLATES #85–#87

CUT *Grain runs with height; all dimensions are given as H × W.* Cut a 2½" × 10" (6.5cm × 25.5cm) strip any color from double-sided crepe. Leaf #86 and 87: Cut 4–6 using a deckle edger from cream/lemon yellow double-sided crepe. Cut four to six 2½" (6.5cm) lengths of 22-gauge wire.

ADD COLOR Using 3 or 4 different colored crayons, draw a plaid pattern on the strip of double-sided crepe. Place on paper towels, and brush water in direction of the grain, to make pattern bleed. Set aside to dry.

BUILD Secure all layers with floral tape. **1.** Cut off a 2½" (6.5cm) square from the plaid paper strip, and make a *Spun-Cotton Center* (p. 130). **2.** Petal #85: Accordion-fold the remainder of the plaid strip to fit the template and cut continuous petal. Trim end of each petal with pinking shears as shown. *Gather and Wrap* (p. 132) around center and slightly *Cup* (p. 134) each petal and secure. **3.** *Scrunch Pleat* (p. 128) all leaves. Attach 1 Leaf #86 to the tip of a full-length wire, and each remaining leaf to the tip of a cut wire, finish wires with tape. **4.** To make leaf clusters, start with shorter stems and *Join Stems* (p. 132) to the longer wire. Repeat steps 3 and 4 as desired to create additional stems of foliage.

PROJECT NOTE To complete the bouquet, we created flowers using a few different double-sided crepe and crayon color combinations. To mix things up even more, we made 6- and 7-petal flowers by adding 1½" (4cm) to the length of the crepe strip for each additional petal, and accordion-folding them to accommodate the extra petals before cutting the template.

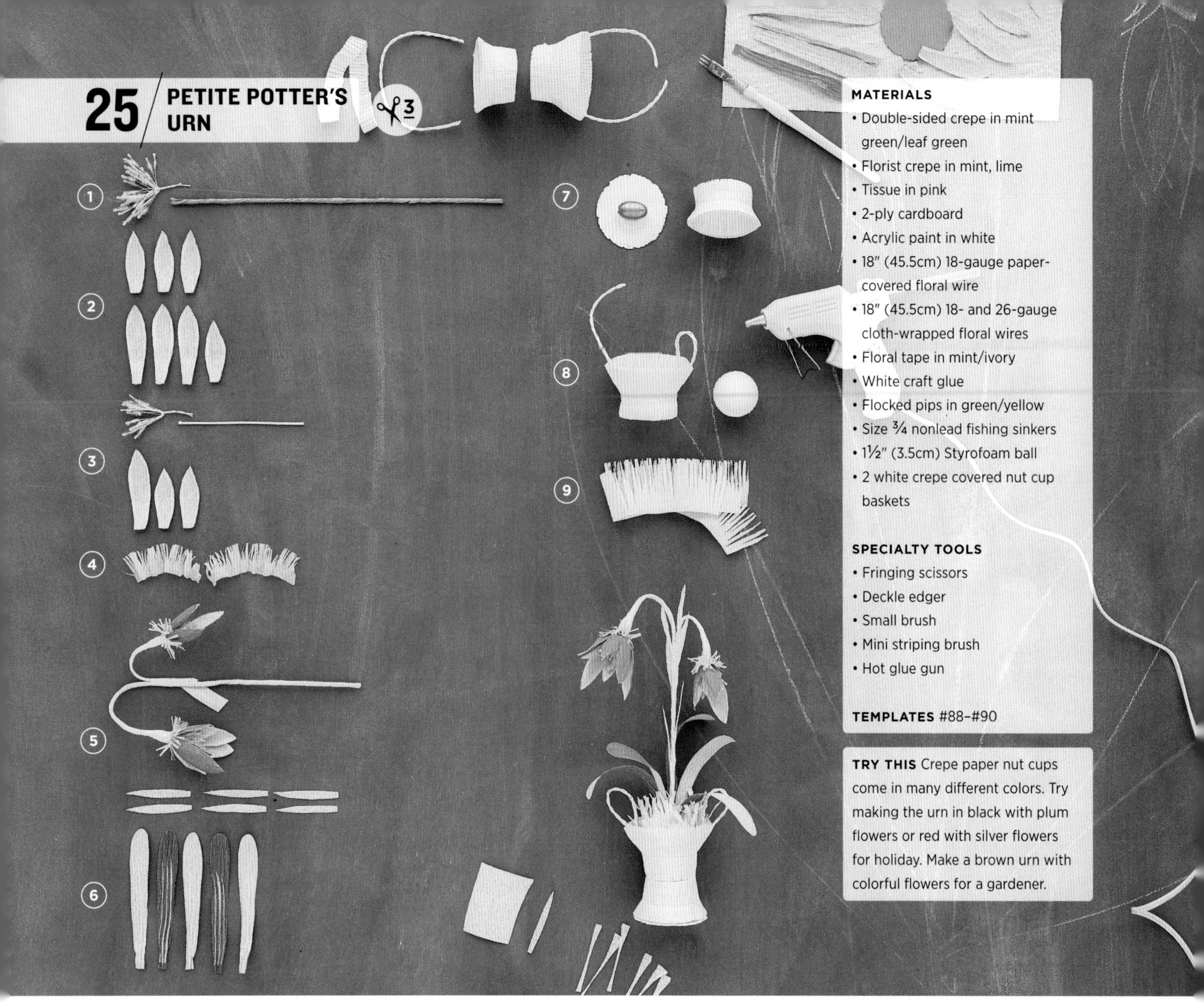

25 / PETITE POTTER'S URN

✂3

MATERIALS
- Double-sided crepe in mint green/leaf green
- Florist crepe in mint, lime
- Tissue in pink
- 2-ply cardboard
- Acrylic paint in white
- 18" (45.5cm) 18-gauge paper-covered floral wire
- 18" (45.5cm) 18- and 26-gauge cloth-wrapped floral wires
- Floral tape in mint/ivory
- White craft glue
- Flocked pips in green/yellow
- Size ¾ nonlead fishing sinkers
- 1½" (3.5cm) Styrofoam ball
- 2 white crepe covered nut cup baskets

SPECIALTY TOOLS
- Fringing scissors
- Deckle edger
- Small brush
- Mini striping brush
- Hot glue gun

TEMPLATES #88–#90

TRY THIS Crepe paper nut cups come in many different colors. Try making the urn in black with plum flowers or red with silver flowers for holiday. Make a brown urn with colorful flowers for a gardener.

CUT *Grain runs with height; all dimensions are given as H × W.* Petal #88: Cut 6 #89: Cut 4 Leaf #90: Cut 5 from mint green/leaf green double-sided crepe. Cut a 1½" × 10" (4cm × 25.5cm) strip each from stretched mint and lime florist crepe. Using fringing scissors, fringe with the grain ¾ of the way down. Cut two 1" × 4" (2.5cm × 10cm) strips from pink tissue. Fold in half lengthwise and finely *Hand Cut Fringe* (p. 127). Cut a 2¼" (6cm) circle from 2-ply cardboard. Trim edge using a deckle edger. Cut a 2" × 3" (5cm × 7.5cm) strip from mint florist crepe. Cut six ¼" (6mm) pointed leaf slivers as shown. Cut a 11" (28cm) length of paper covered wire. Cut a 4" (10cm) length of 18-gauge cloth-wrapped wire. Cut two 2" (5cm) lengths of 26-gauge wire. Two nut cups: One, cut through middle of handle. Two, cut off handles and ruffle that extends beyond the lip of the cup.

ADD COLOR *Dilute* (p. 136) the white acrylic paint. Paint a loose ⅛" (3mm) border on mint side of all petals. Paint entire cardboard circle including edge. Using a striping brush, paint 3 stripes ¾ up the leaves. Let them dry.

BUILD Secure all layers with floral tape. **1.** Make a *Pip Center* (p. 130) with 20 folded pips, a 2" (5cm) 26-gauge wire, and attach to the 11" (28cm) wire. **2.** *Scrunch Pleat* (p. 128) all petals. Secure 3 Petals #88 mint side in evenly around center. Secure 3 Petals #89 and 1 #88 randomly around center. **3.** Repeat step 1 with 10 pips, 2" (5cm) wire, and 4" (10cm) wire. Repeat step 2 with 1 Petal #89 and 2 #88. **4.** *Scrunch Pleat* and *Gather and Wrap* (p. 132) pink tissue around each center, finish stems. **5.** *Join Stem* (p. 132) of short flower to long flower 5" (12.5cm) from flower base. *Style Stems* (p. 133) using a glue bottle. Cover joint with mint florist crepe slivers and attach randomly down stem while finishing. **6.** *Scrunch Pleat* Leaves #90 and secure evenly 1½" (4cm) from stem end. **7.** Hot glue fishing weight to center of cardboard circle and the end of second nut cup to perimeter. **8.** Create 2 side handles on first nut cup by hot gluing handle ends inside cup. Hot glue bases of both cups together and glue foam ball to center of open cup. **9.** Layer mint florist crepe fringe strip over lime strip and fold in half. Squeeze craft glue between the ball and the inside edge of cup. Nestle unfringed edge of strips into space around ball, let it dry. Push stem into foam, secure with hot glue. Ruffle fringe to cover ball and glue to foam if desired.

FEATHERED FASCINATOR / 26

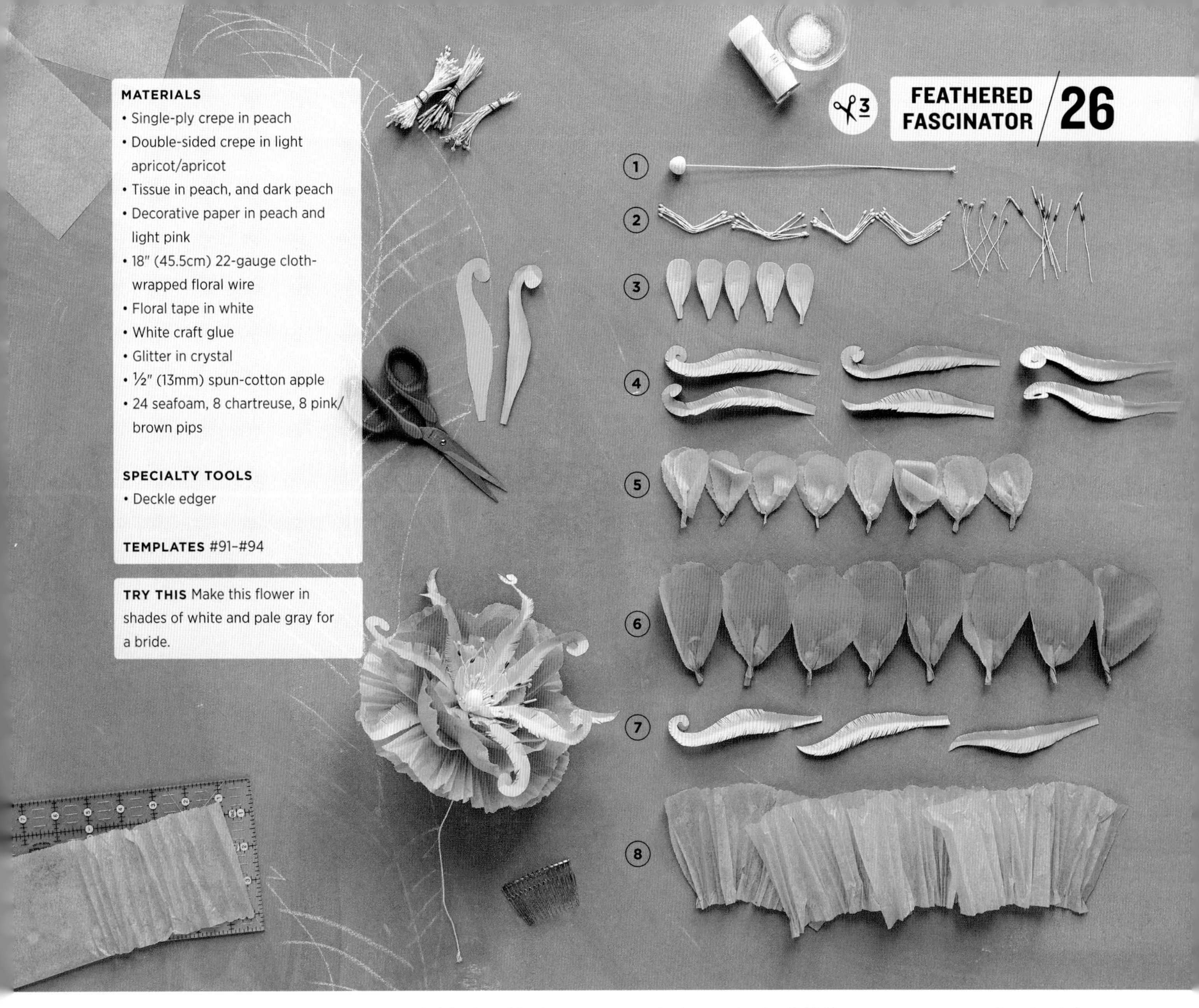

MATERIALS

- Single-ply crepe in peach
- Double-sided crepe in light apricot/apricot
- Tissue in peach, and dark peach
- Decorative paper in peach and light pink
- 18" (45.5cm) 22-gauge cloth-wrapped floral wire
- Floral tape in white
- White craft glue
- Glitter in crystal
- ½" (13mm) spun-cotton apple
- 24 seafoam, 8 chartreuse, 8 pink/brown pips

SPECIALTY TOOLS

- Deckle edger

TEMPLATES #91–#94

TRY THIS Make this flower in shades of white and pale gray for a bride.

CUT *Grain runs with height; all dimensions are given as H × W.* Petal #91: Cut 5 from light-apricot/apricot double-sided crepe. Petal #92: Using a deckle edger, cut 16 from peach tissue. Petal #93: Using a deckle edger, cut 8 from the peach single-ply crepe and 8 from the dark-peach tissue. Cut four 3½" × 10" (9cm × 25.5cm) strips from the peach tissue. Cut 1 long side each with deckle scissors. Feather #94: Cut 5 from the pale-pink decorative paper and 4 from the peach decorative paper. Gently crease the centerlines as shown. *Finely Hand Cut Fringe* (p. 127) along both edges to mimic a feather's shape. Trim off the curled tips from 3 feathers as delineated on template.

BUILD Secure all layers with floral tape. **1.** Glue a spun-cotton apple to the wire tip. Brush the apple with glue and sprinkle it with crystal glitter; let it dry. **2.** Gather 6 seafoam pips and fold them in half; repeat to make 4 sets total. Secure each set evenly around the center. Secure 8 chartreuse and 8 pink/brown pips evenly around the center. **3.** Gently *Cup* (p. 134), *Scrunch Pleat* (p. 128) 5 light-apricot/apricot double-sided crepe petals, and attach them evenly around the center. **4.** Attach the 4 pink feathers and 2 peach feathers randomly around center. **5.** Divide 16 Petals #92 into 8 pairs, offset petals slightly and *Twist* (p. 128) bases. Secure evenly around center. **6.** Gently *Cup* and *Flute* (p. 134) edges of peach single-ply crepe Petals #93 and pair underneath dark peach tissue petals, *Scrunch Pleat* and *Twist* bases. Secure evenly around center. **7.** Attach 2 peach and 1 pink feather randomly around center and secure. **8.** *Table Pleat* (p. 134) 4 peach tissue strips and *Gather and Wrap* (p. 132) 2 evenly around center, repeat with remaining 2 strips. Finish stem.

PROJECT NOTE To make a hair ornament, wrap wire around top section of a small comb multiple times to secure.

CUT *Grain runs with height; all dimensions are given as H × W.* Cut a 4½" (11.5cm) square from white single-ply crepe. Cut a 2¾" × 7" (7cm × 18cm) strip from wood-grain paper, fringe 1 long side ¾ of the way down. Petal #95: Cut a 4" × 17½" (10cm × 44.5cm) strip each from silver and light gray single-ply crepe, accordion-fold to fit template and cut continuous petals, trim petal tips with ripple edger. Cut the silver strip in half. Leaf #96 and #97: Cut 1 each from mint and lime green florist crepe.

ADD COLOR *Dilute* (p. 136) the gray acrylic paint. Use a striping brush to paint rows of dots on a square of white single-ply crepe paper as shown. Set aside to dry.

BUILD Secure all layers with floral tape. **1.** Make a *Spun-Cotton Center* (p. 130) with the 1" ball and dotted white single-ply crepe square. **2.** *Scissor Curl* (p. 135) the wood-grain fringe, with the wood grain facing out. Secure 1 end of the fringe strip, with the wood grain facing out and curling toward the center, to the center with glue and let dry. Wrap it tightly around the center and secure it with tape. **3.** *Scrunch Pleat* (p. 128) and *Gather and Wrap* (p. 132) 1 silver single-ply crepe Petal #95 halfway around center and secure. Repeat with second strip, overlapping ends slightly. Gently *Cup* (p. 134) each petal. **4.** Repeat step 3 with the full-length light-gray single-ply crepe piece. **5.** *Scrunch Pleat* and attach Leaves #96 and #97 randomly in alternating colors while finishing stem.

PROJECT NOTE We crafted additional flowers in different single-ply crepe color combinations with patterned paper fringe centers.

CUT *Grain runs with height; all dimensions are given as H × W.* Cut 10 7" (18cm) lengths of 28-gauge wire. Cut a 4½" (11.5cm) square from prestretched peach florist crepe. Petal #98: Cut a 2½" × 8" (6.5cm × 20.5cm) strip, accordion-fold to fit template, and cut a continuous petal. Petal #99: Cut 7 from cameo pink/apricot double-sided crepe. Trim top edge of the petals with a ripple edger. Petal #100: Cut 9 from peach florist crepe. Trim top edge of the petals with ripple edger. Cut six 6½" (16.5cm) length of 22-gauge wire.

BUILD Secure all layers with 1" (2.5cm) floral tape. **1.** Create a small coil at the end of a 28-gauge wire and bend the coil perpendicular to the wire. Hot glue a gold medallion to the end. Repeat with remaining wires and medallions making 10 total. **2.** Make a *Spun-Cotton Center* (p. 130) with the peach florist crepe square and 1½" ball. Attach 10 medallion wires evenly to center. **3.** Gently *Scissor Curl* (p. 135) the tips of Petals #98, *Gather and Wrap* (p. 132) evenly around the center and secure. **4.** *Stick Curl* (p. 135) the top 1" (2.5cm) of all petals. *Gather and Wrap* 3 Petals #99, spacing evenly around center, secure. Leave ¼" (6mm) space on stem before beginning next layer. *Gather and Wrap* 4 Petals #99, spacing evenly around center, secure. **5.** *Stick Curl* the top 1" (2.5cm) of all petals. Begin layer ½" (13mm) from previous layer. *Gather and Wrap* 4 Petals #100, spacing evenly around center, secure. Leave ¾" (2cm) space on stem before beginning next layer. *Gather and Wrap* 5 Petals #100, spacing evenly around center, secure. Finish stem with gold tape. **6.** With 7 birch leaves *Wire One-Sided Leaves* (p. 133) to 22-gauge wires, 6 to cut wires, and 1 to a full-length wire, let dry. Finish stems with brown tape. *Join Stems* (p. 132) of the 6 short leaves to the main full-length stem as shown.

PROJECT NOTE In addition an oversized Dresden maple leaf was wired on one side and the stem was finished with brown tape. Edges were gently curled with fingers.

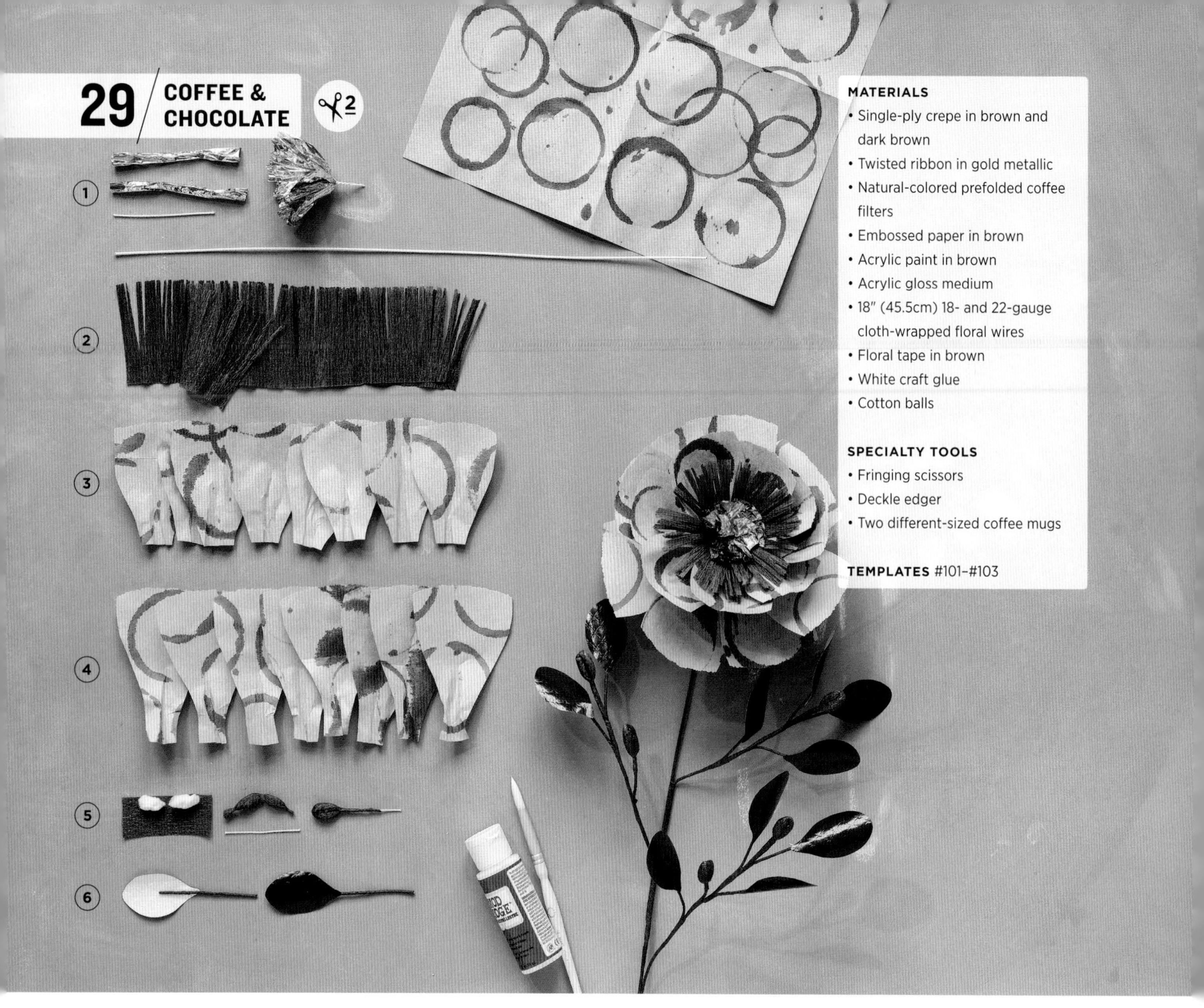

MATERIALS

- Single-ply crepe in brown and dark brown
- Twisted ribbon in gold metallic
- Natural-colored prefolded coffee filters
- Embossed paper in brown
- Acrylic paint in brown
- Acrylic gloss medium
- 18" (45.5cm) 18- and 22-gauge cloth-wrapped floral wires
- Floral tape in brown
- White craft glue
- Cotton balls

SPECIALTY TOOLS

- Fringing scissors
- Deckle edger
- Two different-sized coffee mugs

TEMPLATES #101–#103

ADD COLOR *Dilute* (p. 136) the brown acrylic paint. Pour a small amount of it into a shallow dish. Using 2 mugs that have defined rings on the bottom, dip mugs into paint and make a coffee ring pattern on 3 unfolded natural coffee filters. Set aside to dry.

CUT *Grain runs with height; all dimensions are given as H × W.* Cut two 4" (10cm) lengths of metallic twisted ribbon. Cut two 2½" × 10" (6.5cm × 25.5cm) strips from brown and dark brown single-ply crepe. Trim 1 long edge with deckle edger and fringe, using fringing scissors with the grain, ¾ of the way down. Petals #101 and #102: Cut 8 each from coffee filters, trim petal tops with deckle edger. Cut five 2½" × 1" (6.5cm × 2.5cm) strips from brown single-ply crepe. Cut five 2" (5cm) length of 22-gauge wires. Cut eleven 3" (7.5cm) lengths of 22-gauge wires. Leaf #103: Cut 10 from brown embossed paper.

BUILD Secure all layers with floral tape. **1.** Untwist both lengths of metallic twisted ribbon and fold each in half lengthwise. Use the *Pip Center* (p. 130) method to make a center with both lengths of ribbon and a 3" (7.5cm) wire . Ruffle edges and secure to a full-length 18-gauge wire. **2.** Layer both fringe strips on top of each other, *Gather and Wrap* (p. 132) around center. **3.** *Box Pleat* (p. 128) all Petals #101, and secure evenly around center. **4.** Repeat step 3 with Petals #102. Finish the stem. **5.** Tear off 2 small pieces of cotton ball, form into small ovals, and position over crepe rectangle as shown. Roll cotton inside paper, making a tube. Twist the center 2 times and fold down, twist each end. Nestle a length of 2" (5cm) wire in the base and secure. Brush beans with gloss medium to add sheen, let dry. Make 5 beans total. **6.** *Wire One-Sided Leaves* (p. 133) with ten 3" (7.5cm) lengths of taped wire and Leaves #103 as shown, making 10 leaves total. *Join Stems* (p. 132) of buds and leaves onto 22-gauge wires, before *Joining Stems* to main stem as desired.

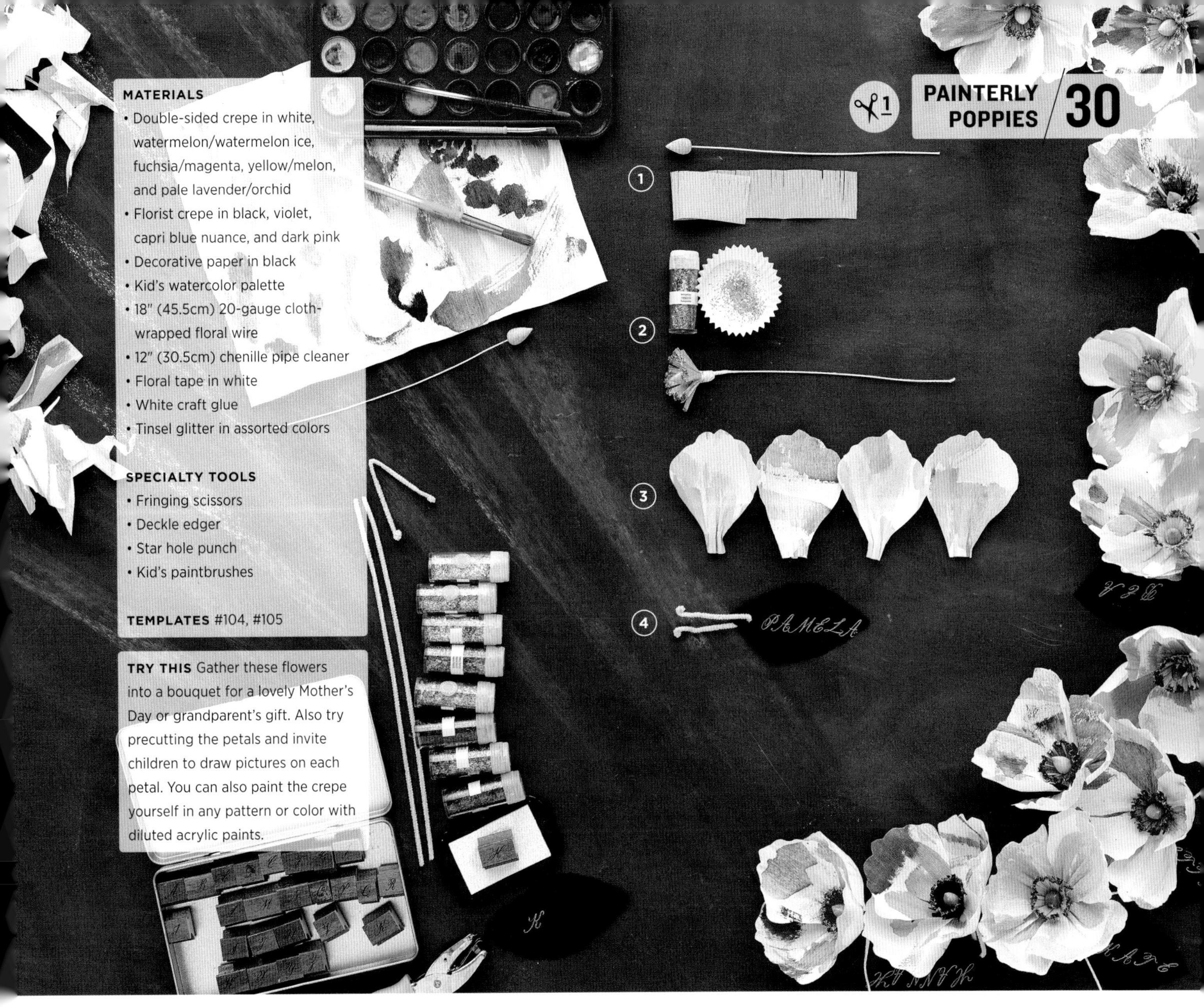

PAINTERLY POPPIES 30

MATERIALS

- Double-sided crepe in white, watermelon/watermelon ice, fuchsia/magenta, yellow/melon, and pale lavender/orchid
- Florist crepe in black, violet, capri blue nuance, and dark pink
- Decorative paper in black
- Kid's watercolor palette
- 18" (45.5cm) 20-gauge cloth-wrapped floral wire
- 12" (30.5cm) chenille pipe cleaner
- Floral tape in white
- White craft glue
- Tinsel glitter in assorted colors

SPECIALTY TOOLS

- Fringing scissors
- Deckle edger
- Star hole punch
- Kid's paintbrushes

TEMPLATES #104, #105

TRY THIS Gather these flowers into a bouquet for a lovely Mother's Day or grandparent's gift. Also try precutting the petals and invite children to draw pictures on each petal. You can also paint the crepe yourself in any pattern or color with diluted acrylic paints.

ADD COLOR Cut a piece of white double-sided crepe 3 folds wide and paint freeform shapes, lines, and dots with kid's watercolor palette. Glue a spun-cotton bud to the tip of a 9" (23cm) length of stem wire and paint with watercolors. Set aside to dry.

CUT *Grain runs with height; all dimensions are given as H × W.* Cut a 1½" × 9" (4cm × 23cm) strip from the yellow/melon double-sided crepe. Using the fringing scissors, fringe, with the grain, ¾ of the way down. Petal #104: Cut 4 from the painted white double-sided crepe. Leaf #105: Cut 1 from the black paper with deckle edger. Punch a hole in the tip. Cut a 4" (10cm) length of chenille pipe cleaner.

BUILD Secure all layers with floral tape. **1.** *Gather and Wrap* (p. 132) the yellow/melon strip around the painted spun-cotton center, and secure. **2.** Using a brush or the applicator tip of a glue bottle, apply the glue to the tips of the fringed strip. Sprinkle the strip with glitter and let it dry. **3.** Gently *Cup* (p. 134), *Flute* (p. 134) the edges, and *Scrunch Pleat* (p. 128) the Petals #104, attaching 2 on opposite sides of the center. Repeat and attach the remaining petals to alternate sides. Finish the stem. **4.** Turn the ends of the chenille pipe cleaner under to hide the wire ends. Thread through the punched hole in Leaf #105, fold it in half, and twist. Twist onto the desired point on the stem.

31 / CONFETTI CAKE

MATERIALS

- Double-sided crepe in white, light apricot/apricot, French vanilla/lemon yellow, pink/bubblegum, peach/light rose, and light yellow/yellow
- Florist crepe in buttercup, pink peony, peach sunset, and peach sorbet
- Decorative paper in dusty plum, mauve, and aqua-gray
- 18" (45.5cm) 24-gauge cloth-wrapped floral wire
- Floral tape in white
- White craft glue
- 4" (10cm) wood skewers
- Toothpicks

SPECIALTY TOOLS

- Fringing scissors
- Deckle edger

TEMPLATES #106–#110

TRY THIS These flowers would make a lovely wedding bouquet in pastel shades crafted on wire stems or try making the petals in white with black confetti.

CUT *Grain runs with height; all dimensions are given as H × W.* Cut all fringe, with the grain, using fringing scissors. Cut a 4" × 2" (10cm × 5cm) piece each from buttercup, pink peony, peach sunset, peach sorbet florist crepe, and pink/bubblegum, peach/light rose, light yellow/yellow double-sided crepe. Fringe ¾ of the way down. Cut across fringe to make confetti. Combine colors as desired. Cut a 2½" × 12" (6.5cm × 30.5cm) piece from white double-sided crepe. Fringe ¾ of the way down. Cut a 1½" × 10" (4cm × 25.5cm) piece from white double-sided crepe. Fringe ¾ of the way down. Petal #106: Cut 5 from peach/light rose crepe. Petal #107: Cut 6 from French vanilla/yellow double-sided crepe. Leaf #108 cut 1 and #109 cut 3 from aqua-gray paper using a deckle edger. Leaf #110: Cut 1 each from the dusty plum and mauve paper. Cut a 3" (7.5cm) length of 24-gauge stem wire.

BUILD Secure all layers with floral tape. **1.** Dot the end of a skewer with glue and *Gather and Wrap* (p. 132) the 2½"H (6.5cm) fringed white double-sided crepe strip and secure to make a center. **2.** Fan out fringe slightly. Using a glue bottle tip apply glue to tips of fringe. Sprinkle with confetti and let dry. **3.** *Stick Curl* (p. 135) the tip of Petal #106 using a skewer. Gently *Cup* (p. 134) and *Scrunch Pleat* (p. 128) each petal. Attach evenly around center and secure with tape as shown. **4.** Repeat step 1 with the 1½"H (4cm) fringed white double-sided strip. **5.** Repeat step 2. **6.** *Stick Curl* the side of Petal #107 on a diagonal using a skewer. Gently *Cup* and *Scrunch Pleat* each petal. Attach evenly around center and secure. **7.** *Single Pleat* (p. 128) Leaves #108 and #109. Attach Leaf #108 to tip of a stem wire and secure. Continue adding leaves to the wire, overlapping them while finishing stem. Trim wire, and secure leaf-covered stem to a skewer with tape. **8.** Crease 1 dusty plum and 1 mauve Leaf #110 in the center. *Single Pleat* and attach pair to a toothpick with tape.

PROJECT NOTE Different foliage configurations were crafted for variety including single leaves attached to toothpicks and smaller groupings of aqua-gray leaves. In addition, we made a flower with Petal #106 in pink/bubblegum double-sided crepe, and a flower with Petal #107 in light apricot/apricot double-sided crepe.

ADD COLOR *Dilute* (p. 136) the berry pink, yellow, and white acrylic paints and fill 3 spray bottles with them. Cut 2 pieces from ivory single-ply crepe, 2 folds wide, and 1 piece from mint/olive double-sided crepe, 3 folds wide. Spray 1 ivory piece with pink paint and the other with yellow paint. Spray the mint/olive piece of crepe with white paint. Let dry.

CUT *Grain runs with height; all dimensions are given as H × W.* Cut all fringe with the grain. Cut twelve 4" × 2" (10cm × 5cm) pieces from rose single-ply crepe. Petal #111: Cut 36 from pink gradated crepe. Cut twelve 3" (7.5cm) lengths of 22-gauge wire. Leaf #112: Using the deckle edger, cut 8 from each speckled crepe paper. Cut twenty 4½" × 4" (11.5cm × 10cm) pieces from mint/olive double-sided crepe. Trim 1 edge with pinking shears against the grain and cut ½" (13mm) wide *Hand Cut Fringe* (p. 127) ¾ of the way down. Cut twenty 4½" × 4" (11.5cm × 10cm) strips from metallic green single-ply crepe, trim 1 edge with pinking shears against the grain. Randomly fringe, using fringing scissors, halfway down, leaving some space between cuts. Cut twenty 4" (10cm) squares from pale green florist crepe, and randomly fringe. Cut twenty 4" × 30" (10cm × 76cm) strips from 3 tissue papers, fold them into eighths widthwise, and randomly fringe.

BUILD Secure all layers with floral tape. **1.** Roll the rose crepe piece lengthwise; twist the paper around on itself to make a loose coil bringing the ends together and secure it to a 22-gauge wire to make a center. **2.** *Scrunch Pleat* (p. 128) then *Cup* (p. 134) 3 Petals #111, attaching them evenly around the center. Repeat steps 1 and 2 for 12 flowers. **3.** *Scrunch Pleat* all Leaves #112. **4.** Fold all 3 crepe papers in half with the grain and *Scissor Curl* (p. 135) the fringed ends; unfold. Leave tissue folded and *Scrunch Pleat* all pieces. **5.** Use 6" (15cm) lengths of tape and start 4" (10cm) from one end of an 18-gauge wire. Begin layering pieces of tissue and crepe, fanning them out side to side and maintaining a "front" side. Every few pieces, add a speckled Leaf #112. Every 5" (12.5cm) add a cluster of flowers. Leave 2" (5cm) from the end of the first wire, overlap a second wire, and glue together, securing with tape. Continue building until you reach 2" (5cm) from the bottom of the second wire. Bend the wires into a circular shape, overlap them, and glue and secure with tape. Once dry, finish covering them. Attach a ribbon or wires to create a hanging loop.

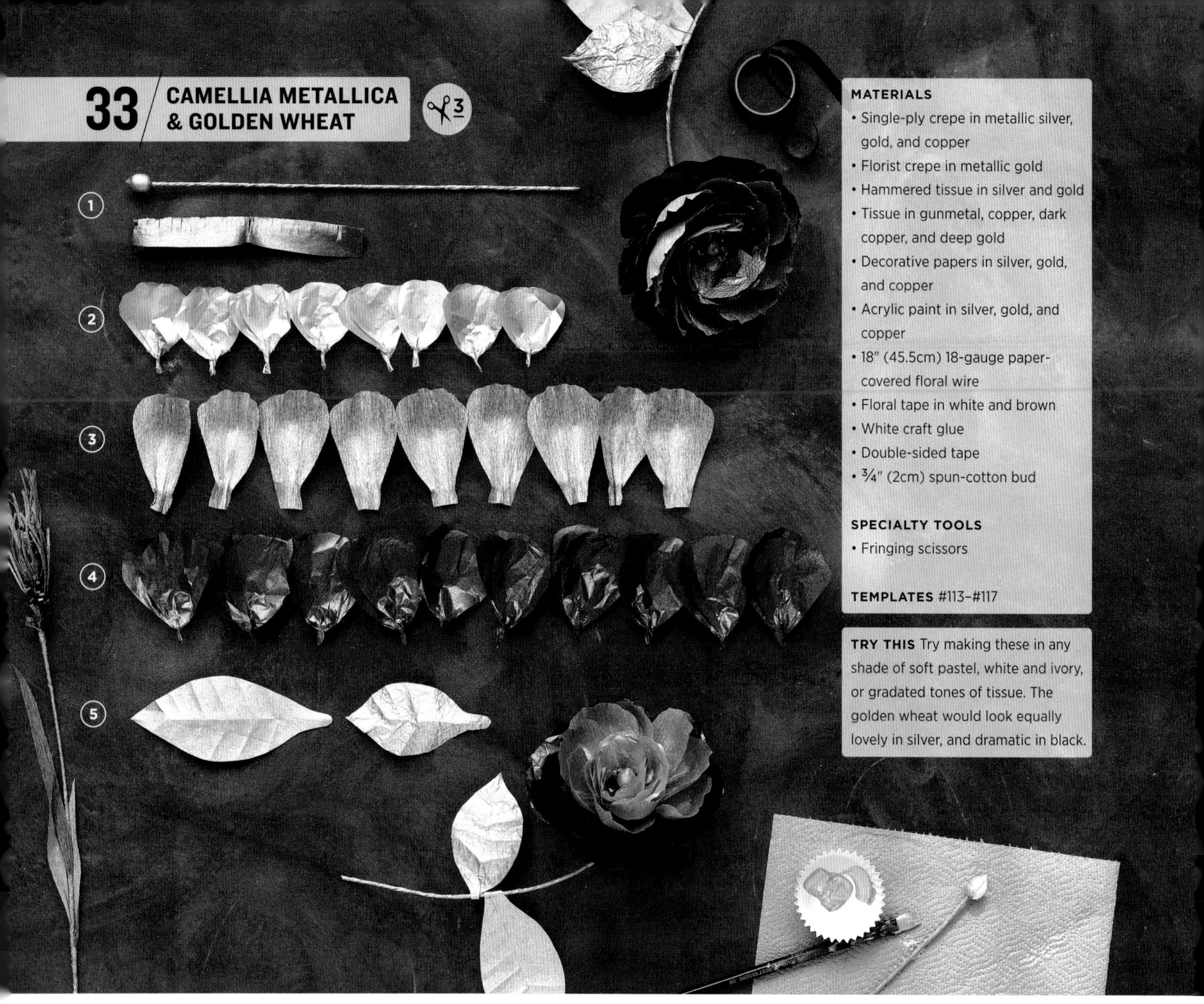

33 / CAMELLIA METALLICA & GOLDEN WHEAT

3

MATERIALS

- Single-ply crepe in metallic silver, gold, and copper
- Florist crepe in metallic gold
- Hammered tissue in silver and gold
- Tissue in gunmetal, copper, dark copper, and deep gold
- Decorative papers in silver, gold, and copper
- Acrylic paint in silver, gold, and copper
- 18" (45.5cm) 18-gauge paper-covered floral wire
- Floral tape in white and brown
- White craft glue
- Double-sided tape
- ¾" (2cm) spun-cotton bud

SPECIALTY TOOLS

- Fringing scissors

TEMPLATES #113–#117

TRY THIS Try making these in any shade of soft pastel, white and ivory, or gradated tones of tissue. The golden wheat would look equally lovely in silver, and dramatic in black.

ADD COLOR Cut a 16" (40.5cm) length of paper-covered wire; secure a spun-cotton bud to the wire tip with glue, let dry. Paint the bud and stem with the silver metallic paint, then set them aside to dry.

CUT *Grain runs with height; all dimensions are given as H × W.* Cut all fringe with the grain using fringing scissors unless specified. Cut a 2" × 7" (5cm × 18cm) strip from the gunmetal metallic tissue, fold it in half lengthwise, fringe it ½ of the way down on the folded side. Petal #113: Cut 16 from the silver metallic tissue. Petal #114: Cut 9 from the metallic silver single-ply crepe, 20 from the gunmetal metallic tissue. Leaf #115: Cut 1 from the metallic silver decorative paper. Leaf #116: Cut 1 from the silver crinkled paper. Cut a 1¾" × 11" (4.5cm × 28cm) strip from the hammered gold tissue, fold it in half lengthwise, fringe ½ way down on folded side. Cut a 3" (7.5cm) square from the gold single-ply crepe and finely *Hand Cut Fringe* (p. 127) it ¾ of the way down; cut the strip into 4 equal pieces, with the grain. Leaf #117: Cut 3–4 short and long from gold single-ply crepe. Cut 1 or more ½" × 12" (13mm × 30.5cm) strips from gold florist crepe.

BUILD Secure all layers with floral tape. **Flower:** Stop taping 2" (5cm) from the flower base in all flower steps to maintain the painted stem. **1.** Leave the fringe folded and *Gather and Wrap* (p. 132) the gunmetal fringe, with the folded edge out, around the painted center. **2.** Crinkle each silver Petal #113 in your hand, then open it. Pair the petals as shown, offsetting slightly, *Twist* (p. 128), and secure evenly around the center. **3.** *Scrunch Pleat* (p. 128), *Flute* (p. 134) Petals #114, and secure evenly around center. **4.** Repeat step 2 with gunmetal tissue Petals #114. **5.** Fold Leaf #115 in half lengthwise, creasing with your fingernail. Create the veining as shown by gently pinching the paper between your index finger and thumb. Repeat step 5 with Leaf #116. To attach the leaves, wrap the base of the leaf around the painted stem and secure with glue. Once complete, cover the visible floral tape at the flower base with silver metallic paint. **Wheat: 6.** Using double-sided tape, secure one end of the folded hammered gold fringe, with folded edge out, to the tip of a full-length wire. Begin wrapping the fringe diagonally down the stem. **7.** Wrap the first ½" (13mm) of the stem and secure 1 of 4 fringed gold single-ply crepe pieces to the

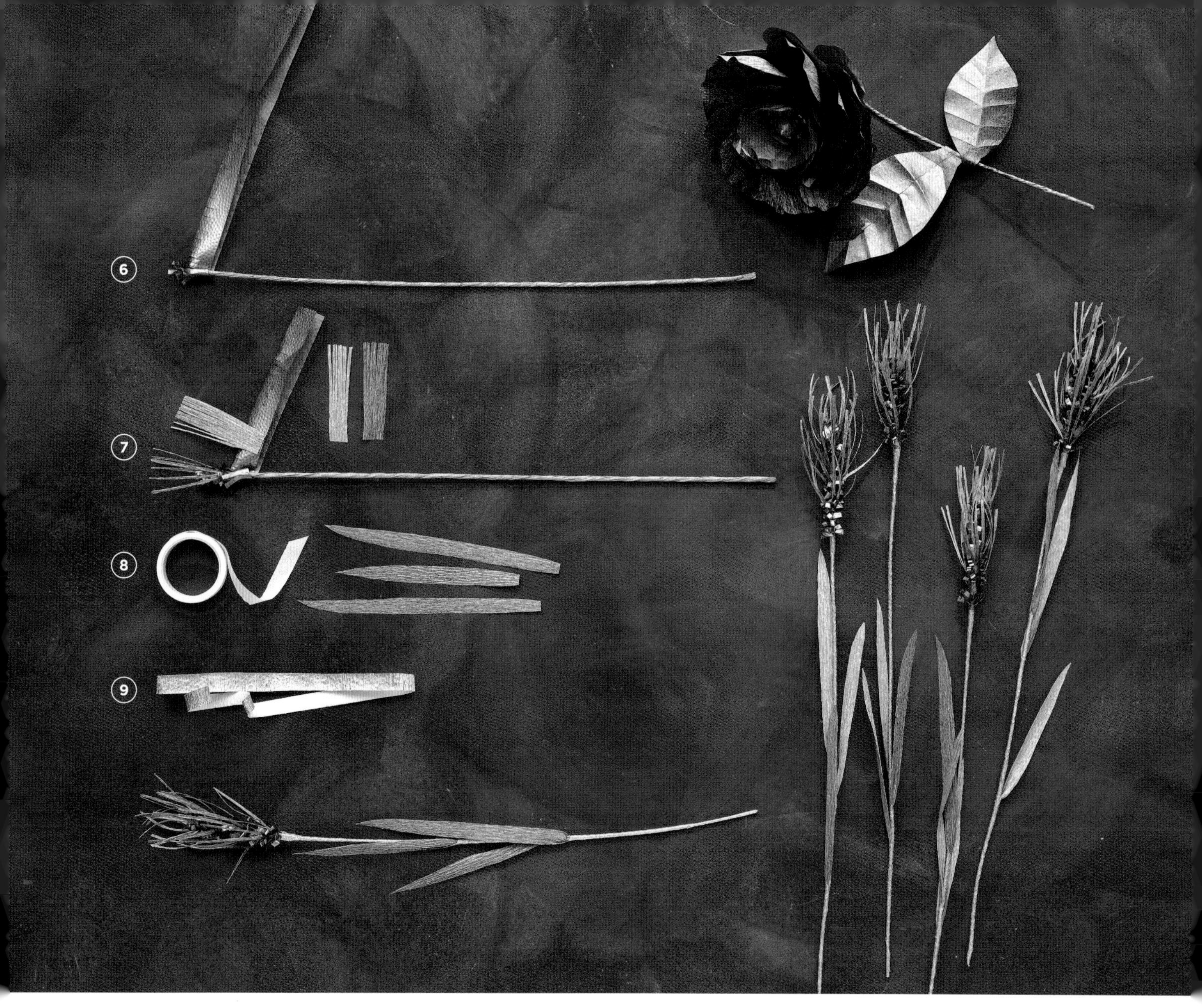

folded fringe with double-sided tape as shown. Continue wrapping and attach the 3 remaining pieces in the same way, spaced apart, adding more double-sided tape to secure the folded fringe as you work. Wrap the end in white tape and continue down the stem. The finished top section of wheat should be 3"–4" (7.5cm–10cm). **8.** *Scrunch Pleat* Leaves #117, and secure to the stem with white tape. **9.** *Cover Stem* (p. 133) with strips of stretched metallic florist crepe. Style the wheat by running your hand gently along the fringe from bottom to top, curling long fringe inward slightly around the short fringe.

PROJECT NOTE We made two additional metallic flowers using the same types of materials but in copper and gold tones.

34 VINTAGE SPRIGS

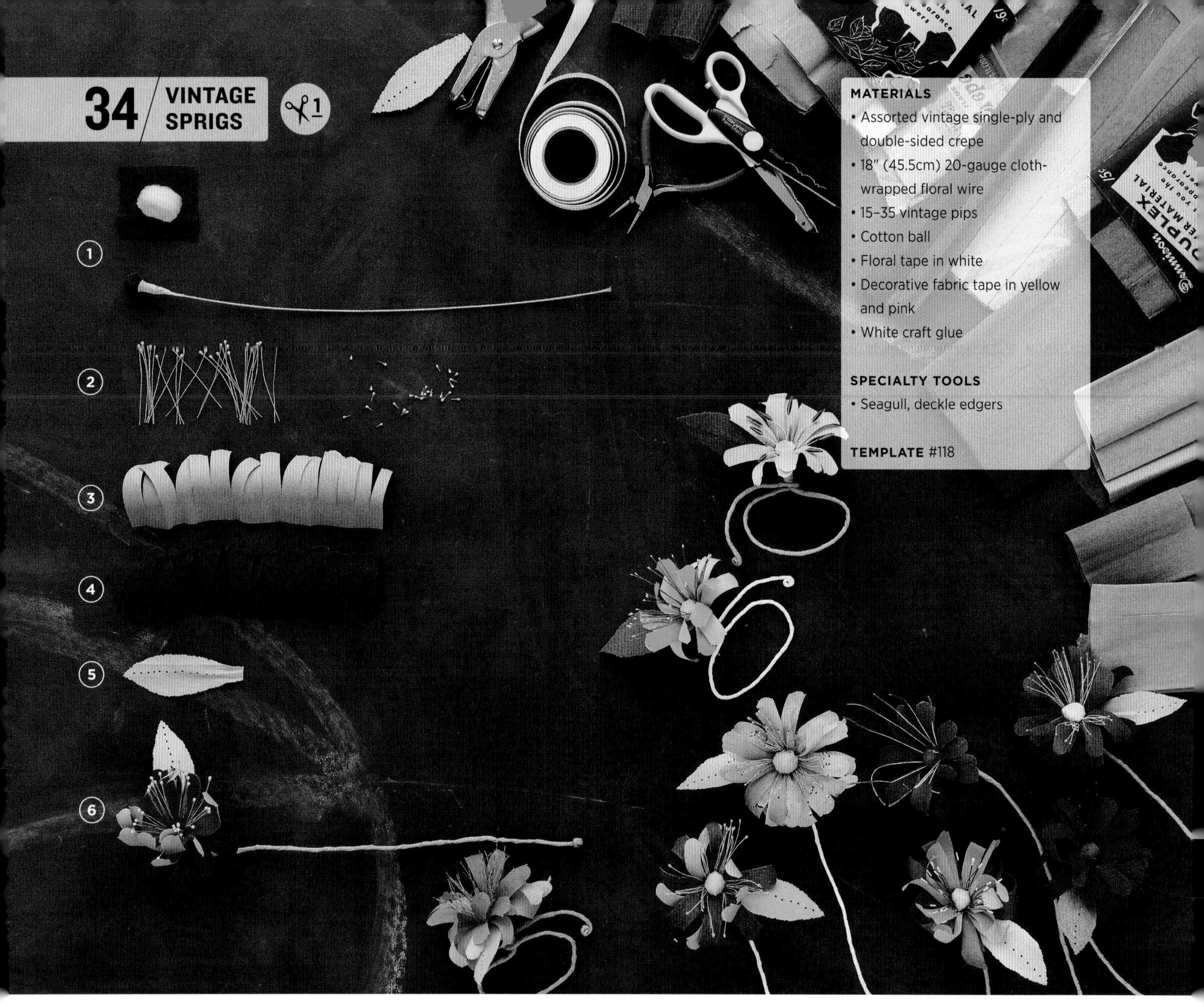

MATERIALS

- Assorted vintage single-ply and double-sided crepe
- 18" (45.5cm) 20-gauge cloth-wrapped floral wire
- 15–35 vintage pips
- Cotton ball
- Floral tape in white
- Decorative fabric tape in yellow and pink
- White craft glue

SPECIALTY TOOLS

- Seagull, deckle edgers

TEMPLATE #118

CUT *Grain runs with height; all dimensions are given as H × W.* Cut a 2" (5cm) square from plum single-ply crepe. Cut a 2½" × 7½" (6.5cm × 19cm) strip from pale pink/pink and plum crepe. Trim 1 long side of each with seagull edger, align pattern as you cut. Cut ¾ of the way down between scallops to form a strip of continuous petals. Tear or cut cotton ball into 4 pieces. Cut a 16" (40.5cm) length of stem wire. Leaf #118: Cut 1 leaf from bisque/blush double-sided crepe using deckle edger. Using a 1⁄16" (1.5mm) hole punch, make a row of holes down center of leaf as shown. If pips are double sided, trim ends.

BUILD Secure all layers with floral tape. **1.** Make a *Cotton Ball Center* (p. 130) with plum single-ply crepe square and 1 piece of cotton ball. **2.** Secure 30 lavender pips evenly around center. **3.** Gently *Scissor Curl* (p. 135) pale pink/pink and plum continuous petals. With curl facing in, *Scrunch Pleat* (p. 128) and *Gather and Wrap* (p. 132) pale pink/pink double-sided crepe petals evenly around center. **4.** Repeat step 3 with plum petals curl facing out. **5.** Attach Leaf #118 to base of flower and secure. **6.** Finish stem with floral tape, then with fabric tape and secure end with glue, curl end on itself to finish.

PROJECT NOTE *Scissor Curl* gently when working with vintage crepe because it can tear more easily. We used assorted colors of vintage crepe and pips to make different color combinations. We varied the scissor curl styling to create these 3 different effects: Double-sided crepe petals were scissor curled in opposite directions every other petal, both layers were scissor curled down, the first layer was scissor curled up and the second layer was scissor curled down. To make the napkin ring, bend the wire to make a squat flat oval large enough to hold a napkin roll if desired. Make a hook on the stem end and loop wire around base of flower to make a ring. These stems can also be tucked into a napkin fold.

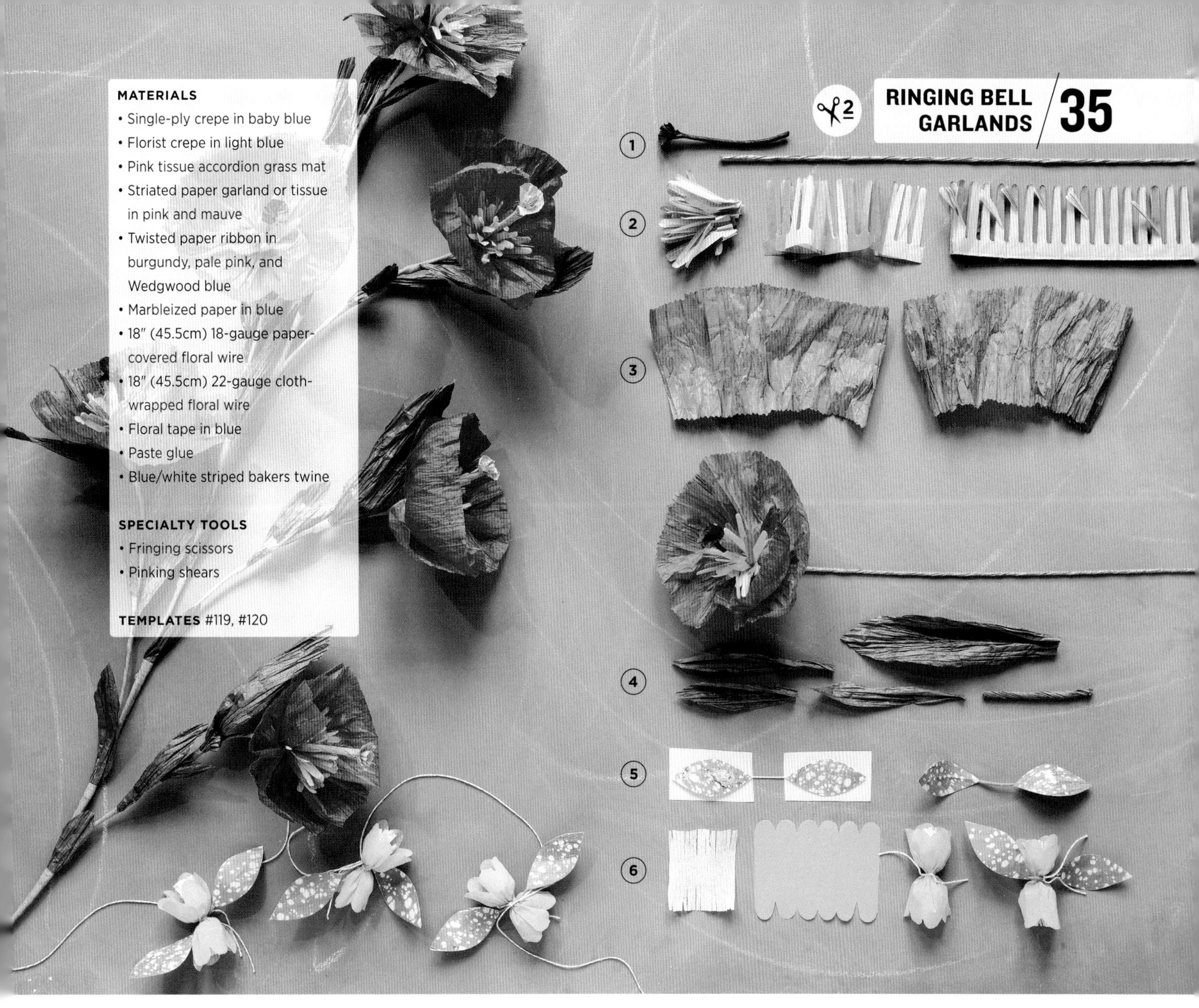

RINGING BELL GARLANDS / 35

✂2

MATERIALS

- Single-ply crepe in baby blue
- Florist crepe in light blue
- Pink tissue accordion grass mat
- Striated paper garland or tissue in pink and mauve
- Twisted paper ribbon in burgundy, pale pink, and Wedgwood blue
- Marbleized paper in blue
- 18" (45.5cm) 18-gauge paper-covered floral wire
- 18" (45.5cm) 22-gauge cloth-wrapped floral wire
- Floral tape in blue
- Paste glue
- Blue/white striped bakers twine

SPECIALTY TOOLS

- Fringing scissors
- Pinking shears

TEMPLATES #119, #120

CUT *Grain runs with height; all dimensions are given as H × W.* Cut a 4" (10cm) length of burgundy twisted paper ribbon. Cut a 20" (51cm) length of unfolded paper grass. Cut two 4" (10cm) lengths of mauve striated garland using pinking shears. Cut six 4"–7" (10cm–18cm) lengths of blue twisted paper ribbon, and untwist. Fold longer lengths in half lengthwise. Round top corners opposite fold using scissors. Cut shorter lengths in half lengthwise. Round top corners. Leaf #119: Cut 2 from marbled paper. Cut two 1¾" × 3" (4.5cm × 7.5cm) pieces from marbled paper. Cut a 5" (13cm) length of 22-gauge wire. Cut a 2½" (6.5cm) square from light blue florist crepe, and fringe it using fringing scissors, with the grain, ¾" (2cm) on opposite sides. Petal #120: Cut a 3½" × 4½" (9cm × 11.5cm) piece from baby blue single-ply crepe, fold it in half, and cut. Cut an 8" (20.5cm) length of bakers twine.

BUILD Secure all layers with floral tape. **1.** Untwist top ¾" (2cm) of burgundy ribbon and fan out. Overlap bottom 1" (2.5cm) with a paper-covered wire and secure. **2.** *Gather and Wrap* (p. 132) paper grass around center. **3.** Pull open both mauve striated garlands, *Gather and Wrap* each halfway around center, overlapping 1"–2" (2.5cm–5cm) on both sides. **4.** Attach leaves randomly while finishing stem. **5.** *Wire Two-Sided Leaves* (p. 133). Spread paste glue on both marbled pieces and place pieces 1" (2.5cm) apart as shown. Center wire between pieces, place Leaves #119 over top, smooth and let dry. Cut excess to match leaf and tape wire. Give each leaf a small bend. **6.** *Scrunch Pleat* (p. 128) center of blue florist crepe strip, *Gather and Wrap* the center of Petal #120 around the florist crepe fringe, tie with bakers twine. *Finesse* (p. 135) base of blue single-ply crepe into a bell shape around fringe on both sides. Place wired leaves over center and tie to flower.

PROJECT NOTE The second coral bells bloom is made with pink striated tissue garland and pink twisted paper ribbon. Finish the large garland by *Joining Stems* (p. 132). Attach the bottom 1½" (4cm) of a stem 4" (10cm) from the end of another stem to connect flowers. Secure with extra tape, cover the joint with a leaf. Continue adding stems and craft in 48" (122cm) lengths and hook sections together into longer swags. Style by gently bending the flowers and leaves. To finish the small garland, tie 1 flower on every 10"–12" (25.5cm–30.5cm) along a length of bakers twine.

36 / FIVE-PETAL SWEETIES

MATERIALS

- Crepe paper of any type and color
- Acrylic paints in assorted colors
- Assorted glitter
- 18" (45.5cm) 20-gauge cloth-wrapped floral wire
- Floral, fabric, and washi tape
- Assorted spun-cotton balls
- Pips of any type and color

TEMPLATE #16

TRY THIS Double or triple the size of the template to make a larger size, or add additional layers to make the flowers more full.

CUT *Grain runs with height; all dimensions are given as H × W.* Cut a 2½" (6.5cm) square from white single-ply crepe. Petal #16: Cut a 2½" × 8" (6.5cm × 20.5cm) strip from red double-sided crepe, accordion-fold to fit template and cut continuous petal.

BUILD Secure all layers with floral tape. **1.** Make a *Spun-Cotton Center* (p. 130) with the white single-ply square. **2.** Fold pips in half and make 5 sets with 3 pips each. Pinch each bundle together and attach tightly and evenly around center. **3.** *Gather and Wrap* (p. 132) Petal #16 around the center and *Cup* (p. 134) petals. **4.** Create a single *Flute* (p. 134) in the center top of each petal.

PROJECT NOTE We love this simple flower for the endless creative possibilities it inspires. It makes the perfect filler flower to add to larger paper flower arrangements. We used a mix of the following treatments to show you how versatile this flower can be. Glitter-smeared petals and centers; rubber-stamped centers and petals; mixed colored pip groupings as well as paper fringe stamen; metallic crepe covered centers; pleated paper covered centers; petals colored with water-soluble crayons; dot and stripe painted petals and centers; hole punched petals; folded crepe crossover covered centers; glitter-glue-lined petals. We used assorted floral, washi, and fabric tapes to finish the stems.

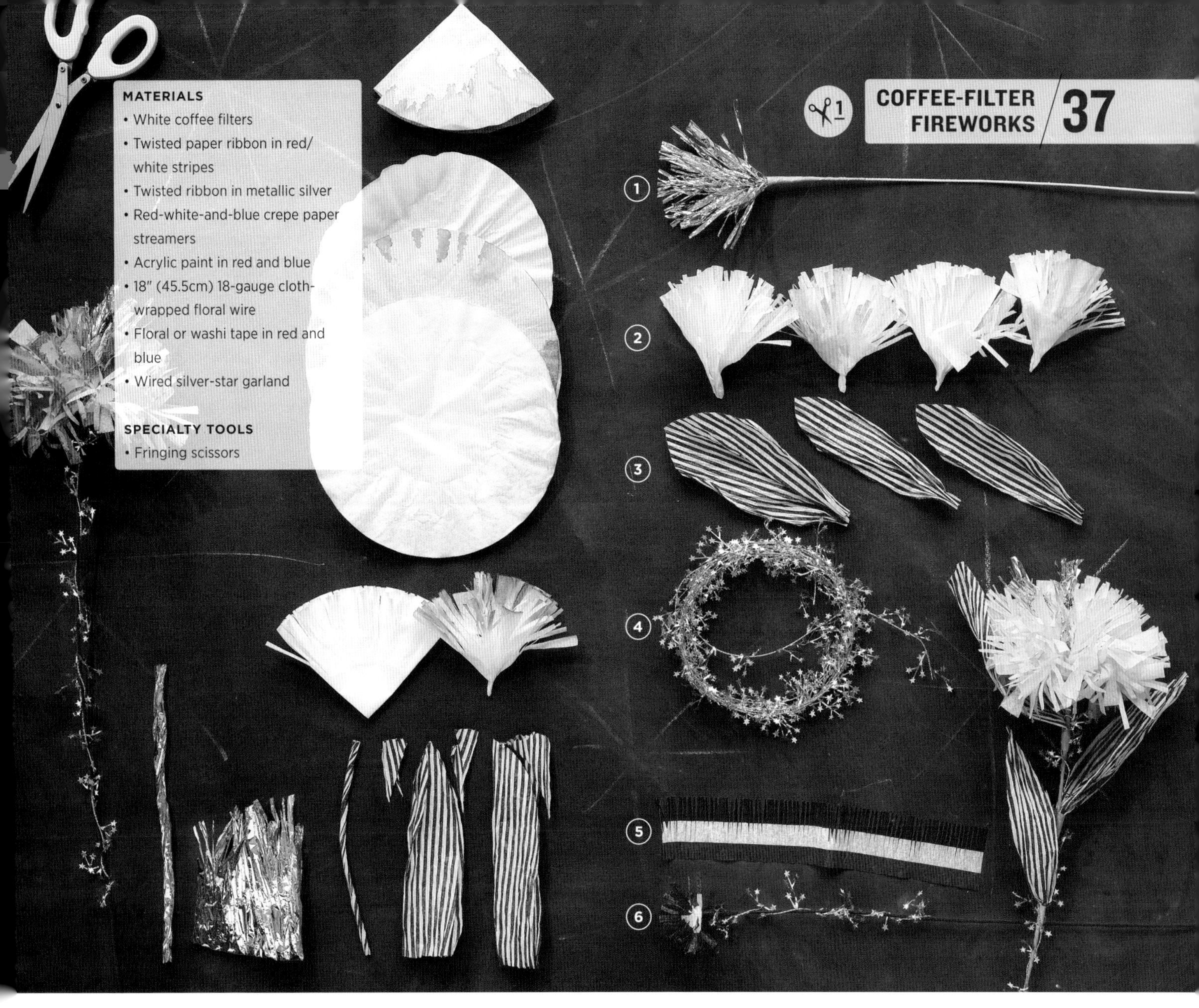

ADD COLOR *Dilute* (p. 136) the blue acrylic paint. Flatten 2 white coffee filters and fold in quarters. *Dip-Dye* (p. 137) the outside edge of the folded filters. Unfold and set aside to dry.

CUT Fold the painted coffee filter into quarters again and, using the fringing scissors, fringe the outside edge halfway down. Repeat with the remaining painted filter. Repeat the fringing step with 2 unpainted filters. Cut a 9" (23cm) length of metallic twisted ribbon and untwist. Fold in half against the "grain" and fringe opposite the fold, ¾ of the way down. Cut two 6" (15cm) lengths of red/white striped twisted paper ribbon, and untwist. Cut 1 in half lengthwise to make 2 strips, place them on top of each other, and round off the corners of both ends, toward the centerline, with scissors to make 2 pointed leaves. Fold the second piece in half lengthwise and round off the top corner opposite the fold to make a larger pointed leaf. Cut a 10" (25.5cm) length of patriotic streamer and fringe it ¾ of the way down on red side.

BUILD Secure all layers with floral tape. **1.** *Gather and Wrap* (p. 132) the folded end of the fringed metallic ribbon to wire tip, and secure. **2.** Unfold coffee filters. Make a C shape with your nondominant hand by touching your index fingertip to thumb. Place the center of a filter over the C. With the index finger of the opposite hand gently push the center of the filter into your open fist. Scrunch the base of filter together and *Twist* (p. 128). Repeat with the remaining 3 filters. Attach filters evenly around center, alternating colors as you build. **3.** *Scrunch Pleat* (p. 128) leaves. Finish stem, adding in leaves. Add larger leaf 3" (7.5cm) from flower base, followed by smaller leaves at 3" (7.5cm) intervals. **4.** Wrap star garland tightly around base of flower and wind down length of stem, wrap tightly at the end of the stem to secure and trim. **5.** *Gather and Wrap* streamer, attach to second wire with red tape, finish stem. **6.** Repeat step 4.

PROJECT NOTE We made blue and red versions of these flowers. Make a red version of the large flower using red paint and follow the build steps using red tape. Omit the leaves. Make a blue version of the small flower by fringing the blue side of the red-white-and-blue streamer, finish with blue tape.

38 / WILD STRAWBERRIES

✂2

MATERIALS

- Single-ply crepe in white, hot yellow, French violet, hot pink, ice blue, sapphire blue, seafoam, and goldenrod
- Double-sided crepe in white
- Florist crepe in capri blue nuance, moss, and pale pink
- 18" (45.5cm) 22-gauge cloth-wrapped floral wire
- Floral tape in white
- Washi tape in gray/white circle
- White craft glue
- Assorted felt tipped markers
- 1"–1½" (2.5cm–4cm) spun-cotton buds, pears, and strawberries
- Cotton ball

SPECIALTY TOOLS

- Lightning edger

TEMPLATES #121–#125

CUT *Grain runs with height; all dimensions are given as H × W.* Cut a 3" (7.5cm) square from white single-ply crepe. Cut a 4" (10cm) square from hot yellow single-ply crepe, round off corners with scissors as shown. Cut a 3" × 1½" (7.5cm × 4cm) piece from white single-ply crepe and *Hand Cut Fringe* (p. 127) with the grain ¾ of the way down. Roll up fringe and cut tiny slivers to make confetti as shown. Petal #121: Cut a 2" × 4½" (5cm × 11.5cm) strip from pale pink florist crepe, accordion-fold to fit template and cut continuous petal. Petal #122: Cut 5 from white double-sided crepe. Petal #123: Using lightning edger, cut 3 from moss florist crepe. Leaf #124: Using lightning edger, cut 3 from capri blue nuance florist crepe. Calyx #125: Cut 1 from capri blue nuance florist crepe. Cut three 7" (18cm) lengths of 22-gauge wire.

ADD COLOR Using a turquoise marker draw random dot "seeds" on hot yellow crepe. Set aside to dry.

BUILD Secure all layers with floral tape. **1.** Make a *Cotton Ball Center* (p. 130) with white single-ply crepe. **2.** Brush center with glue and cover with white crepe confetti and let dry. **3.** With pale pink continuous petal, gently twist one petal at a time from the base up toward the top leaving the oval untwisted; repeat with all petals as shown. *Gather and Wrap* (p. 132) around center. **4.** Crease all Petals #122 down center with a fingernail and *Single Pleat* (p. 128). Attach evenly around center and secure, finish stem. Finish taped stem with washi tape. **5.** Crease all Leaves #123 and #124 down center with a fingernail. Layer Leaf #123 over Leaf #124 to make 3 pairs and *Scrunch Pleat* (p. 128) bases. Attach 1 pair to a wire tip and secure, finish stem. While finishing stem with washi tape attach 2 remaining pairs ¼" (6mm) from base of first leaf. **6.** Make a *Spun-Cotton Center* (p. 130) with strawberry shape and yellow single-ply piece. Finish stem with floral tape followed by washi tape. **7.** Secure Calyx #125 around base of strawberry with glue.

PROJECT NOTE We gave each strawberry cluster 2 wired strawberries, 1 wired set of leaves, and 1 flower. Cover each stem in washi tape, then *Join Stems* (p. 132) together at desired points with white floral tape. Cover joints with washi tape. *Style Stems* (p. 133).

SWEETS BLOOM 39

MATERIALS

- Single-ply crepe in aqua, blush, and whisper pink
- Tissue in peach and burgundy
- 18" (45.5cm) 18-gauge paper-covered floral wire
- 18" (45.5cm) 22-gauge cloth-wrapped floral wire
- Floral tape in pink
- Aqua dyed vintage wood bead
- Rose felt-tipped marker

SPECIALTY TOOLS

- Scallop edger
- Pinking shears

TEMPLATES #126–#128

CUT *Grain runs with height; all dimensions are given as H × W.* Cut a 4" (10cm) length of 22-gauge wire. Cut a 13" (33cm) length of 18-gauge stem wire. Petal #126: Cut a 2" × 10½" (5cm × 26.5cm) strip from aqua single-ply crepe, accordion-fold to fit template, and cut a continuous petal. Petal #127: Cut a 4" × 16½" (10cm × 42cm) strip each from the whisper-pink single-ply crepe and peach tissue, accordion-fold each to fit template, and cut continuous petals. Cut two 3½" × 14" (9cm × 35.5cm) strips from blush single-ply crepe. Trim 1 long side of each petal with scallop edger. Leaf #128: Cut a 2" × 22" (5cm × 56cm) strip, accordion-fold to fit template, and cut a continuous leaf with pinking shears.

ADD COLOR Draw loops and lines on whisper pink single-ply crepe continuous petals using a rose felt-tipped marker.

BUILD Secure all layers with floral tape. **1.** Thread 1 short 22-gauge wire through a bead, bend in half at the center, and twist ends onto 18-gauge stem wire a few times to secure, wrap with tape to finish center. **2.** *Scrunch Pleat* (p. 128) Petal #126 and *Gather and Wrap* (p. 132) evenly around center and secure. Gently *Cup* (p. 134) petals. **3.** Repeat step 2 with whisper pink Petal #127. **4.** *Scrunch Pleat* Petal #127 and *Gather and Wrap* evenly around center and secure. **5.** *Scrunch Pleat* both blush single-ply crepe strips. *Gather and Wrap* 1 strip halfway around center and secure. Repeat with second strip overlapping first strip 1" (2.5cm) on both ends. Finish stem. **6.** Secure 1 end of Leaf #128 to base of flower with glue. Wrap strip around stem pulling leaf points free as you wrap, covering the floral tape. Secure with glue at end of stem.

PROJECT NOTE Clear bags were filled with enough hard candies to weight the bags to support the flower and keep them upright. Insert a flower into a bag and cinch around stem, tying the bag closed with cotton ribbon. We hand-dyed the cotton ribbon in diluted aqua acrylic paint.

40 / PINSTRIPE & PIN DOT

2

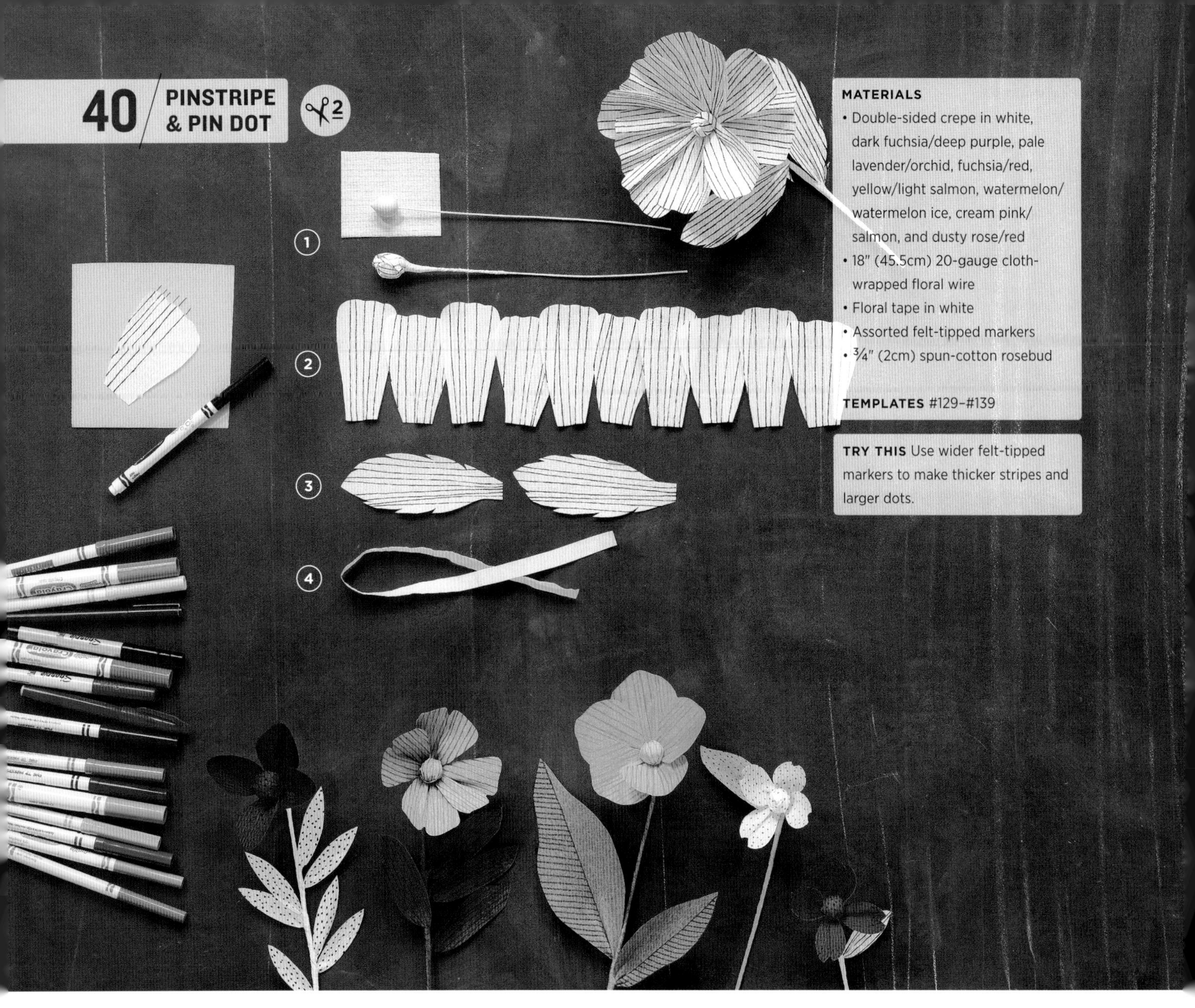

MATERIALS

- Double-sided crepe in white, dark fuchsia/deep purple, pale lavender/orchid, fuchsia/red, yellow/light salmon, watermelon/watermelon ice, cream pink/salmon, and dusty rose/red
- 18" (45.5cm) 20-gauge cloth-wrapped floral wire
- Floral tape in white
- Assorted felt-tipped markers
- ¾" (2cm) spun-cotton rosebud

TEMPLATES #129–#139

TRY THIS Use wider felt-tipped markers to make thicker stripes and larger dots.

CUT *Grain runs with height; all dimensions are given as H × W.* Cut all pieces from white double-sided crepe. Cut a 3" × 2½" (7.5cm × 6.5cm) rectangle. Petals #129 and #130: Cut 5 each. Leaf #131: Cut 2. Cut a ½" × 16" (13mm × 40.5cm) strip. Cut a 9" (23cm) length of wire.

ADD COLOR Work over scrap paper to catch the marker bleeds. Draw randomly spaced lines, with the grain, with a felt-tipped marker on the rectangle, petals, and leaves as shown. Set aside to dry.

BUILD Secure all layers with floral tape. **1.** Make a *Bud* (p. 131) with the marker-striped rectangle. **2.** *Single Pleat* (p. 128) Petals #129 and #130, alternating sizes as you secure evenly around center. **3.** *Scrunch Pleat* (p. 128) leaves. Finish stem with tape, adding first leaf 2½" (6.5cm) from flower base, and second leaf, 2½" (6.5cm) below first leaf. **4.** *Cover Stem* (p. 133) with crepe strips.

PROJECT NOTE Using different colored markers and crepe, as well as a different leaf and petal templates, we created an array of pinstripe and pin-dotted flowers all made from double-sided crepe.

From left to right: Petal #132 in dark fuchsia/deep purple, Leaf #133 and stem in white; Petal #134 in pale lavender/orchid, Leaf #135 and stem in fuchsia/red; Petal #136 in yellow/light salmon, Leaves #137 and #138 and stem in watermelon/watermelon ice; Petal #139 in white, Leaf #135 and stem in cream pink/salmon; Petal #139 in dusty rose/red, Leaf #133 and stem in white.

MATERIALS
- Single-ply crepe in peach batik, yellow, orange, blue batik
- Florist crepe in brown, peach, red, hot pink, yellow, baby pink, and mustard
- Tissue in tangerine, rust, mustard, coral, blue, and burgundy
- Acrylic paint in white
- 18" (45.5cm) 20-gauge cloth-wrapped floral wire
- White craft glue
- Floral tape in pink, blue, yellow, and red
- 40"-long (101.5cm) ¼" (6mm) wood dowels

SPECIALTY TOOLS
- Fringing scissors
- Pinking shears

TEMPLATE #140

TRY THIS Make these sticks with white fringe and pink or green flowers or the reverse for a wedding or birthday party. For a Halloween party craft them with black fringe and orange flowers.

ADD COLOR Paint the dowel with white acrylic paint. Set it aside to dry.

CUT *Grain runs with height; all dimensions are given as H × W.* Cut all fringe with the grain ¾ of the way down. Cut a 1¼" × 3½" (3cm × 9cm) strip from the peach florist crepe; hand-cut a wavy edge on 1 long side. Petal #140: Cut a 2½" × 10½" (6.5cm × 26.5cm) strip from the brown florist crepe; accordion-fold to fit template and cut a continuous petal. Cut four 2½" × 6" (6.5cm × 15cm) strips from peach batik crepe. Fold in half widthwise; trim 1 edge against the grain with pinking shears and randomly *Hand Cut Fringe* (p. 127) along pinked edge. Cut two 5½" × 12" (14cm × 30.5cm) strips from the peach batik crepe. Fold it in quarters widthwise; trim 1 edge against the grain with pinking shears and *Hand Cut Fringe* in ½" (13mm) widths along the pinked edge. Cut two 5½" × 15" (14cm × 38cm) strips from tangerine tissue. Fold in quarters widthwise; trim 1 unfolded edge with pinking shears. Fringe the first piece with fringing scissors along the pinked edge. *Hand Cut Fringe* in ½" (13mm) widths on the pinked edge with the second piece. Cut a 2½" × 12" (6.5cm × 30.5cm) strip from tangerine tissue. Fold in quarters widthwise; trim 1 unfolded edge with pinking shears and randomly *Hand Cut Fringe*. Cut a 9" (23cm) length of wire.

BUILD Secure all layers with floral tape, unless specified. **1.** *Scrunch Pleat* (p. 128) the peach florist crepe strip and attach to wire with tape. **2.** *Gather and Wrap* (p. 132) and *Cup* (p. 134) continuous petal around center, finish stem with pink tape. **3.** Adhere 1 side of fringed peach batik crepe calyx to the flower base with glue. Tightly wrap down and around base 2"–3" (5cm–7.5cm), secure end with glue. Overlap wire and dowel 2" (5cm) and secure with tape. **4.** Starting on the wire 1" (2.5cm) above dowel, *Gather and Wrap* first piece of short tissue. *Gather and Wrap* the next 6 layers, securing each layer with tape, in the order shown. Overlap each layer to cover tape, moving down dowel as you attach. For the final layer, adhere 1 side of fringe to dowel with glue, tightly wrap down and around base 2"–3" (5cm–7.5cm), secure end with glue.

PROJECT NOTE Change the order of the fringe layers to add diversity to your party sticks. We made sticks in multiple playful color combinations.

42 WHITE & BLACK WITH NEON POPS

MATERIALS
- Single-ply crepe in white
- Double-sided crepe in white and watermelon/watermelon ice
- Acrylic paint in neon coral and white
- 18" (45.5cm) 22-gauge cloth-wrapped floral wire
- Floral tape in black
- Black permanent marker

SPECIALTY TOOLS
- Fringing scissors
- Thin brush

TEMPLATES #141–#143

TRY THIS These flowers and pom-poms can be made in any color palette. Try making pom-poms in a range of tonal colors for a party centerpiece or a child's birthday party. Make the lotus bloom with colored crepe and a darker tonal *Dip-Dyed* edge.

CUT *Grain runs with height; all dimensions are given as H × W.* Cut a 1½" × 10" (4cm × 25.5cm) strip from white single-ply crepe, fringe with the grain ¾ of the way down. Petal #141: Cut a 4" × 9" (10cm × 23cm) strip each of white double-sided and single-ply crepe. Fold each in half with the grain to fit template. Cut continuous petal from white double-sided strip down to top cut line on template. Cut continuous petal from white single-ply strip down to the end of the cut line. Cut a 5" (12.5cm) strip 7 folds wide, against the grain, from white single-ply crepe. Leave folded. Using fringing scissors fringe both sides with the grain leaving ½" (13mm) uncut in center to make pom-pom as shown. Leaves #142 and #143: Cut desired number of assorted leaves from white and watermelon/watermelon ice double-sided crepe. Cut 3 11" (28cm) 22-gauge wires.

ADD COLOR *Dilute* (p. 136) the neon coral and white acrylic paints. *Dip-Dye* (p. 137) the tips ½" (13mm) of both Petals #141. Leaves #142 and #143: Paint white veining on Watermelon/watermelon ice crepe leaves, draw black veining with marker on white crepe leaves.

BUILD Secure all layers with floral tape. **1.** Make a *Fringe Center* (p. 130) with white single-ply fringe strip. **2.** *Scrunch Pleat* (p. 128) the double-sided crepe Petal #141 and *Gather and Wrap* (p. 132) it around the center. *Finesse* (p. 135) to create a slight bell shape at base of petal. **3.** *Scissor Curl* (p. 135) the single-ply crepe Petal #141. *Scrunch Pleat* and *Gather and Wrap* the petal around the center with the petals curling down as shown. Finish stem. **4.** To make the pom-pom, start with the folded white single-ply crepe double-edged-fringe piece. Scrunch the center tightly and wrap 2" (5cm) of wire over the center; bend it around and twist tightly to secure as shown. Begin to fan out the fringe one side at a time to create a full pom-pom. Finish stem. **5.** Secure leaves to wire tips, and finish stem.

PROJECT NOTE Make assorted sizes of pom-poms by altering the heights of the double-edged-fringe crepe pom-pom strip: 4" (10cm) and 6 folds wide, 3" (7.5cm) and 5 folds wide, and 2" (5cm) and 4 folds wide. After finishing the stems, *Style Stems* (p. 133) over a rounded shape. *Join Stems* (p. 132). Repeat step 5 for watermelon leaves. Make clusters of 2–3 leaves on each stem.

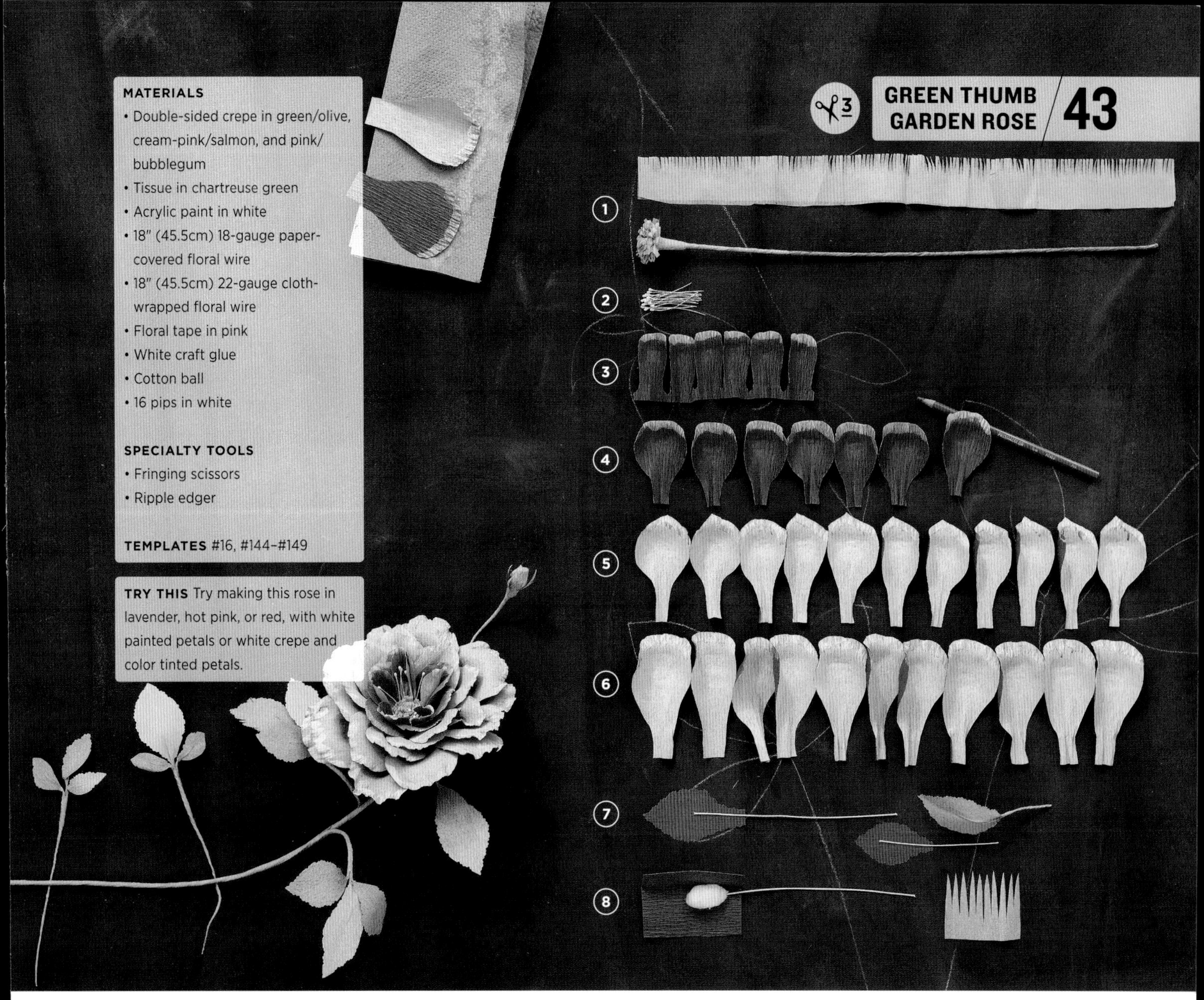

GREEN THUMB GARDEN ROSE / 43

MATERIALS

- Double-sided crepe in green/olive, cream-pink/salmon, and pink/bubblegum
- Tissue in chartreuse green
- Acrylic paint in white
- 18" (45.5cm) 18-gauge paper-covered floral wire
- 18" (45.5cm) 22-gauge cloth-wrapped floral wire
- Floral tape in pink
- White craft glue
- Cotton ball
- 16 pips in white

SPECIALTY TOOLS

- Fringing scissors
- Ripple edger

TEMPLATES #16, #144–#149

TRY THIS Try making this rose in lavender, hot pink, or red, with white painted petals or white crepe and color tinted petals.

CUT *Grain runs with height; all dimensions are given as H × W.* Cut a 3½" × 20" (9cm × 51cm) strip from green tissue. Fold in half widthwise. Using the fringing scissors, fringe the folded side halfway down as shown. Petal #16: Cut a 2½" × 9" (6.5cm × 23cm) strip from the green/olive crepe, accordion-fold to fit template, and cut a continuous petal. Petal #144: Cut 7 from green/olive double-sided crepe. Petal #145: Cut 11 from green/olive double-sided crepe. Petal #146: Cut 11 from green/olive double-sided crepe. Leaves #147 and #148: Using the ripple edger, cut 2 #147 and 1 #148 from the cream-pink/salmon double-sided crepe. Caylx #149: Cut a 2½" × 3" (6.5cm × 7.5cm) strip from the cream-pink/salmon double-sided crepe, fold it in half with the grain, and cut a continuous petal for the calyx. Cut a 3½" × 2½" (9cm × 6.5cm) piece from green/olive crepe to make the bud. Cut an 8" (20.5cm) length and two 4" (10cm) lengths of 22-gauge wire.

ADD COLOR *Dilute* (p. 136) the white acrylic paint to a pale wash. Paint both sides of the tips of all Petals #16, #144, #145, #146. Set aside to dry. Brush again in a few spots to add more color.

BUILD Secure all layers with floral tape. **1.** Make a rolled *Fringe Center* (p. 130) with the green-fringed tissue strip. **2.** Trim off 1 end of 16 white pips and secure them evenly around the center. **3.** *Gather and Wrap* (p. 132) Petal #16 around center, *Cup* (p. 134) and *Flute* (p. 134) top edge. **4.** With Petals #144 olive side up, using a pencil *Stick Curl* (p. 135) out, then *Cup* each petal as shown. *Scrunch Pleat* (p. 128) petals and secure evenly around center. **5.** Repeat step 4 with Petals #145 light green side up. **6.** Repeat step 4 with Petals #146 light green side up. Finish stem. **7.** *Wire One-Sided Leaves* (p. 133) with Leaves #147 and #148 to 22-gauge wires, 1 Leaf #148 to an 8" (20.5cm) wire and 2 Leaves #147 to 4" (10cm) wires. Finish stems. *Join Stems* (p. 132) of short wire leaves to longer wire leaf just below the base. Finish stem. **8.** Make a *Bud* (p. 131) with the green/olive double-sided crepe piece. *Gather and Wrap* Calyx #149 around bud and secure. Finish stem. *Join Stems* of all branches as desired.

44 SPOOKY RAVENS & KITTY CATS

✂2

MATERIALS

- Single-ply crepe in black
- Florist crepe in black and lime green
- Acrylic paint in white
- 18" (45.5cm) 20-gauge cloth-wrapped wire
- Floral tape in black
- Black-and-gold-striped bakers twine

SPECIALTY TOOLS

- Fringing scissors
- Striping brush
- Large sewing needle

TEMPLATES #150–#152

ADD COLOR *Dilute* (p. 136) the white acrylic paint. Cut a 16" (40.5cm) piece of black florist crepe and paint random stripes, with the grain, using a striping brush. Set aside to dry.

CUT *Grain runs with height; all dimensions are given as H × W.* Cut two 3½" (9cm) lengths of wire, and two 1" (2.5cm) lengths of wire per raven. Cut a 2¼" × 6½" (5.5cm × 16.5cm) strip from the painted crepe, and fringe it, with the grain, ¾ of the way down. Petals #150 and #151: Cut 3 each from the painted crepe to the short line on the template. Cut a 1½" × 2¼" (4cm × 5.5cm) piece from the lime-green florist crepe, and fringe it, with the grain, ¼ of the way down. Petal #152: Cut a 2½" × 13½" (6.5cm × 34.5cm) piece from the black single-ply crepe, accordion-fold it to fit the template, and cut a continuous petal.

BUILD Secure all layers with floral tape. **1.** Fully wrap 1" (2.5cm) wires with tape. **2.** Start covering 3½" (9cm) wire with tape, and *Join Stems* (p. 132) attach 1" (2.5cm) wire 1" (2.5cm) from the end of the longer wire as shown. Tape in ¼" (6mm) of the short wire to join it to the longer wire, and finish stem. Repeat with remaining 2 wires. **3.** *Gather and Wrap* (p. 132) fringed strip around tops of both footed wires as shown. **4.** *Cup* (p. 134) petal #150 with stripes facing out. *Scrunch Pleat* (p. 128) each petal and secure evenly around the base with stripes facing out. **5.** Repeat step 4 with Petal #151, attaching at points in between Petals #150. **6.** Using a pencil, *Stick Curl* (p. 135) a few petal tips away from center. **7.** Fold green fringe into thirds widthwise, *Scrunch Pleat* base, flatten fringed side into a "cat eye" shape and secure base with tape. **8.** *Scrunch Pleat* black crepe evenly around green fringe, overlapping edges slightly, and secure tightly with tape. Fan out continuous petal. **9.** Snip off extra tape, leaving ¼" (6mm) of tape as a base. **10.** To make garland, use a thick needle strung with bakers twine, and pass the needle carefully through the green fringe centers.

PROJECT NOTE We made a few ravens from solid black crepe and mixed them in with the striped variety. To secure them to a branch, straddle legs over the branch, and wrap each leg in the opposite direction, up and around the branch. Gently open up and bend the small wires to look like claws.

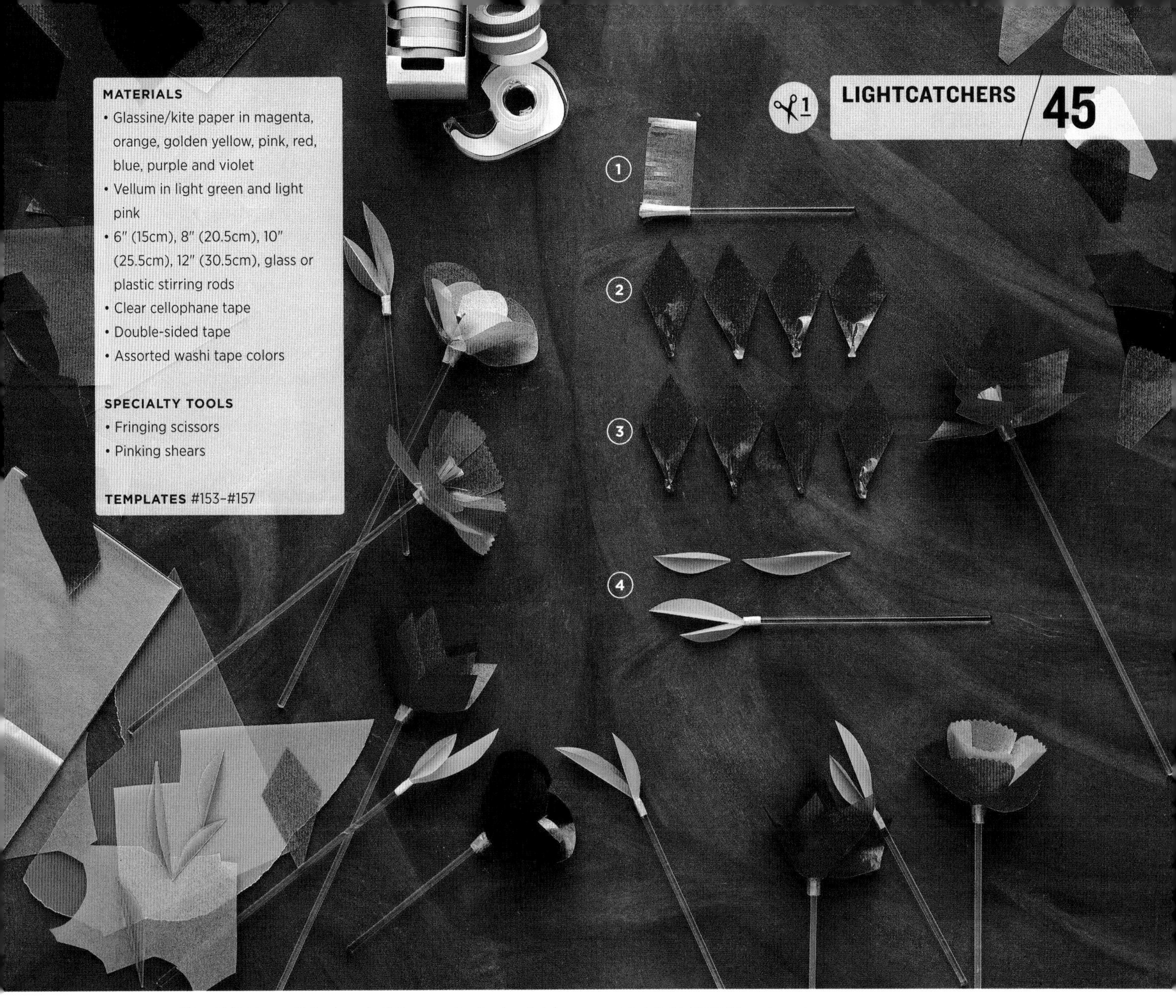

CUT Cut a 1½" × 6½" (4cm × 16.5cm) strip from the golden-yellow glassine. Using fringing scissors fringe ¾ of the way down. Petal #153: Cut 4 each from magenta and orange glassine. Leaves #154 and #155: Cut 1 each from the light green vellum.

BUILD Secure all layers with clear cellophane tape unless noted.
1. Roll a small piece of double-sided tape around the top of the stirring rod. Place three 1"–2" (2.5cm–5cm) strips of double-sided tape along the unfringed base of the fringed strip. Evenly roll the fringe strip around the top of the stir rod as shown and secure to make a center. **2.** *Box Pleat* (p. 128) magenta glassine Petals #153. Attach each petal one at a time to the base of the fringe center with a small piece of cellophane tape. Repeat, attaching all 4 petals evenly around the center. **3.** *Box Pleat* orange glassine Petals #153. Attach each petal at opposite points from first set. Secure each with small piece of cellophane tape. Wrap base with a strip of washi tape, then finish with cellophane tape as shown. **4.** Crease Leaves #154 and #155 down the center. Attach ends to a stirring rod with cellophane tape, cover with a strip of washi tape, and a final strip of cellophane tape.

PROJECT NOTE Four sizes of glass stirring rods were used for our stems. We crafted additional flowers with the same size fringe strip for the center, mixing up the colors. Rounded petals: the first layer uses Petal #156, second layer uses Petal #157. Pinked petals: both layers use Petal #157, with the top edge trimmed with pinking shears. Leaves were also made in light pink vellum.

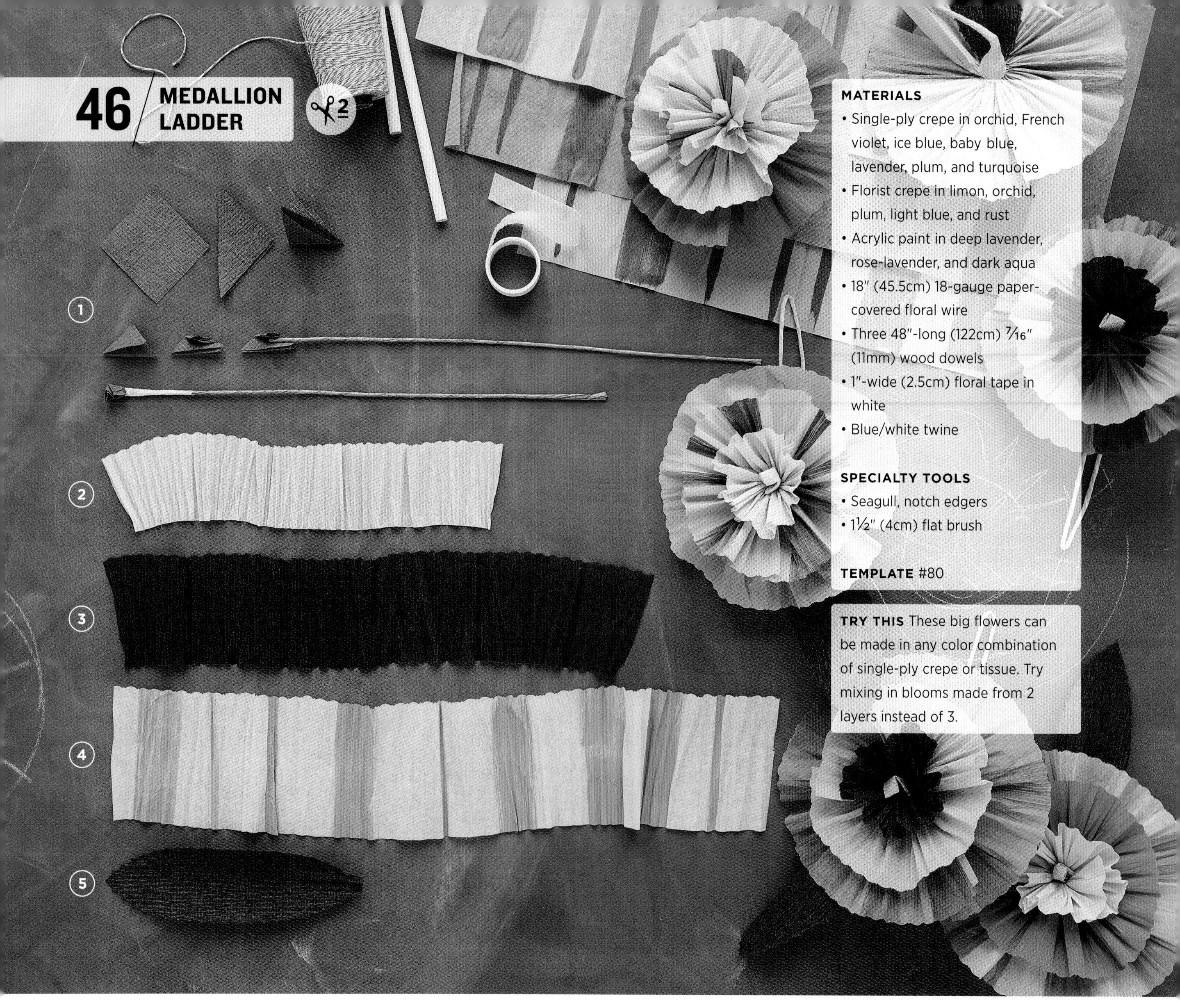

46 MEDALLION LADDER

MATERIALS

- Single-ply crepe in orchid, French violet, ice blue, baby blue, lavender, plum, and turquoise
- Florist crepe in limon, orchid, plum, light blue, and rust
- Acrylic paint in deep lavender, rose-lavender, and dark aqua
- 18" (45.5cm) 18-gauge paper-covered floral wire
- Three 48"-long (122cm) 7/16" (11mm) wood dowels
- 1"-wide (2.5cm) floral tape in white
- Blue/white twine

SPECIALTY TOOLS

- Seagull, notch edgers
- 1½" (4cm) flat brush

TEMPLATE #80

TRY THIS These big flowers can be made in any color combination of single-ply crepe or tissue. Try mixing in blooms made from 2 layers instead of 3.

ADD COLOR *Dilute* (p. 136) the deep lavender, rose-lavender, dark aqua paints. Cut 1 piece each 8 folds wide from orchid, French violet, ice blue single-ply crepe. Paint wide and thin stripes in tonal colors as shown. Set aside to dry.

CUT *Grain runs with height; all dimensions are given as H × W.* Cut a 3" × 20" (7.5cm × 51cm) strip from baby blue single-ply crepe. Trim 1 long edge using seagull edger. Cut a 4" × 25" (10cm × 63.5cm) strip from plum single-ply crepe. Trim 1 long edge using seagull edger. Cut a 5" × 30" (12.5cm × 76cm) strip from painted ice blue single-ply crepe. Trim 1 long edge using seagull edger. Cut a 3" (7.5cm) square from stretched plum florist crepe. Leaf #80: Cut 1 from rust florist crepe using notch edger.

BUILD Secure all layers with floral tape. **1.** Fold plum florist crepe square in half diagonally. Fold again in half diagonally. Fold again. Fold pointed corner over as shown. Tuck wire ¾" (2cm) into folds, pinch base and secure. Push top of triangle point down to create a loose square on top. **2.** *Table Pleat* (p. 134), *Scrunch Pleat* (p. 128), and *Gather and Wrap* (p. 132) baby blue single-ply crepe, overlapping ends by 1"–2" (2.5cm–5cm) and secure tightly. **3.** Repeat step 2 with plum single-ply crepe. **4.** Repeat step 2 with painted ice blue single-ply crepe. **5.** *Scrunch Pleat* and attach rust florist crepe leaf to base of flower. Finish stems.

PROJECT NOTE We made 15 flowers to hang on our ladder. Each bloom has one layer of painted crepe mixed with different colors in our palette. We painted dowels with diluted white acrylic and cut them to the following lengths: 48" (122cm), 39" (99cm), 29" (74cm), 19" (48.5cm), 9" (23cm). They were tied together with blue/white twine to make a suspended ladder. Wires were bent over the dowels allowing the leaves to face different directions and adjusted to hang evenly. After hanging the flowers on the dowels, each flower wire was further adjusted to make the blooms face forward.

PAINTER'S MUSE 47

MATERIALS

- Florist crepe in black
- Tissue in light plum, plum, dark purple, lavender, sage, chartreuse, olive, shell, peach, coral, orange, lemon, butter, golden, Wedgwood blue
- 18" (45.5cm) 18-gauge paper-covered floral wire
- Floral tape in green

SPECIALTY TOOLS

- Fringing scissors

TEMPLATES #158, #159

TRY THIS These flowers could be made in any tissue paper color combination. Change the black stamen to white or a color. Add additional layers of petals to make fuller flowers.

CUT *Grain runs with height; all dimensions are given as H × W.* Cut two 2½" × 8" (6.5cm × 20.5cm) strips each from dark purple and plum tissue, fringe ¾ of the way down. Cut a 3" × 1" (7.5cm × 2.5cm) strip from the black florist crepe. Fully stretch, fold in half with the grain and very thinly *Hand Cut Fringe* (p. 127) with the grain ¾ of the way down. Petal #158: Cut 5 from light plum tissue, and 17 from the lavender tissue. Leaf #159: Cut 2 from chartreuse tissue, and 1 from sage tissue. Loosely fringe leaf tips with fringing scissors as shown.

BUILD Secure all layers with floral tape. **1.** Stack the plum and dark-purple fringe pieces, alternating colors, and make a *Fringe Center* (p. 130). **2.** *Gather and Wrap* (p. 132) the black fringe, spreading it evenly around the center. **3.** Layer the light-plum and lavender petals in 5 pairs offsetting them slightly as shown, and *Scrunch Pleat* (p. 128) then *Twist* (p. 128). Secure each petal evenly around the center. **4.** Layer the lavender petals in 6 pairs offsetting them slightly, as shown, and *Scrunch Pleat* then *Twist*. Secure each petal evenly around the center. **5.** Layer the 3 leaves, sandwiching the sage leaf between the chartreuse leaves. To add body to the leaf, flip the sage leaf over to reverse the fold direction. *Twist* the base of all 3 leaves together. Finish stem with tape, attaching the leaf 4" (10cm) from the flower base.

PROJECT NOTE We re-created the color combinations in the still life painting, pairing up tonal shades of tissue and made leaf combinations with sage and olive tissue.

48 FADING FALL WREATH

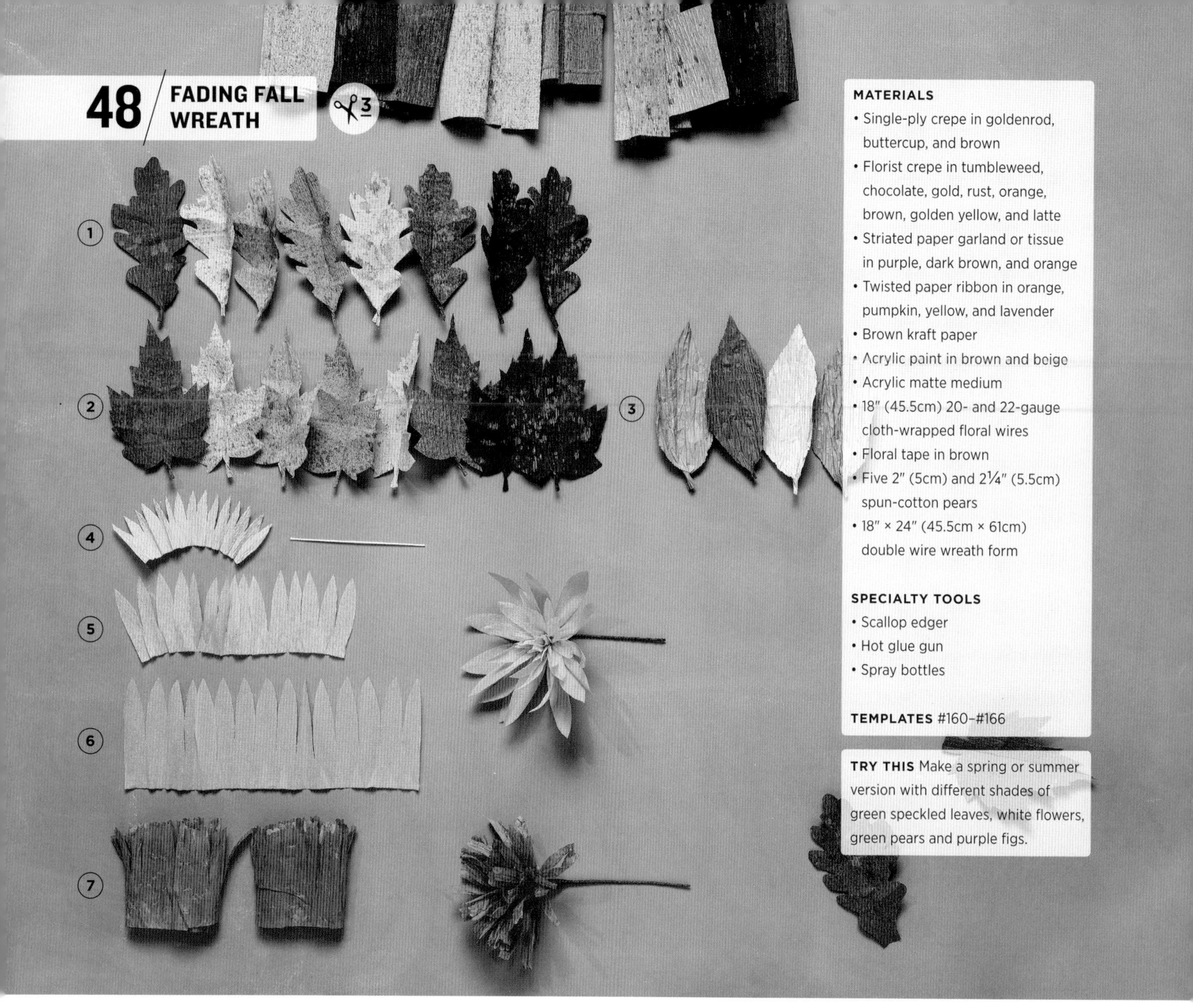

MATERIALS

- Single-ply crepe in goldenrod, buttercup, and brown
- Florist crepe in tumbleweed, chocolate, gold, rust, orange, brown, golden yellow, and latte
- Striated paper garland or tissue in purple, dark brown, and orange
- Twisted paper ribbon in orange, pumpkin, yellow, and lavender
- Brown kraft paper
- Acrylic paint in brown and beige
- Acrylic matte medium
- 18" (45.5cm) 20- and 22-gauge cloth-wrapped floral wires
- Floral tape in brown
- Five 2" (5cm) and 2¼" (5.5cm) spun-cotton pears
- 18" × 24" (45.5cm × 61cm) double wire wreath form

SPECIALTY TOOLS

- Scallop edger
- Hot glue gun
- Spray bottles

TEMPLATES #160–#166

TRY THIS Make a spring or summer version with different shades of green speckled leaves, white flowers, green pears and purple figs.

ADD COLOR *Dilute* (p. 136) the brown and beige acrylic paints, and fill 2 spray bottles with them. Cut 20" (51cm) lengths from all florist crepes. Spray both sides of papers with dark brown paint followed by beige paint. Allow all papers to dry between colors.

CUT *Grain runs with height; all dimensions are given as H × W.* Leaves #160 and #161: Cut strips from all painted crepes to fit the height of the templates, stretch crepe completely. Cut 10 of each leaf from every color totaling 80 oak and 80 maple leaves. Leaf #162: Cut six 6" (15cm) lengths of twisted paper ribbon from all 4 colors; untwist and cut leaves using a deckle edger. Petal #163: Cut 2" × 6" (5cm × 15cm) strips from unpainted florist crepe, 3 golden yellow, 5 latte, and 2 brown, accordion-fold each strip to fit template and cut continuous petals. Cut ten 5" (12.5cm) lengths of 22-gauge wire. Petal #164: Cut 3" × 10" (7.5cm × 25.5cm) strips from single-ply crepe, 3 buttercup and 3 brown; accordion-fold each strip to fit template and cut continuous petals. Petal #165: Cut 4" × 12" (10cm × 30.5cm) strips from single-ply crepe, 5 goldenrod and 5 brown; accordion-fold each strip to fit template and cut continuous petals. Cut 4" × 16" (10cm × 40.5cm) strips from striated paper garland, 8 each from orange, dark brown, and purple, and gently pull folds apart. Fold striated strips in quarters widthwise, trim one edge against the grain with scallop edger, and *Hand Cut Fringe* (p. 127) ½" (13mm) wide, ¾ of the way down on scalloped edge. Cut twelve 5" (12.5cm) lengths of 22-gauge wire. For large pears, cut 5½" × 6½" (14cm × 16.5cm) ovals from striated paper garland, 2 orange, 2 purple, 1 dark brown. For small pears, cut 5" × 6" (12.5cm × 15cm) ovals from striated paper garland, 2 purple, 1 dark brown, 1 orange. Leaf #166: Cut 16 from unpainted tumbleweed florist crepe. Cut nine 4" (10cm) length of 24-gauge wire. Cut five 3" × 24" (7.5cm × 61cm) strips of brown kraft paper, fold in half lengthwise.

BUILD Secure all layers with floral tape. **1 and 2.** Fold and crease all Leaves #160 and #161 in half lengthwise. Unfold, create veining on a diagonal by gently pinching paper between index finger and thumb as shown, and *Twist* (p. 128) each base. **3.** *Twist* base of Leaves #162. **4.** *Gather and Wrap* (p. 132) golden-yellow crepe Petal #163 evenly around a 5" (12.5cm) wire to make a center. **5.** Gently *Scissor*

Curl (p. 135) the buttercup Petals #164, and pinch the tips to create a soft crease. Repeat step 4 with Petal #164. **6.** Repeat step 5 with goldenrod Petal #165. (We made 5 yellow flowers total, replacing the yellow center with latte florist crepe twice, and leaving the second layer out in 2 flowers for variation. We also made 5 brown flowers from brown florist crepe and brown single-ply crepe, and applied the same variations by using latte florist crepe for 3 centers, and making 2 flowers with only the first and third layers.) **7.** *Gather and Wrap* 2 pieces, 1 at a time, of orange striated paper garland around a 5" (12.5cm) wire. Repeat step 7, making 4 orange, 4 dark brown, and 4 purple flowers. **8.** Glue a spun-cotton pear to the end of a full-length 20-gauge cloth-wrapped wire and let it dry. Using a brush, coat a large pear with medium, and center it in a large striated garland oval as shown. Fold up 2 opposite sides at a time, smoothing with medium as needed. Paint medium into creases and fold corners in 1 direction, adhering paper with medium as you wrap the pear. Smooth as much as possible, and twist excess paper at the top around wire. Let dry. Cover excess paper and entire stem with tape. *Scrunch Pleat* (p. 128) 1 Leaf #166 and make a crease up center lengthwise, attach to a 4" (10cm) wire tip, finish with tape. With the leaf and pear *Join Stems* (p. 132) 3" (7.5cm) down from the top of the pear stem. Place a second creased and *Scrunch Pleated* Leaf #166 at the junction of the 2 wires, attach to cover joint. Repeat step 8 to make 5 large pears, and 4 small pears. **9.** Wrap wreath in kraft paper strips as shown, securing with hot glue. Begin layering leaves, flowers and pears on form, in the same direction, creating an ombré fade with the colors. Secure each piece with hot glue. When adhering pear wires, glue 3"–4" (7.5cm–10cm) of wire to wreath form. Add a loop of wire for hanging.

PROJECT NOTE The flower and leaf counts are based on an 18" × 24" (45.5cm × 61cm) wreath form. More or fewer components may be needed based on the size of the wreath you make. If you are working with a different-sized form, lay out your pieces along the form beforehand to make sure there are enough parts to cover it before glueing.

MATERIALS

- Single-ply crepe in white, lavender, purple, and royal purple
- Florist crepe in orchid and plum
- Floral tape in brown
- Found branch

SPECIALTY TOOLS

- Hot glue gun

TEMPLATE #167

TRY THIS These blooms are easy to craft and can be made in any color of crepe. Try all white blossoms with green centers. Craft blossoms in a fade from light to dark pink, try making pale pastels for springtime, or metallic tones for holiday decor. Attach blossoms in any color to smaller branches to mix into other paper flower arrangements.

EVEN EASIER Skip making the rolled and fringe center and just gather and wrap the continuous petal pieces into blossoms and hot glue onto branches.

CUT *Grain runs with height; all dimensions are given as H × W.* Cut sixty 1¾" × 1¼" (4.5cm × 3cm) strips from royal purple single-ply crepe. Cut sixty 1" × 1¼" (2.5cm × 3cm) strips from white single-ply crepe. Finely *Hand Cut Fringe* (p. 127) each strip, with the grain, ¾ of the way down. Petal #167: Cut twelve 2" × 6½" (5cm × 16.5cm) strips from each of the 5 purple-toned crepe papers; accordion-fold strips to fit template and cut continuous petals.

BUILD Secure all layers with floral tape. **1.** Make a *Rolled Center* (p. 131) with purple strip and pinch tightly. **2.** *Gather and Wrap* (p. 132) white fringe around center, tightly secure. **3.** *Gather and Wrap* continuous petal evenly around center and secure tightly. *Cup* (p. 134) petals slightly. **4.** Snip off end of tape, leaving ¼" (6mm) tape at the base as shown. Repeat all steps to complete 60 flowers.

PROJECT NOTE To secure blossoms to the branch, dab a small amount of hot glue on the base of the flower, and place on branch in desired location. Hold until secure. To complete the ombré effect, secure the lightest flowers to the top of the branch, and work from light to dark as you progress down the branch.

To make the buds, cut an additional strip of Petal #167, and snip off 2 petals. *Gather and Wrap* around a piece of white fringe and secure with tape. Snip off end of tape, leaving ¼" (6mm) tape at the base and attach to the branch with hot glue.

PEPPERED PEONY 50

MATERIALS

- Single-ply crepe in white, whisper pink
- Florist crepe in tumbleweed
- Tissue in strawberry pink
- Japanese paper in wood rose and mauve rose
- Acrylic paint in fluorescent pink
- 18" (45.5cm) 18-gauge paper-covered floral wire
- Floral tape in pink
- Vintage feathers

SPECIALTY TOOLS

- Fringing scissors
- Bubbles edger
- Spray bottle

TEMPLATES #168–#171

TRY THIS These can be made in darker shades of single-ply crepe as well. Try diluted white paint on dark pink, burgundy, and plum petals with green leaves.

ADD COLOR *Dilute* (p. 136) the fluorescent pink acrylic paint. Cut 6 folds from ivory single-ply crepe. Using a spray bottle with a fine nozzle finely speckle the paper with paint. Set aside to dry.

CUT *Grain runs with height; all dimensions are given as H × W.* Cut five 2" × 8" (2cm × 20.5cm) strips from the strawberry pink tissue. Trim the 2 long sides with bubbles edger. Cut a 2" × 5" (5cm × 12.5cm) strip from the tumbleweed florist crepe. Using fringing scissors, fringe with the grain ¾ of the way down. Petals #168 and #169: Cut 8 #168 and 5 #169 from speckled single-ply crepe. Leaves #170 and #171: Cut 4 #170 and 5 #171 from both wood rose and mauve rose paper.

BUILD Secure all layers with floral tape. **1.** Gently *Scissor Curl* (p. 135) fringed tumbleweed florist crepe strip. Make a rolled *Fringe Center* (p. 130) with strip and an 18-gauge stem wire. Attach 3 feathers evenly around center and secure. **2.** Twist strawberry tissue strip in the middle twice, fold in half and bring ends together. *Box Pleat* (p. 128) the base to create a cupped shape in the top of the petal. Repeat with all 5 strips. Attach 5 petals evenly around center and secure. **3.** *Flute* (p. 134) top edge of all speckled crepe petals. *Scrunch Pleat* (p. 128) 3 Petals #168 evenly around center and secure. *Cup* (p. 134) at base. Repeat with 3 more petals, attaching at alternate points. Repeat with 2 remaining petals, attaching at alternate points. **4.** Attach 5 Petals #169 evenly around center and secure. *Cup* at base and finish stem. **5.** Secure 2 Leaves #170 and 2 #171 in random colors at base of flower. Continue to add leaves, mixing styles and colors randomly while finishing the stem with a second layer of tape.

PROJECT NOTE We made variations of this flower by decreasing the number of tissue and crepe petals to mimic different stages of bloom, and crafting some petals in whisper pink single-ply crepe.

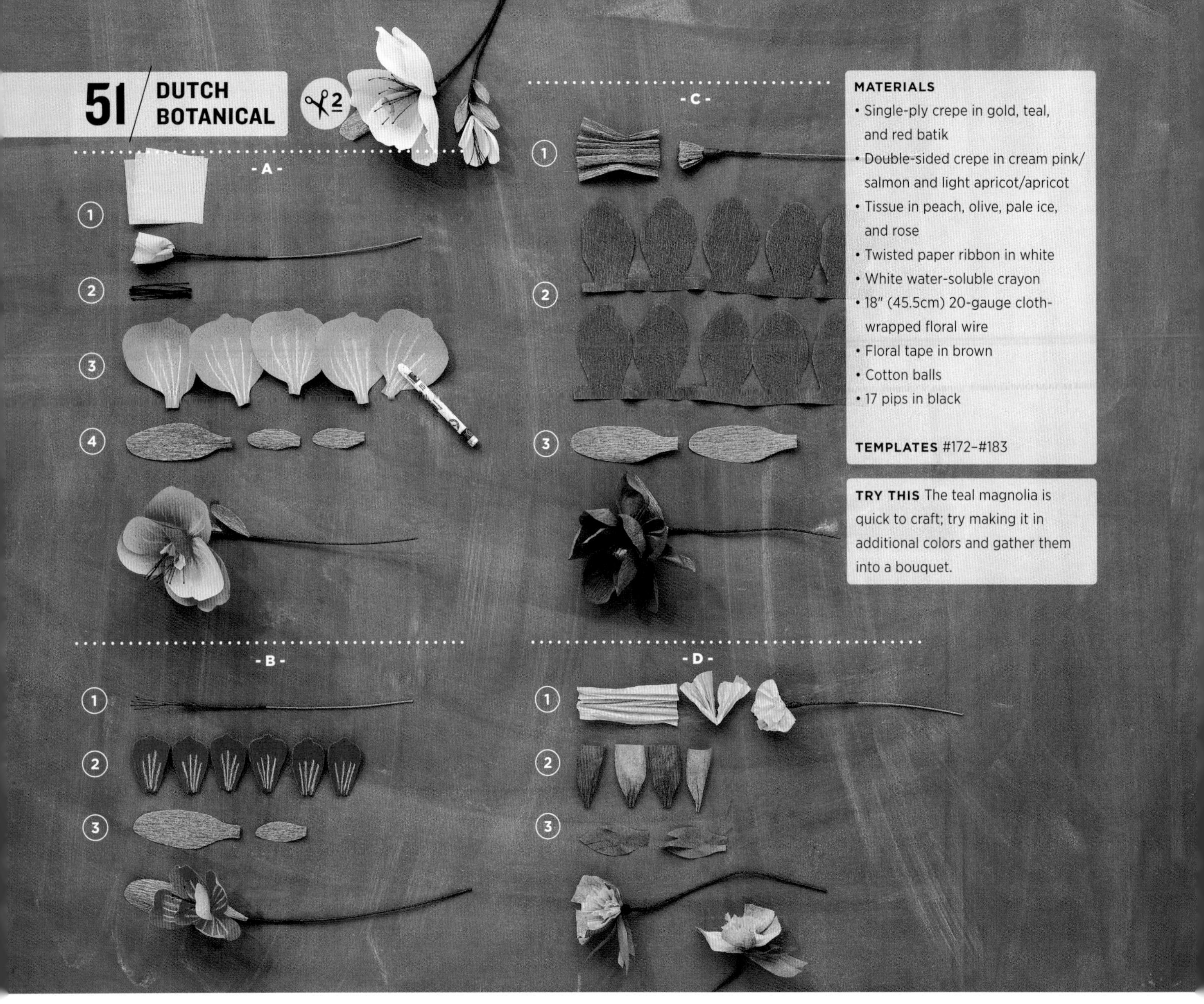

NOTE *Grain runs with height; all dimensions are given as H × W.* Secure all layers and finish stems with floral tape. Cut all wires to desired lengths.

A 1. Cut four 2½" (6.5cm) squares from peach tissue. Stack the squares and fold them in thirds, then *Scrunch Pleat* (p. 128) and secure them to a wire tip to make a center. **2.** Secure 12 pips evenly around the center. **3.** Petal #172: Cut 5 petals from cream pink/salmon double-sided crepe. Using a white crayon, draw lines as shown. Gently *Cup* (p. 134), *Scrunch Pleat*, and attach the petals evenly around the center. **4.** Cut 1 Leaf #173 and 2 #174 from gold single-ply crepe. *Scrunch Pleat* and attach them randomly within the top 3" (7.5cm) of the stem while finishing the stem.

B 1. Make a *Pip Center* (p. 130) with 5 full-length pips. **2.** Repeat step A3 using 6 Petal #175. **3.** Repeat step A4 making 1 each of Leaves #173 and #174.

C 1. Cut a 3" × 4" (7.5cm × 10cm) piece from gold single-ply crepe. *Table Pleat* (p. 134), scrunch together, fold in half against the grain, and secure unfolded ends to a wire tip as shown to make a center. **2.** Petal #176: Cut two 3¾" × 12" (9.5cm × 30.5cm) strips from teal single-ply crepe, accordion-fold to fit template, and cut. *Scrunch Pleat* and *Gather and Wrap* (p. 132) 1 petal around center. Gently *Cup*. Repeat with second teal continuous petal. **3.** Leaf #173: Cut 2 from gold single-ply crepe. *Scrunch Pleat* and attach randomly within the top 3" (7.5cm) of stem while finishing the stem.

D 1. Cut two 3" (7.5cm) squares from peach tissue. *Table Pleat* each square, fold in half, and pinch at the fold. Secure the fold of both pieces to a wire tip. **2.** Petal #177: Cut 4 from red batik single-ply crepe. Gently *Cup* and *Scrunch Pleat* and attached evenly around center. **3.** Leaf #178: Cut 2 from olive tissue. Make a few cuts in the leaf tips as shown. *Scrunch Pleat* and attach to flower base while finishing stem.

E 1. Petal #179: Cut an 8" × 24" (20.5cm × 61cm) strip from pale ice tissue. Fold in half widthwise, accordion-fold to fit the template, with the bottom aligned with the folded edge, and cut. *Gather and Wrap* petal around a stem wire. **2.** Leaf #180: Cut 2 from olive tissue. *Scrunch Pleat* the leaves and attach them to flower base while finishing the stem.

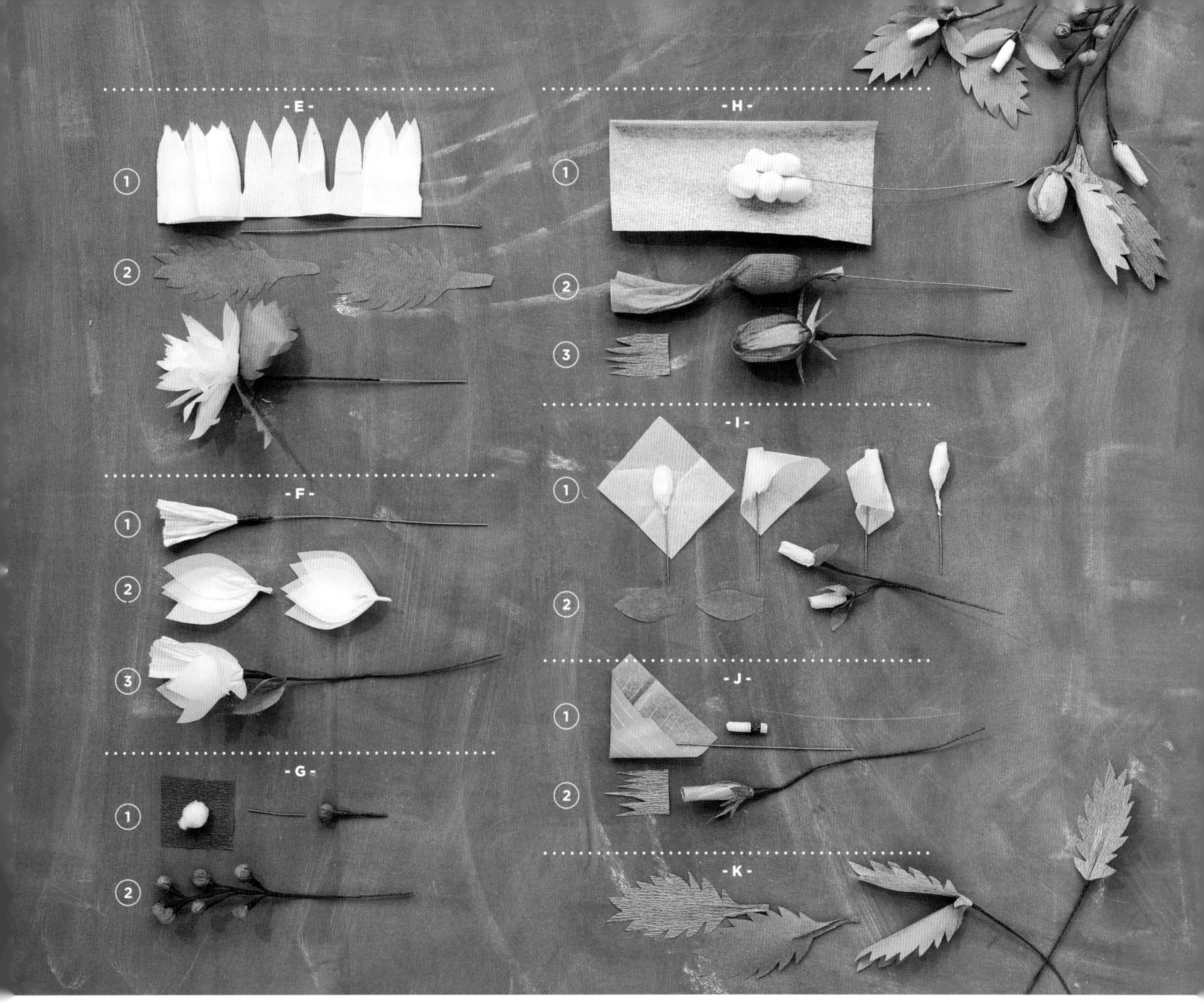

F 1. Cut a 3½" (9cm) length of white twisted paper ribbon. Untwist completely, gather one end, and secure to a stem wire to make a center. **2.** Petal #181: Cut 10 from pale ice tissue. Layer 5 petals, offsetting each slightly as shown, and *Twist* (p. 128) bases. Repeat with remaining 5 petals. Secure 2 layered petals around center. **3.** Leaf #178: Cut 1 from olive tissue. *Scrunch Pleat* and attach 1" (2.5cm) from flower base while finishing the stem.

G 1. Make a *Cotton Ball Center* (p. 130) with a small cotton piece, a 2½" (6.5cm) teal single-ply crepe square, and a 2" (5cm) wire. **2.** Repeat step 1 to make 7 buds total. Attach 1 bud to the tip of a longer stem wire. Make *Connected Buds* (p. 131) with remaining buds as shown, while finishing the stem.

H 1. Cut a 10" × 5" (25.5cm × 12.5cm) strip from red batik single-ply crepe. Place 5 cotton balls and a wire on strip as shown. **2.** Roll paper over cotton to enclose, twisting the base and top several times as shown. Fold long top piece over while continuing to twist, gather at base, and secure. **3.** Leaf #182: Cut 1 from gold single-ply crepe. Attach at base of flower while finishing the stem.

I 1. Make a *Bud* (p. 131) with a 4" × 3" (10cm × 7.5cm) piece from pale ice tissue, ½ cotton ball, and a 3"–6" (7.5cm–15cm) length of wire. Align the tissue and cotton as shown. Repeat to make 2 buds, 1 with a shorter stem. **2.** Leaf #178: Cut 3 from olive tissue. *Scrunch Pleat* all leaves. Attach 2 at the base of short stem bud and 1 at the base of long stem bud while finishing stems. *Join Stems* (p. 132) of short wire to long wire as shown.

J 1. Draw stripes on rose tissue with a white crayon. Make a *Bud* with a 4" × 4½" (10cm × 11.5cm) piece of striped rose tissue, an elongated cotton ball, and a 9" (23cm) length of wire. **2.** Leaf #183: Cut 1 from gold single-ply crepe. *Scrunch Pleat* and secure it to the center. Finish the stem.

K Leaf #180: Cut 1 each from olive single-ply tissue and gold crepe. *Scrunch Pleat* the bases together and attach them to the tip of a stem wire. Finish the stem.

PROJECT NOTE Flowers A and B were also made in light apricot/apricot double-sided crepe.

52 SUMMER SPECKLE

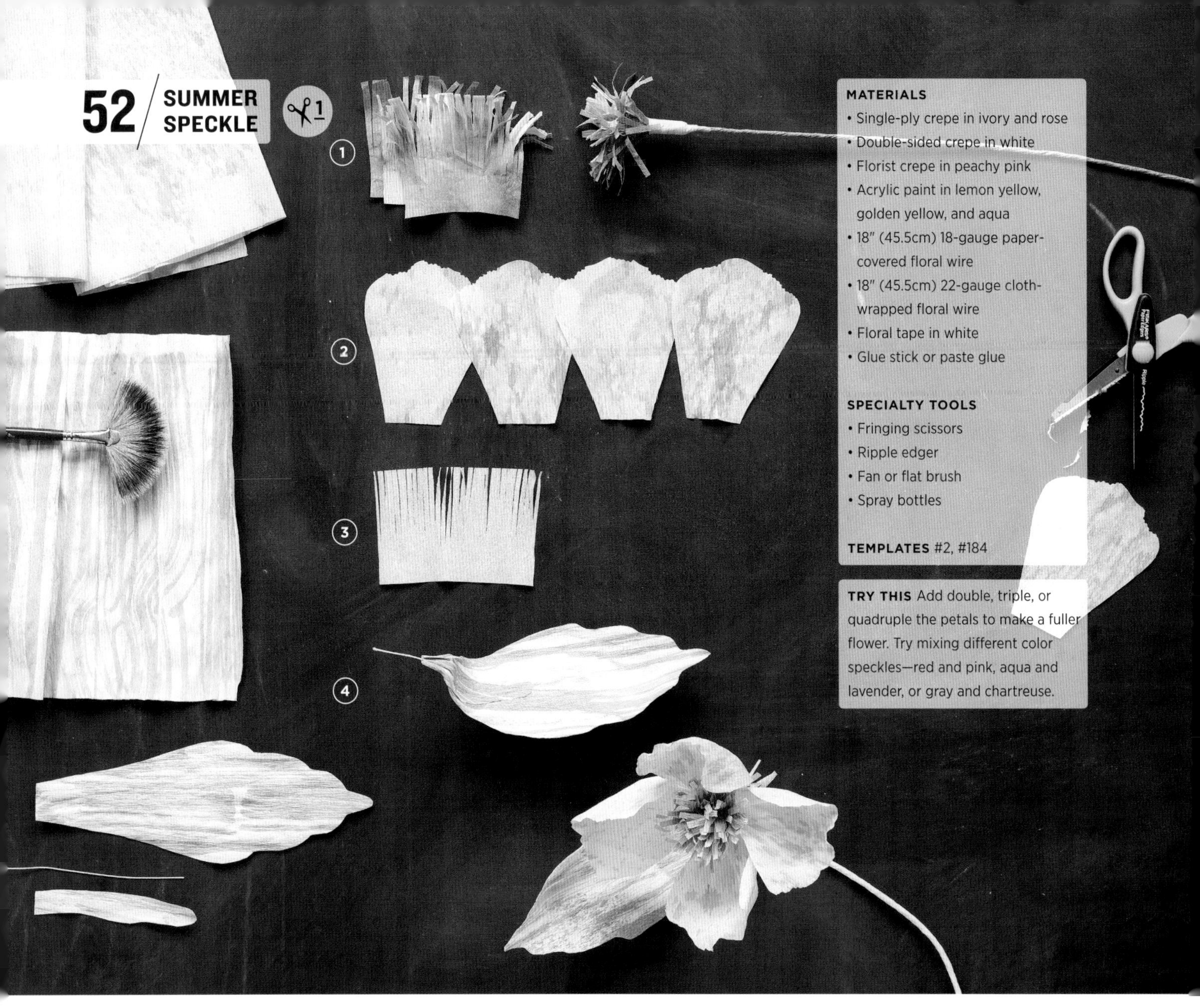

MATERIALS

- Single-ply crepe in ivory and rose
- Double-sided crepe in white
- Florist crepe in peachy pink
- Acrylic paint in lemon yellow, golden yellow, and aqua
- 18" (45.5cm) 18-gauge paper-covered floral wire
- 18" (45.5cm) 22-gauge cloth-wrapped floral wire
- Floral tape in white
- Glue stick or paste glue

SPECIALTY TOOLS

- Fringing scissors
- Ripple edger
- Fan or flat brush
- Spray bottles

TEMPLATES #2, #184

TRY THIS Add double, triple, or quadruple the petals to make a fuller flower. Try mixing different color speckles—red and pink, aqua and lavender, or gray and chartreuse.

ADD COLOR Cut 2 pieces of ivory single-ply crepe, 4 folds wide. *Dilute* (p. 136) the lemon yellow and golden-yellow acrylic paints, and fill 2 spray bottles with them. Spray 1 piece of the crepe with golden-yellow paint and the other with light yellow paint to create a speckled pattern. Set aside to dry. Cut 1 piece of white double-sided crepe, 2 folds wide. *Dilute* the aqua acrylic paint and paint long, loose stripes, with the grain, using a fan brush. Set aside to dry.

CUT *Grain runs with height; all dimensions are given as H × W.* Cut two 3" × 3½" (7.5cm × 9cm) pieces from the rose single-ply crepe, 1 strip from peachy pink florist crepe and fringe all pieces with the grain, using fringing scissors, ¾ of the way down. Petal #2: Cut 2 each from lemon yellow and golden yellow speckled crepe. Snip off top edge of each petal with a ripple edger. Cut a 3" × 4" (7.5cm × 10cm) piece from white single-ply crepe and fringe with the grain, using fringing scissors, ¾ of the way down to make a calyx. Leaf #184: Cut 1 from aqua striped crepe and a 4" × ¾" (10cm × 2cm) organically shaped cut strip to cover the wire. Cut a 5" (12.5cm) length of 22-gauge cloth-wrapped wire.

BUILD Secure all layers with floral tape. **1.** Layer rose single-ply crepe and peachy pink florist crepe strips as shown. *Gather and Wrap* (p. 132) around a full-length paper-covered wire to make a center. **2.** *Scrunch Pleat* (p. 128) each Petal #2, and alternate speckled colors as you attach each petal evenly around center, *Cup* (p. 134) gently, and secure. **3.** *Gather and Wrap* white fringed calyx around base. **4.** With Leaf #184 and a 5" length of wire, *Wire Two-Sided Leaf* (p. 133), cover wire on back with loosely cut strip, let dry. *Scrunch Pleat* base of leaf around wire and curve the base. Begin finishing flower stem with tape, attaching wired leaf 4" (10cm) from flower base, covering the base of leaf in tape. Finish the stem.

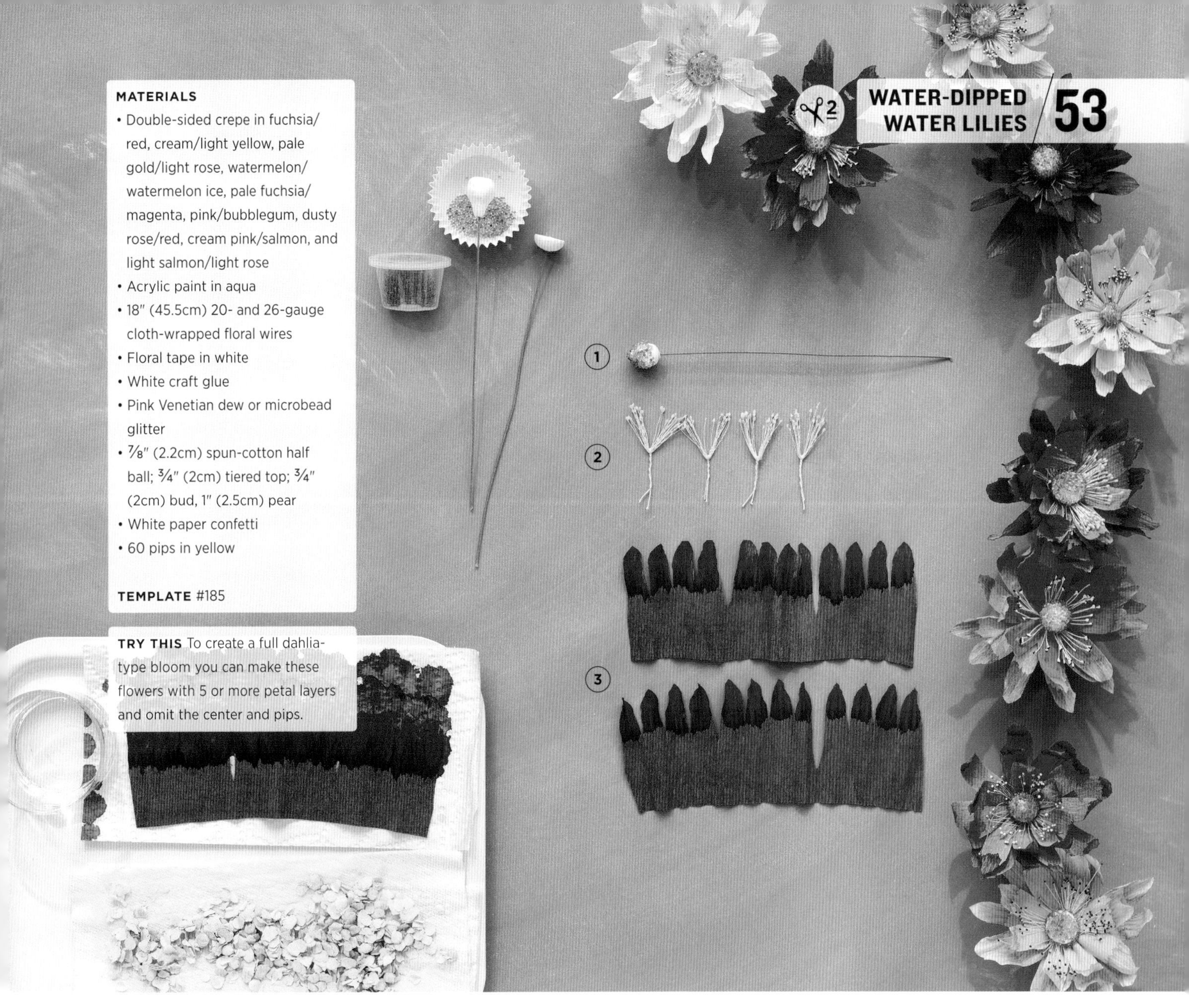

CUT *Grain runs with height; all dimensions are given as H × W.* Petal #185: Cut two 3½" × 9" (9cm × 23cm) strips from fuchsia/red double-sided crepe. Accordion-fold to fit template and cut continuous petal. Cut a 9" (23cm) length of 20-gauge wire. Cut four 4" (10cm) lengths of 26-gauge wires.

ADD COLOR Dip tips of accordion-folded continuous petals ½" (13mm) into water, and gently shake off excess. The water will wick up farther into the paper. Unfold, allow to dry on paper towels. *Dilute* (p. 136) the aqua acrylic paint. Submerge the paper confetti briefly to absorb the color. With your hand, scoop out confetti and squeeze out extra moisture. Spread out on paper towels to dry.

BUILD Secure all layers with floral tape. **1.** Attach a spun-cotton center with glue to the tip of the 20-gauge wire, let dry. Coat center with glue and dip in Venetian dew to cover, or sprinkle with microbead glitter, let dry. **2.** Make 4 *Pip Centers* (p. 130) with 15 yellow pips each and 26-gauge wires. Secure evenly to stem around center. **3.** Gently *Scissor Curl* (p. 135) both continuous Petal #185 tips inward and *Gather and Wrap* (p. 132) evenly around center one layer at a time.

PROJECT NOTE To display flowers upright in shallow bowls bend the stem to make a round flat coil a little smaller than the circumference of the petals that will sit flat and stable in the bottom of a bowl. We made a few varieties of this flower with different spun-cotton shapes, an assortment of vintage pips, and several other colors of double-sided crepe. Lighter colors of double-sided crepe will not have as much color bleed from one side to the next when dipping in water.

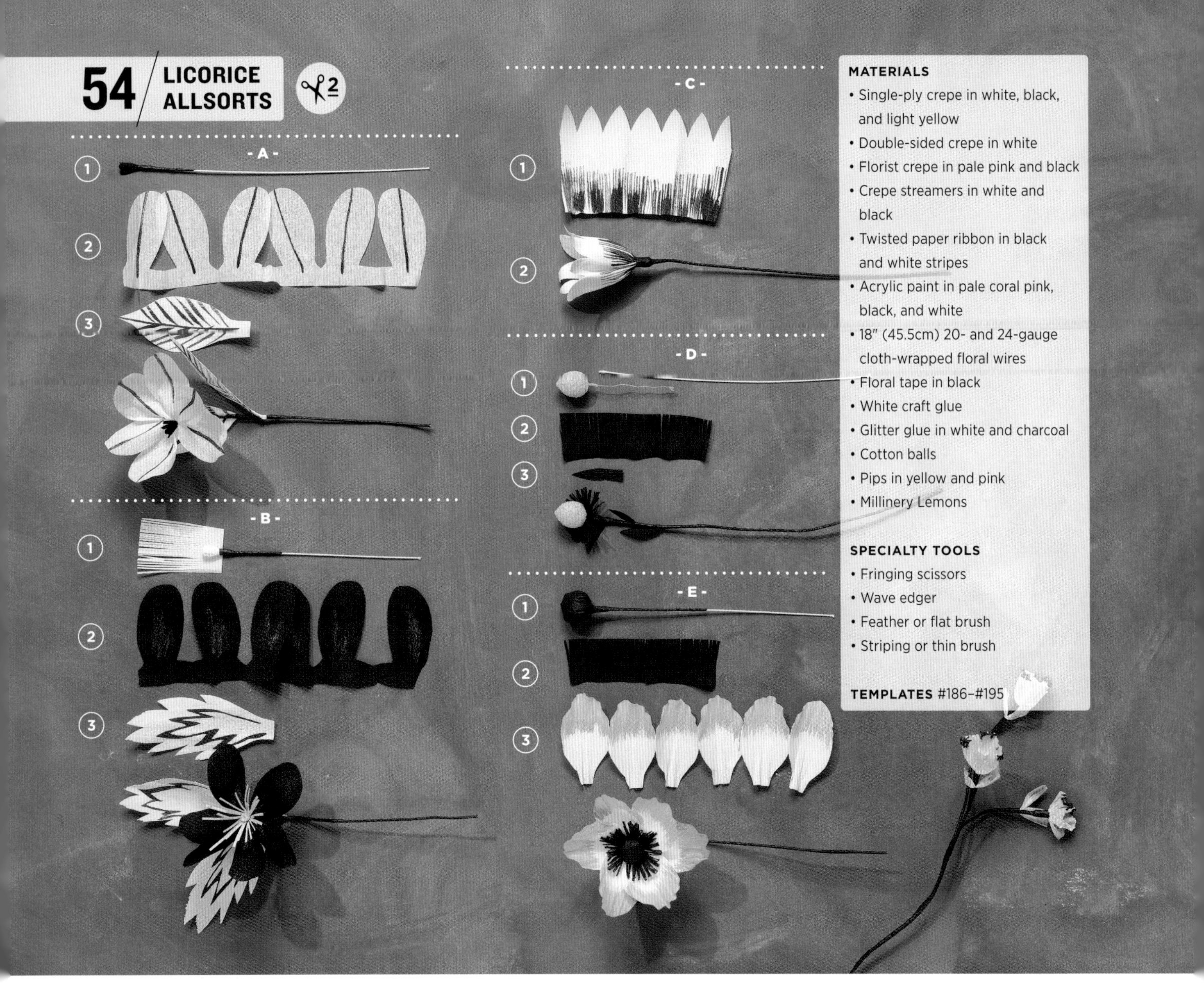

NOTE *Dilute* (p. 136) and paint; let parts dry. *Grain runs with height, unless noted. All dimensions are given as H × W.* Fringe with the grain, ¾ of the way down. Secure all layers and finish stems with floral tape.

A 1. Make a *Rolled Center* (p. 131) with a 2" × 1½" (5cm × 4cm) strip of black florist crepe. **2.** Cut a 3½" × 11½" (9cm × 29cm) strip of white single-ply crepe, accordion-fold to fit Petal #186, and cut. Paint black lines. *Gather and Wrap* (p. 132) it around the center, and *Cup* (p. 134). **3.** Leaf #187: Cut 1 or 2 from white single-ply crepe. Paint black veins. *Scrunch Pleat* (p. 128) the leaves and attach.

B 1. Repeat step A1 with white double-sided crepe. Cut a 2¾" × 1½" (7cm × 4cm) strip of white double-sided crepe and finely *Hand Cut Fringe* (p. 127). *Gather and Wrap* it around the center. **2.** Repeat step A2 with black single-ply crepe and smear it with charcoal glitter glue. *Gather and Wrap* it around the center and *Cup*. **3.** Leaf #188: Cut 2 from white double-sided crepe. Paint black outlines. *Scrunch Pleat* the leaves, attach randomly.

C 1. Cut a 3½" × 5½" (9cm × 14cm) strip of white double-sided crepe, fold it in half, and cut Petal #189. Brush black lines. **2.** *Gather and Wrap* it around stem. *Finesse* (p. 135) into a bell shape. Finger-curl the petal tips.

D 1. Secure lemon to wire. **2.** Cut a 1½" × 5" (4cm × 12.5cm) strip of black single-ply crepe and fringe it. *Gather and Wrap* it around the lemon. **3.** Leaf #190: Cut 3 from black single-ply crepe. *Scrunch Pleat* the leaves, attach randomly.

E 1. Make a *Cotton Ball Center* (p. 130) with a 3½" (9cm) square of black single-ply crepe. **2.** Cut a 1½" × 5" (4cm × 12.5cm) strip of black single-ply crepe and fringe it. *Gather and Wrap* it around the center. **3.** Petal #191: Cut 6 from white double-sided crepe. Brush tops with pink acrylic paint. *Scrunch Pleat* the petals and attach, spacing them evenly.

F 1. Repeat step A1 with black single-ply crepe. **2.** Cut two 3" × 9" (7.5cm × 23cm) strips of white single-ply crepe, accordion-fold to fit Petal #192, and cut. *Gather and Wrap* 1 strip around the center and *Cup*. Repeat with second strip.

G 1. Make a *Fringe Center* (p. 130) with a 3½" × 7" (9cm × 18cm) strip of white single-ply crepe (grain runs lengthwise). *Gather and Wrap* it around the center. **2.** Cut a 3" ×

9" (7.5cm × 23cm) strip of black single-ply crepe, accordion-fold to fit Petal #192, and cut. Smear it with white glitter glue. *Gather and Wrap* it around the center and *Cup*.

H 1. Make a *Rolled Center* with a 2" × 1½" (5cm × 4cm) strip of white single-ply crepe. **2.** Repeat step G2 with white single-ply and double-sided crepe. Paint black borders. *Gather and Wrap* the double-sided strip around the center and *Cup*. Repeat with single-ply strip.
3. Leaves #193: Cut 2 from slightly stretched black florist crepe. Paint white veins. *Scrunch Pleat* the leaves and attach randomly.

I 1. Cut a 3" × 7" (7.5cm × 18cm) strip of white single-ply crepe and trim the top with the wave edger. Paint black lines as shown. *Gather and Wrap* it around the stem and *Cup* the top half. Glue the loose ends. **2.** Leaf #193: Cut 1 from black single-ply crepe. *Scrunch Pleat* the leaf, attach it 1" (2.5cm) from the base. Repeat all steps and reverse colors for the black flower.

J 1. Cut two 3½" (9cm) lengths of streamers, 1 black, 1 white. Cut a 5" (12.5cm) length of 24-gauge wire. *Table Pleat* (p. 134) both streamers and pinch them together. **2.** Wrap the wire around the center of the streamers, fold it down, and twist. Fan the streamers out to create a circle. *Join Stems* (p. 132) of multiple blooms to 1 stem.

K 1. Make a pink *Pip Center* (p. 130). **2.** Cut a 2" × 5" (5cm × 12.5cm) strip of pink florist crepe, accordion-fold to fit Petal #194, and cut. *Gather and Wrap* it around the center and *Cup*. Repeat steps 1 and 2 to make a second flower. **3.** *Join Stems*. Repeat all steps with yellow pips and yellow single-ply crepe.

L Cut a 3½" (9cm) length of 24-gauge wire. Cut a 3" (7.5cm) square of white single-ply crepe. Paint the black stripes as shown. Make 7 *Connected Buds* (p. 131) together to a full-length 18-gauge wire. Cut a 1½" × 5" (4cm × 12.5cm) strip of black single-ply crepe and fringe it. Wrap fringe around stem and secure with glue.

M *On left:* Cut an 8"–10" (20.5cm–25.5cm) length of twisted paper ribbon. Untwist it, fold it in half lengthwise, and round off a corner with scissors. *On right:* Paint black lines on white double-sided crepe as shown. Cut Leaf #195. *Scrunch Pleat* both leaves, attach to individual wires.

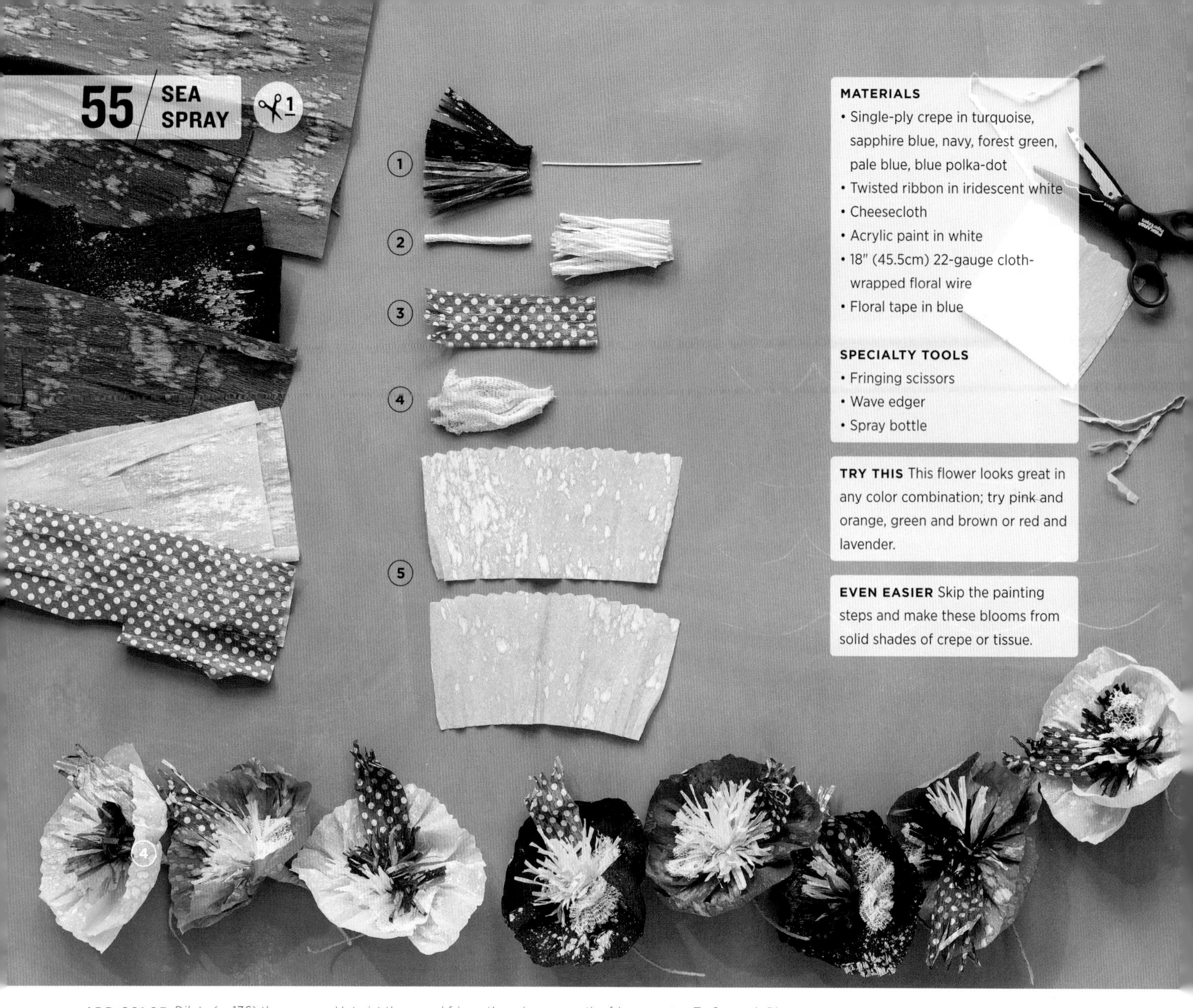

ADD COLOR *Dilute* (p. 136) the white acrylic paint and fill a spray bottle with it. Cut pieces 2–4 folds wide from all 6 crepe papers, and spray with paint to make speckled papers. Set aside to dry.

CUT *Grain runs with height; all dimensions are given as H × W.* Cut all fringe, using fringing scissors, with the grain. Cut a 5" (12.5cm) length of wire. Cut a 3" × 5" (7.5cm × 12.5cm) strip each from the speckled-navy and -turquoise single-ply crepe papers. Stretch the strips and fringe them ¾ of the way down. Cut two 3" (7.5cm) lengths of iridescent twisted ribbon. Untwist them and fringe them in the direction of the twists, ¾ of the way down. Cut a 5" × 1½" (12.5cm × 4cm) strip from polka-dot crepe and fringe it 1" (2.5cm) down. Cut a 3½" (9cm) length of cheesecloth. Cut two 4" × 8" (10cm × 20.5cm) strips of aqua-speckled crepe and trim a long edge lengthwise with a wave edger to make a cuff petal.

BUILD Secure all layers with floral tape. **1.** Make a *Fringe Center* (p. 130) with the speckled-navy and -turquoise fringed strips layered together. **2.** *Scrunch Pleat* (p. 128) the iridescent fringe and attach it as a single piece to one side of the fringe center. **3.** *Scrunch Pleat* the strip of polka-dot crepe and attach it to the center opposite the iridescent fringe. **4.** *Scrunch Pleat* the cheesecloth and attach it next to the polka-dot fringe. **5.** Stretch gently and *Scrunch Pleat* an aqua-speckled crepe cuff and *Gather and Wrap* (p. 132) it halfway around the center. Repeat with the second cuff, overlapping the first cuff by 1" (2.5cm) on both sides. Finish stem with blue tape.

PROJECT NOTE We made this flower in multiple color variations by switching the crepe cuff colors and fringe centers.

PEPPERMINT SNO-CONES / 56

MATERIALS

- Single-ply crepe in white
- Double-sided crepe in red/brick red
- Acrylic paint in candy-cane red, coral red, and fluorescent pink
- Floral tape in white
- White craft glue
- Flake glitter in red and fuchsia
- Assorted decorative straight and corsage pins
- 15" (38cm) Styrofoam cone

SPECIALTY TOOLS

- Fan or thick brush

TEMPLATES #196–#198

EVEN EASIER Skip the painting steps and make these cones from solid shades of red and pink or white and silver crepe.

ADD COLOR *Dilute* (p. 136) the candy-cane red, coral red, and fluorescent-pink acrylic paints in separate containers. Cut 6 pieces of white single-ply crepe, each 4 folds wide. Using fan brush, paint loose stripes in the direction of the grain. Paint 2 pieces of crepe per color. Set aside to dry.

CUT *Grain runs with the height; all dimensions are given as H × W.* Petal #196: Cut twenty 2½" × 9½" (6.5cm × 24cm) strips total from a mix of the 3 painted crepes, accordion-fold to fit template, and cut continuous petals. Petal #197: Cut forty 3" × 14" (7.5cm × 35.5cm) strips total from a mix of the 3 painted crepes, accordion-fold to fit template, and cut continuous petals. Petal #198: Cut ten 2" × 5" (5cm × 12.5cm) strips of red double-sided crepe, accordion-fold to fit template, and cut continuous petals.

BUILD Secure all layers with floral tape. **1.** *Gather and Wrap* (p. 132) Petals #196, as if working with an invisible stem, pinching paper tightly at the base, and secure. Snip off extra tape, leaving ¼" (6mm) of the base as your stem. Fan out flower and gently *Cup* (p. 134) each petal. Repeat with remaining strips. Repeat step 1 with Petal #197. **2.** *Gather and Wrap* Petals #198, as if working with an invisible stem, pinching paper tightly at the base, and secure. Snip off extra tape, leaving ¼" (6mm) as your stem. Fan out flower. Repeat with remaining strips. **3.** Lightly paint the tips of the red blooms with glue. Sprinkle half with red glitter and half with fuchsia glitter. Set aside to dry. **4.** To build the cone, begin with a smaller striped bloom, insert a straight pin through the center, and stick into the top of the cone. Layer and overlap petals slightly and incorporate larger flowers, hiding the foam form, as you work toward the base. Once the cone is covered, add in the red flowers.

PROJECT NOTE We used 9" (23cm), 12" (30.5cm), 14" (35.5cm), and 16" (40.5cm) sizes of cones to complete the project.

57 / TROMPETTES

2

MATERIALS

- Florist crepe in fairy-tale pink metallic nuance, gold, silver, and metallic pink
- Pink tinsel trim
- 18" (45.5cm) 24-gauge cloth-wrapped floral wire
- Acrylic paint in metallic silver and gold
- Floral tape in white, silver, and gold
- White craft glue
- ¼" (6mm), 1" (2.5cm) spun-cotton balls
- ½" (13mm) silver glass wired ball

SPECIALTY TOOLS

- Ripple edger

TEMPLATE #199

TRY THIS Try making these daffodil-inspired flowers in pastel shades of florist crepe for a spring dinner party.

CUT *Grain runs with height; all dimensions are given as H × W.* Cut a 3½" × 4" (9cm × 10cm) piece from the fairy-tale pink metallic nuance crepe. Trim 1 long end with a ripple edger. Petal #199: Cut 7 from fairy-tale pink nuance crepe. Cut a 2½" × 5½" (6.5cm × 14cm) strip from the fairy-tale pink metallic nuance crepe. Trim 1 long end with a ripple edger. Cut an 8" (20.5cm) piece of pink tinsel trim. Cut two 9" (23cm) lengths of stem wire.

ADD COLOR Glue a 1" (2.5cm) spun-cotton ball to the tip of a stem wire to make a center. Paint it with the silver metallic acrylic paint. Paint an additional ¼" (6mm) spun-cotton ball to match. Set them aside to dry.

BUILD Secure all layers with floral tape. **1.** Wrap the 3½" (9cm) fairy-tale pink metallic nuance crepe piece around 1 stem wire ¾" (2cm) from the base of the spun-cotton center. Overlap the edges and hold them stable against the ball with your fingers while you pinch the paper at the base of the ball around the wire to create a trumpet shape as shown. Secure it with white tape. Stretch the top edge of the trumpet to create a flared shape. **2.** *Scrunch Pleat* (p. 128) and curve each Petal #199 gently over a bottle of glue as shown. Attach evenly around the base of the trumpet and secure with white tape. **3.** Finish the stem with silver tape. Glue the painted ¼" (6mm) spun-cotton ball to the bottom end of the stem; let it dry. **4.** Attach the second stem wire to the short wire of a silver glass ball with tape to make a longer stem as shown. **5.** Wrap the tinsel trim around the base of the glass ball and down the wire 4" (10cm). Secure the end with white tape. **6.** *Gather and Wrap* (p. 132) the 2½" (6.5cm) strip of fairy-tale pink metallic nuance crepe around the stem 4" (10cm) from the base of the glass ball. Secure with white tape. **7.** Gently *Cup* (p. 134) to form a bell shape as shown. Finish the stem with silver tape.

PROJECT NOTE Additional color combinations were made with gold painted spun-cotton balls, gold floral tape, and additional colors of metallic crepe. To make these flowers last for many seasons, squeeze craft glue in between the petals and trumpet shape.

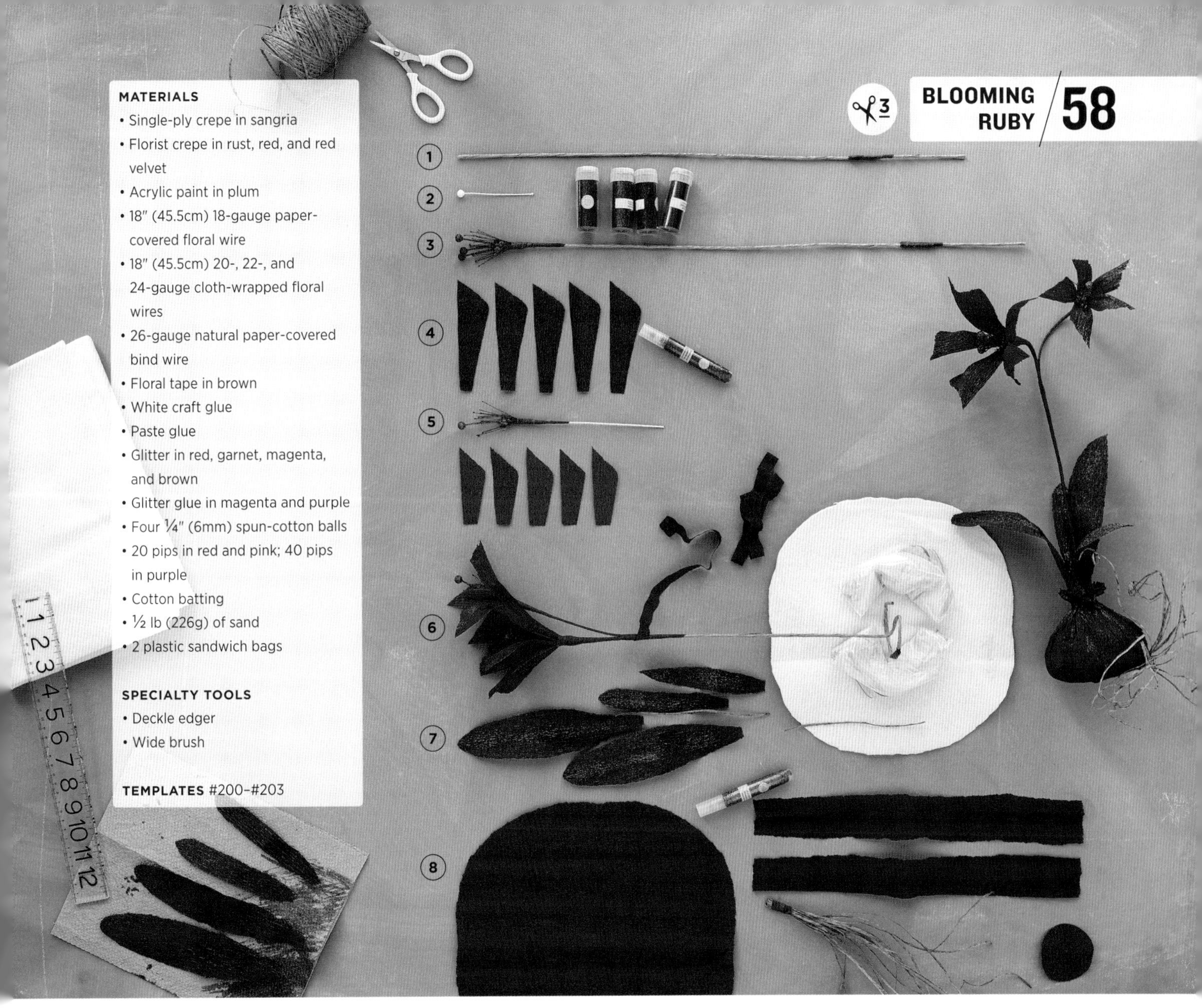

BLOOMING RUBY 58

MATERIALS

- Single-ply crepe in sangria
- Florist crepe in rust, red, and red velvet
- Acrylic paint in plum
- 18" (45.5cm) 18-gauge paper-covered floral wire
- 18" (45.5cm) 20-, 22-, and 24-gauge cloth-wrapped floral wires
- 26-gauge natural paper-covered bind wire
- Floral tape in brown
- White craft glue
- Paste glue
- Glitter in red, garnet, magenta, and brown
- Glitter glue in magenta and purple
- Four ¼" (6mm) spun-cotton balls
- 20 pips in red and pink; 40 pips in purple
- Cotton batting
- ½ lb (226g) of sand
- 2 plastic sandwich bags

SPECIALTY TOOLS

- Deckle edger
- Wide brush

TEMPLATES #200–#203

CUT *Grain runs with height; all dimensions are given as H × W.* Petal #200: Cut 5 from red velvet florist crepe. Petal #201 cut 5 from red florist crepe. Trim top edges using deckle edger. Leaves #202 and #203: Cut 2 each from rust florist crepe using deckle edger. Cut six ½" × 10" (13mm × 25.5cm) strips from sangria single-ply crepe. Using deckle edger, cut a 12" (30.5cm) circle and two 1½" × 14" (4cm × 35.5cm) strips from sangria single-ply crepe. Cut an 11" (28cm) circle from the cotton batting. Cut a 2½" (6.5cm) circle from the rust florist crepe. Cut a 5" (12.5cm) length of 18-gauge wire, a 6" (15cm) length of 20-gauge wire, four 3" (7.5cm) lengths of 24-gauge wire, and eleven 20" (51cm) lengths of bind wire.

ADD COLOR *Dilute* (p. 136) the plum acrylic paint. Paint the leaves as shown, then let them dry. Smear purple glitter glue on both sides.

BUILD Secure all layers with floral tape. **1.** *Join Stems* (p. 132) using 1 full-length and 5" (12.5cm) 18-gauge wires. **2.** Glue a spun-cotton ball to a 3" (7.5cm) wire tip; make 4 total. Coat 3 balls and stems with glue. *Glitter* (p. 137) 1 each using red, brown, and garnet glitter. Secure to the end of the stem. **3.** Secure 20 red folded pips and 20 purple pips to the center. **4.** *Scrunch Pleat* (p. 128) Petals #200. Secure evenly around the center, *Cup* (p. 134) them out. Smear them with magenta glitter glue. **5.** Repeat steps 2, 3, and 4 using 1 magenta-glittered ball and 20-gauge wire, 10 pink and 20 purple pips, and Petals #201. **6.** *Join Stem* to the long flower 4" (10cm) from the base. *Cover Stems* (p. 133) using ½" (13mm) crepe strips. Bend the bottom 6" (15cm) of the stem to create a coil. Fill each bag with ¼ lb (113g) of sand, form into logs, roll out the air, and seal. Stand the flower upright and center the coil on the batting and curve the bags over the coil. Fold the batting up the sides to the base of the stem; secure using bind wire. **7.** *Scrunch Pleat* leaves, secure at batting joint using bind wire. **8.** Center the bulb on the crepe circle and gather around the bulb; secure with bind wire. Spread the paste glue up the centerline of a 14" (35.5cm) strip of sangria crepe, center under the bulb, wrap up the sides using the ends to cover the bind wire. Trim excess using a deckle edger. Repeat with the second strip perpendicular to the first. Ruffle all edges and smear purple glitter glue on the bulb. Bend 8 lengths of bind wire in half, tape the bend, and glue to the bottom of the bulb. Glue the rust crepe circle over the joint.

59 / STARBURST WREATH

MATERIALS
- Single-ply crepe or tissue in star print
- Card stock in gold
- Thin gold tinsel trim
- Floral tape in white
- White craft glue

SPECIALTY TOOLS
- Pinking shears
- Large and small star craft punch
- Hot glue gun

TEMPLATE #204

TRY THIS This wreath would look lovely in silver and white. Try making it from solid or printed papers in any color. To increase the wreath's size, attach the flowers to a painted or paper-covered standard Masonite wreath form for more stability.

CUT *Grain runs with height; all dimensions are given as H × W.* Trace a dinner plate or other similar round object onto gold card stock. Draw a second circle 2½" (6.5cm) outside the first circle and cut along both circles, using pinking shears, to make a wreath form. Cut fifteen to twenty-five 2½" (6.5cm) lengths of gold tinsel trim. Petal #204: Cut fifteen 4" × 12" (10cm × 30.5cm) strips from star pattern single-ply crepe, accordion-fold to fit template, and cut continuous petals. Punch 30 small and large stars from gold card stock using craft punches.

BUILD Secure all layers with floral tape. **1.** Fold the tinsel strip in half and secure the ends together to make a center. **2.** *Gather and Wrap* (p. 132) Petal #204 evenly around the tinsel center, pinch tightly, and secure. *Cup* (p. 134) the petals gently. **3.** Snip off the end of the floral tape, leaving ¼" (6mm) of tape as the base as shown. Repeat steps 1 and 2 to make 15 flowers using 2 strips of tinsel in the centers of a few flowers for variation. **4.** Attach the flowers evenly around the wreath with hot glue, holding them in place until the glue sets. Affix gold stars randomly on the petals with craft glue, holding each in place until the glue sets. Add a printed or hand-lettered banner by tucking it into the flowers and securing with glue. Attach a length of wire or decorative cording to the back for hanging.

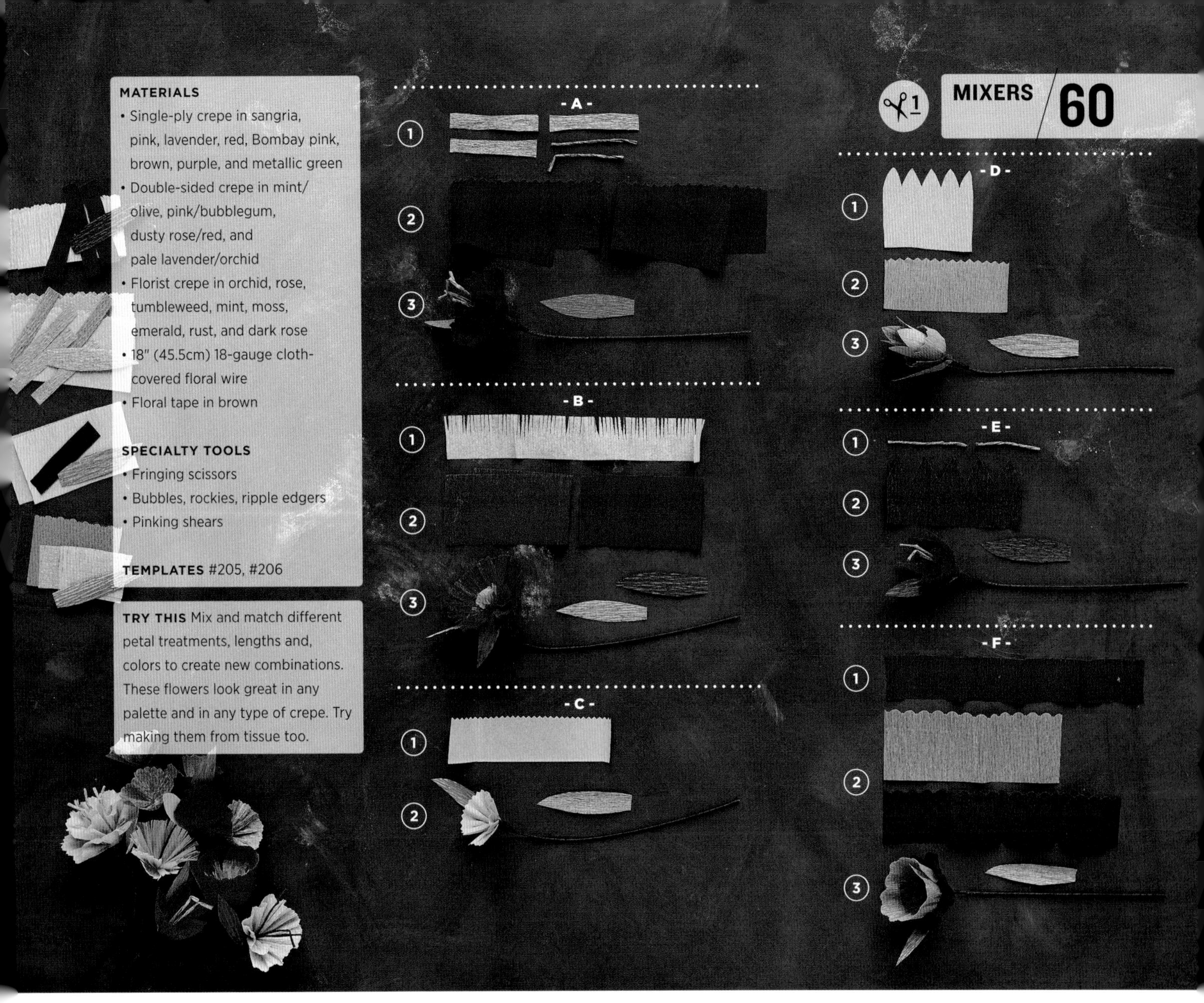

NOTE *Grain runs with height; all dimensions are given as H × W.* Cut fringe with fringing scissors, with the grain, ¾ of the way down. Cut wires to 9" (23cm). Secure all layers with floral tape. Leaf #205: Cut 1 or 2 from green crepe as desired and attach at base of flower while finishing stem.

A 1. Cut five 3" × ½" (7.5cm × 13mm) strips from orchid florist crepe. Tightly roll strip widthwise twisting into a thin cord. Fold top ½" (13mm) at right angle. Make 5 total, attach to wire tip to create center. **2.** Cut two 2½" × 10" (6.5cm × 25.5cm) strips from sangria single-ply crepe. Trim 1 long side each using rockies edger. **3.** *Gather and Wrap* (p. 132) each strip around center.

B 1. Cut a 1½" × 10" (4cm × 25.5cm) strip from pink single-ply crepe and fringe. *Gather and Wrap* around wire tip to create center. **2.** Cut a 2½" × 9" (6.5cm × 23cm) strip each from Bombay pink and red single-ply crepe, fringe each strip ½" (13mm) down on one long side. **3.** *Gather and Wrap* each around center.

C 1. Cut a 1¾" × 6" (4.5cm × 15cm) strip from pink/bubblegum double-sided crepe. Trim 1 long edge using rockies edger. **2.** *Gather and Wrap* strip to wire tip, overlap edge ¼" (6mm) and fan out.

D 1. Petal #206: Cut 1 from pale lavender/orchid double-sided crepe. *Gather and Wrap* around wire tip to create center. *Finesse* (p. 135) into bell shape. **2.** Cut a 1½" × 3½" (4cm × 9cm) strip from pale lavender/orchid double-sided crepe. Trim 1 long edge with pinking shears. **3.** *Gather and Wrap* around center and *Finesse*.

E 1. Repeat step A1 with rose florist crepe, make 2 total. **2.** Cut a 2½" × 5" (6.5cm × 12.5cm) strip from rust florist crepe. Accordion-fold 5 times, trim corners ¾" (2cm) from top to create point. **3.** *Gather and Wrap* around center. *Finesse* into bell shape.

F 1. Repeat step B1 with sangria single-ply crepe. **2.** Cut a 2½" × 7" (6.5cm × 18cm) strip from orchid florist crepe. Trim 1 long edge using seagull edger. *Gather and Wrap* around center. **3.** Repeat step 2 with a 2" × 10" (5cm × 25.5cm) purple single-ply crepe strip.

61 / STARGAZER LILIES

✂3

MATERIALS

- Single-ply crepe in metallic silver, gray, and navy blue
- Double-sided crepe in white
- Florist crepe in black
- Tissue in silver star-printed white
- 18" (45.5cm) 18-gauge paper-covered floral wire
- Floral tape in white and black
- Glue stick
- White ink stamp pad

SPECIALTY TOOLS

- Star rubber stamp

TEMPLATES #150, #151, #207

EVEN EASIER Skip gluing the tissue to the crepe and omit the bud. Craft these tall flowers in solid colors and cluster in a vase for holidays, springtime, or a wedding.

ADD COLOR Cut 1 piece of white double-side crepe 2 folds wide and 1 piece of star-printed tissue sized to match the crepe. Apply the glue stick to 1 side of the crepe, working in 3" (7.5cm) sections. Lay tissue, right side up, over the crepe. Starting at one side, smooth the tissue onto the crepe in one direction. Repeat the process to make 2 pieces. Weight the sheets to keep them flat while drying.

CUT *Grain runs with height; all dimensions are given as H × W.* Cut seven 3" × ½" (7.5cm × 13mm) strips from metallic silver single-ply crepe. Cut a 4" × 1¼" (10cm × 3cm) strip from gray single-ply crepe. Petal #150 and #151: Cut 3 each from star tissue/crepe. Cut 4 pieces from star tissue crepe using the top section (7.5cm) of Petal #151. Leaf #207: Cut 40–50 from metallic silver single-ply crepe. Cut a 12" (30.5cm) length of wire.

BUILD Secure all layers with floral tape. **1.** Tightly roll the metallic silver single-ply strip widthwise, twisting it into a thin cord. Fold the top ½" (13mm) at a right angle as shown. Repeat step 1 to make 7 stamen. **2.** Fold the gray crepe into thirds, with the grain, then round off one end. Unfold the scalloped strip and cut ½" (13mm) down each notch. Roll it tightly into a coil and fold the scalloped tips down as shown. **3.** Secure 5 silver stamen around 1 gray stamen to a full-length wire. **4.** *Single Pleat* (p. 128) Petals #150 with tissue side up. Gently curl the petals with your fingers and secure evenly around the center with the star pattern facing in. **5.** Repeat step 4 with Petals #151 and attach at opposite points from Petals #150. Gently curl all petals outward with your fingers. **6.** Secure 2 silver stamen to the cut wire. **7.** *Single Pleat* the Petal #151 tops with the tissue side up, secure to the stem with the star pattern facing out, and curl them inward to form a bud. **8.** Cover the top 10" (25.5cm) of both stems with Leaves #207, while finishing stems. *Join Stems* (p. 132) 4" (10cm) from the bottom of the longer stem. Add leaves to cover joint while finishing stems. Make the flower taller using *Join Stems* with an additional full-length wire overlapping 3" (7.5cm).

PROJECT NOTE Make the black flower: We used a star rubber stamp to stamp petals with white ink on stretched black florist crepe. Three Petals #151 were cut from black sparkly tulle and layered with the crepe petals. Leaves were cut from navy single-ply crepe and stem was finished with black tape.

DELFT & FLOW BLUE 62

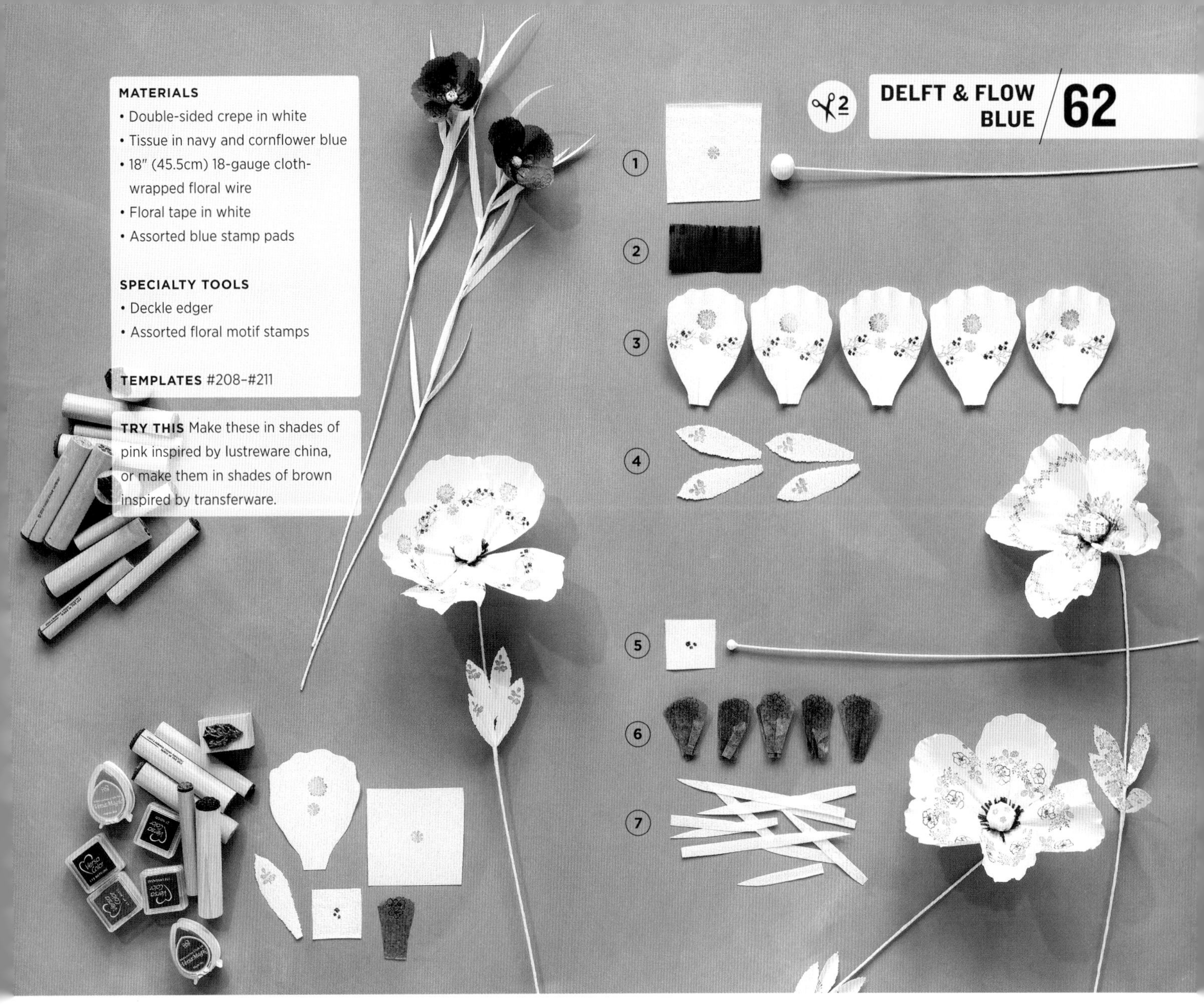

MATERIALS

- Double-sided crepe in white
- Tissue in navy and cornflower blue
- 18" (45.5cm) 18-gauge cloth-wrapped floral wire
- Floral tape in white
- Assorted blue stamp pads

SPECIALTY TOOLS

- Deckle edger
- Assorted floral motif stamps

TEMPLATES #208–#211

TRY THIS Make these in shades of pink inspired by lustreware china, or make them in shades of brown inspired by transferware.

CUT *Grain runs with height; all dimensions are given as H × W.* Cut a 3" (7.5cm) square from white double-sided crepe. Cut a 1½" × 5" (4cm × 12.5cm) strip from navy-blue tissue. Fold it in half lengthwise and finely *Hand Cut Fringe* (p. 127) ¾ of the way down. Petal #208: Cut 5 from white double-sided crepe. Leaf #209: Cut 4 from white double-sided crepe using a deckle edger. Cut a 1¾" (4.5cm) square from white double-sided crepe. Petal #210: Cut 10 from cornflower blue tissue and round the tops with a deckle edger. Leaf #211: Cut 8–10 assorted lengths from white double-sided crepe, 1"–3" (2.5cm–7.5cm) longer and shorter than the template.

ADD COLOR Ink all stamps generously. Let the stamped papers dry thoroughly. Stamp 1 pattern in the center of both the 3" (7.5cm) and the 1¾" (4.5cm) crepe square. Work with Petal #208, stamping 1 or several designs in various colors. Keep the pattern and layout consistent on each petal. Repeat with Leaf #209 and Petal #210 creating different patterns.

BUILD Secure all layers with floral tape. **1.** Make a *Spun-Cotton Center* (p. 130) with the larger stamped crepe square, centering the stamped pattern over the top of the cotton center. **2.** *Gather and Wrap* (p. 132) the tissue fringe around the center. Trim fringe slightly to tailor. **3.** *Flute* (p. 134) the top edges of the stamped Petals #208. *Box Pleat* (p. 128) and secure evenly around the center. **4.** *Scrunch Pleat* (p. 128) Leaves #209 and attach them in pairs halfway down the stem, while finishing the stem with tape. **5.** Repeat step 1 with the smaller crepe square. **6.** Layer Petals #210 on top of one another offsetting slightly; make 5 pairs as shown. *Single Pleat* (p. 128) and secure evenly around the center. **7.** *Scrunch Pleat* Leaves #211, and attach them randomly as you finish the stem.

63 / NOM DE BLOOM

✂3

MATERIALS

- Single-ply crepe in white
- 18" (45.5cm) 18-gauge paper-covered floral wire
- 18" (45.5cm) 20-gauge cloth-wrapped floral wire
- Floral tape in white
- White craft glue
- Glittered vintage pips
- Glitter paint in aquamarine and copper
- Glitter glue in gold
- Glitter in light and medium aqua, gold, copper, and brown
- 1⅞" (4.7cm) spun-cotton mushroom cap
- Prewired silver pressed-paper leaves
- Glitter alphabet stickers

TEMPLATES #212–#214

TRY THIS Make this flower using diluted paint instead of glitter.

CUT *Grain runs with height; all dimensions are given as H × W.* Cut a 6" (15cm) square from white crepe. Petal #212: Cut 16 from white crepe. Petal #213: Cut 20 from the white crepe. Petal #214: Cut 26 from white crepe.

ADD COLOR After glittering, set pieces aside to dry. With 8 Petals #212, draw thin centerlines on each one using a tube of gold glitter glue, as shown. With the remaining 8 petals, smear gold glitter glue ¼"–½" (6mm–13mm) along the top edges with a finger. Using a brush, paint the top edges of all 20 Petals #213 with copper glitter paint. Repeat with all 26 Petals #214 with aquamarine glitter paint. Coat the top of the pressed leaf with glue and fully cover it with *Glitter* (p. 137). Cover the large leaves: 7 with light-aqua glitter and 8 with dark-aqua glitter. Cover the small leaves: 3 with gold glitter, 7 with copper glitter, and 6 with brown glitter, or as desired.

BUILD Secure all layers with floral tape. **1.** Glue the mushroom cap center to the end of a full-length 18-gauge wire; let dry. Cover with the white single-ply crepe square and secure. Attach the monogram stickers to finish the center. **2.** Layer the centerline Petals #212 over the glitter-edged Petals #212, offset slightly, as shown. *Scrunch Pleat* (p. 128) and *Twist* (p. 128) attach 8 pairs, securing them evenly around the center. **3.** Layer the painted Petals #213 in pairs, offset them slightly, and *Twist* to make 10 pairs. Leave ½" (13mm) of space on the stem between layers. Secure petals evenly around the center. **4.** Repeat step 3 with Petals #214. **5.** Group 2 or 3 light and medium aqua leaves and 1 glittered pip and *Join Stems* (p. 132) to a 20-gauge wire. Coat the top 4" (10cm) of the wire in glue and sprinkle with aqua glitter. Repeat the process to make leaf branches with the remaining leaves, grouping like colors together, and *Glittering* the stems with matching glitter. Attach the leaf branches by *Joining Stems* 2"–4" (5cm–10cm) from the flower base to form a ring around the flower. Trim stems as needed. Secure the stem with several layers of tape and trim as desired.

CANDY CENTER 64

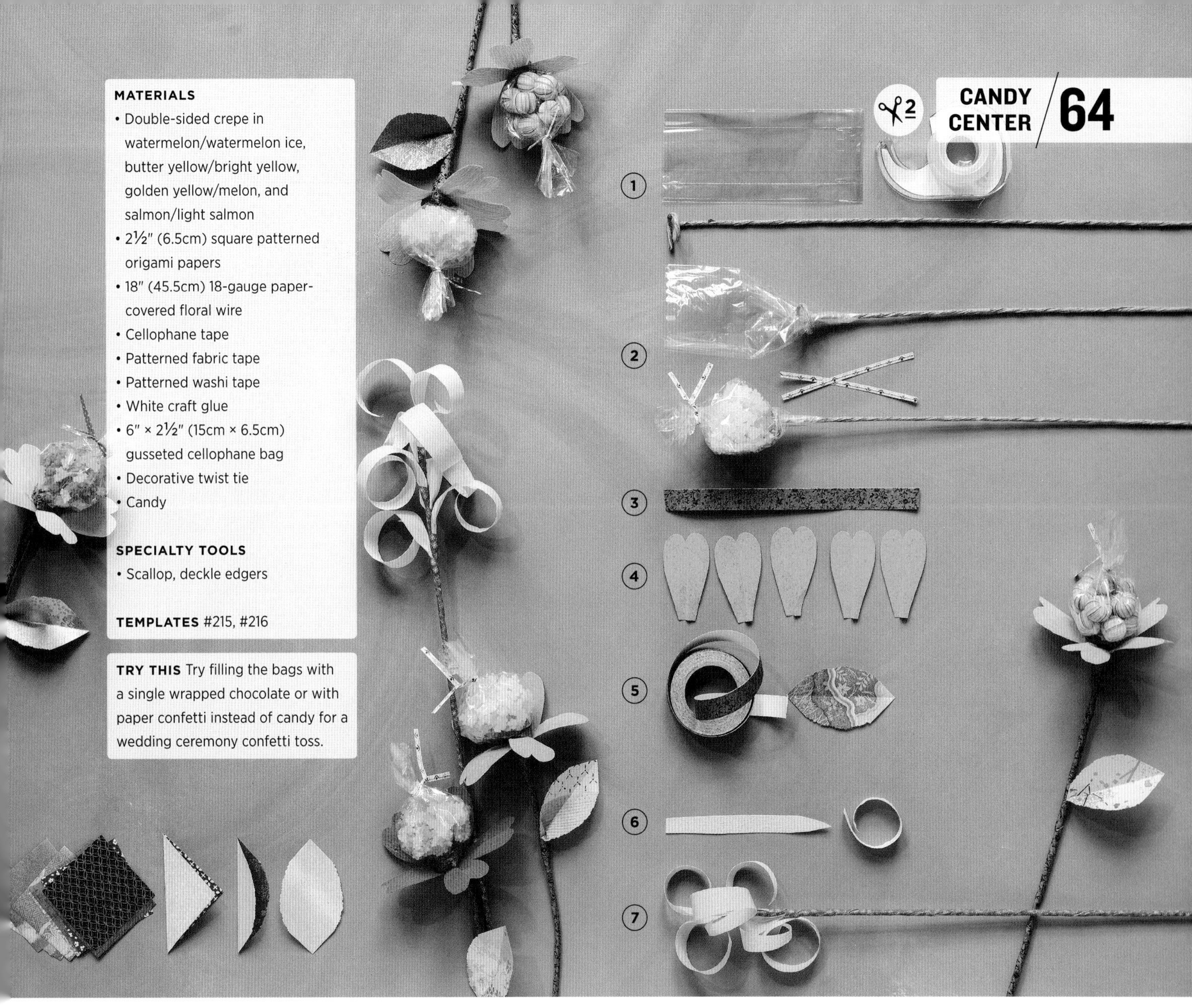

MATERIALS

- Double-sided crepe in watermelon/watermelon ice, butter yellow/bright yellow, golden yellow/melon, and salmon/light salmon
- 2½" (6.5cm) square patterned origami papers
- 18" (45.5cm) 18-gauge paper-covered floral wire
- Cellophane tape
- Patterned fabric tape
- Patterned washi tape
- White craft glue
- 6" × 2½" (15cm × 6.5cm) gusseted cellophane bag
- Decorative twist tie
- Candy

SPECIALTY TOOLS

- Scallop, deckle edgers

TEMPLATES #215, #216

TRY THIS Try filling the bags with a single wrapped chocolate or with paper confetti instead of candy for a wedding ceremony confetti toss.

CUT Trim top of bag with scalloped shears. Petal #215: Cut 5 from watermelon double-sided crepe. Fold origami paper diagonally and round off both corners opposite the fold with a deckle edger to create a leaf, as shown. Leaf #216: Cut 6–8 from yellow crepe. Create assorted lengths by cutting 1"–2" (2.5cm–5cm) from the bottom of half of the full-sized leaves.

BUILD 1. Create an open circle with a 2½" (6.5cm) section at the end of a stem wire. Bend into a 1" (2.5cm) circle and bend again at a right angle to the stem as shown. Scrunch bottom of cellophane bag and thread 1" (2.5cm) of bag through circle. Pinch bag tightly around stem below circle and secure with several layers of cellophane tape. **2.** Open bag and fill with a small amount of candy. Twist top of bag and secure with a decorative twist tie. Tape bottom ½" (13mm) of bag to the wire circle, down onto stem, using cellophane tape. **3.** Cover visible wire with a 5"–8" (12.5cm–20.5cm) length of fabric tape at top of stem. **4.** *Single Pleat* (p. 128) Petals #215 and attach below fabric tape-covered wire with more fabric tape. **5.** Continue finishing stem with fabric tape, attach *Single Pleated* origami leaf 3"–5" (7.5cm–12.5cm) from flower base. Secure fabric tape with glue at bottom of wire. **6.** *Scissor Curl* (p. 135) all Leaves #216 into coils. **7.** *Scrunch Pleat* (p. 128) leaves and attach randomly, using washi tape, 4"–7" (10cm–18cm) from the top of a full-length wire to create a cluster of coiled leaves. Finish the stem with washi tape and secure end with glue.

PROJECT NOTE Use a small amount of lightweight candy in the candy centers. Avoid overfilling the bags or the centers may pull the flower down. Choose crepe and origami colors to complement the sweets. We used additional colors of double-sided crepe to make our flowers.

MATERIALS

- Single-ply crepe in pale pink, light blue, navy blue, ice blue, baby blue, red, black, light gray, dark gray, brown, hot pink, and teal
- Double-sided crepe in yellow/bright yellow, red/brick red, and white
- Florist crepe in white, coral, and gold
- 3½" (9cm) paper ribbon in white, red, and gold
- 18" (45.5cm) 18-gauge paper-covered floral wire
- Floral tape in white
- White craft glue
- 2 cotton balls

SPECIALTY TOOLS

- Fringing scissors
- Deckle edger

TEMPLATES #217–#224

TRY THIS Craft these on longer stems in any palette and group them together in an arrangement. Try making the petals from thicker double-sided or florist crepe for a crisper look and feel.

CUT *Grain runs with height; all dimensions are given as H × W.* Cut a 9" (23cm) length of stem wire. Cut a 4" (10cm) square of light-blue single-ply crepe. Cut a 2½" × 5" (6.5cm × 12.5cm) strip of white florist crepe and fringe it, with the grain, using fringing scissors, ¾ of the way down. Trim the fringed edge with a deckle edger. Cut two 4" (10cm) lengths of white paper ribbon. Petals #217, #218, #219, #220, and #221: Cut 2 each from light-pink single-ply crepe. Leaves #222, #223, and #224: Cut 1 each from navy single-ply crepe using a deckle edger. Cut three ½" × 10" (13mm × 25.5cm) strips from light blue single-ply crepe.

BUILD Secure all layers with floral tape. **1.** Fold two ¼" (6mm) overlapping pleats, with the grain, across the middle of the 4" (10cm) light blue single-ply square, as shown. Make an oval-shaped *Cotton Ball Center* (p. 130) with 2 cotton balls. Carefully fold the pleated sides down first when making the center in order to keep the pleats intact. **2.** *Gather and Wrap* (p. 132) the white florist crepe fringe around the center. **3.** Fold the paper ribbon in half, against the grain, to create 2 loops. *Scrunch Pleat* (p. 128) ribbon petals, and attach them on either side of the oval center. **4.** *Cup* (p. 134) and then *Flute* (p. 134) the center tip of each petal. *Scrunch Pleat* the petals and attach them evenly around the base in the order as shown. **5.** Attach the leaves randomly while finishing the stem. **6.** *Cover Stem* (p. 133) with light blue crepe strips.

PROJECT NOTE We made additional flowers varying the order of the petals in step number 4 in the following color combinations: The red flower is made from red, black, and ice blue single-ply crepe with white florist crepe and paper ribbon. The gray flower is made from light gray and dark gray single-ply crepe, yellow double-sided crepe, and white florist crepe and paper ribbon. The blue flower is made from baby blue, brown, and navy single-ply crepe with white florist crepe and paper ribbon. The hot pink flower is made from hot pink and black single-ply crepe, red/brick red double-sided crepe, and coral florist crepe and red paper ribbon. The teal flower is made from teal, dark gray, and navy single-ply crepe with white florist crepe and paper ribbon. The black flower is made from black and dark gray single-ply crepe, white double-sided crepe, and gold florist crepe and paper ribbon.

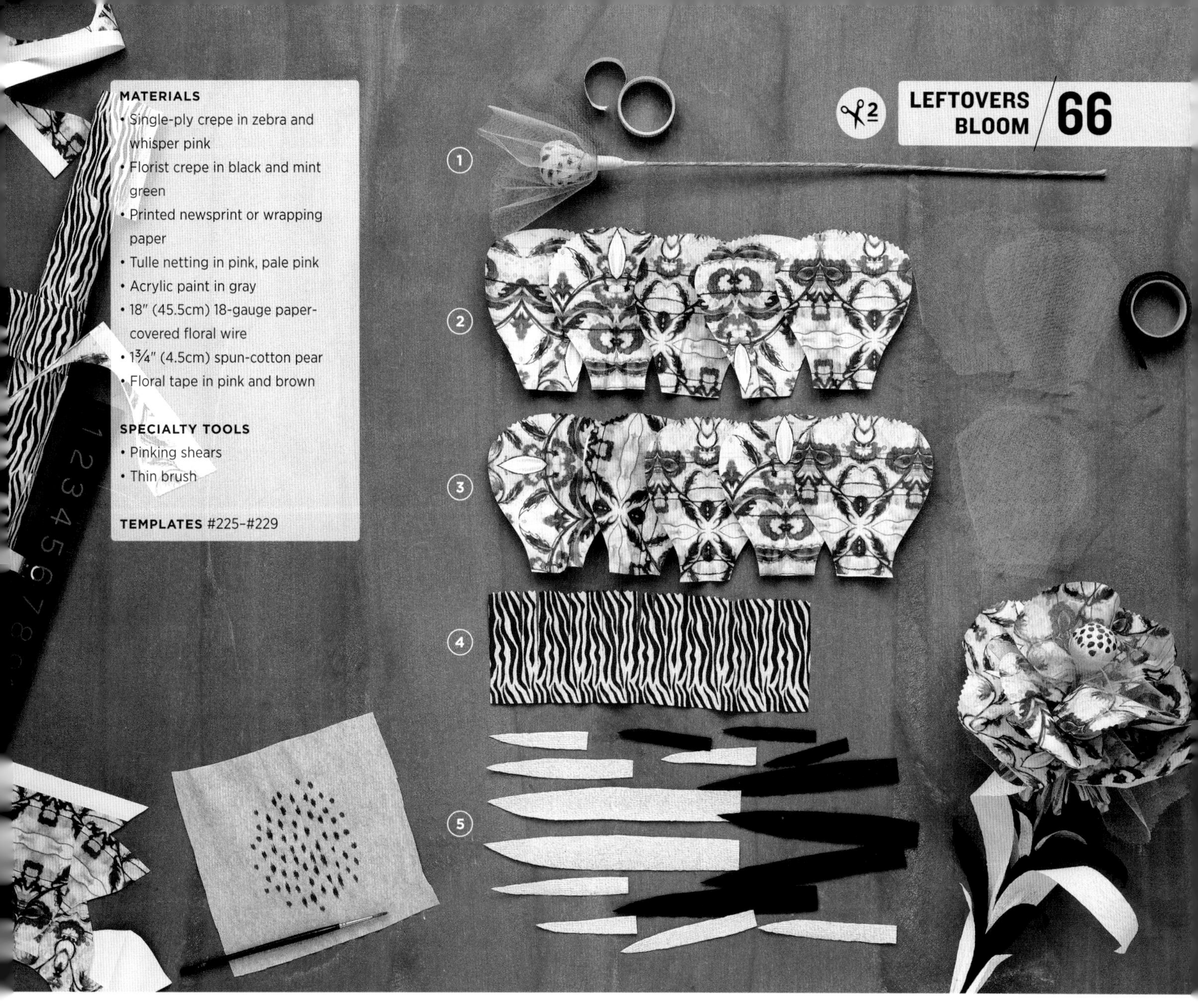

LEFTOVERS BLOOM 66

MATERIALS
- Single-ply crepe in zebra and whisper pink
- Florist crepe in black and mint green
- Printed newsprint or wrapping paper
- Tulle netting in pink, pale pink
- Acrylic paint in gray
- 18" (45.5cm) 18-gauge paper-covered floral wire
- 1¾" (4.5cm) spun-cotton pear
- Floral tape in pink and brown

SPECIALTY TOOLS
- Pinking shears
- Thin brush

TEMPLATES #225–#229

CUT *Grain runs with height; all dimensions are given as H × W.* Cut a 7" (18cm) square of whisper pink single-ply crepe. Petal #225: Cut 6 each from pink and light-pink tulle. Cut 10 from the printed newsprint wrapping paper. Randomly snip the top edges with pinking shears. Cut a 4" × 11" (10cm × 28cm) strip from zebra single-ply crepe. Using pinking shears, cut one long edge. *Hand Cut Fringe* (p. 127) this strip, with the grain, ¼"–½" (6mm–13mm) wide ¾ of the way down from the pinked edge. Leaf #226: Cut 3 from mint green and 3 from black florist crepe. Leaf #227: Cut 4 from mint green florist crepe. Leaf #228: Cut 4 from black florist crepe. Leaf #229: Cut 2 from mint green florist crepe.

ADD COLOR *Dilute* (p. 136) the gray acrylic paint. Using a thin brush, paint small dots randomly in the center of the whisper pink single-ply square, as shown.

BUILD Secure all layers with floral tape. **1.** Make a *Spun-Cotton Center* (p. 130) with a pear shape and dotted square of whisper pink single-ply crepe paper; finish with pink tape. *Gather and Wrap* (p. 132) 4 Petals #225 evenly around the center, alternating pink and light pink tulle and securing them with pink tape. **2.** *Box Pleat* (p. 128) 5 wrapping paper Petals #225 and attach them evenly around the center; secure with brown tape. *Gather and Wrap* (p. 132) 4 tulle Petals #225 evenly around the center, alternating pink and light pink tulle, secure with brown tape. **3.** Leave ¾" (2cm) of space on the stem and repeat step 2 with the 9 remaining Petals #225. **4.** *Gather and Wrap* the strip of zebra single-ply crepe around the center and secure with brown tape. **5.** *Scrunch Pleat* (p. 128) all the leaves. Finish stem with brown tape while attaching all leaves, mixing 4 sizes and both colors, to cover stem.

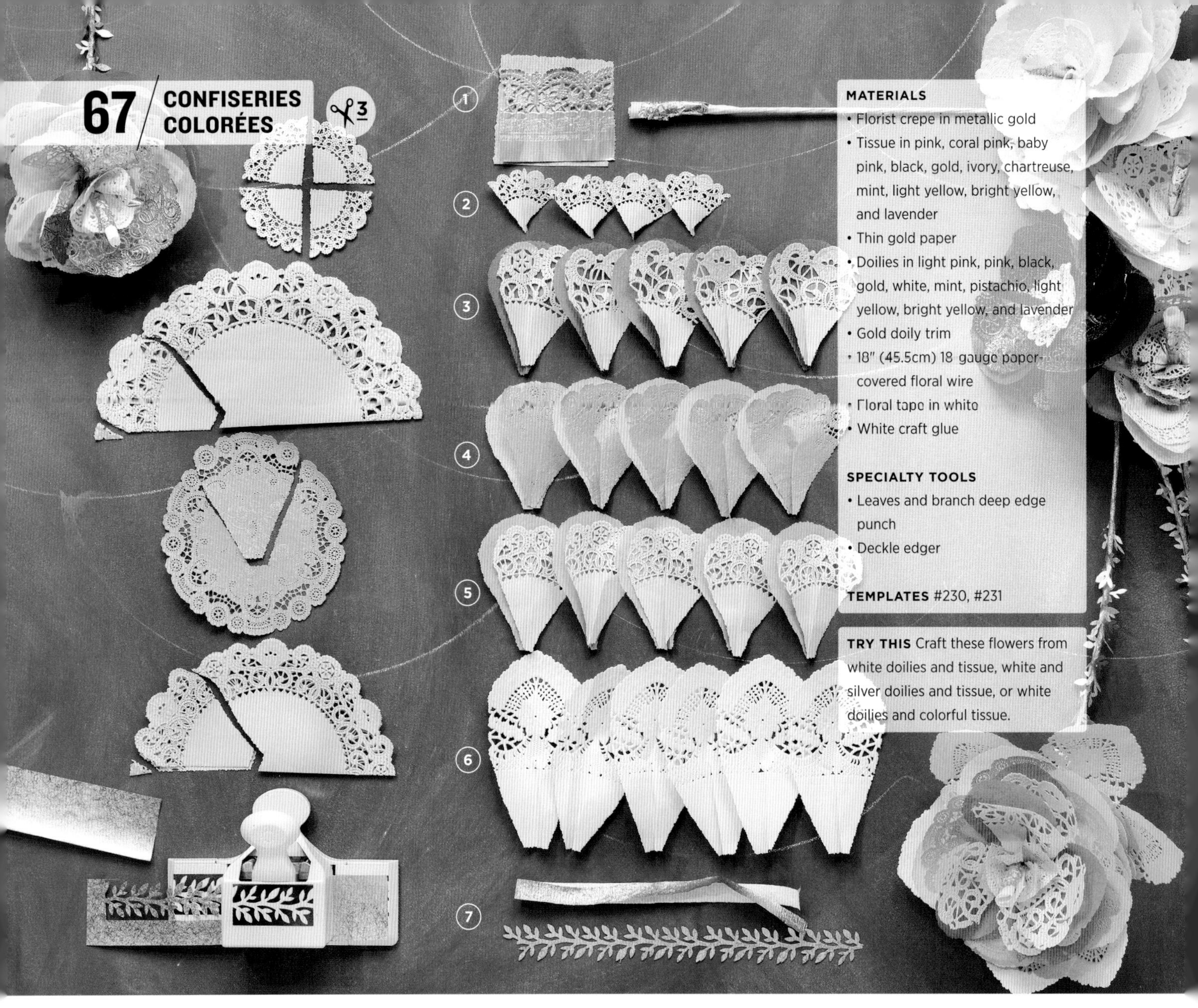

67 CONFISERIES COLORÉES

3

MATERIALS

- Florist crepe in metallic gold
- Tissue in pink, coral pink, baby pink, black, gold, ivory, chartreuse, mint, light yellow, bright yellow, and lavender
- Thin gold paper
- Doilies in light pink, pink, black, gold, white, mint, pistachio, light yellow, bright yellow, and lavender
- Gold doily trim
- 18" (45.5cm) 18 gauge paper-covered floral wire
- Floral tape in white
- White craft glue

SPECIALTY TOOLS

- Leaves and branch deep edge punch
- Deckle edger

TEMPLATES #230, #231

TRY THIS Craft these flowers from white doilies and tissue, white and silver doilies and tissue, or white doilies and colorful tissue.

CUT *Grain runs with height; all dimensions are given as H × W.* Cut a 2¾" × 3½" (7cm × 9cm) strip from gold doily trim using a deckle edger. Cut a 3½" (9cm) square from pale pink tissue using a deckle edger. Cut a 4" (10cm) pink doily into quarters. Petal #230: Using a deckle edger, cut 5 each from 3 different pink doilies and 3 different colored pink tissue papers. Align the top of the template with the top of the doily curves, as shown. Petal #231: Cut 6 from a large pink doily. Cut a ½" × 18" (13mm × 45.5cm) strip of metallic florist crepe. Stretch this strip completely. Using a continuous deep edge punch, punch two 12" (30.5cm) lengths from thin gold paper.

BUILD Secure all layers with floral tape. **1.** Layer the gold doily trim piece on top of the light pink tissue square as shown. Flip them over and position a wire at 1 edge, 1" (2.5cm) from the bottom, and wrap it tightly around the wire at first and then wrap it looser as you finish; secure it to make a center as shown. **2.** *Single Pleat* (p. 128) the smallest petals and attach them evenly around the center. **3.** Pair 1 set of doily Petals #230 with 1 set of tissue petals, offset slightly, as shown. *Single Pleat* them together and attach them evenly around the center. Leave ¼"–½" (6mm–13mm) of space on the stem between the petal layers. **4 and 5.** Repeat step 3 with a different pairing of doily and tissue. **6.** *Single Pleat* Petals #231 and attach them evenly around the stem. Finish stem. **7.** *Cover Stem* (p. 133) with a length of the stretched gold crepe. Attach the punched garland to the base of the flower with glue and hold it in place until it sets. Gently wrap down the stem, dot it with glue every 2" (5cm), and secure the end with glue.

PROJECT NOTE We created a range of pastel flowers, all with rolled gold doily trim centers, in the following additional variations. The black bloom is made from black doilies and tissue. The gold flower is made from layers of white and gold doilies with gold and ivory tissue. The green flower is made from layers of chartreuse and mint tissue and mint and pistachio doilies. The yellow flower is a mix of light and bright yellow doilies and yellow tissue. Lastly, the purple bloom is a mix of lavender doilies and tissue.

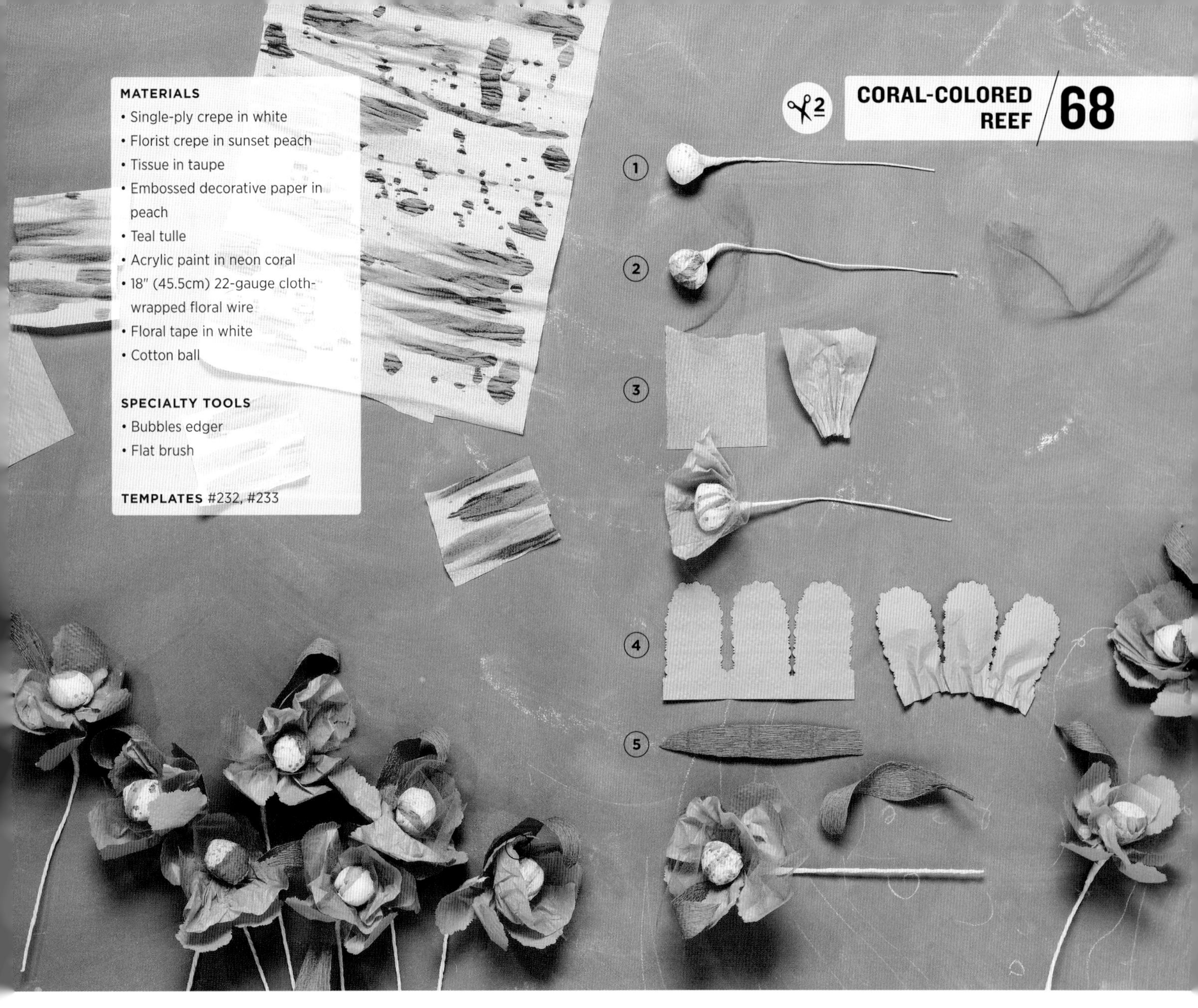

ADD COLOR *Dilute* (p. 136) the neon coral acrylic paint. Cut 2 folds of white single-ply crepe. With a wide, flat brush, paint loose stripes, splatters, and dots. Set aside to dry.

CUT *Grain runs with height; all dimensions are given as H × W.* Cut a 3" (7.5cm) square from the painted white single-ply crepe. Cut a 2" × 7" (5cm × 18cm) strip from the teal tulle. Cut a 4" × 3" (10cm × 7.5cm) strip from the taupe tissue and tear off the top edge to make a ripped edge. Petal #232: Cut two 4" × 6" (10cm × 15cm) strips from the peach embossed paper, accordion-fold to fit template, and cut a continuous petal with a bubbles edger. Leaf #233: Cut 1 from sunset peach florist crepe. Cut a 9" (23cm) length of 22-gauge wire.

BUILD Secure all layers with floral tape. **1.** Make a *Cotton Ball Center* (p. 130) with the painted white single-ply crepe square. **2.** Thread the tulle onto the stem by poking the stem through the tulle piece; pull it up around the center. **3.** *Scrunch Pleat* (p. 128) the strip of taupe tissue, attach it to the center, and secure. **4.** *Scrunch Pleat* 1 Petal #232 and *Gather and Wrap* (p. 132) it halfway around the center. Repeat with the second peach continuous-petal strip. **5.** Using a pencil, *Stick Curl* (p. 135) the top 2" (5cm) of Leaf #233, *Cup* (p. 134) the center slightly, and *Scrunch Pleat* the base. Finish stem while attaching the leaf at the base of the flower.

MATERIALS

- Single-ply crepe in copper
- Double-sided crepe in white
- Tissue in taupe, caramel, bronze, and burnished gold
- Decorative paper in zebra print
- Acrylic paint in black
- 18" (45.5cm) 18-gauge paper-covered floral wire
- 18" (45.5cm) 20-gauge cloth-wrapped floral wire
- 1½" (4cm) spun-cotton apple
- Floral tape in black

SPECIALTY TOOLS

- Fringing scissors
- Bubbles, sunflower edgers
- Thin brush

TEMPLATE #234

ADD COLOR *Dilute* (p. 136) the black acrylic paint. Cut 2 folds from white double-sided crepe. Paint ½" (13mm) triangles as shown.

CUT *Grain runs with height; all dimensions are given as H × W.* Cut all the fringe, with the grain, using fringing scissors. Cut a 6" (15cm) square from copper single-ply crepe. Cut a 2½" × 7½" (6.5cm × 19cm) strip from bronze tissue and fringe ¾ of the way down. Petal #234: Cut 3 from zebra paper as shown, and fringe the edge ¼" (6mm). Cut three 4" × 5" (10cm × 12.5cm) pieces from copper single-ply crepe. Trim 1 long edge and 2 short edges of all strips with bubbles edger. Cut three 5" × 10" (12.5cm × 25.5cm) strips from caramel tissue. Trim one long edge of each strip with sunflower edger. Cut three 5½" × 12" (14cm × 30.5cm) strips from taupe tissue. Trim one long edge of each strip with sunflower edger. Cut three 6½" × 12" (16.5cm × 30.5cm) strips from burnished gold tissue. Trim one long edge of each strip with sunflower edger. Cut two 7½" × 15" (19cm × 38cm) strips from copper single-ply crepe. Trim 1 long edge and 2 short edges of all strips with bubbles edger and fringe ½" (13mm) down on trimmed edge. Make 2 additional 2" (5cm) deep cuts 5" (12.5cm) from both short edges on the fringe edge. Leaf #234: Cut 3 from painted white double-sided crepe.

BUILD Secure all layers with floral tape. **1.** Make a *Spun-Cotton Center* (p. 130) with an apple shape, a square of copper single-ply crepe, and 18-gauge wire. **2.** *Gather and Wrap* (p. 132) the fringed bronze tissue strip around the center and secure. **3.** *Box Pleat* (p. 128) 3 Petals #234, attach evenly around the center, and secure. **4.** *Scrunch Pleat* (p. 128) and *Gather and Wrap* 3 strips of copper single-ply crepe, attach evenly around the center, and secure. **5.** Leave ½" (13mm) of space on the stem and repeat step 4 with 3 strips of caramel tissue. **6.** Repeat step 5 with 3 strips of taupe tissue. **7.** Repeat step 5 with 3 strips of burnished-gold tissue. **8.** Repeat step 5 with 2 strips of copper crepe. Finish stem. **9.** Attach Leaf #234 to the tip of a 20-gauge wire, cut stem to desired length, and finish the stem.

PROJECT NOTE We made two additional leaf stems cut to 9" (23cm). A few smaller hand cut leaves were attached to the tips of 20-gauge wires. *Join Stems* (p. 132) of wired leaves to the main flower stem at desired points.

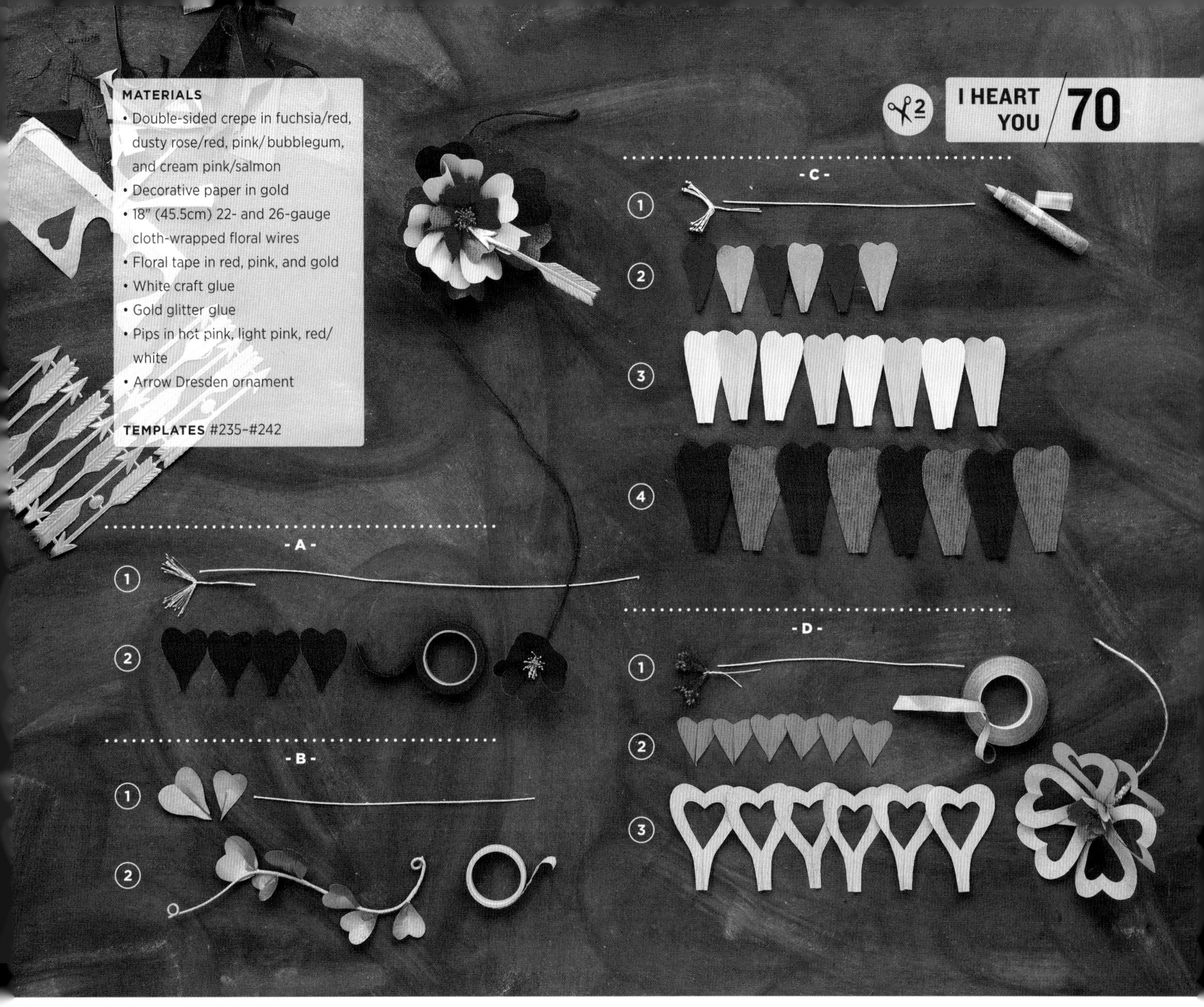

NOTE *Grain runs with height; all dimensions are given as H × W.* Secure all layers and finish stems with floral tape. Cut wires to desired lengths.

A 1. Make a *Pip Center* (p. 130) with a 4" (10cm) length of 26-gauge wire and 20 light pink pips. Secure to a 22-gauge stem wire with red tape. **2.** Petal #235: Cut 4 from fuchsia/red crepe, *Single Pleat* (p. 128) all the petals and attach them evenly around the center. Finish stem with red tape.

B 1. Leaf #236: Cut 2 from the gold paper. Leaf #237: Cut 4 from the gold paper. *Single Pleat* all of the leaves. Cut a 9" (23cm) length of 22-gauge wire. **2.** Begin covering the wire with pink tape and attach 1 Leaf #236 3" (7.5cm) from the end; continue to add Leaves #236 and #237 randomly while finishing the stem. Tightly curl the stem ends and curve the stem, as shown.

C 1. Make a *Pip Center* with a 4" (10cm) length of 26-gauge wire and 10 red and white pips. Secure to a 22-gauge stem wire with red tape. Using a tube, brush the tops of the pips with gold glitter glue and let them dry. **2.** Petal #238: Cut 6 from the dusty rose/red crepe paper. Turn half of them over and *Single Pleat* the petals. Alternating colors, attach them evenly around the center, and secure. **3.** Petal #239: Cut 8 from pink/bubblegum crepe. Turn half of them over and *Single Pleat* the petals. Alternate the colors, attach them evenly around the center, and secure. **4.** Petal #240: Cut 8 from fuchsia/red crepe. Turn half of them over and *Single Pleat* the petals. Alternate colors, attach them evenly around the center, and secure. Finish stem with red tape. Attach the Dresden arrow with glue as shown.

D 1. Make a *Pip Center* with a 4" (10cm) length of 26-gauge wire and 24 hot pink pips. Secure them to 22-gauge stem wire with gold tape. **2.** Petal #241 and #242: Cut 6 from cream pink/salmon crepe (the template yields 1 inner and 1 outer petal from a single cut step). *Single Pleat* the inner Petals #241 with the salmon side up and attach them evenly around the center. **3.** *Single Pleat* the outer Petals #242 with the cream-pink side up and attach them evenly around the center. Finish stem with gold tape.

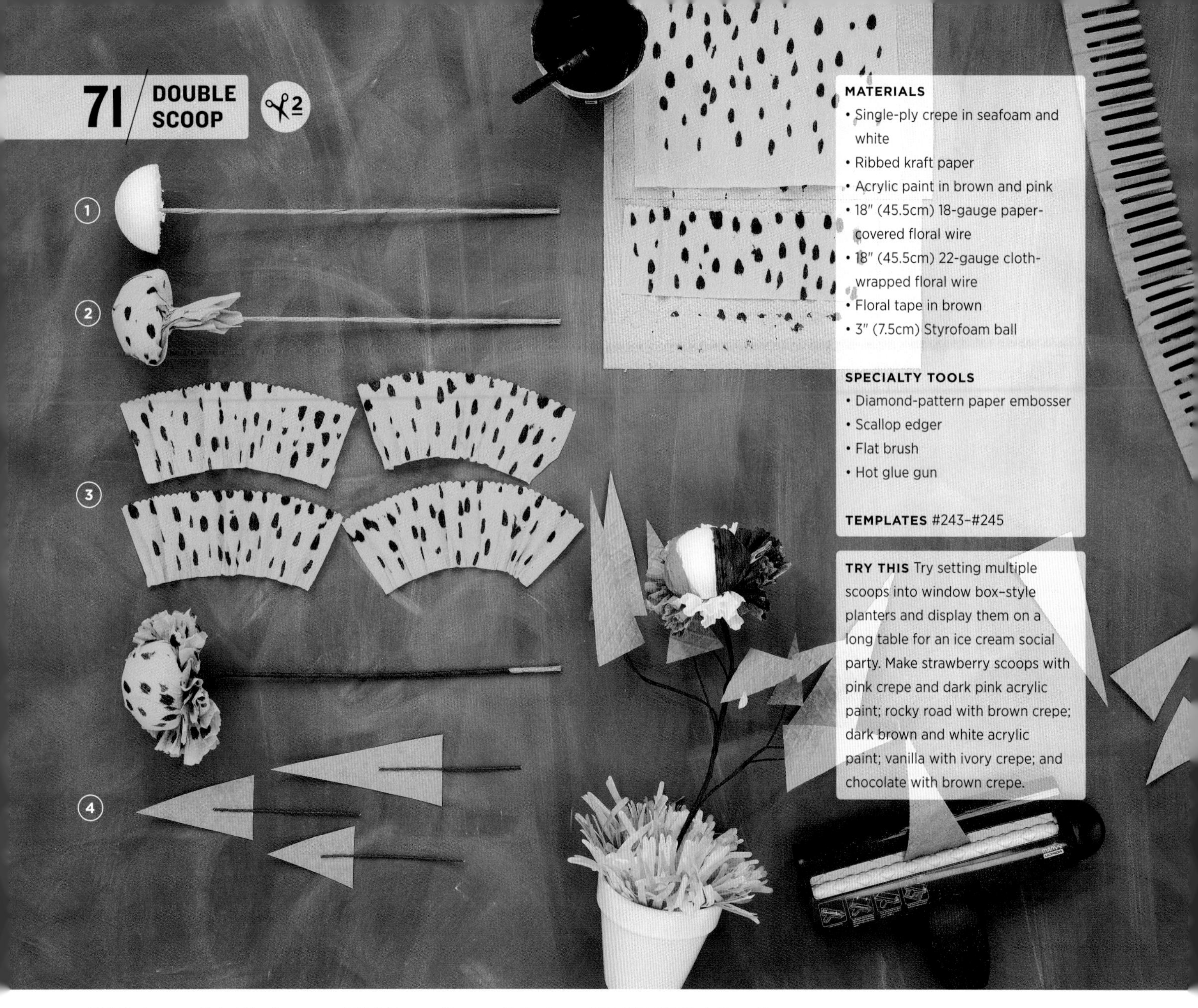

71 / DOUBLE SCOOP ✂2

MATERIALS

- Single-ply crepe in seafoam and white
- Ribbed kraft paper
- Acrylic paint in brown and pink
- 18" (45.5cm) 18-gauge paper-covered floral wire
- 18" (45.5cm) 22-gauge cloth-wrapped floral wire
- Floral tape in brown
- 3" (7.5cm) Styrofoam ball

SPECIALTY TOOLS

- Diamond-pattern paper embosser
- Scallop edger
- Flat brush
- Hot glue gun

TEMPLATES #243–#245

TRY THIS Try setting multiple scoops into window box–style planters and display them on a long table for an ice cream social party. Make strawberry scoops with pink crepe and dark pink acrylic paint; rocky road with brown crepe; dark brown and white acrylic paint; vanilla with ivory crepe; and chocolate with brown crepe.

CUT *Grain runs with height; all dimensions are given as H × W.* Cut a 9" (23cm) square from the seafoam single-ply crepe. Cut four 3" ×10" (7.5cm × 25.5cm) strips from the seafoam single-ply crepe and trim one long edge of each strip with a scallop edger. Cut the foam ball in half. Cut nine 5" (12.5cm) lengths of 22-gauge wire. Leaves #243, #244, #245: Cut 3 each from the ribbed kraft paper.

ADD COLOR *Dilute* (p. 136) the brown acrylic paint. Using a small, flat paintbrush, paint loose oval dots on the seafoam single-ply crepe square and strips. Set them aside to dry.

BUILD Secure all layers with floral tape. **1.** Poke the wire into the ball ¾" (2cm) and hot-glue it at the joint. **2.** Wrap the painted seafoam single-ply crepe square over half of the ball, twist at the base, and secure. **3.** *Scrunch Pleat* (p. 128) the 4 painted strips of seafoam single-ply crepe. *Gather and Wrap* (p. 132) 1 strip at a time in quarters evenly around the stem. Finish the stem. **4.** Cover the 22-gauge wires with tape. Pass the kraft paper through the embosser. *Wire One-Sided Leaves* (p. 133) and let them dry. *Join Stems* (p. 132) of the leaves at the desired attachment points to the ice cream stem.

PROJECT NOTE A Neapolitan scoop was made by painting wide pink-and-brown stripes on a 9" (23cm) square of white single-ply crepe to cover the center, surrounded by petals made from 4 strips of white single-ply crepe, 2 unpainted, 1 painted pink, and 1 painted brown. A rolled, embossed paper cone was made around the stem wire and secured with floral tape at the base of the stem and hot glued at the base of the flower head. The flowers were stuck into dry floral foam placed into ceramic glazed pots and covered with pink tissue grass mat sections adhered with hot glue.

CANDY STRIPES / 72

✂1

MATERIALS

- Double-sided crepe in white, golden yellow/melon, lavender/pink lilac, and dusty rose/red
- Decorative textured paper in white
- Acrylic paint in rose, white, pink, and yellow
- 18" (45.5cm) 20-gauge cloth-wrapped floral wire
- Floral tape in white
- White craft glue
- Butter and peach super-bulky cotton/wool yarn

SPECIALTY TOOLS

- Deckle edger
- Flat brush
- Double striping brush

TEMPLATES #246–#248

EVEN EASIER Skip the painting step and make these in any type of crepe with different color yarn centers. Try mixing different yarn colors and thicknesses within the same bloom.

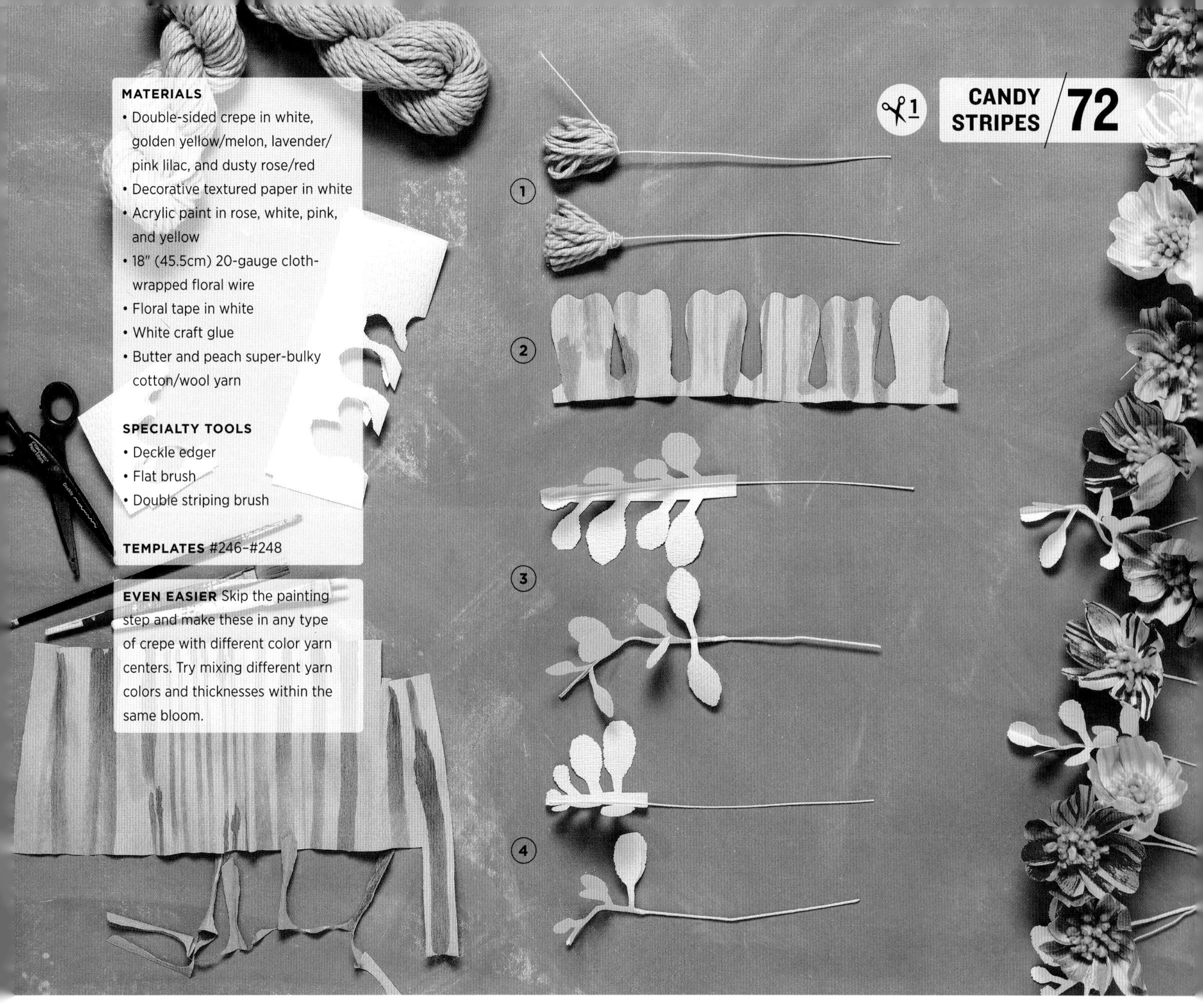

ADD COLOR *Dilute* (p. 136) the rose acrylic paint. Cut 4 folds from the golden-yellow/melon double-sided crepe. Using a double stripe and flat brushes, loosely paint wide and thin mixed strips with the grain as shown. Set aside to dry.

CUT *Grain runs with height; all dimensions are given as H × W.* Cut a 54" (137cm) length of butter yarn. Cut three 12" (30.5cm) wires. Petal #246: Cut a 4" × 15" (10cm × 38cm) strip from golden yellow/lemon double-sided crepe, accordion-fold to fit template, and cut a continuous petal. Leaves #247 and #248: Cut 1 each from the white textured decorative paper. Use a deckle edger to cut the leaves and a scissors to cut the stem area.

BUILD Secure all layers with floral tape. **1.** Wrap the entire length of yarn continuously around 3 fingers. Remove the yarn from your fingers and thread the first 3" (7.5cm) of a 22-gauge wire through the yarn circle; fold the wire over and twist it 1 or 2 times to secure. Bend the short arm of the wire up, wrapping it around the base of the yarn bunch to keep it from unraveling. Cut all the loops to make a yarn-fringe center. **2.** *Scrunch Pleat* (p. 128) Petal #246, *Gather and Wrap* (p. 132) it evenly around the center, and secure. Gently *Cup* (p. 134) the petals and *Flute* (p. 134) the center tips. Finish stem. **3.** Unfold Leaf #247. Draw a thin line of glue up the center crease area of the shape and lay a 22-gauge wire in the glue line. Add a bit more glue to the wire, then fold the leaf in half, pressing the stem and fold line to secure it. Leave the leaf areas unglued. Let them dry. Finish stem. **4.** Repeat step 3 with Leaf #248.

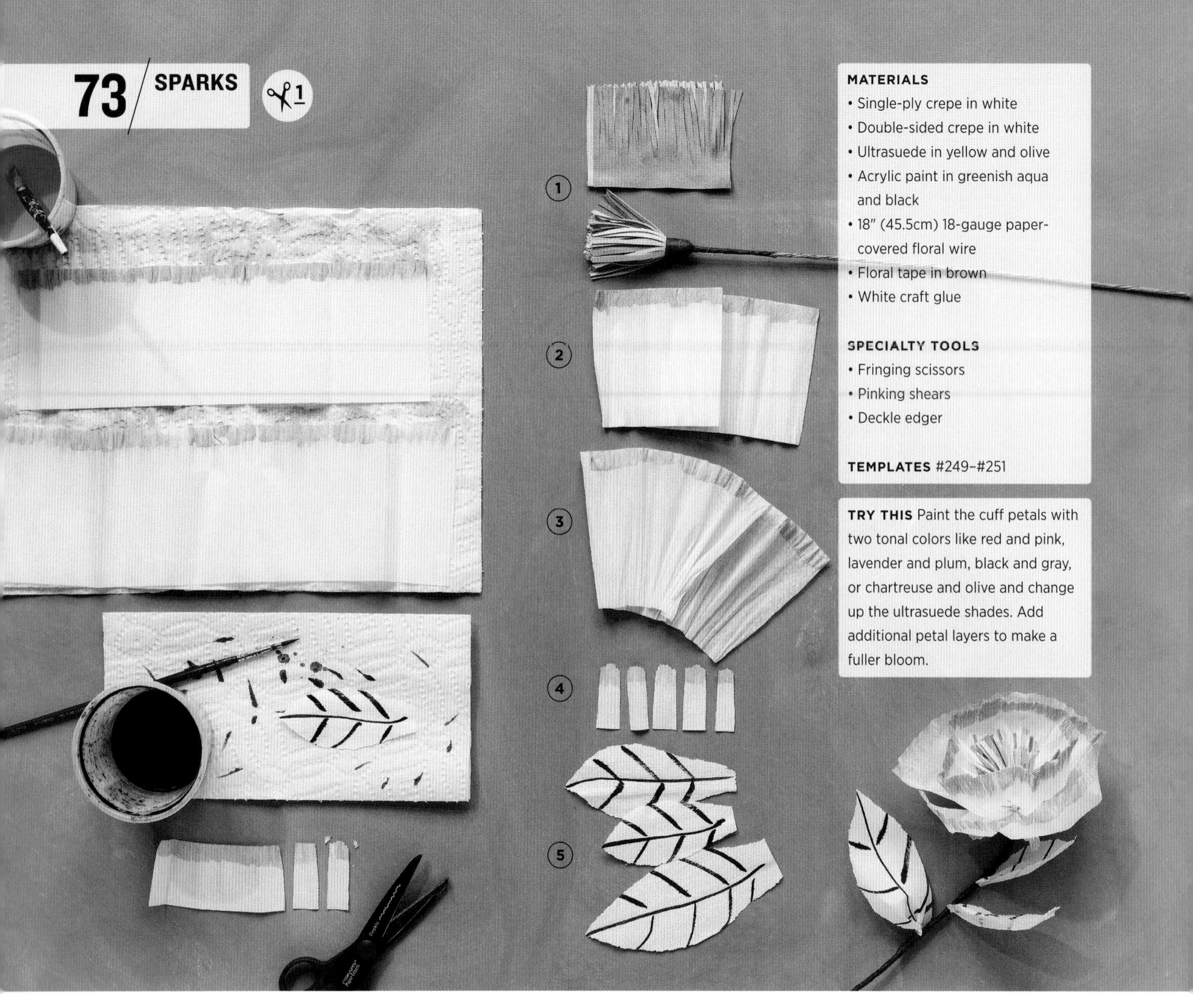

73 / SPARKS

MATERIALS
- Single-ply crepe in white
- Double-sided crepe in white
- Ultrasuede in yellow and olive
- Acrylic paint in greenish aqua and black
- 18" (45.5cm) 18-gauge paper-covered floral wire
- Floral tape in brown
- White craft glue

SPECIALTY TOOLS
- Fringing scissors
- Pinking shears
- Deckle edger

TEMPLATES #249–#251

TRY THIS Paint the cuff petals with two tonal colors like red and pink, lavender and plum, black and gray, or chartreuse and olive and change up the ultrasuede shades. Add additional petal layers to make a fuller bloom.

CUT *Grain runs with height; all dimensions are given as H × W.* Cut a 3" × 4" (7.5cm × 10cm) strip from each color of ultrasuede. Trim one long edge with pinking shears and fringe it ¾ of the way down using fringing scissors. Cut a 4½" × 15" (11.5cm × 38cm) strip of white single-ply crepe. Cut a 4" × 12" (10cm × 30.5cm) strip of white double-sided crepe. Cut a 2" × 4½" (5cm × 11.5cm) strip of white double-sided crepe. Leaves #249, #250, and #251: Cut 1 each from white double-sided crepe using a deckle edger.

ADD COLOR *Dilute* (p. 136) the greenish aqua and black acrylic paints. Loosely paint ½" (13mm) aqua stripes along one edge of the 3 crepe strips, as shown. Turn the pieces over and repeat the process on the same edge. Let them dry. Paint the black veining on the leaves, as shown. Set them aside to dry.

BUILD 1. Secure all layers with floral tape. Layer both the ultrasuede fringe strips and glue them together at the base. Let them dry. Attach a full-length stem wire with glue to one side at the bottom ¾" (2cm) of the fringe strip. Roll the fringe tightly around the wire, adding glue as you roll. Secure the end with glue and wrap the base in tape to finish the center. **2.** *Scrunch Pleat* (p. 128) the 12" (30.5cm) strip of double-sided crepe and *Gather and Wrap* (p. 132) it evenly around the center overlapping the ends slightly. Gently *Cup* (p. 134) the base of cuff petal to create a bowl shape. **3.** Repeat step 2 with the strip of single-ply crepe and attach it at a different starting point. **4.** Cut five ¾" (2cm) strips, with the grain, from the 4½" (11.5cm) strip of double-sided crepe to make 5 petals. Round off each painted side with a deckle edger, as shown. *Scrunch Pleat* each petal and attach them evenly around the center, and secure. **5.** *Scrunch Pleat* Leaves #249, #250, and #251. Attach them randomly while finishing the stem.

DELICATE DIP-DYE / 74

MATERIALS

- Single-ply crepe in white
- Double-sided crepe, in white
- Acrylic paints in pink, smoky blue, golden yellow, green, and gray
- 18" (45.5cm) 18-gauge cloth-wrapped floral wire
- Floral or washi tape in pink

SPECIALTY TOOLS

- Fringing scissors

TEMPLATES #252–#259

TRY THIS This technique can be used with almost any color combination. Try darker colors of crepe and paint or pink crepe with dark pink paint and dark green crepe with plum paint. With white crepe as a base *Dip-Dye* black and gray paints or neon shades of color instead of pastels.

CUT Cut a 3" (7.5cm) square from white single-ply crepe. Petal #252: Cut 5 from white double-sided crepe. Leaf #253: Cut 3 from white double-sided crepe. Cut a 9" (23cm) length of wire.

ADD COLOR *Dilute* (p. 136) the pink and smoky blue acrylic paints using the pale-wash formula. *Dip-Dye* (p. 137) the bases of the petals with pink, and the bases of the leaves with smoky blue. Set aside to dry.

BUILD Secure all layers with floral tape. **1.** Make a *Cotton Ball Center* (p. 130) with the white single-ply crepe square. Once complete, *Dip-Dye* the center loosely into the pink paint, and let dry. **2.** Gently *Cup* (p. 134) and *Scrunch Pleat* (p. 128) each Petal #252, and secure evenly around the center. **3.** Begin finishing the stem with tape, attaching Leaf #253 2" (5cm) from the flower base and the remaining leaves in 1" (2.5cm) increments below the first leaf.

PROJECT NOTE All of the flowers displayed are made from a mix of 5 petal and 4 leaf styles. *From left to right, the flower groupings shown:* Petal #254; 2" × 6" (5cm × 15cm) strip fringed with fringing scissors, with the grain, ¾ of the way down; Petals #252; Petals #255; and Petals #256. The 4 leaf shapes, Leaves #253, #257, #258, and #259, are randomly paired with different petals to create a varied and fun look. Using assorted paint colors, we experimented by dipping different sections of the petals, leaves and centers into the paint, creating a number of design variations. To create a straight line down the center of a petal or leaf, fold the piece in half, and dip the folded portion into the paint, unfold and let dry. We also made covered fruits and *Connected Buds* (p. 131).

75 / BUTTERFLY NEST

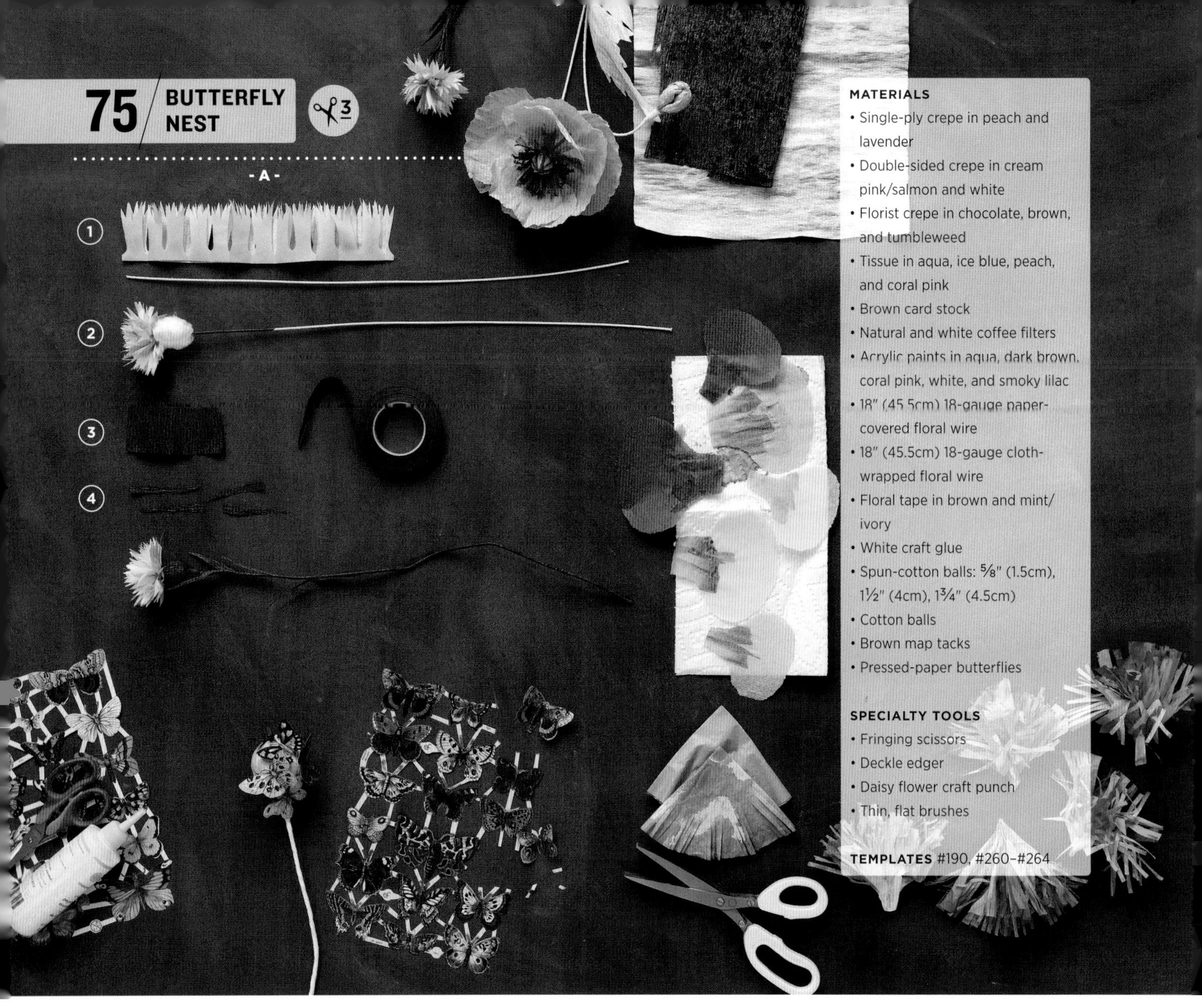

MATERIALS
- Single-ply crepe in peach and lavender
- Double-sided crepe in cream pink/salmon and white
- Florist crepe in chocolate, brown, and tumbleweed
- Tissue in aqua, ice blue, peach, and coral pink
- Brown card stock
- Natural and white coffee filters
- Acrylic paints in aqua, dark brown, coral pink, white, and smoky lilac
- 18" (45.5cm) 18-gauge paper-covered floral wire
- 18" (45.5cm) 18-gauge cloth-wrapped floral wire
- Floral tape in brown and mint/ivory
- White craft glue
- Spun-cotton balls: ⅝" (1.5cm), 1½" (4cm), 1¾" (4.5cm)
- Cotton balls
- Brown map tacks
- Pressed-paper butterflies

SPECIALTY TOOLS
- Fringing scissors
- Deckle edger
- Daisy flower craft punch
- Thin, flat brushes

TEMPLATES #190, #260–#264

NOTE *Dilute* (p. 136) and paint; let parts dry. *Grain runs with height; all dimensions are given as H × W.* Secure all layers and finish stems with floral tape. Cut wires to desired lengths and vary the wire thicknesses. Cut fringe using fringing scissors.

A 1. Petal #260: Cut a 4½" × 10" (11.5cm × 25.5cm) strip each from ice blue and aqua tissue. Fold each in half widthwise, accordion-fold to fit template, and cut continuous petals. Layer both strips and *Gather and Wrap* (p. 132) them around the cloth-wrapped wire. **2.** Pull a cotton ball open and evenly wrap it around the base of the center. **3.** Cut a 1¾" × 3½" (4.5cm × 9cm) strip from a piece of prestretched chocolate florist crepe and trim one long side with a deckle edger. Wrap the strip around the cotton ball to cover it, with the deckle edge up, then twist the bottom tightly, and secure. **4.** Leaf #190: Cut 4–6 leaves from prestretched chocolate florist crepe. Attach the leaves randomly while finishing stem.

B 1. Cut a 3" (7.5cm) square from the chocolate florist crepe. Using a thin brush and white acrylic paint, draw 4 crossing lines on the crepe as shown. Round off the corners to create a circle. Make a *Spun-Cotton Center* (p. 130) with the painted crepe circle, ⅝" (1.5cm) spun ball, and a cloth-wrapped wire. **2.** Cut a 1¼" × 5½" (3cm × 14cm) strip from prestretched brown florist crepe and fringe it, with the grain, ¾ of the way down. *Gather and Wrap* the fringe around the center and secure. **3.** Cut a 2" (5cm) square from tumbleweed florist crepe and *Hand Cut Fringe* (p. 127) it, with the grain, halfway down. Roll the fringe strip tightly and snip the fringed end to make confetti, as shown. Brush the tips of the fringe attached to the center with glue and sprinkle them with confetti. Let it dry. **4.** Petal #261: Cut 2 from coral pink tissue, 2 from cream pink/salmon double-sided crepe. Using a flat brush, paint the lower ⅔ of the petals with loose brush strokes in coral pink acrylic paint and let it dry. Crumple the petals in your hand, then unfold them. Layer the petals, offsetting slightly, 1 pair with the crepe on top, 1 pair with tissue on top, to make 2 pairs and *Scrunch Pleat* (p. 128) each pair at the base. Secure the pairs opposite each other around the center. **5.** Petal #262: Repeat step 4 and secure them on opposite points from Petals #261. Finish the stem. **6.** To make the bud: Cut a 4½" × 2½" (11.5cm × 6.5cm) piece from the chocolate florist crepe. Tear a cotton

ball into 2 pieces and elongate each piece slightly. Place them as shown on the crepe piece, leaving space between the cotton pieces. Roll the crepe strip tightly, with the grain, over the cotton and twist it in the center a few times, before twisting both ends to secure. Bend this in half and secure it to a cloth-wrapped wire to make a bud. Finish stem. **7.** Leaf #263: Using a spray bottle, spray both sides of a 12" (30.5cm) piece of brown florist crepe with dark brown acrylics. Let it dry between sides. Cut 1 leaf from a stretched section of the painted brown florist crepe and *Scrunch Pleat* the base. **8.** Trim the bud stem to the desired length and *Join Stem* (p. 132) to the main stem 6" (15cm) from the base of the flower. *Style Stem* (p. 133) of the bud. Cover the joint with Leaf #263 and secure it. Affix a paper butterfly with slightly folded wings at the base of the leaf with glue.

C 1. Cut a 5" (12.5cm) square from the coral pink tissue. Round off corners to create a circle. Crumple this in your hand, and then unfold it. Make a *Spun-Cotton Center* with the tissue circle, the $1\frac{1}{2}$" (4cm) spun ball, and paper-covered wire. Finish the stem. **2.** Leaf #264: Cut 1 from brown florist crepe. Attach it with glue at the base of the center. **3.** Using a punch, cut 1 daisy from the brown card stock. Pinch each punched daisy petal to slightly crease up the centerline to add depth. Attach the brown card stock daisy to the top of the flower with a map tack. **4.** Leaf #263: Cut the template at the short marker, cut 1 leaf from the prestretched brown florist crepe painted in step B7. *Scrunch Pleat* the base. **5.** Secure Leaf #263 8" (20.5cm) from the base of the flower. *Style Stem* with opposing bends, as shown.

PROJECT NOTE Make additional flowers in mixed colors, adding paper butterflies to achieve the effect shown in our planter. Glue paper butterflies to the buds, pods, and stems. To make the peach poppies, we used peach single-ply crepe and tissue petals; lavender single-ply crepe and smoky-lilac acrylic center; brown florist crepe–fringed center tipped with chocolate crepe confetti; white double-sided crepe leaves painted with sprayed aqua acrylic paint; tumbleweed florist crepe buds. The finished arrangement was secured in dry floral foam placed in a hollowed-out log planter. To cover the floral foam, we *Dip-Dyed* (p. 137) and fringed coffee filters (Coffee-Filter Fireworks, p. 179) with shades of aqua acrylic paint.

156

TEMPLATES/

ABOUT TEMPLATES Templates are displayed in the order of the projects. Grain direction is indicated with three parallel lines. Solid lines are cut lines, dashed lines indicate where the folds are when accordion-folding paper to make continuous petals or shapes that are folded before cutting (e.g., #14, #16). Broken solid lines indicate cut lines for templates that are used full size and also used cut down (e.g., #7, #9). Some templates require enlarging where noted. Download templates at papertopetal.com/book-templates.

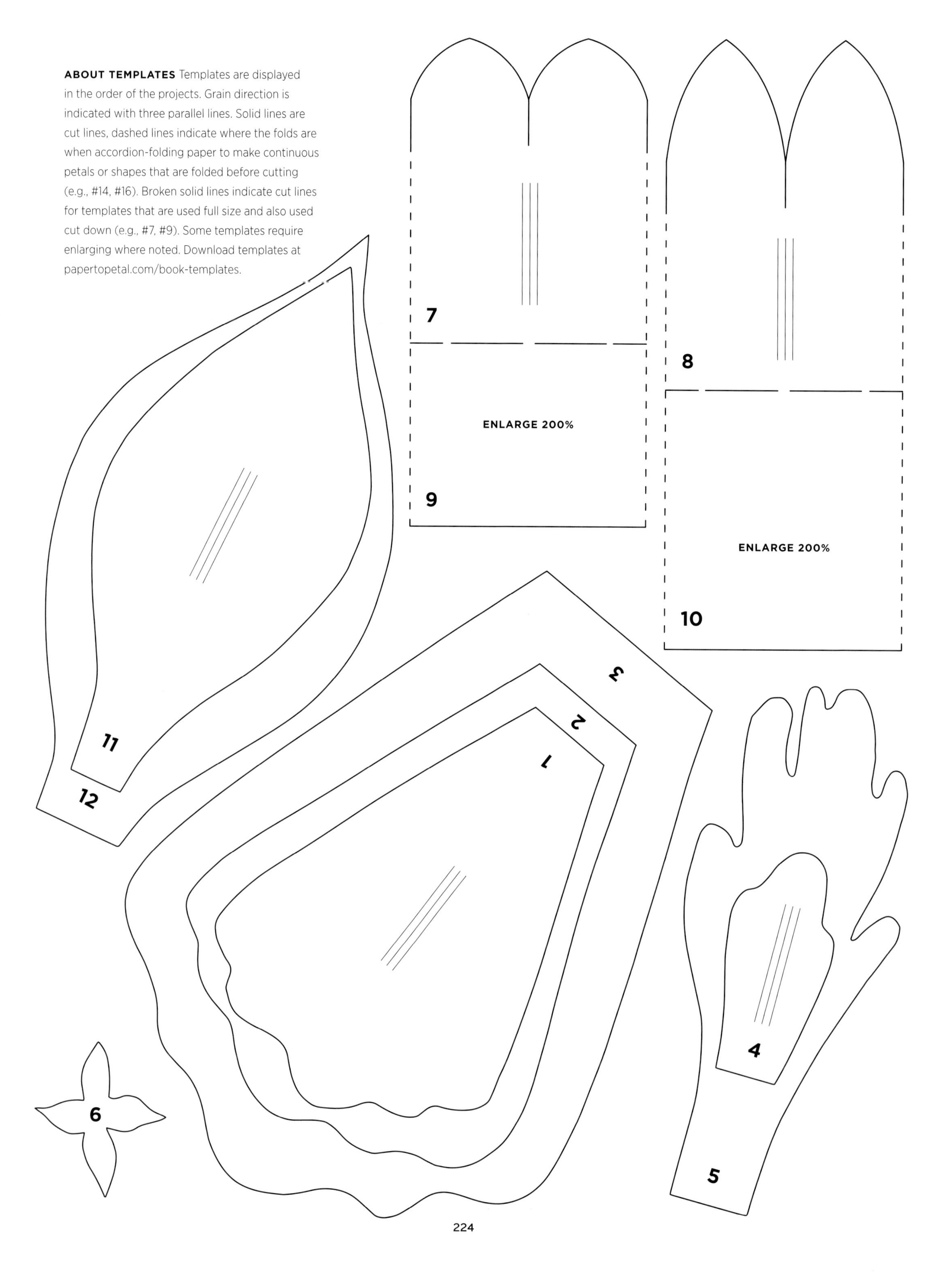

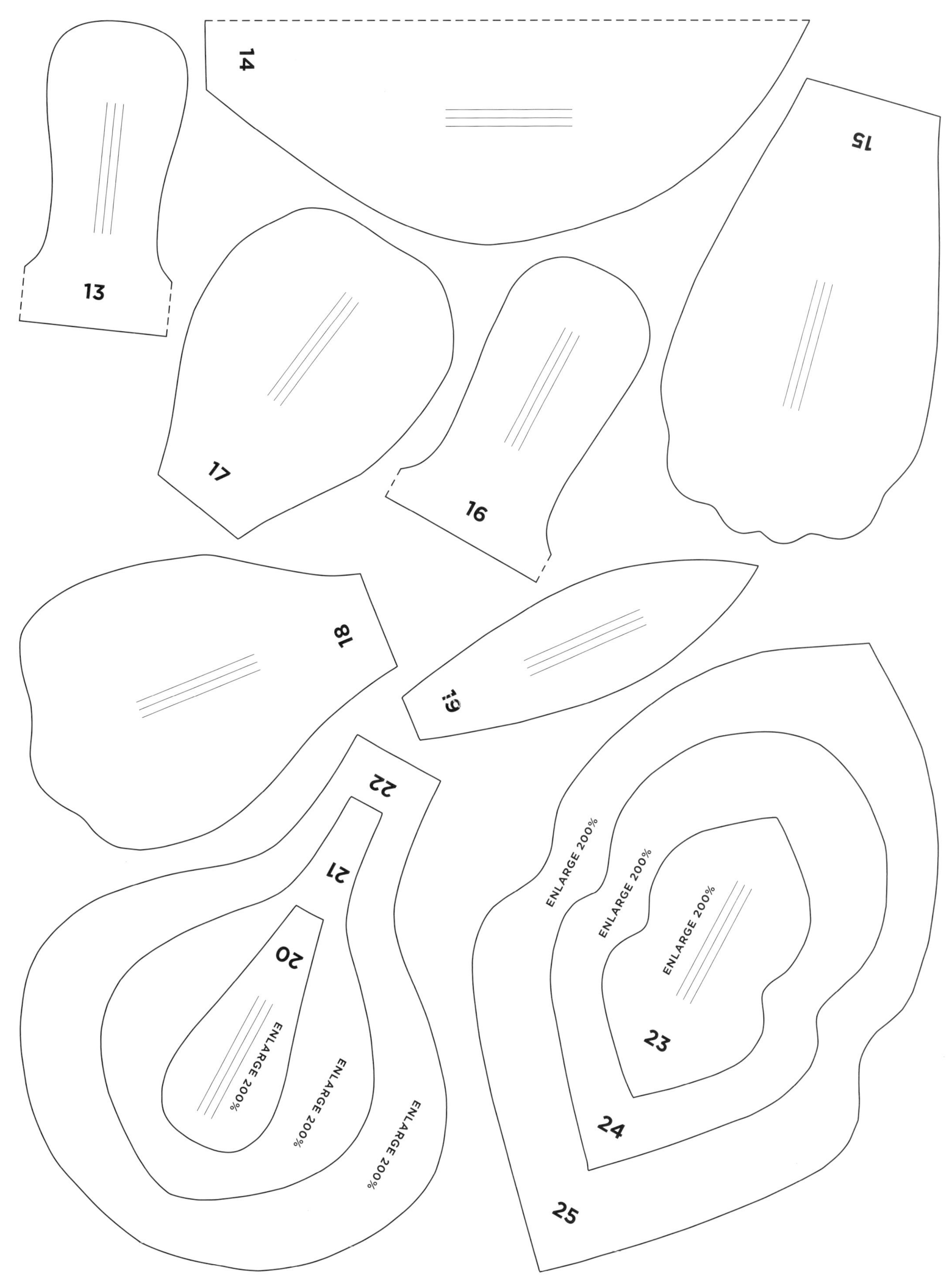
13
14
15
17
16
18
19
22
21
20
ENLARGE 200%
ENLARGE 200%
ENLARGE 200%
ENLARGE 200%
ENLARGE 200%
ENLARGE 200%
23
24
25

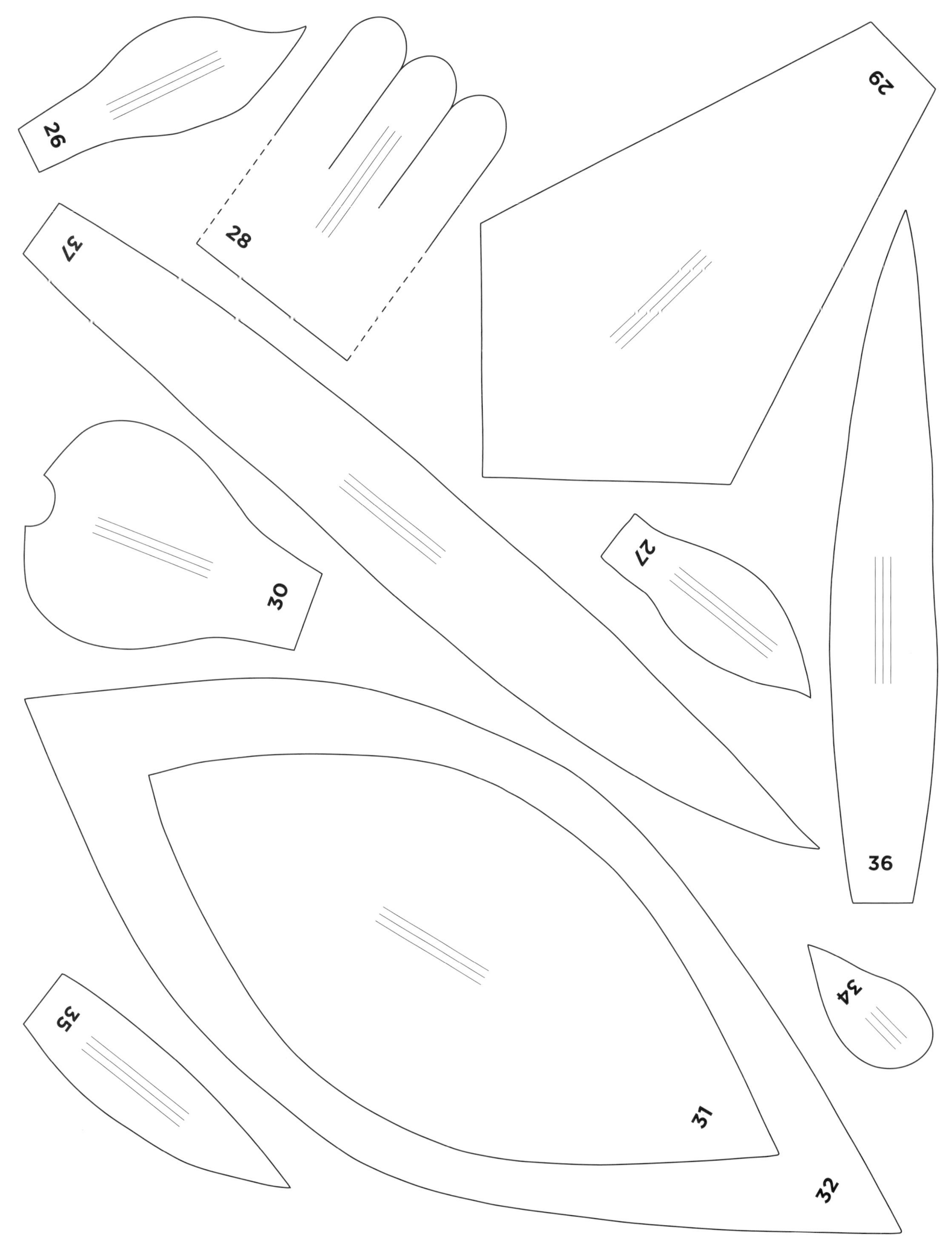
26
28
29
37
30
27
36
31
32
35
34

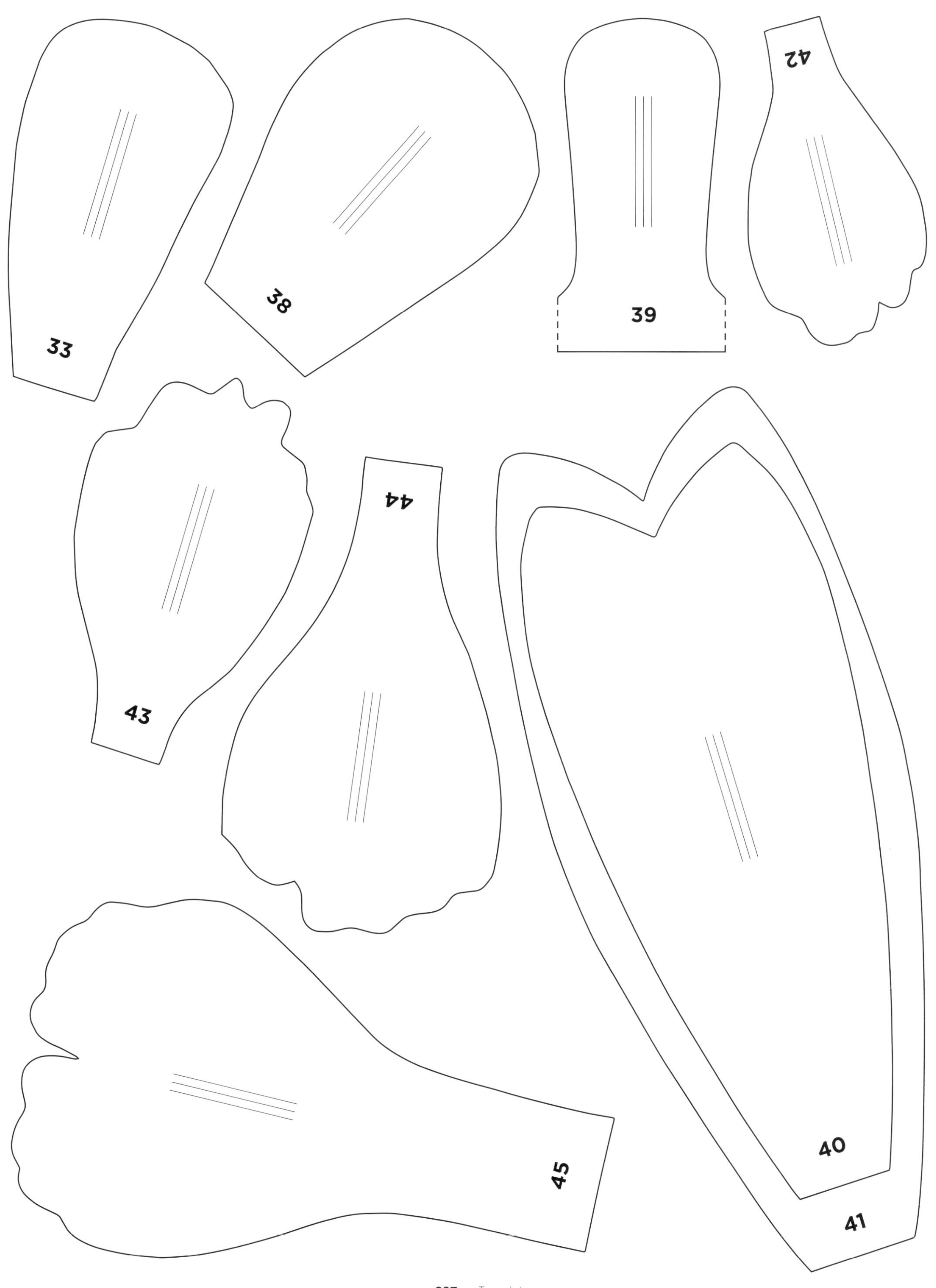
33
38
39
42
43
44
40
41
45

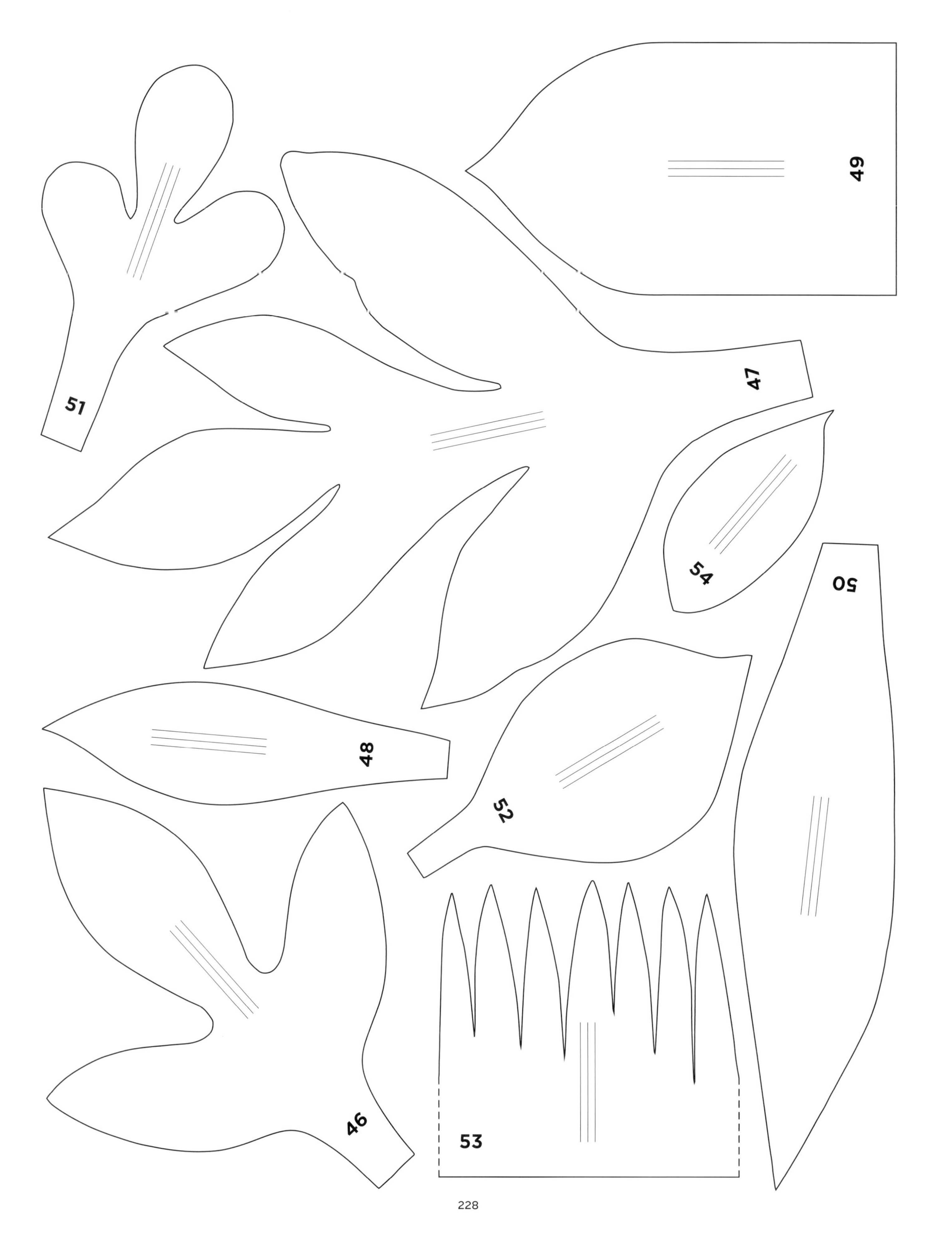
49
51
47
54
50
48
52
46
53

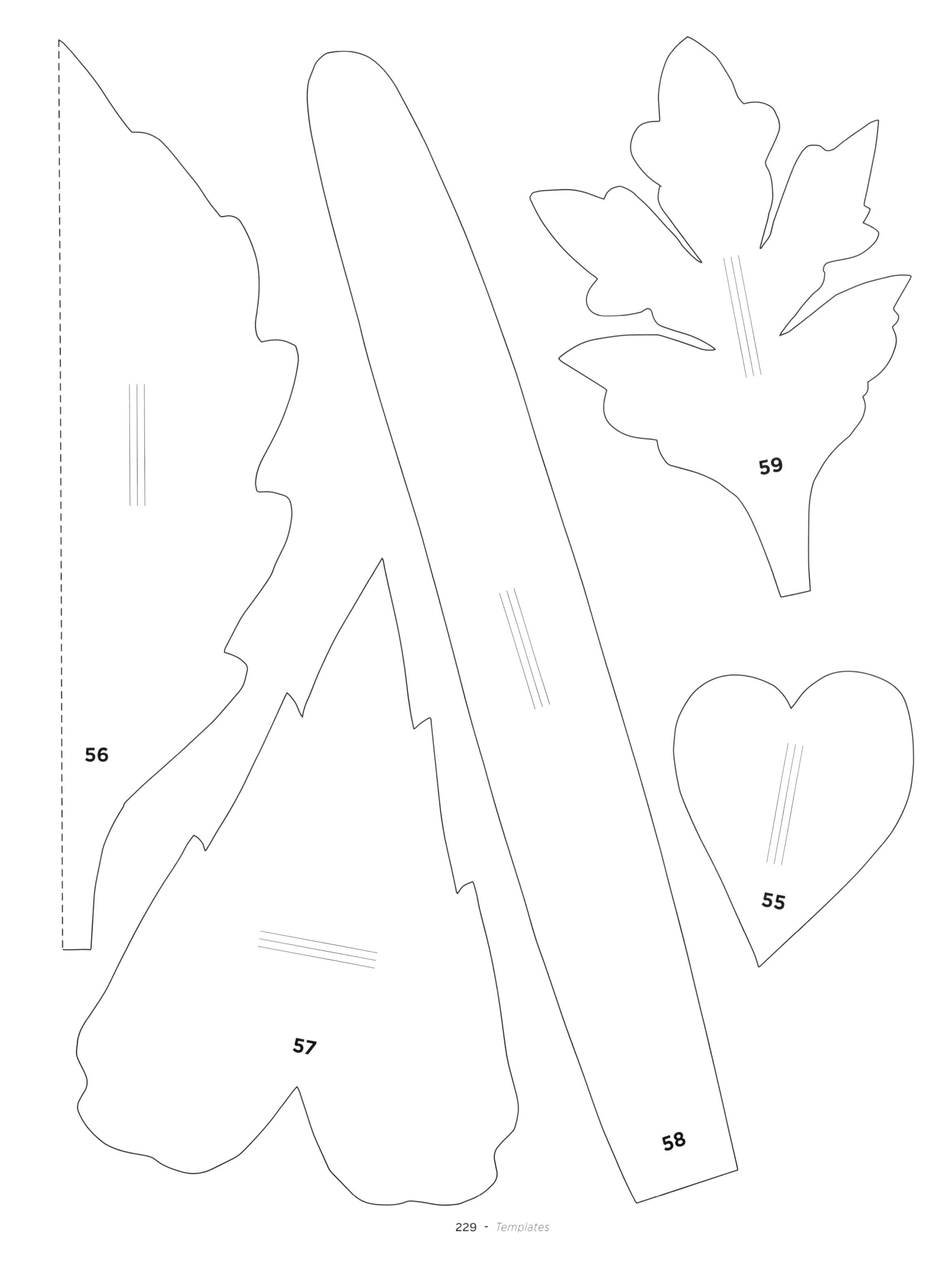
56
57
58
59
55

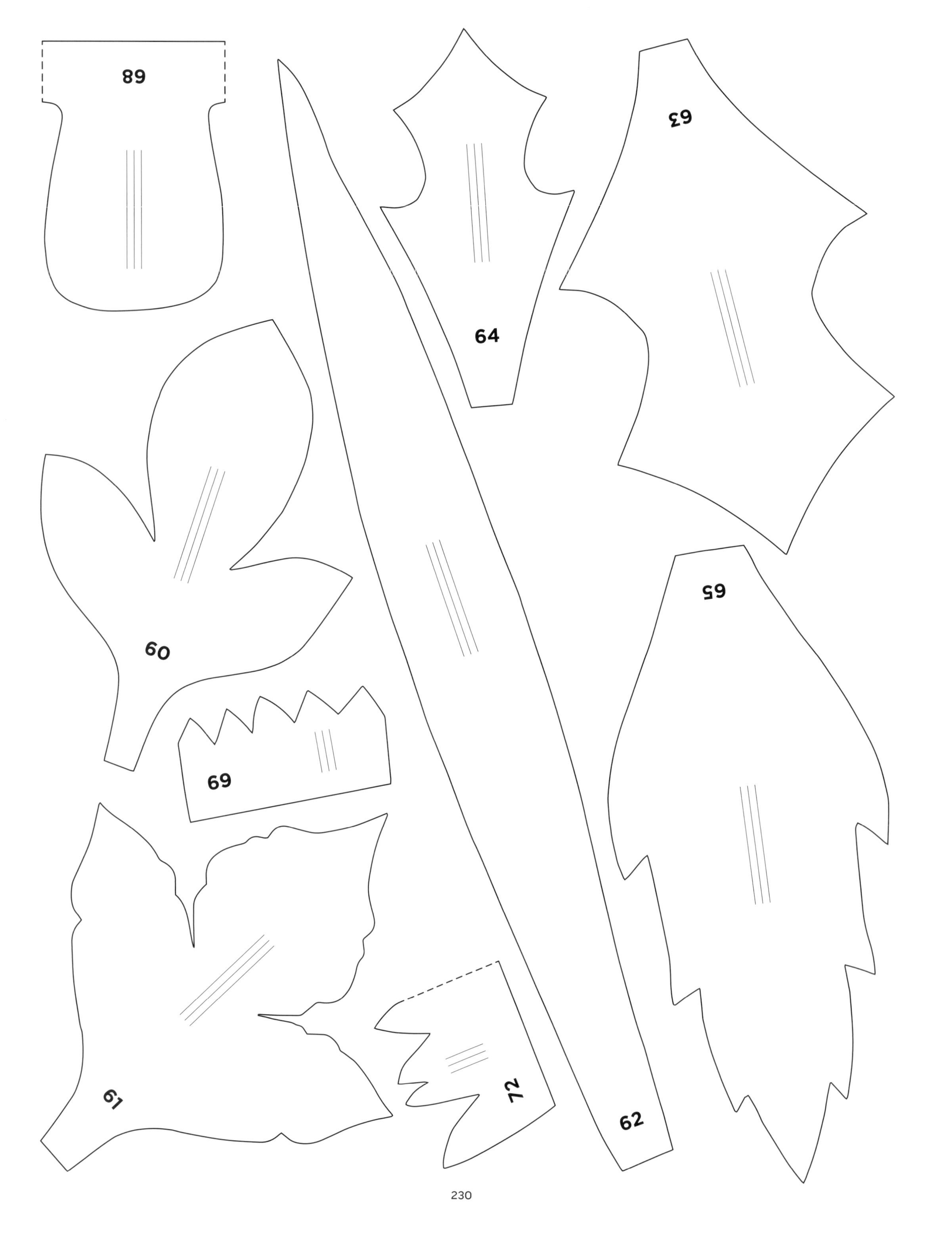
68
64
63
60
65
69
61
72
62

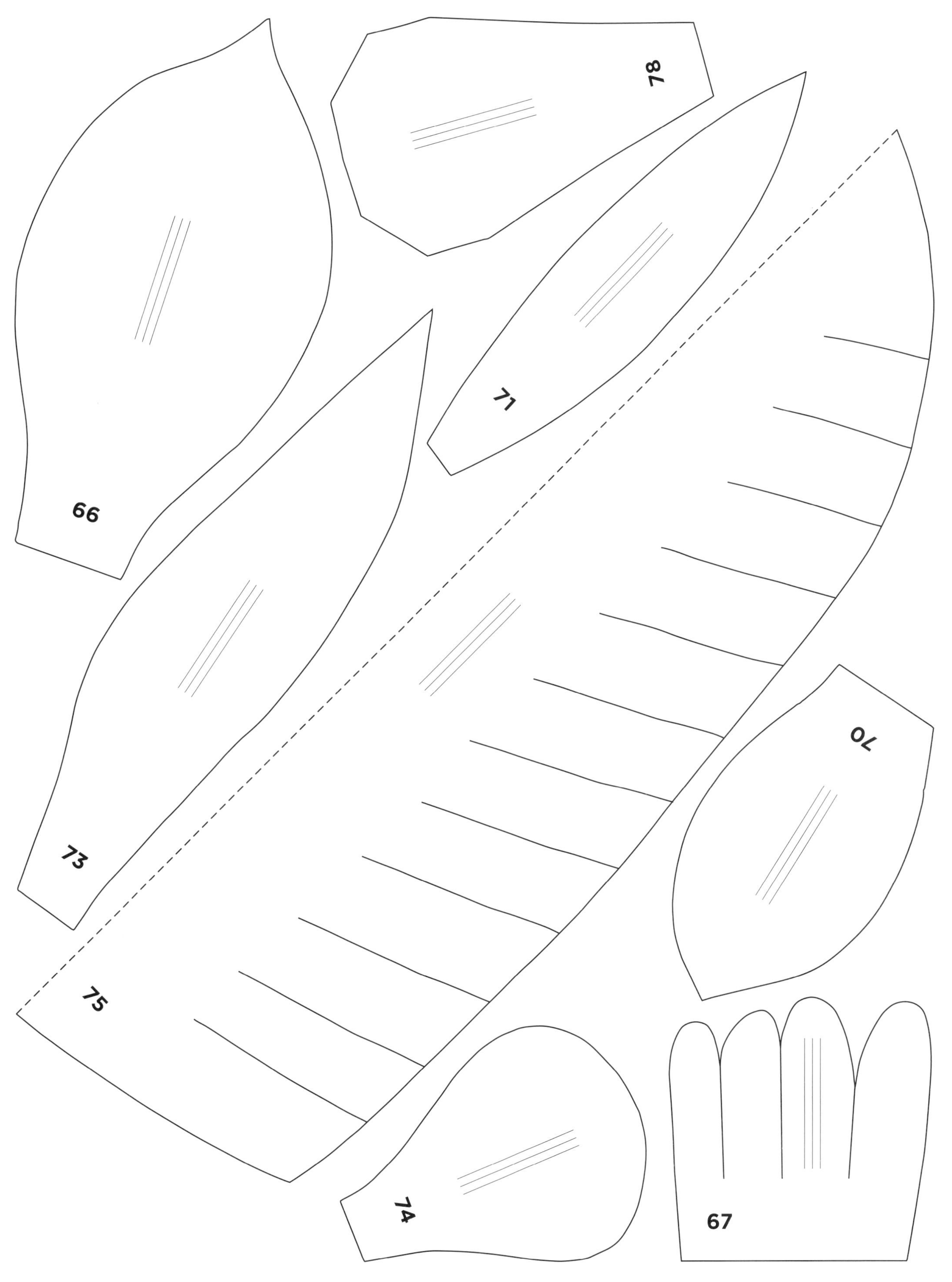
78
66
71
73
70
75
74
67

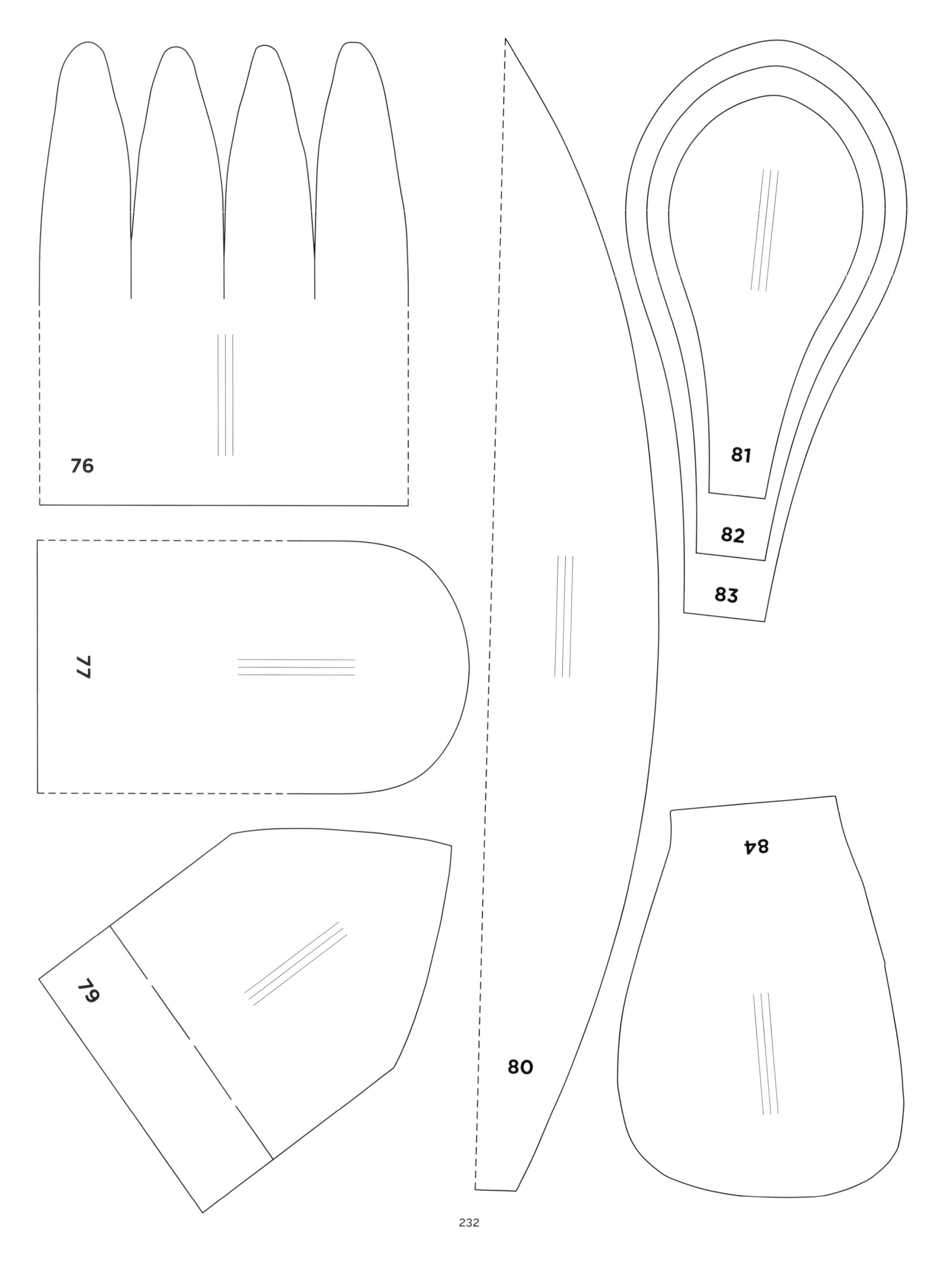

76
77
79
80
81
82
83
84

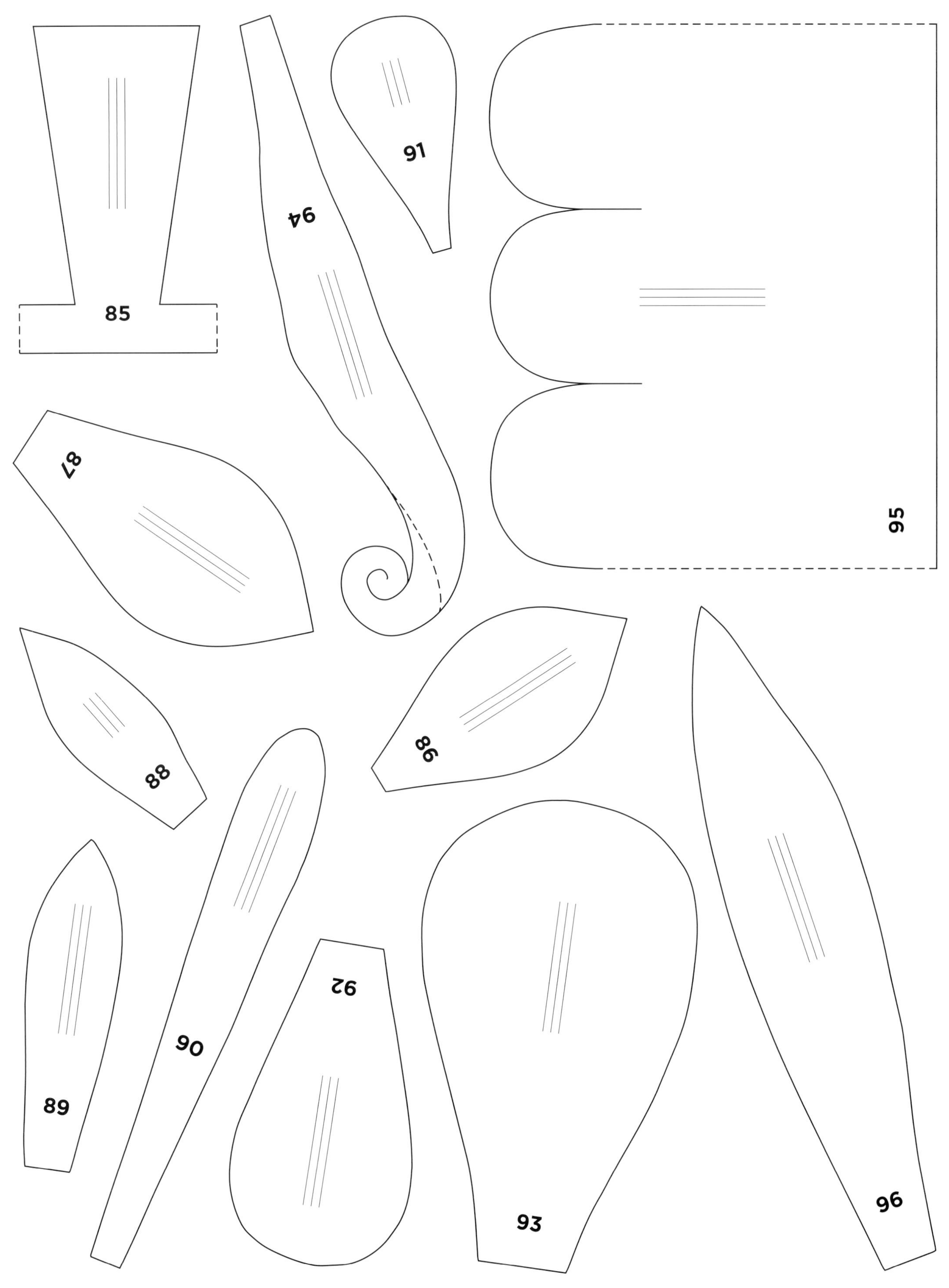

85
94
91
95
87
86
88
96
90
92
93
89

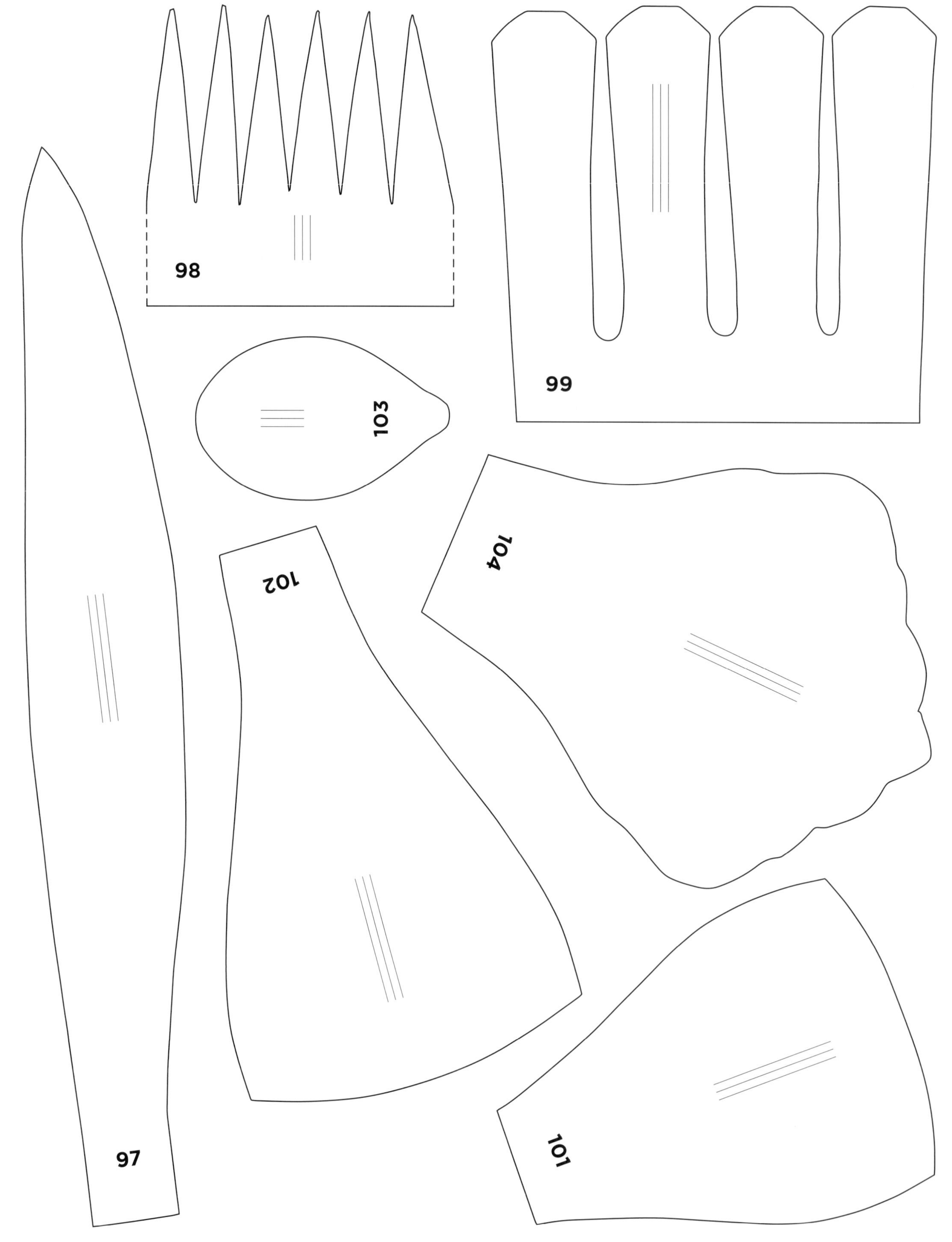
98
99
103
104
102
97
101

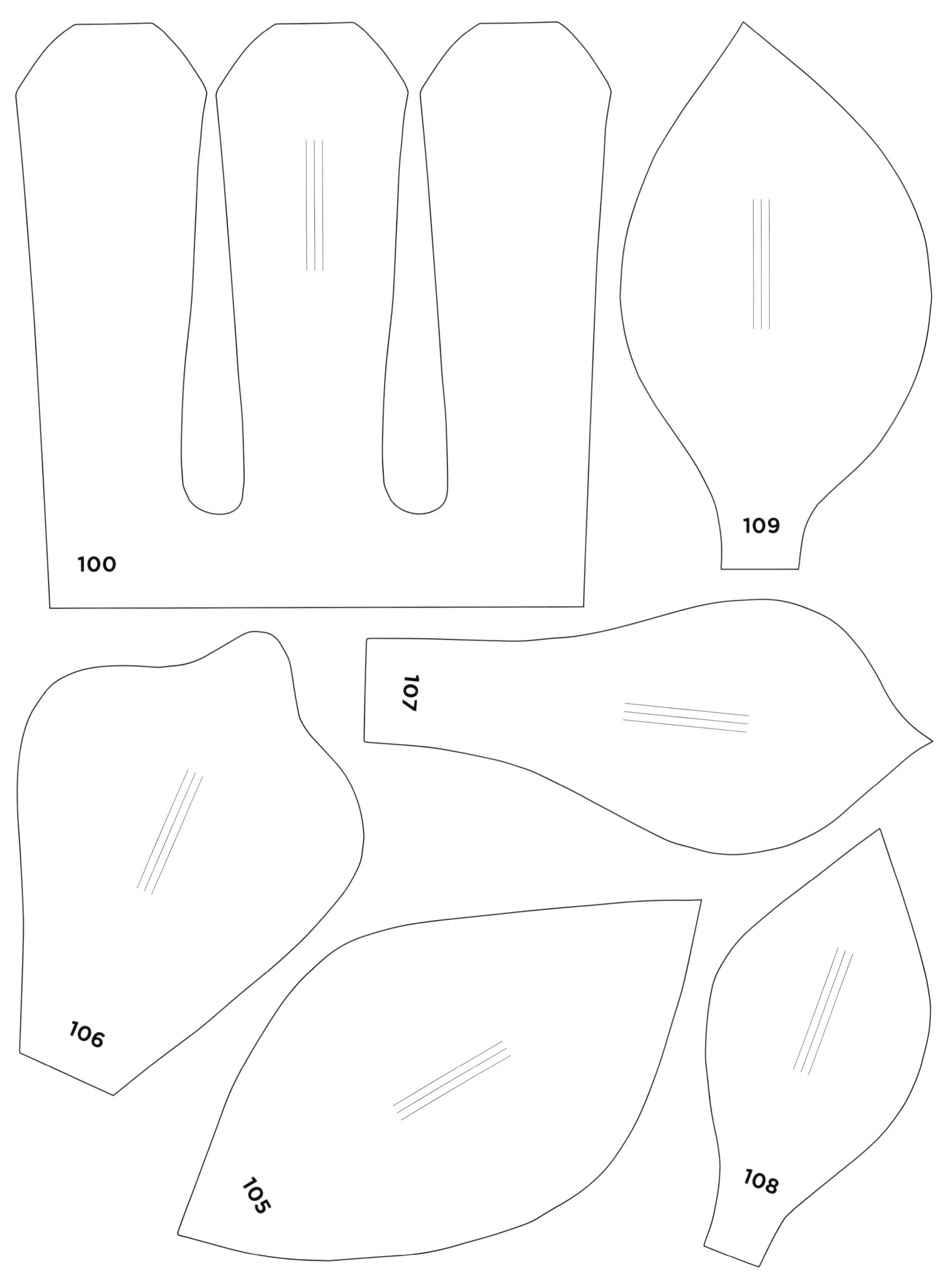
100
109
107
106
105
108

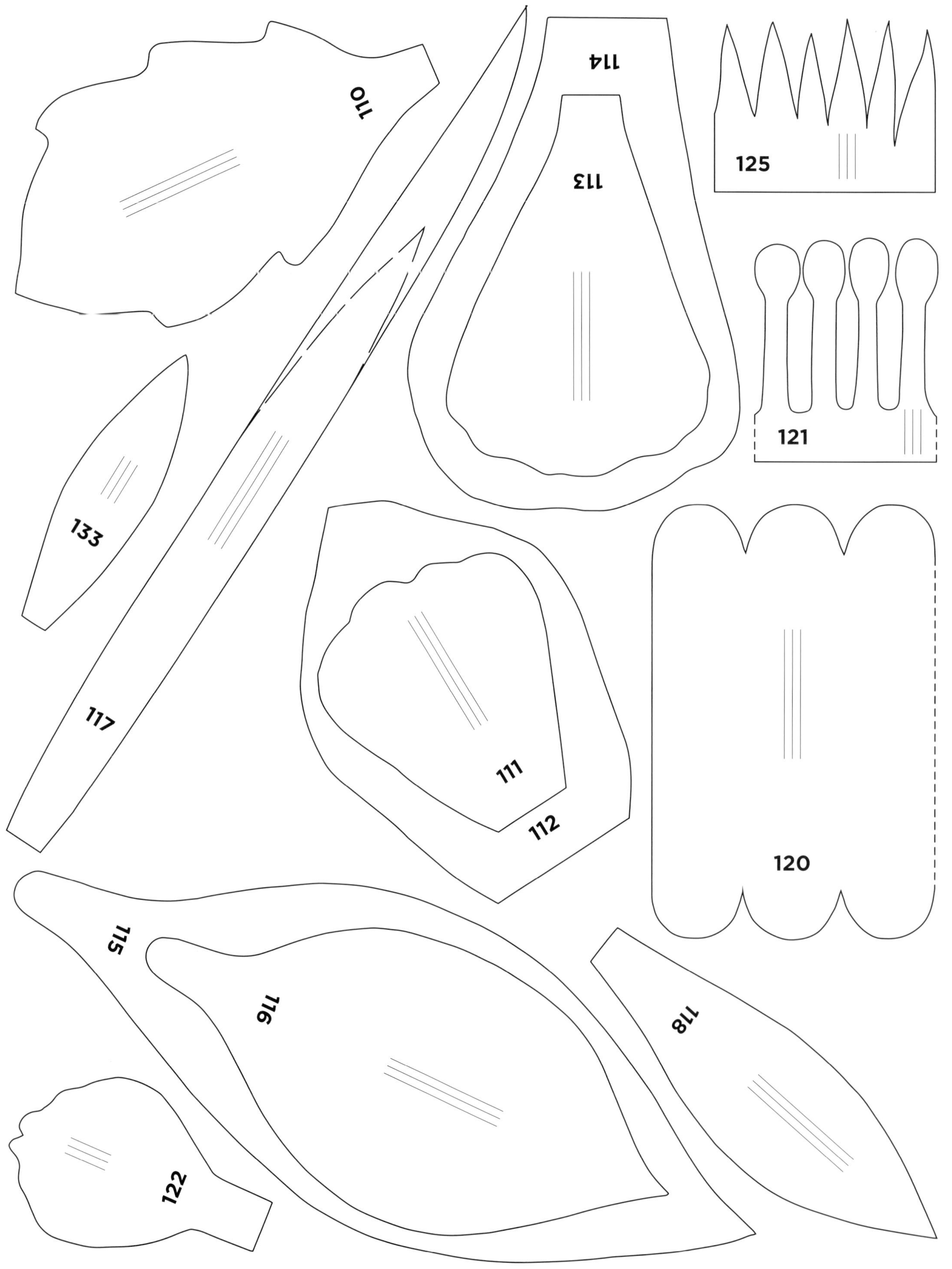
110
114
113
125
121
133
117
111
112
120
115
116
118
122

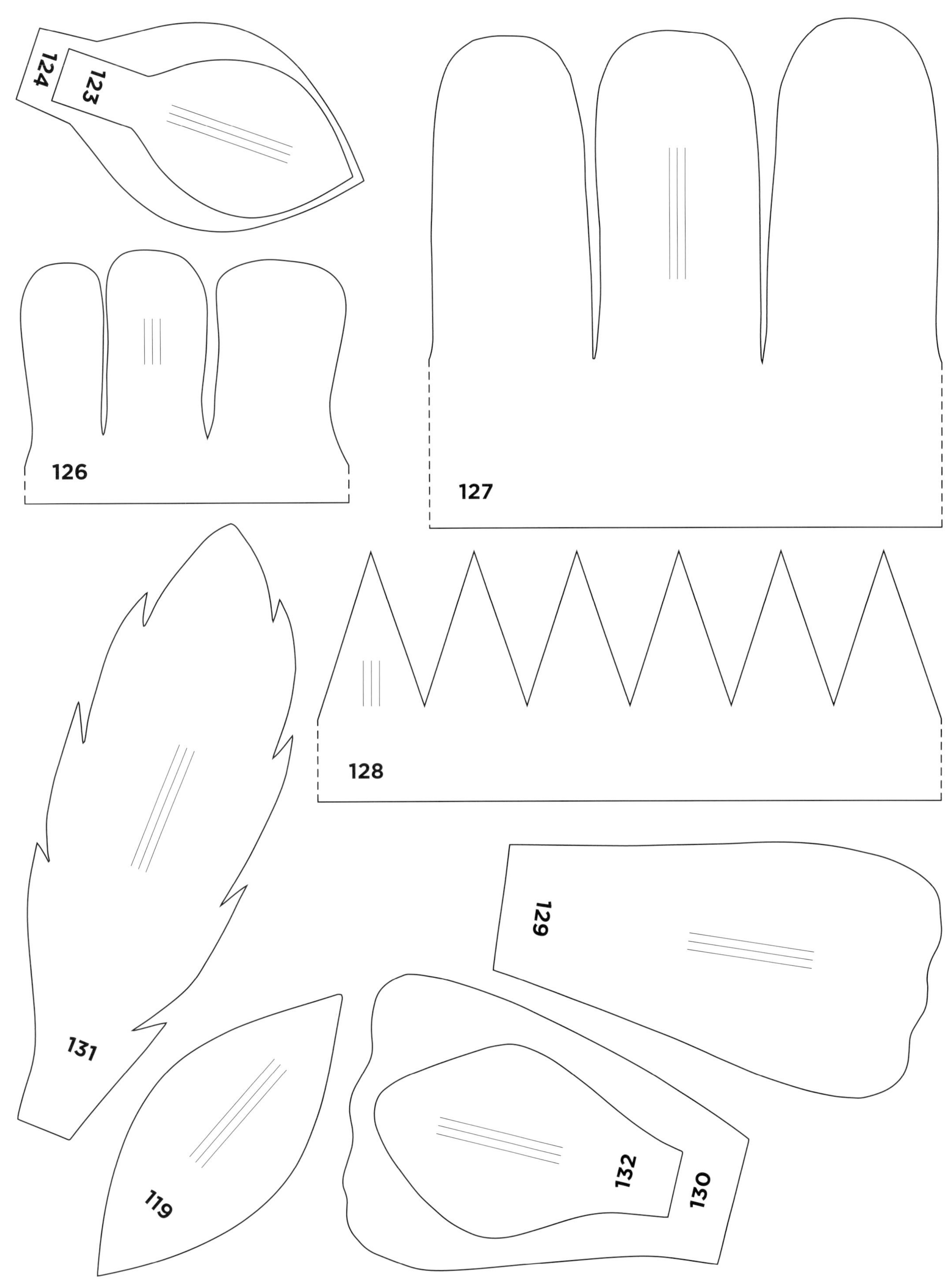
124
123
126
127
128
129
131
119
132
130

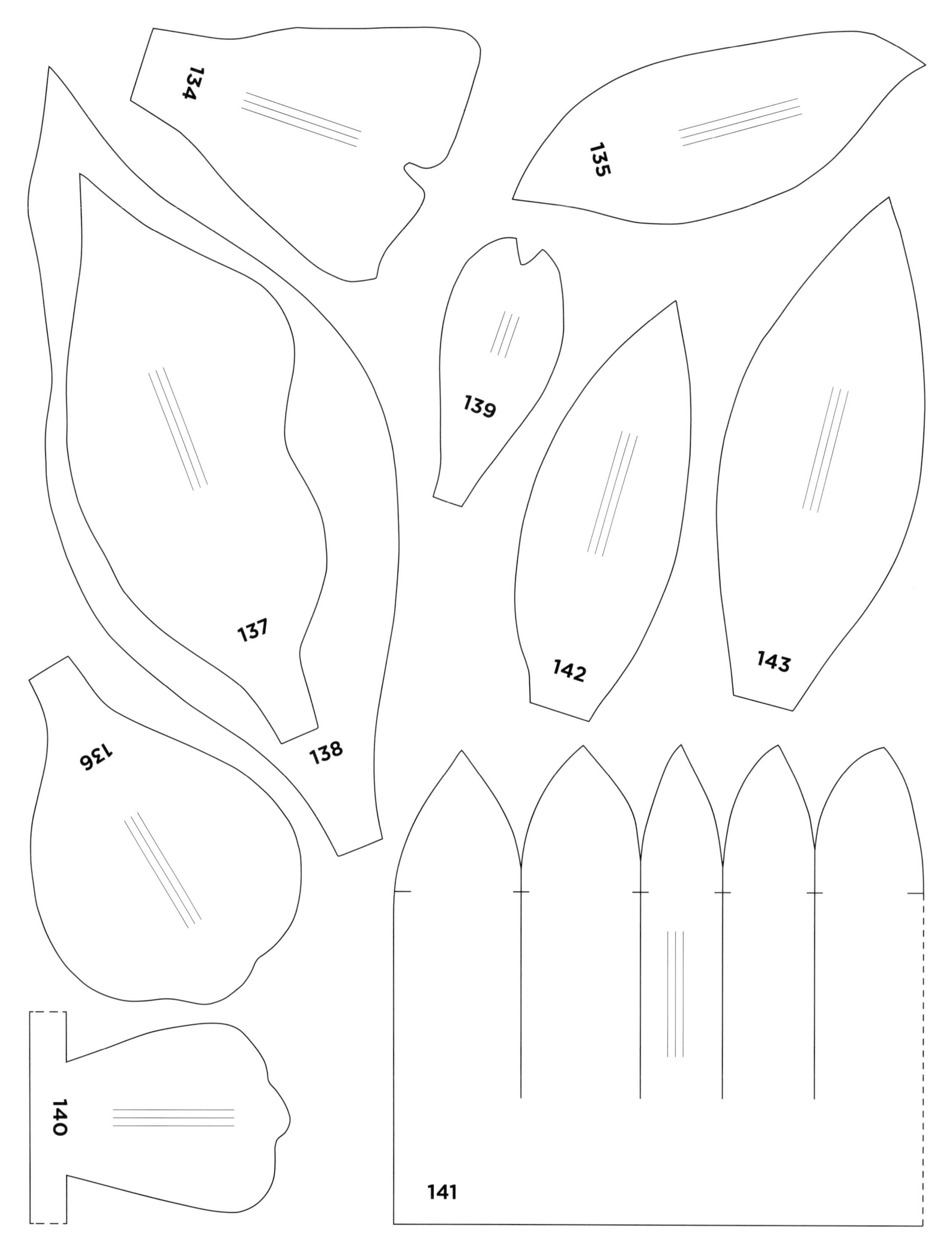
134
135
139
137
142
143
136
138
140
141

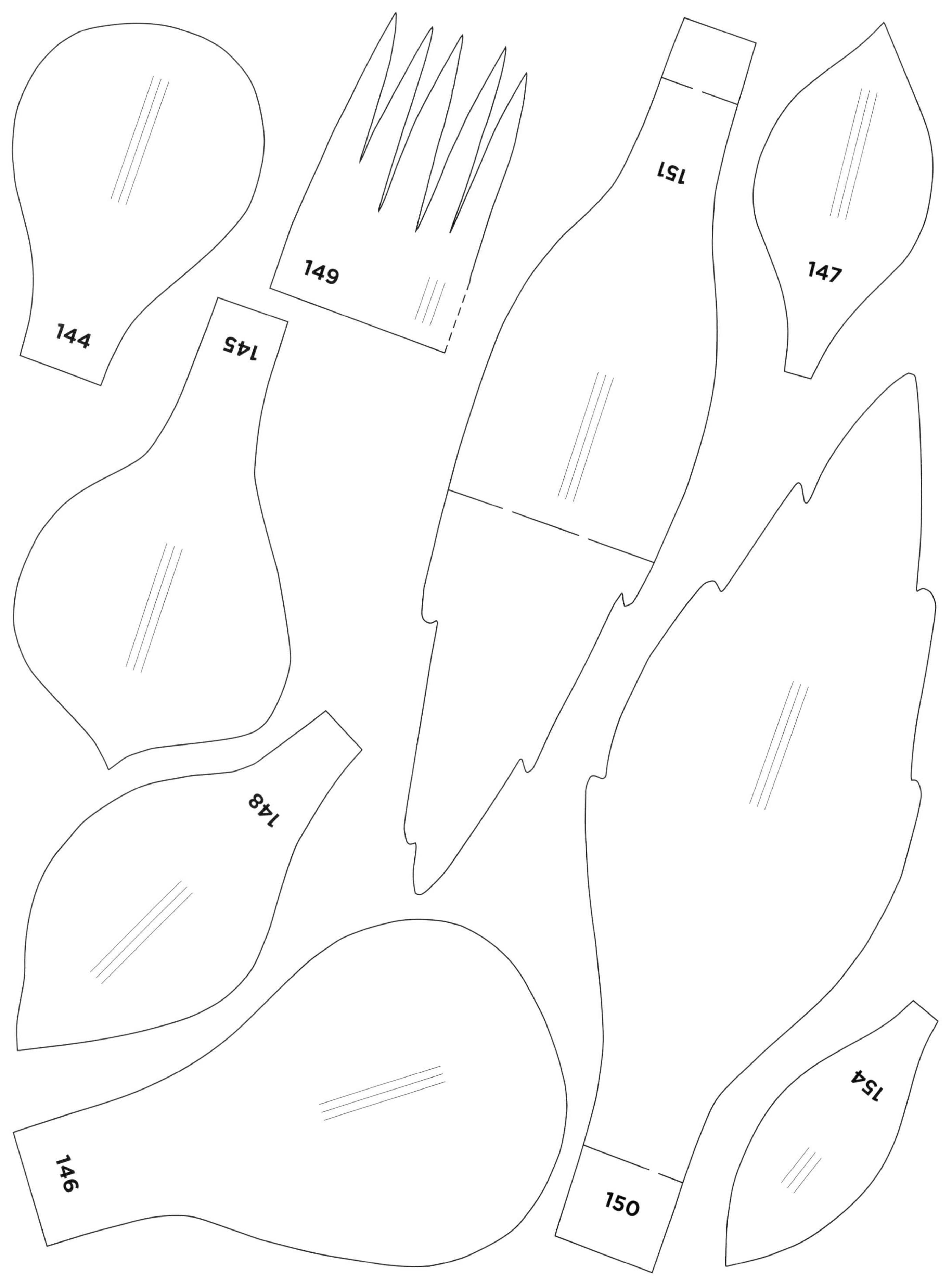
144
149
151
147
145
148
146
150
154

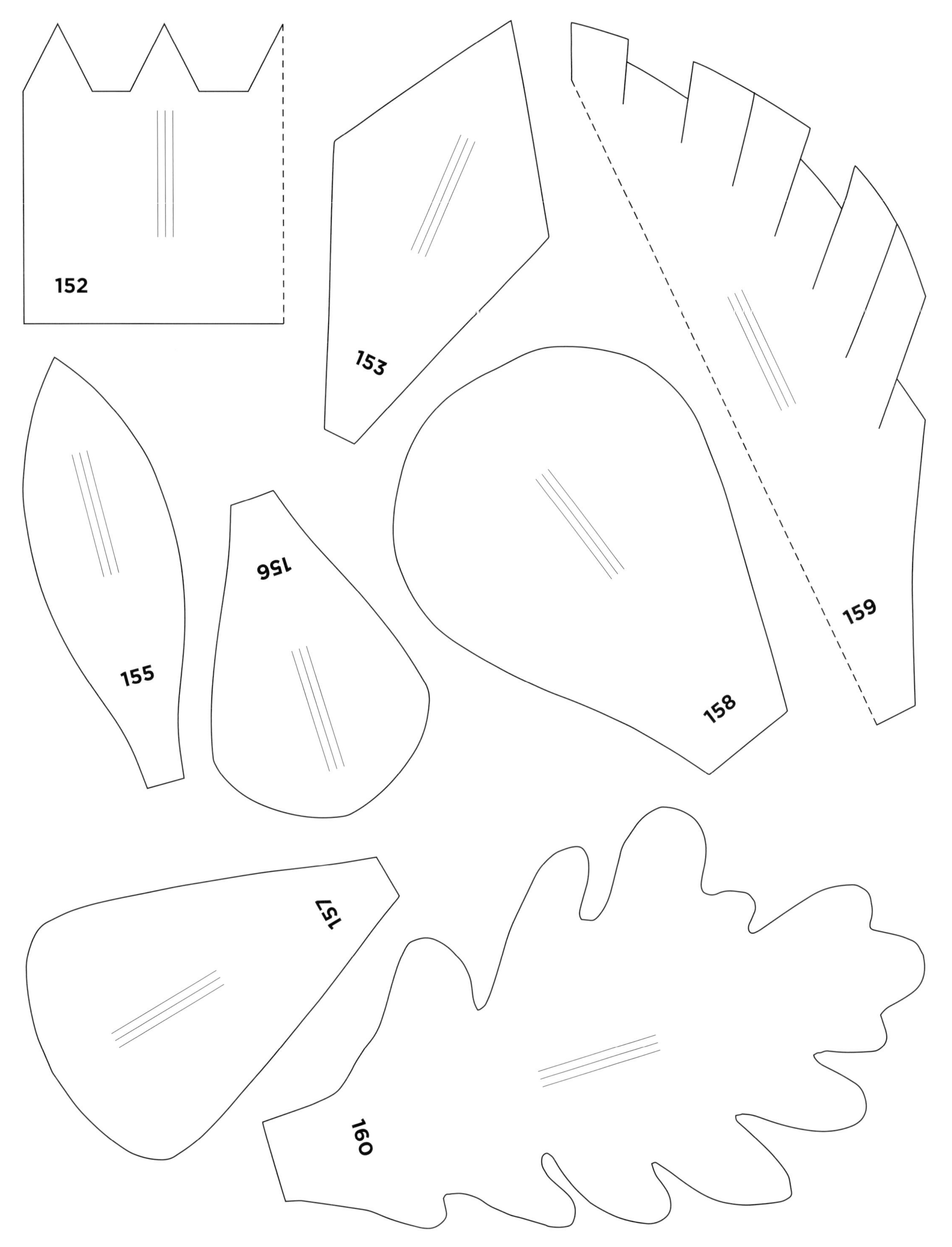
152
153
159
155
156
158
157
160

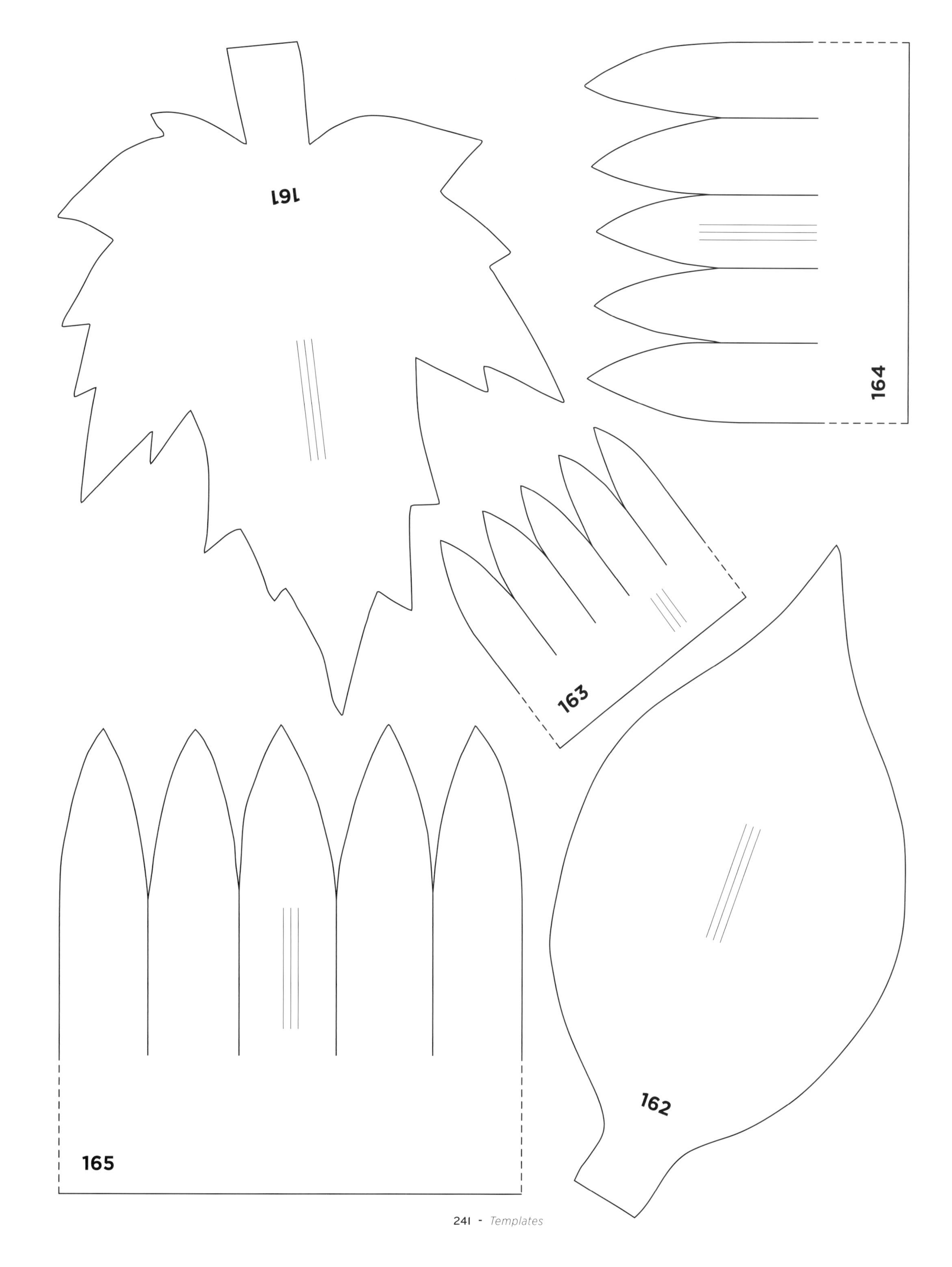
161
164
163
162
165

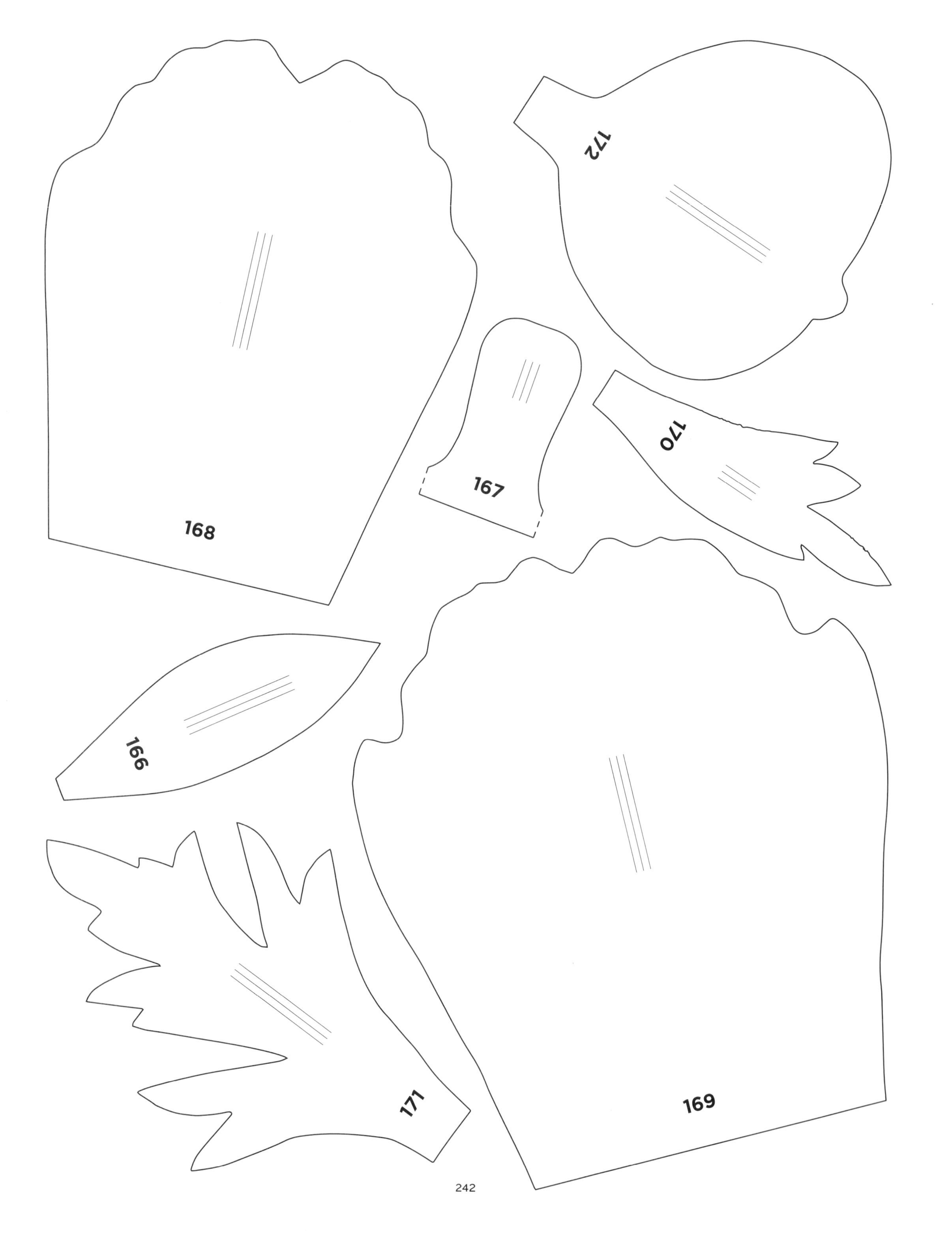
168
172
167
170
166
169
171

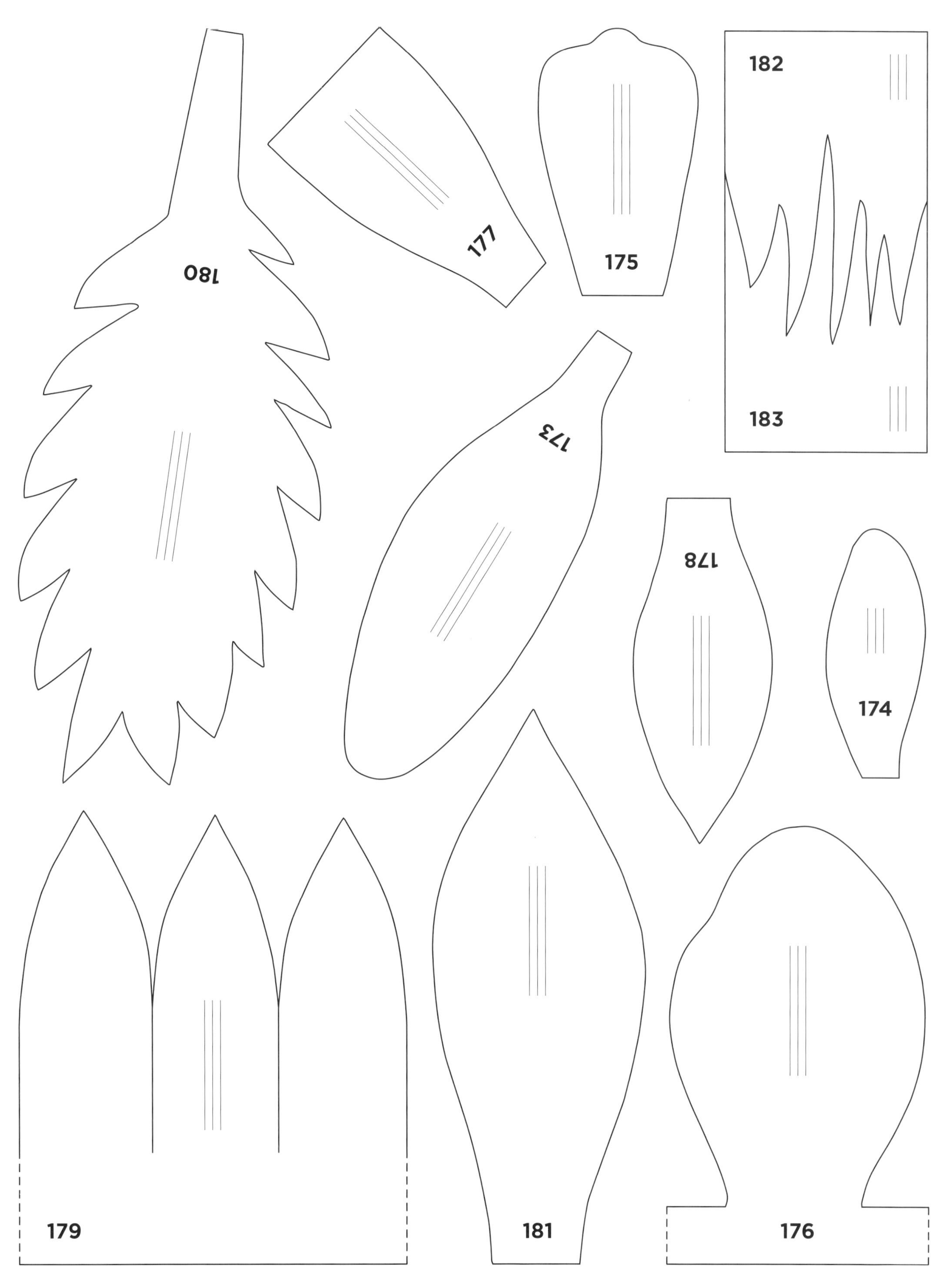
180
177
175
182
183
173
178
174
179
181
176

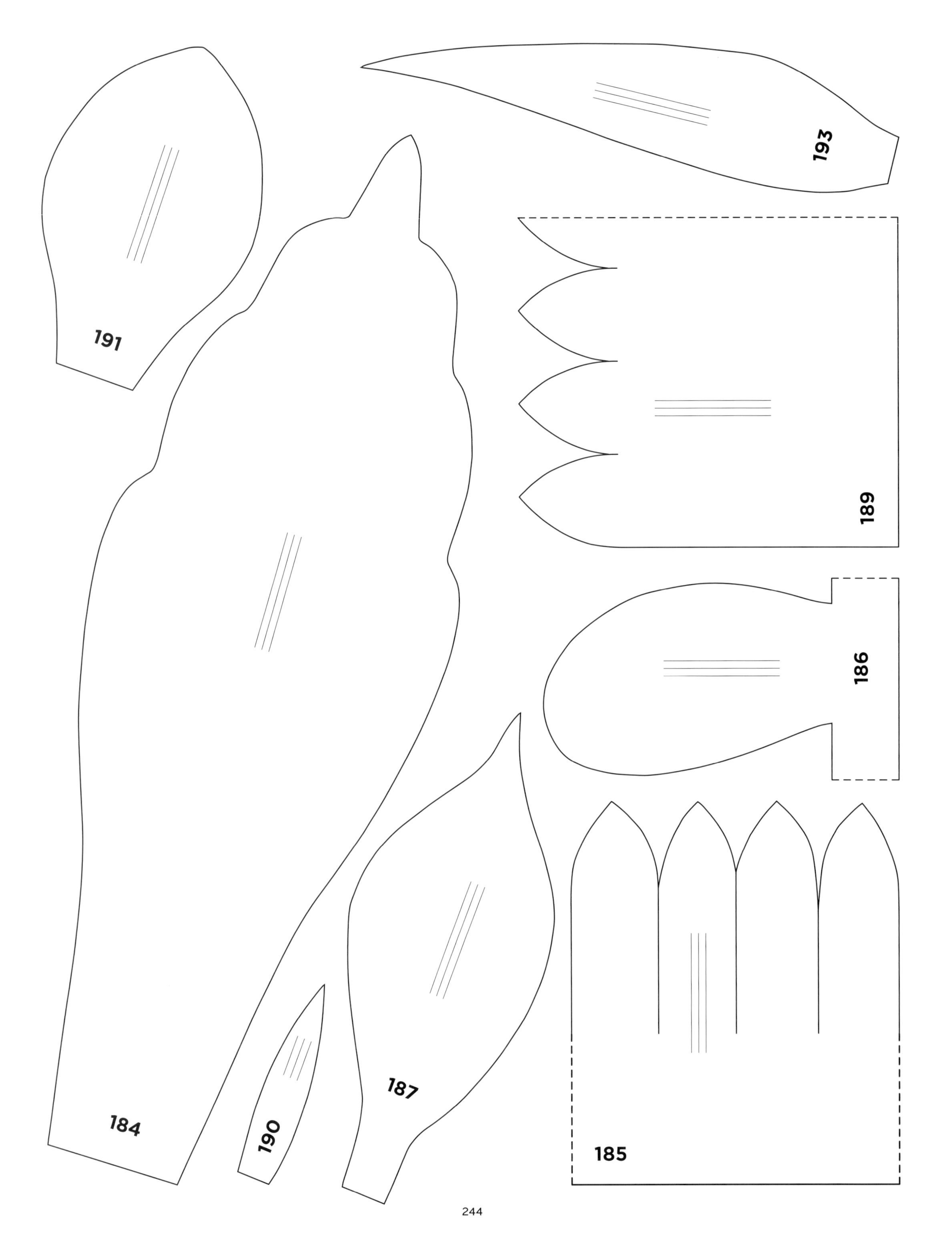
191
193
189
186
184
190
187
185

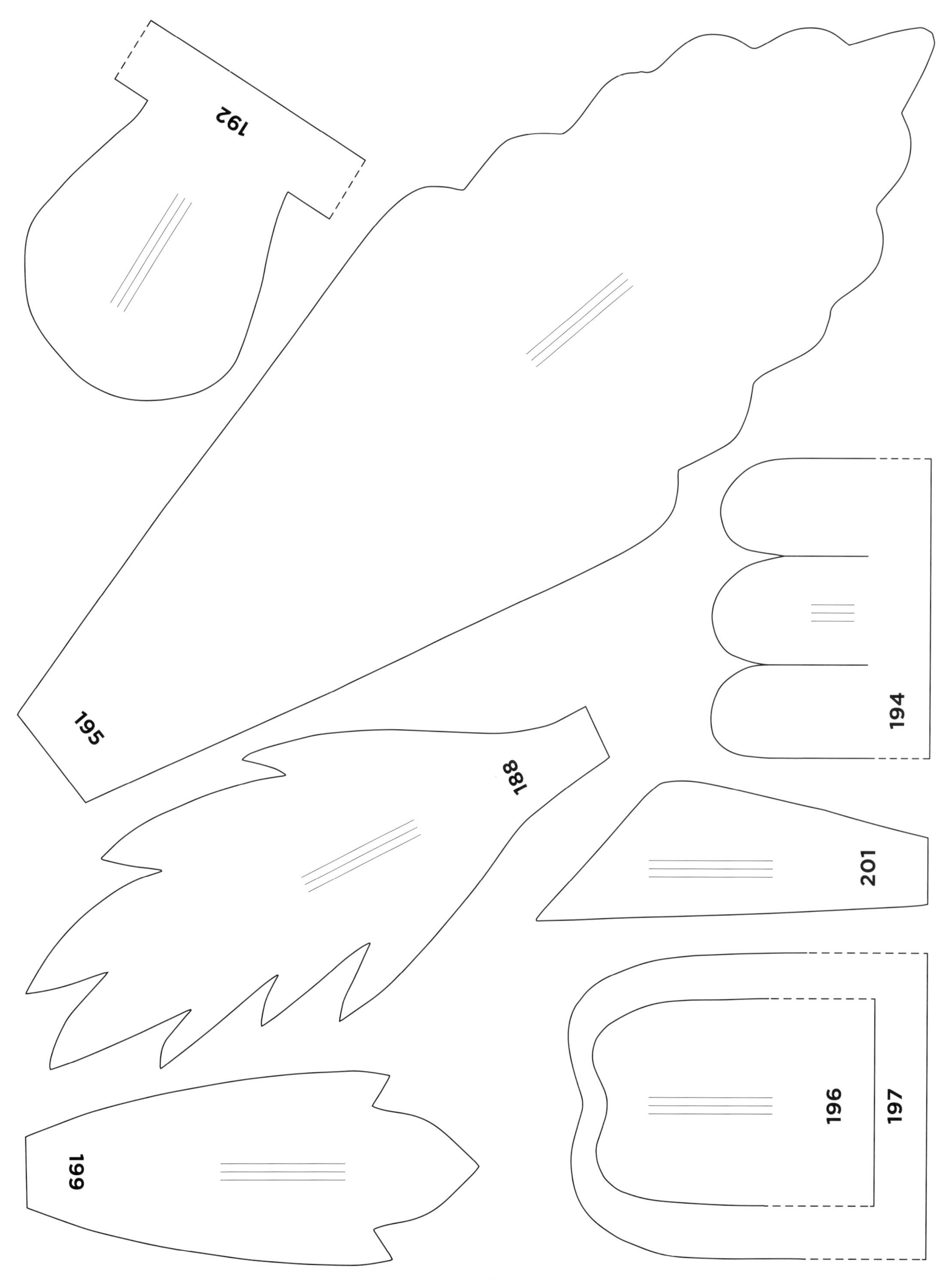
192
195
194
188
201
199
196
197

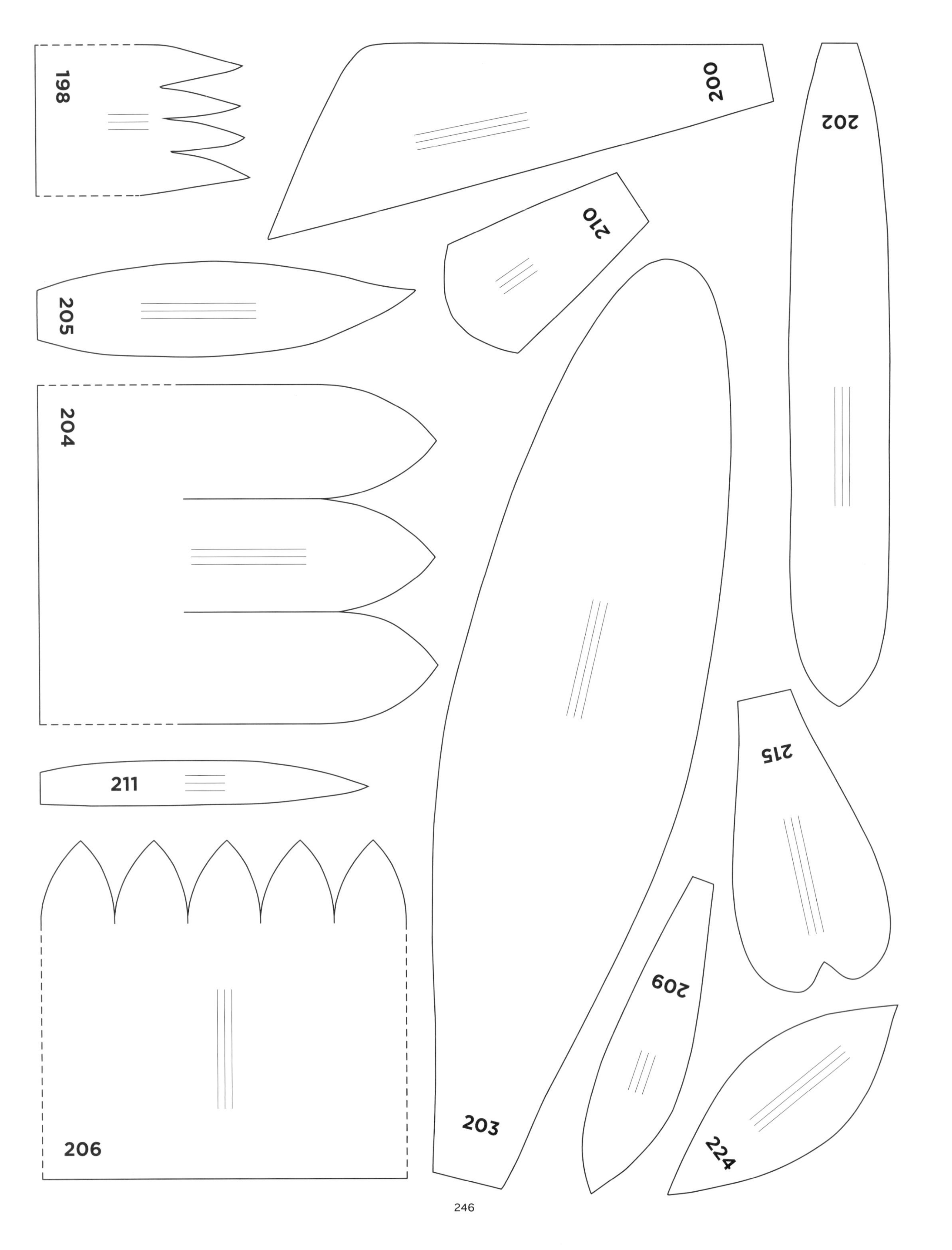
198
200
202
210
205
204
211
206
203
215
209
224

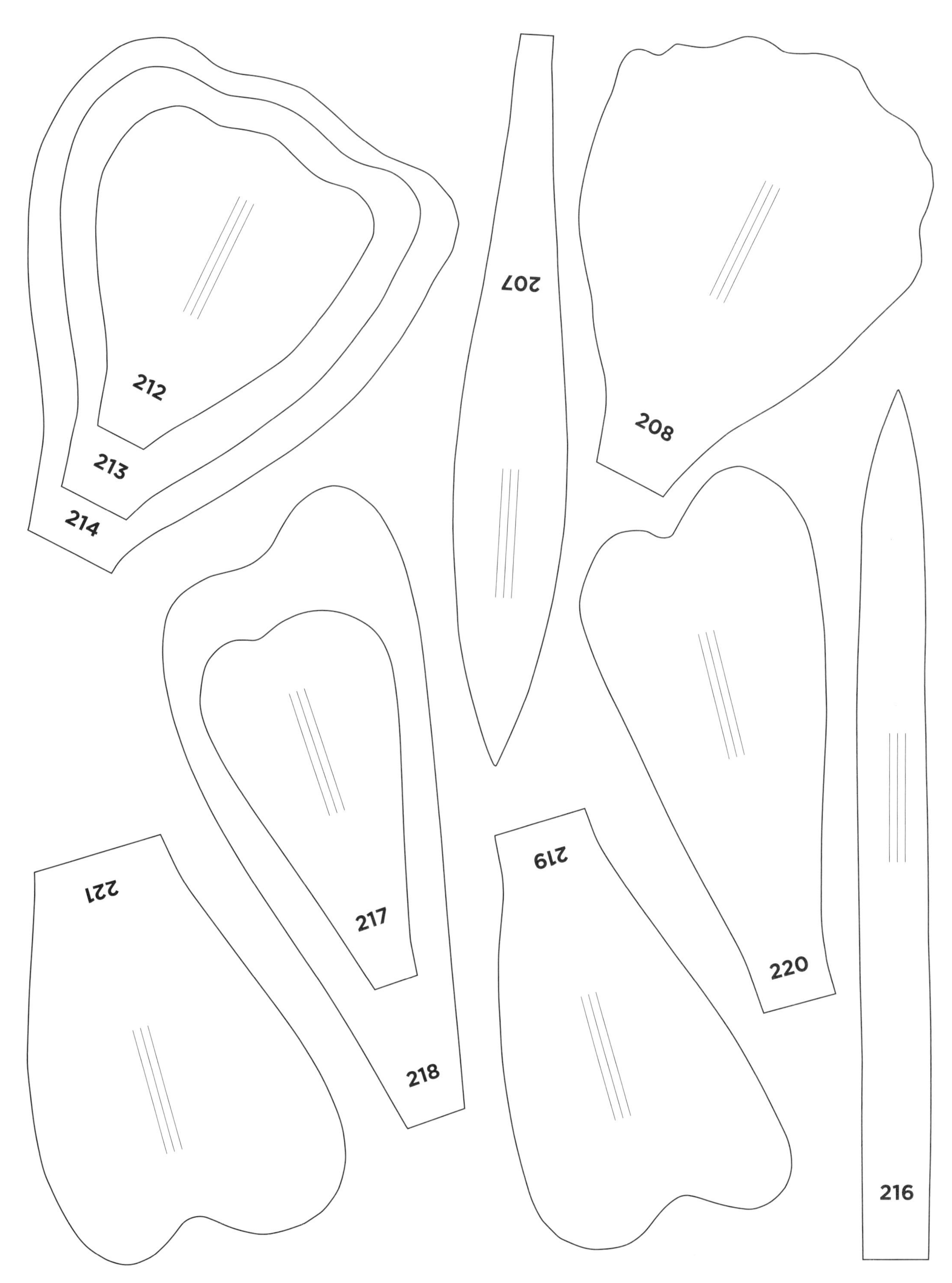
212
213
214
207
208
217
218
219
220
221
216

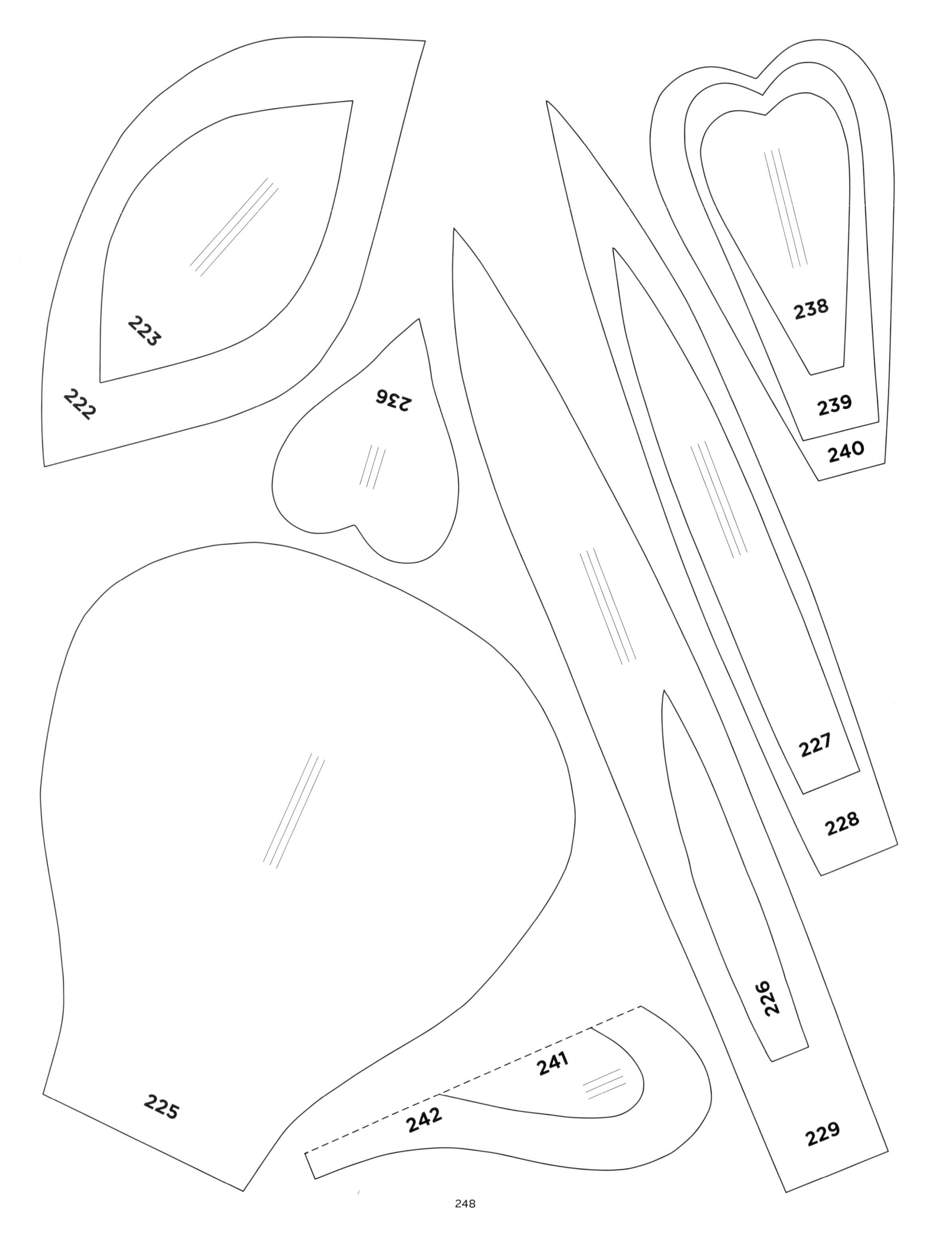
222
223
236
225
241
242
226
227
228
229
238
239
240

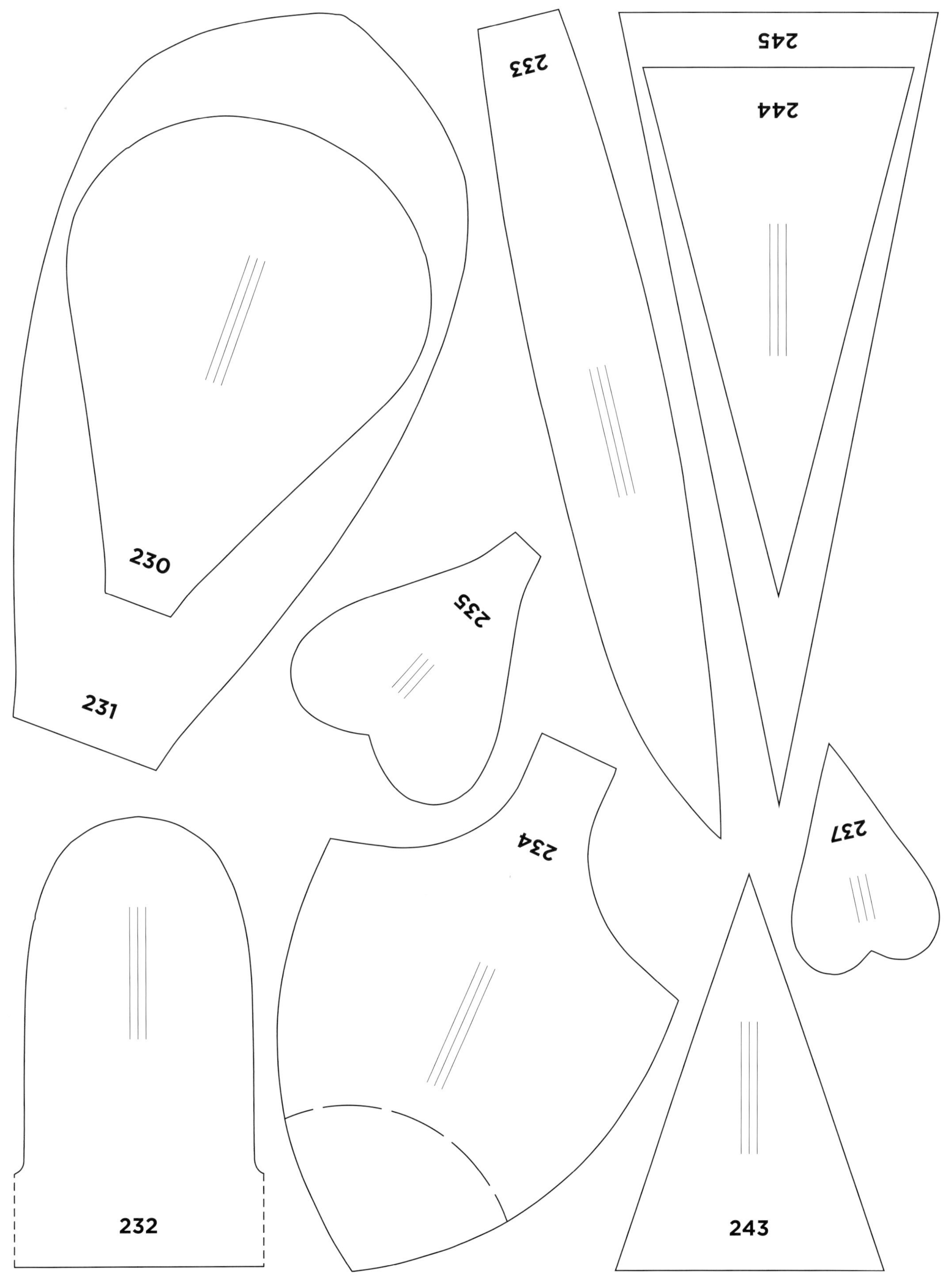
230
231
233
245
244
235
234
237
232
243

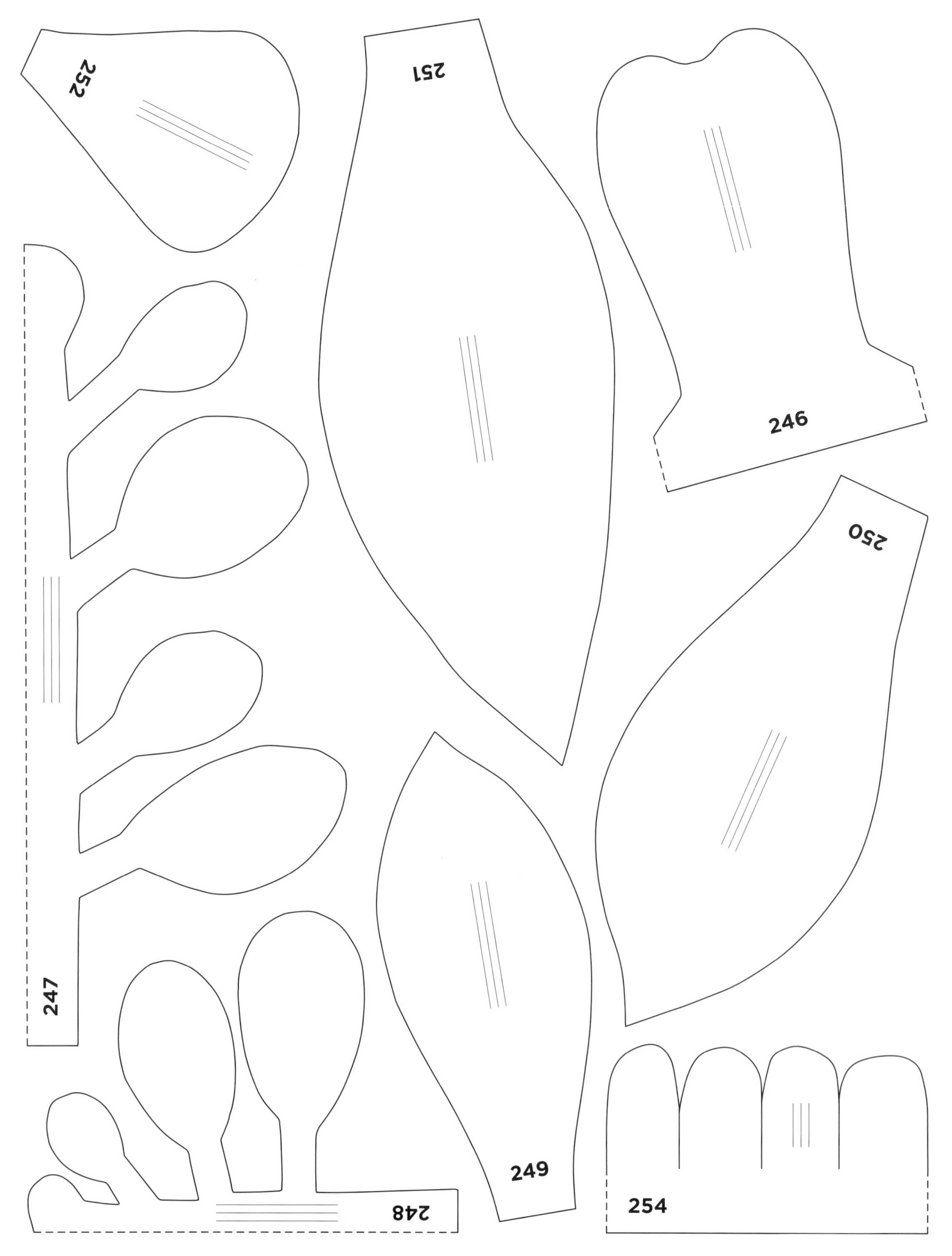
252
251
246
250
247
249
248
254

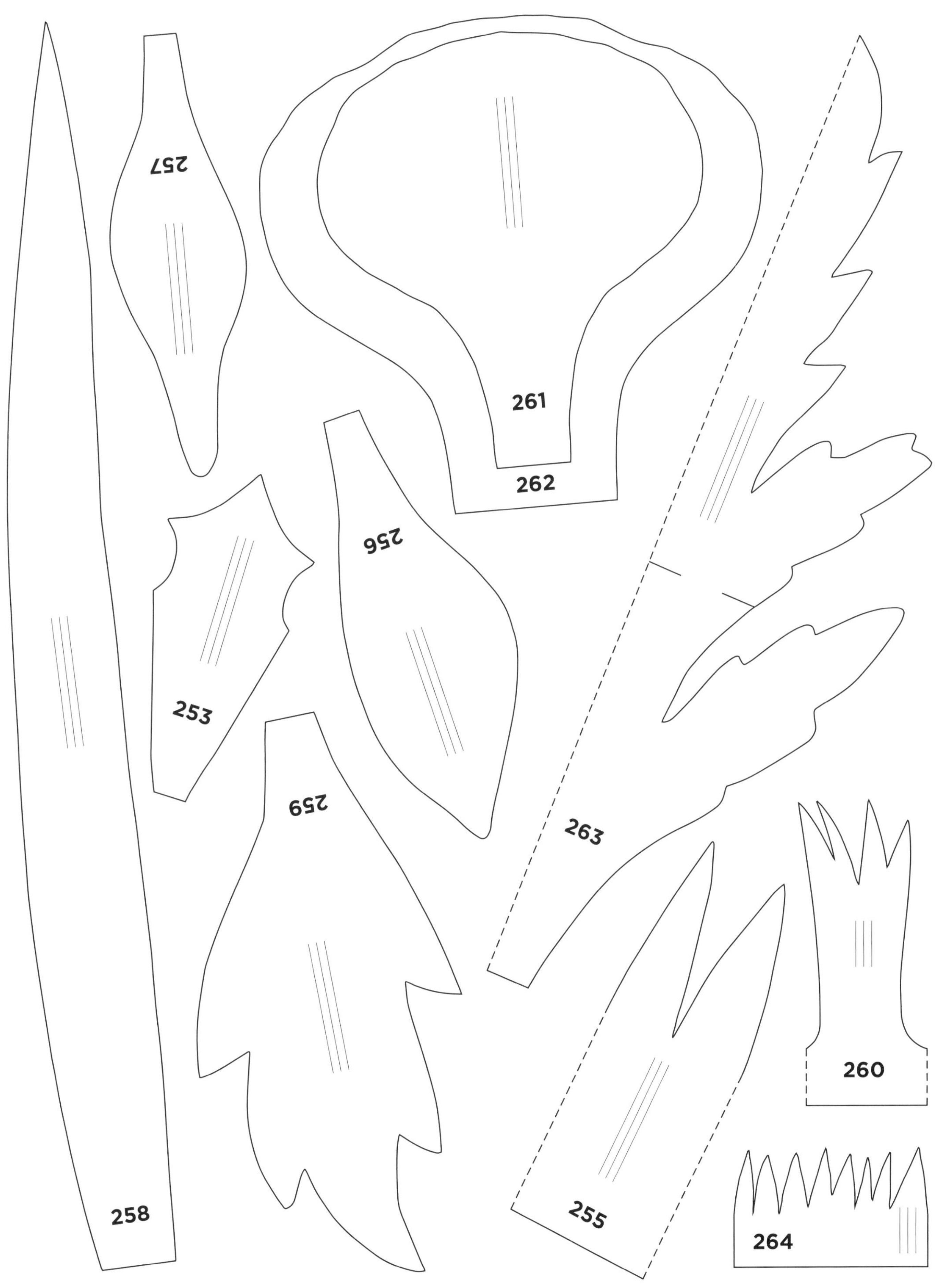
257
261
262
256
253
258
259
263
260
255
264

SOURCES

PAPERS

Crepe, tissue, decorative paper, paper ribbon

A CHILD'S DREAM COME TRUE
achildsdream.com
Glassine (kite paper)

ACORN SPRING RANCH
acornspring.com
1-866-820-1807
Patterned tissue

BELL'OCCHIO
bellocchio.com
1-415-864-4048
French matelassé paper, tissue

CARTE FINI
cartefini.com
1-888-284-6532
Italian florist crepe (180 grams), metallic florist crepe, gradated nuance crepe

CASTLE IN THE AIR
castleintheair.biz/shoppe/
1-510-204-9801
Italian florist crepe (160 and 180 grams); Gloria double-sided German crepe; single-ply, metallic, and patterned crepe; decorative paper

CREPE PAPER STORE
crepepaperstore.com
1-812-547-2445
Florist crepe (180 grams), single-ply crepe, tissue, crepe paper streamers

D. BLUMCHEN & COMPANY
blumchen.com
1-866-OLD-XMAS
Dennecrepe brand single-ply crepe, and Gloria double-sided German crepe

ESKAYEL
eskayel.com
1-347-703-8084
Newsprint wrapping paper

ETSY
etsy.com
Vintage crepe, vintage papers

MISTER ART
misterart.com
1-800-721-3015
Cindus brand single-ply crepe, Bleeding Art Tissue

NASHVILLE WRAPS
nashvillewraps.com
Tissue

NEW YORK CENTRAL ART SUPPLY
nycentralartsupply.com
1-800-950-6111
Decorative, Japanese, Chinese, Indian, German, Italian, kozo, momi, metallic, and marbleized papers; glassine; origami paper

PAPERMART
papermart.com
1-800-745-8800
Florist crepe (100 and 180 grams), tissue, twisted paper ribbon, paper ribbon, striated tissue paper garland

PAPER SOURCE
paper-source.com
1-888-727-3711
Tissue; decorative, Japanese, Chiyogami/Yuzen, and wrapping papers; origami paper

FLORAL SUPPLIES

Floral wire, floral stem wrap tape, specialty tape

CREATE FOR LESS
createforless.com
1-866-333-4463
Panacea brand cloth-wrapped and paper-covered floral wire

CUTE TAPE
cutetape.com
Washi tape, decorative fabric tape

JAMALI GARDEN
jamaligarden.com
1-212-996-5534
Paper-covered bind wire, Atlantic brand and Floratape brand floral stem wrap tape

SAVE ON CRAFTS
save-on-crafts.com
1-831-768-8428
Panacea cloth-wrapped and paper-covered floral wire, Atlantic brand floral stem wrap tape

SWEET LULU
shopsweetlulu.com
Washi tape

SPI SUPPLIES
2spi.com
1-610-436-5400
Floratape brand floral stem wrap tape

CENTER MATERIALS

Stamen pips, spun-cotton shapes

32º NORTH
vintage-ornaments.com
1-760-487-8580
Stamen pips, spun-cotton shapes and fruits

CASTLE IN THE AIR
castleintheair.biz/shoppe/
1-510-204-9801
Spun-cotton fruits

D. BLUMCHEN & COMPANY
blumchen.com
1-866-OLD-XMAS
Spun-cotton (watte) shapes, stamen pips

TINSEL TRADING
tinseltrading.com
1-212-730-1030
Stamen pips

CRAFT SUPPLIES

Adhesives, glitter, paint, paint brushes, punches, ribbon, rubber stamps, tools, yarn, paper ornaments, and more

32º NORTH
vintage-ornaments.com
1-760-487-8580
Paper doilies, Dresden paper ornaments, paper paste glue, millinery fruits, spun-cotton face beads, paper butterflies, glitter

AMAZON.COM
Caran d'Ache brand water-soluble crayons, Do-A-Dot brand dot stampers, Martha Stewart Crafts brand products, markers

BELL'OCCHIO
bellocchio.com
1-415-864-4048
Fringing scissors, notions, ribbon

CARTA, INC. ANGELA LIGUORI
angelaliguori.com
1-617-730-3788
Italian cotton ribbon, cotton twine

CASTLE IN THE AIR
castleintheair.biz/shoppe/
1-510-204-9801
Dresden paper ornaments, millinery fruits

CREATE FOR LESS
createforless.com
1-866-333-4463
Martha Stewart Crafts brand products, craft punches, rubber stamps and stamp pads, polystyrene cones and balls, origami paper, Fiskars brand decorative paper edgers

D. BLUMCHEN & COMPANY
blumchen.com
1-866-OLD-XMAS
Chenille pipe cleaners, crepe paper nut cups, pressed paper butterflies, paper doilies, paper leaves, tinsel

trimming, accordion-paper grass mat, Venetian dew microbeads, glitter

ECONOMY HANDICRAFTS
economyhandicrafts.com
1-800-216-1601
Doll head wood beads

FANCY FLOURS
fancyflours.com
1-406-587-0118
Doilies, crepe paper nut cups, wood berry baskets, cellophane bags

FISKARS BRANDS, INC.
fiskars.com
Scissors, decorative paper edgers, punches

LAKESHORE LEARNING
lakeshorelearning.com
(800) 778-445
Kids texture sponge brushes, dot stampers

MAINEWREATHCO.COM
1-877-846-3797
Wreath forms

MARTHA STEWART CRAFTS
marthastewartcrafts.com
Craft glue, glitter glue, craft paint, fringing scissors, craft punches; tinsel, flake, microbead, and fine glitter; alphabet stickers

MASTERSTROKE CANADA
masterstrokecanada.com
1-866-249-7677
Ribbon

MICHAELS
michaels.com
1-800-MICHAELS
Martha Stewart Crafts brand products, craft paint, glitter eyelash yarn, alphabet stickers, glitter, striping brush, patterning brushes, beads

MISTER ART
misterart.com
1-800-721-3015
Fiskars brand paper edgers, diamond paper crimper, fan brushes, Caran d'Ache brand water-soluble crayons, Mod Podge brand mediums, Americana brand acrylic craft paints, markers

NEW YORK CENTRAL ART SUPPLY
nycentralartsupply.com
1-800-950-6111
Paint brushes, adhesives

ORIENTAL TRADING
orientaltrading.com
1-800-875-8480
Curvy cut scissors (decorative paper edgers), paper confetti

PAPERMART
papermart.com
1-800-745-8800
Metallic star garland, tulle, metallic twisted ribbon, corsage and cake boxes, paper cord, metallic film, cellophane bags

PAPER SOURCE
paper-source.com
1-888-727-3711
Rubber stamps, stamp pads, craft punches

PLAID
plaidonline.com
1-800-842-4197
Martha Stewart Crafts brand products; adjustable striping, decorative, patterning, feather and detail paint brushes; craft paint

PURL SOHO
purlsoho.com
1-800-597-7875
Yarn, ribbon, floral print fabric, pinking shears, cotton batting

RUBBER STAMP TAPESTRY
rubberstamptapestry.com
1-910-464-2608
Floral rubber stamps, stamp pads

SAVE ON CRAFTS
save-on-crafts.com
1-831-768-8428
Corsage decorative pins

SWEET LULU
shopsweetlulu.com
Paper straws, bakers twine, doilies, crepe paper nut cups, glitter, pom-poms

TINSEL TRADING
tinseltrading.com
1-212-730-1030
Ribbon, trimmings, vintage notions, Dresden paper ornaments

WALNUT HOLLOW
walnuthollow.com
1-800-395-5995
Wood carving blocks and beads

ADDITIONAL SOURCES

ANTHROPOLOGIE
anthropologie.com
Vases, containers

MERCI
merci-merci.com
Vases, linens

MIDDLE KINGDOM PORCELAIN
middlekingdomporcelain.com
Porcelain vases

MOON RIVER CHATTEL
moonriverchattel.com
1-718-388-1121
Vases, containers, linens

TERRAIN
shopterrain.com
Vases, containers

WENDY KROMER SPECIALTY CONFECTIONS
wendykromer.com
1-419-609-0450
Wedding cakes, confections

WEST ELM
westelm.com
Vases, containers

INDEX

Page numbers in *italics* indicate projects, and page numbers in parentheses indicate project templates.

THANK YOU!

Kathryn Thuss, thank you from the bottom of our hearts for the countless hours of thoughtful crafting, listening, writing, unending support, and patience.

Marilyn and Richard Thuss, and Pamela and Keith Leinauer, we are so grateful for the innumerable days and weeks that you generously gave us. The gift of your time and unwavering support allowed us to make this project a reality.

Thank you to Martha Stewart for years of inspiration and opportunity. Thank you for building a brand that inspires so many to make the time to hand-craft and bring the joys of crafting into their daily lives.

Thank you to Hannah Gordon for your commitment and excitement for our project and Yfat Reiss Gendell for perspective in times of need.

Thank you to Betty Wong and the entire Potter Craft team for believing in us, giving us this opportunity, and seeing it through.

Thank you to our friends and family for their love, patience, commitment to us, and their many contributions, particularly Stephanie Adams, Jane Folk, Matthew Robbins, the Faust-Fogel family, Christina Dalle Pezze, Wendy Kromer, Andrew Farrell, and John Farrell.

Poet, our muse and inspiration, thank you.

ABOUT THUSS+FARRELL

THUSS + FARRELL are husband and wife team Rebecca Thuss and Patrick Farrell, a photography and design duo who have worked together since 1991. In addition to still-life, portraiture, and travel and lifestyle photography, their work together encompasses a wide variety of creative disciplines, including set design, furniture design, crafting, creative direction, and graphic design.

Their clients include Chronicle Books, Landor Associates, Procter & Gamble, Corcoran, Daniel Boulud, Per Se, Random House, Abrams: Stewart, Tabori & Chang, EMG, Martha Stewart Living Omnimedia, Keri Levitt Communications, Bonpoint, and the *New York Times*.

Rebecca and Patrick live in New York with their daughter, Poet.

www.papertopetal.com
www.thussfarrell.com
www.marriedtocraft.com